MW01039932

Civil War in Europe, 1905–1949

This is the first account in any language of the civil wars in Europe during the era of the world wars, from 1905 to 1949. It treats the initial confrontations in the decade before World War I, the confusing concept of "European civil war," the impact of the world wars, the relation between revolution and civil war, and all the individual cases of civil war, with special attention to Russia and Spain. The civil wars of this era are compared to and contrasted with earlier internal conflicts, with particular attention to the factors that made this era a time of unusually violent domestic contests, as well as those that brought it to an end. The major political, ideological, and social influences are all treated, with a special focus on violence against civilians.

Stanley G. Payne has taught history in several universities, including Columbia University, UCLA, and the University of Wisconsin. He is a member of the American Academy of Arts and Sciences and a corresponding member of Real Academia Española de la Historia, Madrid. He has received various awards and prizes, most recently the Marshal Shulman Book Award of the American Association for the Advancement of Slavic Studies (2005) and the Gran Cruz de Isabel la Católica from the Spanish government (2009). He has been coeditor of the *Journal of Contemporary History* since 1999. Professor Payne is the author of some twenty books and many articles, as well as other edited, coedited, and coauthored books. Most recently, he is the author of *The Collapse of the Spanish Republic, 1933–1936: Origins of the Civil War*; *Franco and Hitler*; and *Spain: A Unique History*.

Civil War in Europe, 1905–1949

STANLEY G. PAYNE

University of Wisconsin, Madison

CAMBRIDGE
UNIVERSITY PRESS

CAMBRIDGE UNIVERSITY PRESS
Cambridge, New York, Melbourne, Madrid, Cape Town,
Singapore, São Paulo, Delhi, Tokyo, Mexico City

Cambridge University Press
32 Avenue of the Americas, New York, NY 10013-2473, USA

www.cambridge.org
Information on this title: www.cambridge.org/9781107648159

First published 2011

Printed in the United States of America

A catalog record for this publication is available from the British Library.

Library of Congress Cataloging in Publication data
Payne, Stanley G.
    Civil war in Europe, 1905–1949 / Stanley G. Payne.
        p.   cm.
    Includes bibliographical references and index.
    ISBN 978-1-107-01090-1 (hardback)
    1. Civil war – Europe – History – 20th century.   2. Europe – History, Military – 20th
century.   3. Europe – Politics and government – 1871–1918.   4. Europe – Politics and
government – 1918–1945.   5. Europe – Social conditions – 20th century.   6. Violence –
Europe – History – 20th century.   7. Revolutions – Europe – History – 20th
century.   8. Civilians in war – Europe – History – 20th century.   9. War and society – Europe –
History – 20th century.   10. Social conflict – Europe – History – 20th century.   I. Title.
    D424.5.P39   2011
    303.6′409409041 – dc22   2011000377

ISBN 978-1-107-01090-1 Hardback
ISBN 978-1-107-64815-9 Paperback

Contents

Preface

The notion of a "European civil war" during the decades 1914–45 has become rather popular with certain historians during the past generation; the most recent book bearing this title appeared in Spain in 2010. The concept is applied primarily to the world wars, and secondarily to the conflict between Nazism and Communism. None of the works involved devotes much attention to the numerous civil wars and insurgencies that in fact took place during these years. This study therefore represents an initial attempt to treat them all, however briefly, within a single volume.

The entire manuscript has been read by David Gress, Juan Linz, and Michael Seidman, and Stathis Kalyvas has critiqued the section on Greece. Each of them has made valuable criticisms, suggestions, and corrections, for which I am grateful. This book ranges far across European history and politics, and, in the years to come, further research will undoubtedly correct deficiencies and fill gaps.

Madison, Wisconsin
November 2010

Chronology of Events

1926	Pilsudski coup d'etat in Poland; new authoritarian governments in Lithuania, Portugal, and (briefly) Greece
1928	"Third Period" of world revolution declared by Comintern
1930–33	Depression crisis in Germany
April 1931	Second Republic in Spain
1933	Authoritarian regime in Austria
February 1934	Socialist insurrection in Austria
October 1934	Revolutionary insurrection in Spain
August 1935	Comintern announces tactic of Popular Front
February 1936	Popular Front electoral victory in Spain
July 1936	Spanish civil war begins
September 1936	Franco made commander-in-chief by military junta
November–December 1936	Battle of Madrid
March 1937	Battle of Guadalajara
March–October 1937	Franco conquers northern Republican zone
May 1937	"May Days" anarchist revolt in Barcelona
	Juan Negrín prime minister of Republican government
April 1938	Offensive by Franco splits Republican zone in two
July–November 1938	Battle of the Ebro
March 1939	Overthrow of Negrín
April 1, 1939	Spanish civil war ends
August 1939	Nazi-Soviet Pact
1939–45	World War II
1939–45	Ethnic conflict in Western Ukraine
1941–45	Yugoslav war of resistance and civil war
1943–44	First round of Greek civil war
1943–45	Civil war in northern Italy
December 1944–February 1945	Second round of Greek civil war
1946–49	Third round of Greek civil war
1944–50s	Insurgency against Communist regimes by resistance movements in Poland, Ukraine, Lithuania, Latvia, and Estonia
1944–52	Insurgency of *Maquis* in Spain

Glossary of Political Acronyms

AVNOJ	Anti-Fascist Council for the National Liberation of Yugoslavia
CEDA	Spanish Confederation of Autonomous Rightist Groups
CHEKA	Special Commission for Security (Soviet Union)
CNT	National Confederation of Labor (Spain)
CPY	Communist Party of Yugoslavia
CTV	Corps of Volunteer Troops (Italy)
DAG	Democratic Army of Greece
EAM	National Liberation Front (Greece)
ECCI	Executive Commission of the Communist International
ELAS	National People's Liberation Army (Greece)
FAI	Iberian Anarchist Federation (Spain)
FET	Traditionalist Spanish Phalanx
IMRO	Internal Macedonian Revolutionary Organization (Bulgaria)
IRA	Institute of Agrarian Reform (Spain)
JONS	Juntas of National Syndicalist Offensive (Spain)
JSU	United Socialist Youth (Spain)
KAPD	Communist Workers Party of Germany
KKE	Communist Party of Greece
KPD	Communist Party of Germany
NDH	Independent State of Croatia
NEP	New Economic Policy (Soviet Union)
NKVD	People's Commissariat for Internal Affairs (Soviet Union)
NSDAP	National Socialist German Workers Party ("Nazi Party")
PASOK	Panhellenic Socialist Movement (Greece)
PCE	Spanish Communist Party
PCF	Communist Party of France
PCL	Political Combat Leagues (Germany)
PNF	National Fascist Party (Italy)
POUM	Worker Party of Marxist Unification (Spain)
PSI	Socialist Party of Italy
PSOE	Socialist Workers Party of Spain

PSUC   Unified Socialist Party of Catalonia (Spain)
RFB   Red Front-fighters League (German Communist militia)
RILU   Red International of Labor Unions
SA   Storm Detachment (Nazi militia)
SPD   Social Democratic Party of Germany
SR   Socialist Revolutionaries (Russia)
SS   Protection Squads
SSR   Soviet Socialist Republic
UGT   General Union of Labor (Spain)
USPD   Independent Social Democratic Party of Germany
USSR   Union of Soviet Socialist Republics

Introduction

Revolution and Civil War as Forms of Conflict

Civil war, as a form of armed conflict within a single political unit rather than a foreign war between two different polities, is one of the oldest forms of strife. It may take one or more of many different forms, which include "most revolutions, sustained peasant insurrections, 'revolutionary' or ethnic insurgencies, anti-colonial uprisings, and resistance wars against foreign occupiers."[1] Significant political violence alone, however, is not enough to constitute genuine civil war, which must involve an extended contest of arms to win state power, even if waged by means of irregular warfare.

Historically, the most important civil wars have tended to cluster in three different sorts of conflicts: a) dynastic succession conflicts, b) wars of secession or national liberation, and c) full-scale political or ideological civil wars to impose or thwart the imposition of a new or revised model on the polity. In some of them more than one kind of conflict has been combined, or other features have been added to give them an even more complex character. Any of these conflicts, for example, may include secondary mini–civil wars fought to some degree within one of the contending sides, as in the internal civil war in some regions that attended the war of independence of the American colonies. Similarly, there may be mini–civil wars within a greater civil war, as happened during the Spanish civil war in May 1937 in Barcelona and in March 1939 in Madrid.[2]

The oldest and historically most common form of civil war has been succession conflict, for struggles over succession to the throne were frequent in traditional polities. They were often relatively uncomplicated contests for power, though exceptions might be found. In Castile, the greatest civil war was the dynastic succession struggle of the 1360s, which ended with the defeat and death of Pedro the Cruel. The famous Wars of the Roses that dominated

---

[1] S. Kalyvas, *The Logic of Violence in Civil War* (Cambridge, 2006), 19.

[2] There is no better brief discussion of the phenomenon than that in Gabriele Ranzato's introductory study, "Un evento antico e un nuovo oggetto di riflessione," in his edited work, *Guerre fratricide: Le guerre civili in età contemporanea* (Turin, 1994), ix–lvi.

the politics of fifteenth-century England were exclusively a dynastic struggle, though the Catalan civil war of that century was somewhat different insofar as it involved greater changes in policy and institutions. Something similar might be said about the revolt of the Communities of Castile in 1520–21. The greatest of all Spanish succession conflicts, which grew into the international war of 1702–14, was initially traditional in character, though it eventually produced major institutional changes in the Aragonese principalities. Beginning in the fifteenth and sixteenth centuries, even civil wars that stemmed from succession problems began to develop more complex agendas regarding religion, institutions, and state formation.

The second most common form of war within a polity have been struggles to achieve secession, which in recent times have often been called national liberation wars. Secession wars of one kind or another have been found in all periods of history, and were relatively common, for example, in the Middle Ages. They have often involved attempts to break away from empires or multinational states, but there have also been numerous efforts to secede from nonimperial polities. Secession struggles have sometimes been involved in dynastic succession conflicts, as well. In traditional societies, they have not usually sought to alter the institutional structure so much as to draw new boundaries.

In more recent times, beginning no later than seventeenth-century England, armed rebellion and civil war have sometimes sought to introduce radically different political models. The greatest civil war of the nineteenth century, however – the war that took place in the United States from 1861 to 1865 – was a purely secessionist struggle, and thus in principle not a full civil war, despite the terminology normally employed in the United States.[3] At no time did the seceding Confederacy propose to conquer the United States and impose on it a new political model. The Confederate Constitution was largely a copy of the United States Constitution, though with slightly greater rights for individual states and explicit guarantees for slavery. The struggle waged by the Confederacy may also be seen as the most extensive national liberation war to have ended in failure, just as the Spanish civil war of 1936 featured the most extensive revolution ever to have ended in failure.

The third type of civil war – ideological or revolutionary civil war – which seeks to alter the system drastically or introduce completely new ideas and policies, was rare to nonexistent in traditional polities. It might nonetheless be found in truncated form in the guise of slave or peasant revolts, the latter often seeking to regain aspects of a perceived earlier order. There seem to have been brief conflicts of this sort in some Greek city-states. Radical new political, social, and ideological features began to appear, sometimes in religious form or due to religious motivation, in Europe in the time of the Reformation, starting with the Bohemian Hussite rebellions of the fifteenth century. Such

---

[3] The term "American War of Secession," or variants thereof, sometimes found in European historiography, is more accurate than the common American usage.

features appeared in other Reformation-era struggles, particularly in the French Wars of Religion[4] and the Dutch revolt, even as the Bohemian and Dutch rebellions (especially the latter) became secessionist struggles.

In modern times this would take the form of the revolutionary civil war. "Revolution" is a term that passed into the general political lexicon during the seventeenth century.[5] For some time it was used to refer to violent and fundamental changes in government and political institutions, though this came increasingly to embrace basic changes in culture, values, and myths and symbols. The first major example was the English civil war and political revolution of the 1640s, so categorically different from the Wars of the Roses.[6] The first complete modern secular example, in which secular or political religion replaced traditional religion, was the great French Revolution of 1789, followed by the French civil war of 1793–94,[7] and later by various revolutionary urban insurrections, particularly in Paris in 1848, reaching a final climax in the bloody Paris Commune of 1871. By that time, the concept of revolution had been expanded to refer especially to violent attempts to bring about drastic changes in social and economic structures, and subsequently this expanded concept became fundamental to the definition of a "true revolution," as distinct from mere coups d'etat or takeovers. During the first half of the twentieth century Europe was the scene not merely of two great world wars, but also of several major revolutions, revolutionary civil wars, and other internal wars and insurrections.[8] During the second half of the twentieth century violent

---

[4] The conceptual relation between Calvinism and political revolution is treated in J. Witte, Jr., *The Reformation of Rights: Law, Religion, and Human Rights in Early Modern Calvinism* (Cambridge, 2007).

[5] For the origins of the modern use of the term "revolution," see A. Rey, *"Révolution." Histoire d'un mot* (Paris, 1989), and I. Rachum, *"Revolution": The Entrance of a New Word into Western Political Discourse* (Lanham, Md., 1999).

[6] Recently Steven Pincus, in his *1688: The First Modern Revolution* (New Haven, Conn., 2009), has sought to claim this status for what has normally been called the "Glorious Revolution of 1688," but his elaborate effort is unpersuasive. The changes of 1688–89 were much less extensive than those of the Civil War, and merely restabilized and reformed English institutions following the moderate counterrevolution of 1660–88, which, as Pincus shows, entered a more radical phase under James II in 1685–88. They introduced significant reforms that became permanent and were fundamental to the rise of modern Britain, but they overturned not a single existing institution.

[7] The historiography of the French Revolution is immense. S. Neely, *A Concise History of the French Revolution* (Lanham, Md., 2008), provides an excellent recent summary. For the battle of interpretation, see A. Gérard, *La Révolution française: Mythes et interpretations, 1789–1970* (Paris, 1975); F. Furet, *Penser la Révolution française* (Paris, 1978); and S. L. Kaplan, *Farewell, Revolution: The Historians' Feud, France 1789–1989* (Ithaca, N.Y., 1995).

[8] The sociologist Pitirim Sorokin made an attempt to quantify the violence of this era as compared to other periods of history in "Quantitative Measurement of Internal Disturbances," in his *Social and Cultural Dynamics*, abr. ed. (Boston, 1957), 573–604. Writing around 1930, his conclusion was that "the first quarter of the twentieth century, 1901–1925, was not only the bloodiest period in the entire history of the international conflicts of mankind but also, when internal disturbances are considered, was one of the very turbulent periods" (p. 602).

revolutionary struggle became a worldwide phenomenon, as did national wars of liberation and secession.

Philosophers and historians have discussed the problems of civil war for nearly two and a half millennia, beginning with Thucydides[9] and Aristotle. Much more recently, the outbreak of modern revolutionary conflict led to attempts to understand and interpret the problem of revolution, the first major achievement being the work of Alexis de Tocqueville in the mid nineteenth century.[10] During the era of the Cold War, when the focus of struggle was increasingly transposed to the internal conflicts in what was then called the Third World, the effort to understand civil war and revolution became a growth industry. Taxonomies were developed,[11] multiple case studies published,[12] and numerous explanations and interpretations advanced. These ranged from economic arguments to speculations concerning social structure or historical sequences, and the formation of various political models.[13]

And worse was yet to come. Certainly the absolute number of people killed was greater than in any previous time, but the common perception that this was proportionately the most violent era known to the West is more a common perception than a measured reality, as David Gress reminds me. Death and violence were very common in the seventeenth century, but cannot be measured as accurately in proportionate terms. There is evidence of very high rates of deaths by violence in certain Paleolithic societies.

[9] J. J. Price, *Thucydides and Internal War* (Cambridge, UK, 2001).

[10] For an interesting new evaluation of the achievement of Tocqueville, see J. Elster, *Alexis de Tocqueville, the First Social Scientist* (Cambridge, UK, 2009).

[11] Perhaps the best taxonomy is M. N. Hagopian, *The Phenomenon of Revolution* (New York, 1974). See also M. Edmonds, "Civil War, Internal War, and Intrasocietal Conflict: A Taxonomy and Typology," in R. Higham, ed., *Civil Wars in the Twentieth Century* (Lexington, Ky., 1972), 11–26. On terminology, see R. Koselleck, "Revolution, Rebellion, Aufruhr, Bürgerkrieg," in *Geschichtliche Grundbegriffe: Historisches Lexikon zur politisch-sozialen Sprache in Deutschland* (Stuttgart, 1984), 5:653–788.

[12] The best book on the history of modern revolutions is M. Malia, *History's Locomotives: Revolutions and the Making of the Modern World* (New Haven, Conn., 2006). Miscellanies may be found in R. Martins, *História das grandes revoluçoes* (Lisbon, 1953), 2 vols.; Col. G. Bonnet, *Les guerres insurrectionnelles et révolutionnaires de l'antiquité à nos jours* (Paris, 1958); M. Kossok, ed., *Revolutionen der Neuzeit 1500–1917* (Berlin, 1982); F. Martins and P. Aires Oliveira, eds., *As revoluçoes contemporâneas* (Lisbon, 2005); and more systematically in C. Tilly, *European Revolutions, 1492–1992* (Cambridge, 1993). J. DeFronzo, *Revolutions and Revolutionary Movements* (Boulder, Colo., 2007) is a textbook, and D. Close and C. Bridge, eds., *Revolution: A History of the Idea* (London, 1985), a collection of examples. On civil wars, see H. Eckstein, *Internal War: Problems and Approaches* (New York, 1964); R. Higham, ed., *Civil Wars in the Twentieth Century* (Lexington, Ky., 1972); S. Neumann, "The International Civil War," *World Politics* (1948), 33–51; and J. N. Rosenau, ed., *International Aspects of Civil Strife* (Princeton, N.J., 1964). I. E. Shavrova, ed., *Lokalnye voiny. Istoriya i sovremennost* (Moscow, 1981), offers a lengthy compendium of internal wars from 1898 to 1975.

[13] Crane Brinton, *The Anatomy of Revolution*, rev. ed. (New York, 1965), was an early classic. One of the best collections is G. A. Kelly and C. W. Brown, eds., *Struggles in the State: Sources and Patterns of World Revolution* (New York, 1970). Principal studies include G. S. Pettee, *The Process of Revolution* (New York, 1938); W. E. Mühlmann, *Chiliasmus und nativismus. Studien zur Psychologie, Soziologie und historischen Kasuistik der Umsturzbewegungen* (Berlin, 1961); P. Amann, "Revolution: A Redefinition," *Political Science Quarterly*, 77 (March 1962), 36–53; C. Johnson, *Revolution and the Social System* (Stanford, Calif., 1964); L. Stone, "Theories of Revolution," *World Politics*, 18 (1965), 159–77; H. Arendt,

In the later twentieth century, as the Cold War came to an end and the interest in and support for revolution dwindled in most regions of the world, studies of revolution declined. Nonetheless, as civil war and internal conflict became the normative kind of conflict in much of the world, studies of "internal war" soon proliferated once more.

The term "internal war" came to be preferred by some social scientists for two reasons. The first was the obvious one that this term was more flexible and might include more marginal phenomena whose status or classification could otherwise be a subject for debate. The second was that established governments, whatever their nature, that faced civil war insurgencies sometimes alleged that there was no civil war but simply a conspiracy or rebellion against legitimate government. This argument had first been used in 1793 by Robespierre and the French Jacobins, who maintained that a government that had a constitution and a parliament and had held elections could never be faced with a true civil war, no matter what its policies, for it legitimately represented "the people." Over the years, there have been many variations on this theme, most notably by Spanish Republicans in 1936–39.

Harry Eckstein has grouped all explanations of revolution and internal war into five categories: 1) hypotheses that emphasize "intellectual" factors, 2) hypotheses that emphasize economic factors, 3) hypotheses that emphasize aspects of social structure, 4) hypotheses that emphasize political factors, and 5) hypotheses that emphasize general characteristics of social process.[14] More broadly and simply, they can be divided into hypotheses and theories that stress economic and structural factors, which imply a certain determinism, and those that emphasize behavioral factors. In early twentieth-century Europe, the great catalyst of revolution was war, but war was only a precipitant, not the cause, for most states at war did not experience revolution.

On Revolution (New York, 1965); C. J. Friedrich, ed., *Revolution* (New York, 1966); R. Tanter and M. Midlarsky, "A Theory of Revolution," *Journal of Conflict Resolution*, 11:3 (1967), 154–75; J. Ellul, *Autopsie de la révolution* (Paris, 1969) and *De la révolution aux révoltes* (Paris, 1972); K. Griewank, *Der neuzeitliche Revolutionsbegriff. Entstehung und Entwicklung* (Frankfurt, 1969); P. Calvert, *A Study of Revolution* (Oxford, 1970); T. R. Gurr, *Why Men Rebel* (Princeton, N.J., 1970); J. C. Davies, ed., *When Men Revolt and Why: A Reader in Political Violence and Revolution* (New York, 1971); J. Dunn, *Modern Revolutions: An Introduction to the Analysis of a Political Phenomenon* (Cambridge, 1972); K. von Beyme, ed., *Empirische Revolutionsforschung* (Opladen, 1973); A. S. Cohan, *Theories of Revolution: An Introduction* (London, 1975); T. Skocpol, *States and Social Revolutions: A Comparative Analysis of France, Russia, and China* (Cambridge, 1979); E. Zimmermann, *Krisen, Staatsstreiche und Revolutionen. Theorien, Daten und neuere Forschungsansätze* (Opladen, 1981); J. Krejci, *Great Revolutions Compared: The Search for a Theory* (New York, 1983); N. O'Sullivan, ed., *Revolutionary Theory and Political Reality* (New York, 1983); J. A. Goldstone, ed., *Revolutions: Theoretical, Comparative and Historical Studies* (San Diego, Calif., 1986); and N. Bobbio, *Sulla rivoluzione. Problemi di teoria politica* (Milan, 1990). The Marxist-Leninist approach may be found in M. Kossok, ed., *Vergleichende Revolutionsgeschichte – Probleme der Theorie und Methode* (Berlin, 1988), and that of fascists in J. Streel, *La révolution du vingtième siècle* (Brussels, 1942).

[14] H. Eckstein, "On the Etiology of Internal Wars," *History and Theory*, 4:2 (1965), 133–63.

The classic behavioral theory of the origins of revolution was formulated by Alexis de Tocqueville in 1856, when he observed regarding France that "it was precisely in those parts of France where there had been the most improvement that popular discontent ran highest. This may seem illogical – but history is full of paradoxes." Tocqueville explains that deteriorating conditions do not generally provoke revolution, but that complaints tend instead to increase after conditions have begun to improve. "The regime destroyed by a revolution is almost always better than the one that immediately preceded it and experience teaches us that the most hazardous moment for a bad government is normally when it is beginning to reform."[15] The absolutist government of Louis XIV provoked much less resentment than the mild, semiliberal reign of Louis XVI. In other words, revolution is less likely when things are getting worse than it is after they have begun to get better. Fundamental is the revolution of rising expectations and the raising of consciousness, which are more important than objective conditions in themselves. Once such attitudes have taken hold, some new crisis or setback, which may or may not be of profound importance in itself, triggers revolution.

James C. Davies has elaborated the point: "Revolutions are most likely to occur when a prolonged period of objective economic and social development is followed by a period of sharp reversal.... The actual state of socioeconomic development is less significant than the expectation that past progress, now blocked, can and must continue into the future."[16] Theodore S. Hamerow concurs: "Economic privation is not the key factor in the downfall of established authority any more than political repression.... What makes the economic situation seem intolerable is not deteriorating conditions but rising expectations." He further points out that "Leon Trotsky, the sharpest analytical mind produced by the revolutionary movements of the twentieth century, openly acknowledged this primacy of perception over actuality in the decline of established authority.... A revolution of expectations thus prepares the way for a revolution of deeds."[17]

Harry Eckstein concludes that "despite the fact that there is a danger that the behavioral approach might lead to naïve conspiracy theory ..., the arguments against a primary emphasis on structural theories are very strong.... Purely structural theories have generally been found difficult to sustain whenever they have been applied." He argues that the strongest reason to support

---

[15] A. de Tocqueville, *The Ancien Regime and the Revolution* (London, 2008), 174–75.

[16] J. C. Davies, "Toward a Theory of Revolution," *American Sociological Review*, 27:1 (February 1962), 5–19. Davies tried to illustrate this conclusion in his article "Revolution and the J-Curve," the J-Curve being a graph revealing the difference between the extent to which expectations go up and opportunities either do not go up or do not go up as far and fast, in H. D. Graham and T. R. Gurr, *Violence in America: Historical and Comparative Perspectives* (Washington, D.C., 1969), 2:547–77.

[17] T. S. Hamerow, *From the Finland Station: The Graying of Revolution in the Twentieth Century* (New York, 1990), 7, 24. On pages 6–24 Hamerow describes various pre-revolutionary situations in terms of improving conditions, the relationship between modernization and destabilization, and changes in expectations.

behavioral theories is that "so many different objective social conditions seem capable of generating" revolution and civil war.[18] Karl Marx also reflected on the influence of behavioral factors, when he observed that even an increase in wages can stimulate the radicalization of workers, if other sectors gain even more, because the psychological effect is relative rather than absolute.[19] Very severe oppression and extreme hunger usually atomize a society, whereas improving conditions and greater education may stimulate political reactions, sometimes of a severely adversarial nature.

Modern revolutions do not take place in traditional societies, but only in polities in which a certain amount of modernization has already occurred. Some degree of modernization is a sine qua non for the preliminary revolution of rising expectations, though in revolutionary or pre-revolutionary situations there has almost always been a strong feeling that the existing degree of modernization has been inadequate. A sense of comparative backwardness or, alternatively, "disadvantaged positions within international arenas"[20] is also usually present, though the form taken by the latter may be simply military defeat.

Nearly all interpretations of revolution agree upon certain common preconditions, such as the loss of elite support, a rebellious intelligentsia, the rise of radical, often millenarian, expectations, and the existence of a weak and divided old order that has lost its nerve. Strongly organized revolutionary groups are important, but not always indispensable. The most crucial factor is, to use Jonathan Israel's term, "a revolution of the mind."[21]

Revolutions occur only when the old order has become relatively weak. Thus the initial revolution that accomplishes its overthrow is sometimes comparatively easy and often not accompanied by great disorder or bloodshed. Sometimes this is not the result of any great new exertion by the revolutionaries themselves; rather, the downfall of the old order is only the beginning of the revolutionary process, which usually leads to greater radicalization and more and more bloodshed, often involving civil war and sometimes major international war as well. The revolution often stimulates not merely opposition, but in some cases a competing new counterrevolutionary movement that may be almost as radical, though with a very different program, so that the struggle, as in Spain during the 1930s, may become a vicious contest of competing radicalisms.

[18] Eckstein, "Etiology of Internal Wars," 182–83.
[19] K. Marx and F. Engels, "Wage Labour and Capital," in *Selected Works in Two Volumes* (Moscow, 1955), 1:94, quoted in Davies, "Toward a Theory."
[20] Skocpol, *States and Social Revolutions*, 19.
[21] J. Israel, *A Revolution of the Mind: Radical Enlightenment and the Intellectual Origins of Modern Democracy* (Princeton, N.J., 2009). Israel notes the continued insistence by more than a few scholars upon the preeminence of structural factors in bringing about the American, Dutch, and French revolutions of the late eighteenth century, but argues convincingly that the most crucial and decisive factor was the prior "revolution of the mind," an argument that may be extended to almost every modern revolution.

Europe had earlier gone through two periods of protracted international war accompanied by violent internal conflict, during the era of the Thirty Years War[22] in the first half of the seventeenth century and later during the quarter-century of the French revolutionary wars. In the first, intense religious strife added a certain dimension of ideological civil war, but, with the exceptions of England and Holland, the traditional order generally prevailed.[23] The French revolutionary and Napoleonic era introduced modern revolutionism on an international scale, but this was largely restricted to politics and culture, and ended with universally triumphant counterrevolution, at least for some years. The twentieth-century conflict era, by contrast, extended war on a previously unimagined scale and produced political breakdown and continuing revolutionary confrontation to a degree totally unprecedented.

The era of twentieth-century revolutions began in 1905–11, with the First Russian Revolution of 1905, the Iranian quasi-revolution of 1906–11, the great Romanian peasant revolt of 1907, the successful Young Turk revolt of 1908, the Greek military coup for a more liberal system in 1909, and the beginning of the Mexican and Chinese revolutions in 1910–11, together with the successful republican revolt of 1910 in Portugal. The clustering of these events in the same years was not fortuitous, but in different ways the by-product of processes of change and modernization in underdeveloped societies, either on the periphery of Europe or outside it altogether,[24] just as the civil wars, national liberation movements, and national unification drives in the years between 1775 and 1871 had been the product of changes in the more developed societies. Most of these new cases were also accompanied by major outbreaks of political violence – the worst in peacetime since the Paris Commune of 1871 – involving trial runs for genocide in Turkey between 1894 and 1909 in which more than 200,000 Armenians were slaughtered in the twentieth century's first gigantic outbreak of jihadist violence, while between 1904 and 1907 Russia was the scene of the century's first large-scale systematic political

---

[22] P. H. Wilson, *The Thirty Years War: Europe's Tragedy* (Cambridge, Mass., 2009).

[23] The early and middle decades of the seventeenth century constituted an era of war and internal rebellion on an enormous scale, affecting not merely Europe but also Russia, the Middle East, and Asia. It was the period of the most extreme worldwide turmoil during the modern era prior to the twentieth century. Jack Goldstone, in *Revolution and Rebellion in the Early Modern World* (Berkeley, Calif., 1991), argues that such extensive conflict was provoked above all by a crisis in resources resulting from demographic and environmental catastrophe, while Geoffrey Parker contends that it was crucially influenced by major shifts in environment and climate: Goldstone, "Crisis and Catastrophe: The Global Crisis of the Seventeenth Century Reconsidered," *American Historical Review*, 104:4 (October 2008), 1053–79; and Parker, *The Global Crisis: War, Climate, and Catastrophe in the Seventeenth-Century World* (New Haven, Conn., 2010). In general, the consequences were not revolutionary change, despite the major reformist breakthrough in England and the pronounced shift toward absolutism and centralism in numerous European states, two kinds of change that moved in opposite directions. The aftermath is treated in T. K. Rabb, *The Struggle for Stability in Early Modern Europe* (New York, 1975).

[24] The only recent study that attempts to treat these cases together (with the exceptions of Greece and Romania) is C. Kurzman, *Democracy Denied, 1905–1915* (Cambridge, Mass., 2008).

terrorism. The Young Turk regime soon became one of the most sinister of the twentieth century, its one-party state a partial precursor of Bolshevism and Fascism, its "Teshkilat" squads to some extent forerunners of the Cheka and the SS.

Revolution is usually not an event but a process.[25] In every case, none of these developments of the years 1905–11 was decisive, but merely marked the beginning of a process that either began to erode, or had initially accomplished the overthrow, of the old regime. In some cases, the full development of these processes would require decades to complete. They would usually lead to civil war or other convulsive internal conflict, though this was not so in every case, and in some the eventual civil war would not develop for years or decades. Forms of civil strife might continue for many years.

Twentieth-century revolutionary/counterrevolutionary civil wars began in Finland and in Russia in 1917–18, and would eventually spread around much of the world, but would not afflict any of the advanced countries save, to a degree, Germany. Among the various patterns of revolutionary conflict to appear was that of the east Baltic peoples, where the dominant goal was national liberation, with foreign powers playing major military roles, while a different one appeared in the societies of established states like Germany and Italy. In Hungary, where a complete revolutionary takeover briefly occurred, there was little civil war, but multiple liberation movements by the nationalities, accompanied by foreign intervention. In countries as far apart as Poland and Portugal political conflict was sometimes violent, but did not involve social revolution and never led to full civil war (except for two months in Portugal), while attempted Communist insurrections in Bulgaria and Estonia (1924) failed to reignite civil conflict. The last revolutionary civil war of the era took place in Spain from 1936 to 1939, though perceptions of it were heavily influenced by the foreign interventions that took place, so that in some interpretations the Spanish war is folded into World War II and is not treated simply as the bridge between two epochs. Within the strange world of the Soviet Union, massive violence and also a degree of insurgency (unable to achieve civil war) persisted, not merely because of the proclivity of the Soviet state to wage a kind of war against its own citizens, but also because of the continuing resistance of sectors of the Muslim nationalities. Outside Europe, the process of the Mexican revolution went on for years, with limited civil war reignited in the late 1920s, when the new regime sought to suppress Catholicism. The process was most chaotic of all in China, with complete disintegration a danger for some years. The eventual civil war between the new revolutionary Nationalist (Kuomintang) regime and the Communist movement began in 1927 and would weave its way through varying stages for more than two decades, a war in which the original revolutionaries would find themselves cast in the role of counterrevolutionaries.

[25] R. D. Hopper, "The Revolutionary Process: A Frame of Reference for the Study of Revolutionary Movements," *Social Forces*, 28 (March 1950), 270–79.

During World War II a form of multisided revolutionary civil war developed in occupied Yugoslavia, and then also in Greece. A limited sort of civil war was waged in occupied northern Italy between 1943 and 1945, while in the western borderlands of the Soviet Union various forms of internal conflict and violence persisted throughout the 1940s. During the next two generations, during the Cold War, revolutionary insurrections broke out in many different parts of what was called the Third World – such places as Vietnam, the Philippines, Malaya, Cuba, Yemen, Nicaragua, Angola, and Mozambique, to provide only a partial list – in most of these countries creating conditions of internal war or insurgency and in some cases full-scale civil war. Revolutionary terrorist organizations created severe conflict in Turkey, in various Latin American countries, and indeed in a sizable part of the world, including Spain, though this did not produce conditions approximating civil war, except in several Latin American cases. When these instances involved national liberation struggle as well, the conflict became even more intense.

Twentieth-century revolutionary civil wars typically featured a struggle between revolutionary collectivists (usually, but not always, Communists) and various kinds of more conservative, or at least anti-Communist, counterrevolutionary forces, ranging from liberal democrats to fascists. In some major cases, such as Russia and China, the revolutionaries won, though counterrevolutionaries were normally successful in Europe (Finland, the Baltic, Hungary, Spain, Greece), and later revolutionary insurrections were suppressed in the Philippines, Malaya, Central America, and elsewhere.

One major way in which revolutionary civil wars have differed from both international conflicts and more traditional civil wars has been their greater tendency to dehumanize opponents and the proportionate extent of their atrocities against civilians, though of course there are some atrocities against civilians in nearly all conflicts. In traditional civil wars, as in many international wars, there was sometimes greater willingness to recognize the common humanity of the other side, whereas revolutionary civil wars have been waged as wars between two totally different concepts of state, society, and culture that brook no compromise. Their protagonists have tended to regard the opposition not merely as a political foe but as the bearer of an entire adversarial culture or religion, a totally different system of belief, values, and morality, which threatens every dimension of life. Thus the goal is often not merely military victory but complete extirpation in one form or another, often leading to massive repression and executions. Even before the advent of modern revolutions, such a tendency in civil war was noted by a good many commentators.[26]

Two other aspects increase the potential bloodiness of civil wars. One is the absence of a clear demarcation between two contenders in the same country,

---

[26] The most thorough and intellectually sophisticated comparative analysis of this phenomenon will be found in S. Kalyvas, *The Logic of Violence in Civil War* (Cambridge, UK, 2007). See his discussion of "barbarism" in civil war, 52–86.

so that the potential for the existence of an "internal enemy" is much greater than in international wars, an almost ubiquitous circumstance dramatized especially by the concept of the "Fifth Column" in Spain in 1936. Beyond that, the breakdown of law and order in civil wars permits, and sometimes encourages, the growth of private violence, involving strictly personal, sometimes totally nonpolitical vindictiveness.

As Dan Diner and others have pointed out, it was the American Civil War that gave birth to the phrase "unconditional surrender." This "rules out any compromise that might allow for the continued existence of both parties. In an undivided polity, only one party can hold a monopoly on ... use of force.... For that reason, civil wars are the most brutal wars possible, intensifying animosities and the exercise of violence to a radical degree." In wars between two established states there often exists a certain mutual recognition, including a rule of war that "does not strive for the enemy's total destruction." Civil wars, by contrast, "generate an unlimited degree of radicalization." Civil wars and international wars "are conceptual antipodes," the former "propelled by questions of religion and values, of ideology and principles."[27]

In his essay *Ex Captivitate Salus* (1949), Carl Schmitt emphasized that civil war is especially cruel because it has a tendency to overturn the legal system, justifying extreme means and demanding total triumph that requires the absolute political, and sometimes physical, elimination of the enemy, to show pity for whom is held to be a sign of weakness and lack of commitment. This was initially pointed out by Thucydides in his *History of the Peloponnesian War*, the first account of such conflict that we have. He wrote that in the civil war in Corcyra (Corfu) in 427 B.C. all laws were overthrown, permitting conditions of massive violence in which murder was committed with abandon, combatants seeking to prove their commitment and loyalty by murdering fellow citizens.[28]

André Malraux has quoted Mao Zedong as declaring that "revolution is the mobilization of hatred." The resultant revolutionary violence is important in its symbolism and in its religious role, both as sacrificial and as redemptive violence, and in the expurgative killing of scapegoats. Counterrevolutionaries, in turn, condemn the violence employed by revolutionaries because it pursues redemptive scapegoating, while conversely viewing the victims of this process, depending on their identity and behavior, as martyrs whose sacrifice is in turn redemptive for the counterrevolutionary cause.[29] This latter feature

---

[27] D. Diner, *Cataclysms: A History of the Twentieth Century from Europe's Edge* (Madison, Wis., 2007), 12–13.

[28] These two examples are pointed out in E. Traverso, *A ferro e fuoco: La guerra civile europea 1914–1945* (Bologna, 2007), 66.

[29] This problem is treated in J. Goldhammer, *The Headless Republic: Sacrificial Violence in Modern French Thought* (Ithaca, N.Y., 2005). On the redemptive role of the sacrificial scapegoat, see R. Girard, *The Scapegoat* (Baltimore, 1986) and *I See Satan Fall like Lightning* (Maryknoll, N.Y., 2001), and G. Baillie, *Violence Unveiled: Humanity at the Crossroads* (New York, 1997).

appeared most fully in the aftermath of the Spanish civil war, with the great number of beatifications of members of the martyred clergy. The phenomenon was first seen in modern Europe during the wars of religion in the sixteenth and seventeenth centuries,[30] and then fully revealed in the Terror of the French Revolution, which may have slain 40,000 people,[31] while as many as 300,000 perished in the accompanying civil war, with its mass slaughters.[32] The counterrevolution of repressive violence occurred not immediately after the revolution but three generations later in the bloody repression of the Commune of Paris in 1871, which may have produced as many as 20,000 summary executions.[33]

During the Cold War and especially afterward, as international war became less and less frequent, forms of civil war emerged as the most common kind of armed conflict. Powerful factors discouraged direct international war after 1945, but decolonization and the formation of an increasing number of new states, the rapid growth of political consciousness and mobilization, together with the destabilizing effects of new social, economic, and cultural changes, have in varying ways combined to produce ever more internal violence. By the end of the twentieth century this was no longer primarily triggered by the classic revolutionary movements, but more commonly by racial, ethnic, religious, and other factors.[34] Civil war had become the predominant form of violent conflict.[35]

[30] D. Crouzet, *Les guerriers de Dieu: La violence au temps des troubles de religion, vers 1525 – vers 1610* (Seyssel, 1990).

[31] P. Gueniffey, *La politique de la Terreur. Essai sur la violence révolutionnaire, 1789–1794* (Paris, 2000), and A. J. Mayer, *The Furies: Violence and Terror in the French and Russian Revolutions* (Princeton, N.J., 2000).

[32] Then approximately 500,000 French troops and untold numbers of Europeans died in the revolution's wars between 1792 and 1799, and about the same number in the endless wars of Napoleon that followed, out of a population of nearly 29 million. J. Dupâquier, "Le coût humain de la Révolution française," in E. Vilquin, ed., *Révolution et population. Aspects démographiques des grandes révolutions politiques* (Louvain, 1990), 37–53.

[33] A. Horne, *The Fall of Paris: The Siege and the Commune 1870–71* (London, 1965); R. L. Williams, *The French Revolution of 1870–1871* (New York, 1969); and R. Tombs, *The War Against Paris: 1871* (Cambridge, UK, 1981). The Commune also inspired Karl Marx's classic account, *The Civil War in France* (1871).

[34] The revolutionary civil wars of the first half of the twentieth century may of course be seen as wars of political or secular religion, and there is little doubt that the Spanish war of 1936 also involved a war of religion, as will be discussed later in this book.

[35] For further discussion of the reasons for the prevalence of civil war, see N. Sambanis and I. Elbadawi, "How Many Wars Will We See? Explaining the Prevalence of Civil War," *Journal of Conflict Resolution*, 46:3 (2002), 307–34.

PART ONE

WORLD WAR I AND AN ERA OF INTERNAL CONFLICT, 1905–1935

I

World War, Revolution, Civil War, 1905–1918

The era of world war and revolution in Europe was a time of unprecedented transformation. The four decades 1890–1930 constituted a sort of "Axial Age" of classical modernity, for most of the inventions and technological advances that made the difference between traditional life and the way in which modern people have lived ever since were first introduced or generalized during these years. Innovations included much broader use of electricity, the telephone, movies, automobiles, airplanes, the radio, refrigeration, and such basic conveniences as generalized indoor plumbing. Medical science also made vital breakthroughs. At the beginning of this period, most fatalities in warfare stemmed from disease; at its close, this was no longer true. There have been comparatively few decisive, absolutely new inventions since that time, for the computer was initially developed, and nuclear fission discovered, only a few years later.

There were similarly decisive innovations in politics, culture, and social organization. Political democracy first became a major feature of European life during this period, even though it met frustration or failure in many countries. The emergence of the masses altered social relations, accompanied by mass culture and mass politics. The origins of artistic "modernism" date from the mid nineteenth century, but modernism became a common artistic style only after the fin de siècle. Mass publicity and the arts of mass propaganda were introduced around the same time.

Modern political and social ideologies had been developing since the second half of the eighteenth century, but became genuine mass movements only in this first era of classical modernity, producing intense conflict, revolution, civil war, and novel new radical dictatorships. No new ideologies have been introduced since that time, with the possible exception of postmodern, post-Marxist Political Correctness, which crystallized only in the late twentieth century and lacks the canonical definition of the classic ideologies.

The convergence of so many new ideas and influences was profoundly destabilizing – more so, in fact, than any set of new social and cultural conditions that had ever before existed at a single time in human history. It helped to spark profound unrest, which for many led to hope for drastic transformation, with a higher standard of living and novel diversions, or for an absolute new utopia. For others, the political, social, and international changes of the era of world war, followed later by unprecedented economic depression, generated great pessimism, foreboding, and fear.

The sense of a great mutation – politically, culturally, or both – was widespread, the sense not merely of the ending of the old era but of the ending of traditional culture and society in general, producing an increasing mood of apocalyptic expectation among cultural and social elites. This mood was strongest among Russian cultural elites before 1917, among German elites afterward. In the revolutionary movements it was translated into millenarian expectations. Altogether, the convergence of such influences, when combined with an unprecedented level of international conflict, produced profound destabilization, demands for radical change or improvement, and widespread internal strife, which some historians have called – with a degree of exaggeration – a climate of general European civil war.

Ever since the French Revolution, the danger of internal revolt, convulsion, or civil war had been a latent threat for much of Europe.[1] During the nineteenth century, such concerns had focused on three different kinds of conflict: the division between liberals and traditionalists; the rebellions and wars of nationalists seeking either secession or unification (and sometimes of minorities opposed to that); and later increasingly the rise of the "social question," which referred to the mounting resentment of workers in industrializing areas and also of poor peasants in the most backward countries.

The twentieth-century era of revolution began with the abortive Russian Revolution of 1905. Though the tsarist empire had continued to expand, it had fallen prey to grave internal pressures, both horizontally and vertically. Vicious internal wars had been waged during the preceding century to maintain control of subject nationalities, particularly the Poles, as well as Muslims in the Caucasus, while vertical social discontent grew apace, especially among enserfed Russian peasants, who scarcely considered themselves an imperial *Herrenvolk*. There were more small peasant revolts in nineteenth-century Russia than during any equivalent period in any land in history, and the terms of peasant emancipation in 1861 had not solved the problem, for severe issues of land tenure and credit remained. Rapid industrialization from the close of the nineteenth century generated a new class of disaffected and exploited urban workers, whose numbers expanded rapidly, while political resentment against the imperial autocracy – the only European state to deny any form of parliamentary government – had mounted ever since the 1860s.

---

[1] For a broad philosophical and historical approach, see H. Kesting, *Geschichtsphilosophie und Weltbürgerkrieg. Deutungen der Geschichte von der Französischen Revolution bis zum Ost-West Konflikt* (Heidelberg, 1959), and R. Schnur, *Revolution und Weltbürgerkrieg. Studien zur Ouvertüre nach 1789* (Berlin, 1983).

The combined explosion of political, urban social, and agrarian discontents came to a head in the semi-spontaneous rebellion of 1905, whose catalyst was imperial defeat in the Russo-Japanese War. For the first time the tsarist regime temporarily lost control and was forced to grant major concessions, though most of the army remained loyal, and Nicholas II was able to regain dominance by 1907. Revolutionary terrorism had begun in the 1860s and reached a high point during these years in the greatest outburst of terrorist activity since the French Revolution, a variety of organizations killing nearly 8,000 people over a period of years, many of them low-level state employees. There was a degree of continuity between this terrorism and the subsequent state terrorist apparatus of the Bolsheviks, with some of the same personnel involved.[2] After 1905, the resultant state repression officially executed at least 4,500 people, and in fact probably many more, but for the first time since the France of the 1790s, revolutionaries had shown that their propensity for violence was as great or greater than the repression of the previously established regime.

The great Romanian peasant revolt of the late winter of 1907 was a simpler affair, stemming from massive peasant protests against oppressive terms of land leases. As in Russia, sizable units of the army had to be called out, even employing artillery, and in a brutal repression approximately 11,000 peasants were killed. Proportionate to the population, the loss of life was considerably greater than in Russia.[3]

The decade prior to World War I was a time of widespread rebelliousness, though all successful revolts were more specifically political than social, beginning with the limited Persian political revolution initiated in 1906, partly under the influence of events in Russia, and the Young Turk rebellion of 1908 that began to impose a new modernizing nationalist elite on the Ottoman state. The Greek military revolt of 1909 and the Portuguese republican insurrection of 1910 brought to power more advanced and radical forms of liberalism, while the revolutions that began in China and Mexico in 1910–11 were much broader and more open-ended processes that would not play out fully for many years.

Nationalism played a major role in all these convulsions of 1906–11, and indeed for much of the nineteenth century, prior to the rise of socialism and anarchism, the dominant form of European revolutionism had been nationalism, manifested in movements of liberation or secession, of unification, of domestic transformation, and of irredentism or external expansion.[4] Late eighteenth- and nineteenth-century nationalism often advanced the idea that the

---

[2] The best study of revolutionary terrorism in Russia prior to 1917 is A. Geifman, *Thou Shalt Kill: Revolutionary Terrorism in Russia, 1894–1917* (Princeton, N.J., 1993). See also her *Death Orders: The Vanguard of Modern Terrorism in Revolutionary Russia* (Santa Barbara, Calif., 2010).

[3] See P. G. Eidelberg, *The Great Rumanian Peasant Revolt of 1907: Origins of a Modern Jacquerie* (Leiden, 1974), and, for a brief account, K. Hitchins, *Rumania 1866–1947* (Oxford, 1994), 176–79.

[4] J. H. Billington, *Fire in the Minds of Men: Origins of the Revolutionary Faith* (New York, 1980), 126–364.

nation would introduce a new politics and a new culture, something expressed in varying ways by the French Revolution, by liberal nationalists, by Russian Slavophils and Pan-Slavists, and by the idea of the new Germany as a dynamic cultural and political force that would overcome the perceived decadence of the West, ushering in a new order.[5]

By 1914–15 a new concept would contend that war itself would be the mother of radical transformation and revolution by achieving mass mobilization, the shattering of institutional barriers, and an opening for new social and cultural forces.[6] This stemmed in part from the "cultural revolution of the 1890s" that served as the conceptual matrix of fascism,[7] emphasizing vitalist philosophy, the priority of conflict, and the cult of violence.

Concern over the relationship between war and revolution led to quite divergent conclusions. After the folly of 1905, Russian conservatives urged the tsar to avoid war like the plague, agreeing with the radicals that war would bring another and greater revolution. Concern about socialism was the main reason why, proportionate to national population, the standing army of Germany was smaller than that of France. About half the German population, a higher proportion than in any other large continental country, was made up of workers, mostly attracted to socialism, and thus the military establishment had preferred not to draft its full quota but to rely on what it considered the more reliable social sectors. This was also one of several factors that stimulated a decision for preemptive war in 1914 in order to unify the nation and to provide the best chance, even if a somewhat desperate one, to preserve established institutions. In Italy, however, radical nationalists viewed the war from the opposite perspective, as the midwife of revolution that would achieve a mass mobilization of society otherwise impossible, breaking down the barriers of the old order. Russian Bolsheviks viewed the war as the icebreaker of revolution, rejecting any involvement, keeping their hands free to exploit the breakdown and chaos they hoped would result.

The German government was certainly original in some of its designs during World War I. If revolutionaries dreamed of major war to precipitate the end of the old order, officials in the German Foreign Ministry put their own twist on the concept. They developed a broad, if not entirely integrated, strategy of subversion, sabotage, and revolution to promote the collapse of enemy home fronts and of opposing empires from within. This was a goal not of universal civil war, but of multiple targets for subversion, by far the

---

[5] Certain origins of this idea are treated in P. L. Rose, *Revolutionary Antisemitism in Germany from Kant to Wagner* (Princeton, N.J., 1990).

[6] E. Gentile, *L'apocalisse della modernità. La grande guerra per l'uomo nuevo* (Milan, 2008); M. Eksteins, *Rites of Spring: The Great War and the Birth of the Modern Age* (New York, 1989).

[7] The term was coined by Zeev Sternhell with regard to the intellectual background of fascism in his "Fascist Ideology," in W. Laqueur, ed., *Fascism: A Reader's Guide* (Berkeley, Calif., 1986), 315–76. See S. G. Payne, *A History of Fascism, 1914–1945* (Madison, Wisc., 1995), 23–34, and, more broadly, P. Blom, *The Vertigo Years: Europe, 1900–1914* (New York, 2008).

most elaborate strategy of sabotage on an international level ever conceived to that point in history, designed especially to bring down the existing order in Russia and to undermine the British and French empires.[8] This encompassed the preaching of jihad (holy war) against the imperial overlord in the Muslim domains of Britain, France, and Russia (extending the jihad to Shiite Muslims with the goal of bringing Shiite Iran into the war on the side of Germany and Turkey);[9] domestic sabotage of war industry, accompanied by an abortive effort at biological warfare, in the United States;[10] colonial revolt against France (and also Spain) in Morocco;[11] inciting rebellion in and running guns to Ireland; secretly funding pacifists and socialists in order to subvert the war effort in France; fomenting of class war and terrorism in Barcelona to undermine Spanish war production for the Allies;[12] and subsidizing revolution in Russia.[13] This last involved not merely financial support of revolutionary socialism, but also efforts to incite the various national minorities,[14] as well as a half-hearted attempt to stimulate the subversive potential of Russian Jews. Only in Russia did this strategy meet with success,[15] even though the revolution of 1917 was due overwhelmingly to internal causes.

If the limitations of its navy fundamentally restricted Germany to a war in Europe, the German government sought by these and other means to extend the war much farther abroad, because in a broader war the empires of the Entente powers had even more to lose. From the earlier concept of *Weltpolitik* (world policy), German leaders moved to the idea of *Weltkrieg*, a "world war." Upsetting the established international order was the goal, in order to achieve not merely security but hegemonic status, and hence the paradox that

[8] F. Fischer, *Germany's Aims in the First World War* (New York, 1967), 120–54.

[9] P. Hopkirk, *Like Hidden Fire: The Plot to Bring Down the British Empire* (New York, 1994); D. M. McKale, *War by Revolution: Germany and Great Britain in the Middle East in the Era of World War I* (Kent, Ohio, 1998); T. Ludke, *Jihad in Germany: Ottoman and German Propaganda and Intelligence Operations in the First World War* (Münster, 2005); M. Aksakal, *The Ottoman Road to War in 1914: The Ottoman Empire and the First World War* (Cambridge, UK, 2008); U. Gehrke, *Persien in der deutschen Orientpolitik während des Ersten Weltkrieges* (Stuttgart, 1960), 2 vols.; T. G. Fraser, "Germany and Indian Revolution, 1914–18," *Journal of Contemporary History*, 12 (1977), 255–72.

[10] C. Millman, *The Detonators: The Secret Plan to Destroy America and an Epic Hunt for Justice* (Boston, 2006); R. L. Koenig, *The Four Horsemen: One Man's Mission to Wage the Great War in America* (New York, 2006).

[11] H. L. Müller, *Islam, gihad ("Heiliger Krieg") und Deutsches Reich: Ein Nachspiel zur wilhelmischen Weltpolitik im Mahgreb, 1912–1918* (New York, 1991); E. Burke, "Moroccan Resistance, Pan-Islam and German War Strategy, 1914–1918," *Francia. Forschungen zur West-europäische Geschichte*, 3 (1975), 434–64.

[12] F. J. Romero Salvadó, *Spain 1914–1918: Between War and Revolution* (London, 1999).

[13] Z. A. B. Zeman, *Germany and the Revolution in Russia, 1915–1918* (London, 1958); W. Hahlweg, *Lenins Rückkehr nach Russland 1917. Die deutschen Akten* (Leiden, 1957).

[14] S. Zetterberg, *Die Liga der Fremdvölker Russlands 1916–1918. Ein Beitrag zu Deutschlands antirussischen Propagandakrieg unter den Fremdvölkern Russlands im Ersten Weltkrieg* (Helsinki, 1978).

[15] Even though the twenty-six million marks spent in Russia was only a fraction of the total funding for the multiple subversion programs.

a fundamentally conservative and nondemocratic power was in fact playing a revolutionary role in world affairs.

War discourse in Germany repeated some of the concepts developed by nineteenth-century German nationalism, presenting the conflict as a *Weltanschauungskrieg*, a kind of war of ideology and values to preserve and expand the higher form of German culture, of German idealism over and against Russian despotism or Anglo-French commercialism, materialism, and market imperialism. For German nationalists this was far superior to the ideals of 1789, and in October 1914 more than 4,000 German professors and intellectuals signed a manifesto that declared the end of the "long nineteenth century" of materialism and the beginning of a great struggle waged by an heroic spirit and high ideals to triumph over materialism and the mediocrity of political liberalism. The same contrast might be found in Werner Sombart's *Händler und Helden* (Traders and Heroes, 1915) and in the Jewish writer Nachum Goldmann's *Der Geist des Militarismus* (The Spirit of Militarism, 1915), which heralded military spirit as truly progressive, combining equality of opportunity with meritocracy, a victory not just for Germany but for all mankind.[16]

For Germany the world war became a struggle free from conventions identified with the archenemy England: a banally experienced world, a materialism averse to everything metaphysical, a despicable reality of exchange, trade, and money earning. Germany wanted to change the world; England was straining to preserve it. ... From this perspective, the Great War can indeed be viewed as a war between cultures – in the words of Franz Marc, a "European civil war."[17]

Whether justified or not, Germans were the first to use this concept, derived at least to some extent from the idealist and purposeful German philosophy of history. A leftist spin was placed on it by the Socialist Paul Lensch, in his *Drei Jahre Weltrevolution* (1917), which suggested that the drastic alterations wrought by the war might enable a semisocialist Germany to lead a new era of progress as the most modern and progressive country, by contrast with capitalist Britain and bourgeois France. This would represent "true socialism" or "German socialism."

The concept of "international civil war" – in itself oxymoronic – can be advanced only from a universalist perspective or concept that projects the same policy or doctrine in a continental or world dimension. Within the realm of culture, followers of Friedrich Nietzsche during the preceding generation

[16] H. Strachan, *The First World War* (London, 2003), 61. Strachan also points out that Walther Rathenau, who was in charge of mobilizing raw materials for war production, postulated that Germany's wartime economic policy was creating "a new form of economic organization which would combine the best features of capitalism with those of collectivism in a managed economy." For further discussion, see R. Rürup, "Der Geist von 1914 in Deutschland: Kriegsbegeisterung und Ideologisierung des Krieges im Ersten Weltkrieg," in B. Huppauf, ed., *Ansichten vom Krieg. Vergleichende Studien zum Ersten Weltkrieg in Literatur und Gesellschaft* (Königstein im Taunus, 1984), 4–23.

[17] Diner, *Cataclysms*, 25.

had argued that the transvaluation of values and deconstruction of traditional culture that his philosophy promoted would lead to an "international civil war" in culture. During the course of the nineteenth century a kind of political and historical philosophy had begun to emerge in Germany, drawn from idealist philosophy and its concept of world history. In the war years quite different perspectives developed in the Western democracies on the basis of liberal democratic doctrine, then later in Russia on the basis of revolutionary Marxism. By comparison, the political content of the German position remained remarkably vague, and had difficulty going beyond the projection of idealized power. From the beginning, therefore, the idea of German revolution in the modern world threatened to become a sort of revolution of nihilism.

Another way in which both world wars resembled civil wars is that, unlike most preceding international wars, both conflicts were pressed by their major participants toward absolute victory. There were exceptions, such as that of Austria-Hungary in 1917, but the rejection of limited goals, otherwise characteristic of most international conflicts, and the orientation toward total victory bore some similarity to civil wars.

The war soon came to be experienced as something of a revolution by people who were in no way revolutionaries, because it was destroying the common fabric of a European culture that in recent generations had developed more fully and had become more closely interconnected than in any previous time. Achievement of the first economic globalization, the tendency toward convergence of political and legal systems, the expansion of a common scientific and educational culture, and even the intermarriage of the ruling dynasties had all produced an increasingly interassociated European society. An awareness among some that life was not so very dissimilar in enemy society created a sensation akin to civil war. For some Europeans what was being destroyed was not only countless lives but also the very form of civilization itself. The war gave impetus to a cultural revolution of nihilism and placed in question the belief in a common Western civilization. The temporary stabilization that would take place in the 1920s would be inadequate to restore what had been lost, so that historians as diverse as Eric Hobsbawm, François Furet, Ernst Nolte, and Enzo Traverso have employed the concept of "international civil war" to the entire era, beginning either in 1914 or 1917 and extending to 1945.[18]

Standards of legitimacy and justice are frequent casualties of war, but this seemed especially the case in 1914, as the concepts of just war and civilized conflict began to be cast aside. European theorists had generally held that all sovereign states or rulers had the right to wage war (*jus ad bellum*), but that this was limited by norms for the proper conduct of war (*jus in bello*). Such standards had recently been violated primarily in colonial wars, which in some cases had been conducted with absolute ruthlessness, as in the recent

---

[18] E. Nolte, *Der europäische Bürgerkrieg 1917–1945. Nationalsozialismus und Bolschewismus* (Frankfurt, 1987); E. Traverso, *A ferro e fuoco: La guerra civile europea 1914–1945* (Bologna, 2007).

campaign by the Germans in southwest Africa,[19] though there were examples
by other powers as well.[20] World War I broke many of the rules and brought
the standards of colonial war home to Europe. Neutral countries were invaded
(and not just by Germany), rights and laws of the sea violated, a loose blockade – illegal under international law – imposed on Germany, civilians arrested
and shot, chemical warfare employed and biological warfare attempted, and
the bombing of cities initiated.

Some years before the war it had been noted that the German General
Staff manual on the conduct of war of 1902 apparently ignored the restrictions regarding bombardments of cities, reprisals, and the rights of neutrals
as established by the First Hague Conference in 1899.[21] In their invasion of
Belgium and France the Germans took civilian hostages and executed 6,427
civilians, including at least 43 priests, during the first weeks.[22] Similar things
happened in the initial invasion of Serbia[23] and in the campaigns of all three
armies on the eastern front.[24]

Ethnic cleansing and genocide are the most extreme forms of internal war.
The tsarist government revealed what cynics might say is the standard Russian
tendency toward sadomasochism as it practiced a form of ethnic cleansing
on some of its own subjects, applying scorched-earth policies to the homes of
many Polish, Jewish, and Baltic people in its western provinces during 1914–15,
some three million of whom were forcibly displaced to distant parts of Russia,
which only added to the growing confusion and chaos within its borders.[25]
Moreover, the tsarist government was the only participant in the war except
Britain that had to suppress a major internal revolt, brutally putting down a
rebellion against conscription in Russian Central Asia, a revolt in which tens of
thousands of Muslim civilians perished, though the deportations planned for
the aftermath were canceled owing to the collapse of the regime.[26]

[19] I. V. Hull, *Absolute Destruction: Military Culture and the Practices of War in Imperial Germany* (Ithaca, N.Y., 2005), 7–90.
[20] V. R. Berghahn, *Europe in the Era of Two World Wars: From Militarism and Genocide to Civil Society, 1900–1950* (Princeton, N.J., 2006), 18–25.
[21] Though the government of William II always tended to blow hot and cold, as when at the Second Hague Conference of 1907 it took the initiative in proposing sanctions against those who violated the laws of war. Comment by Eric Thiers in S. Audoin-Rousseau et al., eds., *La violence de guerre 1914–1945* (Brussels, 2002), 52–54; and see, more broadly, Hull, *Absolute Destruction*, 110–58.
[22] J. Horne and A. Kramer, *German Atrocities, 1914: A History of Denial* (New Haven, Conn., 2001); J. Lipkes, *Rehearsals: The German Army in Belgium, August 1914* (Leuven, 2007).
[23] Though apparently behavior by the Austro-Hungarians soon moderated, seeking to conciliate and incorporate the Serbs. J. E. Gumz, *The Resurrection and Collapse of Empire in Habsburg Servia, 1914–1918* (Cambridge, UK, 2009).
[24] A. Kramer, *Dynamic of Destruction: Culture and Mass Killing in the First World War* (New York, 2007), offers a broad approach.
[25] P. Gatrell, *A Whole Empire Walking: Refugees in Russia during World War I* (Bloomington, Ind., 1999); V. Thurstan, *The People Who Run: Being the Tragedy of the Refugee in Russia* (New York, 1916).
[26] E. D. Sokol, *The Revolt of 1916 in Russian Central Asia* (Baltimore, 1953).

The first major modern European ethnic cleansing had apparently taken place during the rolling back of the Islamic frontier in eastern Europe in the nineteenth century, initially in parts of the Caucasus and later in the Balkans, followed by similar processes of deportation in the Balkan wars of 1912–13, conducted ruthlessly. Nearly all the victims had been Muslims. Massive slaughters of Armenians then took place in Turkey between 1895 and 1909, as Turkish leaders cynically employed Islamist and jihadist notions to try to strengthen central control. On the eve of World War I, Turkish government leaders debated the possibility of undertaking widespread ethnic cleansing of the several Christian minorities within their country, viewing mass deportation of Greeks, Armenians, and perhaps also Assyrian Christians as the best way to achieve unity and cohesion in a modern nationalist Turkey. Under severe wartime conditions, this led in 1915–16 to wholesale deportation of nearly all Armenians. Most adult males were liquidated outright, in a manner soon to be replicated in whole or in part by Soviet Communists and by German Nazis, the operation quickly escalating into a genocide that may have claimed as many as a million lives,[27] a horrific process in which Turkey's ally Germany played an indirect and inadvertent role.[28] A further example that remained only latent might be found in Bulgaria, where during the war officials debated ethnic cleansing in newly occupied Macedonia, briefly contemplating a scheme for liquidation of part of the population by means of mobile gas chambers, a project fortunately never put into practice. These cases in World War I have been seen by some historians as trial runs for the greater genocide and truly massive ethnic cleansing of World War II.

It is nonetheless necessary to distinguish between the experience of World War I as a profound rupture, a mass destruction both of human ideals and of millions of lives, of the breakdown of social structures and the overthrow of empires, on the one hand, and the growth of internal war, on the other. Conditions for the latter fully emerged in the tsarist empire only in 1917, and in some other countries only by the end of the war itself. Strictly speaking, there can be no question of World War I being a European or international civil war, since it was a classic contest among states, empires, and international alliances. When all is said and done, the idea of "European civil war" as applied to the events of 1914–17 is an exaggeration.

---

[27] The most important studies are T. Akçam, *A Shameful Act: The Armenian Genocide and the Question of Turkish Responsibility* (New York, 2006), and G. Lewy, *The Armenian Massacres in Ottoman Turkey: A Disputed Genocide* (Salt Lake City, 2005). Other principal works include R. Melson, *Revolution and Genocide: On the Origins of the Armenian Genocide and the Holocaust* (Chicago, 1992); V. N. Dadrian, *The History of the Armenian Genocide: Ethnic Conflict from the Balkans to Anatolia to the Caucasus* (Providence, R.I., 1995); M. Mann, *The Dark Side of Democracy: Explaining Ethnic Cleansing* (Cambridge, UK, 2005); and D. Bloxham, *The Great Game of Genocide: Imperialism, Nationalism, and the Destruction of the Ottoman Armenians* (Oxford, 2005). For an overview of political violence in the Middle East during this era, see H. Bozarslan, *Una historia de la violencia en Oriente Medio. Del fin del Imperio Otomano a Al Qaeda* (Barcelona, 2009), 15–72.

[28] Hull, *Absolute Destruction*, 263–90.

So long as this is understood, it is appropriate to bear in mind the afore-mentioned experience of the war as something more than and different from the standard military conflicts of the eighteenth and nineteenth centuries, marking a caesura as had no other. The war assumed dimensions only dimly foreseen at the outset, but one dimension common to both the beginning and the end in Germany was that the decision to precipitate events in 1914 reflected a determination to bar the path to the advance of socialism through extreme preemptive action that would unify the country and guarantee its existing institutions and social structure. To that extent, the Central Powers began World War I in the spirit of counterrevolution, but not in the sense of a simple reaction or return to the past. Rather, their decision reflected the sense of Joseph de Maistre's trenchant observation that "the counterrevolution is not the opposite of a revolution, but is an opposing revolution."[29]

The war had been intended by Berlin to revolutionize not society but the international power structure, establishing German dominance on the conti-nent of Europe. To that end, it was Berlin and not Bolshevist Moscow that ini-tiated the first project of world revolution and subversion, though the German project was selective and varied and in no way as systematic as the Bolshevik idea. Nearly all the German plans failed, and the war moved inexorably toward the destruction of the existing dynasties and empires of central and eastern Europe, and finally toward the threat of sociopolitical revolution and civil war, so that the era of potential civil war – often more latent than actual – embraced the years 1917–23, not the main period of the war itself.

Two new universalisms that stressed categorical internal change in European countries emerged in 1917. One was revolutionary Communism in Russia, which insisted on withdrawing from the European war to encourage interna-tional class war. The other was the democratic universalism led by Woodrow Wilson in the United States, which entered the war immediately after Russia first began to withdraw from it. Wilson developed a war aims program, the Fourteen Points, completely different from the secret deals of imperial aggran-dizement made by the other powers. His stress on political democracy and national self-determination reflected the traditional moralistic and "suprater-ritorial" policies of the United States, which periodically showed a penchant for "recognizing not states but only governments considered 'lawful' accord-ing to its own perception of legality."[30] Wilsonianism proposed its own form

---

[29] There is very little theoretical discussion of counterrevolution. See J. H. Meisel, *Counter-revolution: How Revolutions Die* (New York, 1966), and T. Molnar, *The Counter-revolution* (New York, 1969). For a discussion of De Maistre, see R. A. Lebrun, ed., *Joseph de Maistre's Life, Thought and Influence: Selected Studies* (Montreal, 2001).

[30] Diner, *Cataclysms*, 14. There is a considerable literature on this tendency in American foreign policy. See R. Kagan, *Dangerous Nation: America's Place in the World from Its Earliest Days to the Dawn of the Twentieth Century* (New York, 2006); R. M. Gamble, *The War for Righteousness: Progressive Christianity, the Great War, and the Rise of the Messianic Nation* (Wilmington, Del., 2003); and K. Krakau, *Missionsbewusstsein und Völkerrechtsdoktrin in den Vereinigten Staaten von Amerika* (Frankfurt, 1967).

of *Weltanschauungskrieg*, which was also revolutionary, at least in a political sense, and, outside of Russia, carried the day in 1918–19. Social revolution and civil war was largely, though not entirely, restricted to the lands of the former tsarist empire, where the first revolutionary civil war was waged and resolved in Finland.

THE FINNISH REVOLUTION AND CIVIL WAR OF 1918[31]

In one sense the pluriform insurrections that made up the Russian revolution of 1905 constituted the first of Europe's revolutionary civil wars of the twentieth century, but the Russian insurgency did not produce a clear-cut civil war fought between two opposing organized forces. That distinction belongs to Finland in 1918.

Finland had been the only semi-autonomous part of the tsarist empire after the latter incorporated it in 1809. During the nineteenth century semi-autonomy permitted Finland to lay the roots of a self-governing modern national society, administered by its own laws, courts, and senate under a constitutional separation of powers. From 1863 the traditional four-estate Finnish Diet (parliament) resumed regular meetings, and a major national awakening took place as the economy began to develop more rapidly. Despite an abortive program of Russification attempted by the tsarist government at the end of the century, Finland continued to enjoy much greater freedom than the rest of the empire. The elite Swedish-speaking minority began to identify themselves as Finnish, and an incipient sense of nationhood was encouraged by the consequences of the Russian Revolution of 1905, for in the following year Tsar Nicholas II authorized a modern unicameral parliament for Finland, to be elected by universal suffrage (not simply male suffrage) for all citizens over twenty-four years of age. Though the functioning of parliament was largely suppressed by the Russian reaction that followed, Finnish society was on its way to becoming one of the most democratic in the world. When new elections were finally authorized in 1916, the Finnish Social Democratic Party (SDP) became the first socialist party in the world to win a parliamentary majority, gaining a plurality of the popular vote and 103 of the 200 seats in parliament.

The outbreak of the Russian Revolution in 1917 had a dramatic effect, stimulating worker mobilization and activism, but above all energizing the Finnish independence movement. The Russian provisional government rejected the latter's demands and dissolved the Finnish parliament, then authorized new elections for October 1917, in which the Socialists lost their narrow majority, the center and moderate right returning 108 deputies, leading to a new

---

[31] Sources in Western languages are limited. For the following narrative and analysis I have primarily relied on C. J. Smith, Jr., *Finland and the Russian Revolution 1917–1922* (Athens, Ga., 1958), and A. F. Upton, *The Finnish Revolution, 1917–1918* (Minneapolis, 1980). See also R. Alapuro, *State and Revolution in Finland* (Berkeley, Calif., 1988).

center-right government. Strikes and disorder of all kinds increased, some of it
associated with the nearly 50,000 Russian soldiers and sailors stationed in the
country, who were by that point on the verge of mutiny. The Socialists formed
a militia of Red Guards, as they had earlier in 1905 (the term was apparently
first coined in Finland), while the center and right organized a separate militia
of Home Guards (later dubbed the White Guards in opposition to the Reds).
Hunger became a major problem, for Finland had to import a significant part
of its food, and supplies were interrupted by the war and then further reduced
by a poor harvest and the economic breakdown of Russia. Radical workers in
the cities of southern Finland charged that conservative farmers in the interior
were systematically trying to starve them.

The Socialists bitterly resented losing their short-lived political hegemony,
and maintained a loose association with Lenin's Bolsheviks in Russia, who
promised to support Finland's independence. They accepted Lenin's request
that they come out in opposition to the democratic Russian Provisional
Government and also that they totally reject further participation in World
War I. This stance embraced the goal of turning the world war into an international revolutionary civil war, though for months the Finnish Socialists did little
to advance that objective. As soon as he seized power in Russia in November,
Lenin urged the Socialists to do the same in Finland. On 9 November they
formed a Revolutionary Central Council of Workers in Helsinki, a broader
and more radical "soviet"-type organization that began to outflank the SDP
itself, but the Council would go no further than a week-long general strike in
mid-November, which produced widespread disorder and numerous acts of
violence, the Red Guards killing thirty-two people while suffering two fatalities of their own. Politically, the strike was a failure but initiated a process of
profound polarization, something like the effect of the 1934 agrarian general
strike and revolutionary insurrection in Spain.

At the end of November, the moderate P. E. Svinhufvud became prime
minister[32] of a coalition of the center and right, which declared Finnish independence early the following month. At the beginning of 1918 the new government announced the formation of a national army ("Protective Corps"),
though at first it was little more than a paper creation. Meanwhile, the Red
Guards, who operated largely outside the control of the Socialist leadership,
continued to engage in illegal raids, extortion, and arbitrary arrests, which
further stimulated the organization of the Home Guards, though serious
clashes were still avoided.

The Socialists sternly rejected what they called the government's decision
to create a "class-war army," though all independent states of course seek to
form some sort of security force. Lenin's official policy was noninterference
with Finland, but on 20 January he promised to send a shipment of arms to
the Red Guards six days later. In the face of impending hostilities, the Finnish

---

[32] Technically president of the senate, since the small appointive senate served as government
council, or council of ministers.

government officially recognized the Home Guards as the nucleus of a new Finnish army on 25 January, and the next day some of the cabinet ministers abandoned Helsinki for more secure territory, the rest going into hiding as the Red Guards began to take over the capital city.

The Finnish Socialist leaders were themselves semimoderates but could not withstand the pressure of radicals in their own movement (much like the later situation of moderate and semimoderate Socialist leaders in Spain), so that on the evening of 27 January 1918, as Russian arms entered the country, the Socialists announced their revolutionary seizure of power. They were the first Socialists to launch a revolutionary insurrection against a democratically elected government; the Spanish Socialists would be the second. They were able to seize the southern part of the country, with nearly half the total population and almost all the larger cities. The revolutionary leaders announced a one-party state (termed, at Lenin's suggestion, the Finnish Socialist Workers Republic) and the introduction of a mixed economy that would recognize most private property, including a rural economy based primarily on small property holders. Compared to what was developing in Russia, the economic program was moderate, but it was based on a violent, revolutionary one-party state.

The Red government prepared the draft of a new constitution providing for nominal parliamentary democracy but stipulating that "only the Left parties can form a democratic parliamentary majority," briefly making official in Finland what would be the firm and continuing position of the left in Spain after 1931. It then warned that a new democratically elected parliament might "try to restore minority rule" (Socialist terminology for a non-Socialist government), in which case "the nation" should "dissolve that parliament" and hold new elections, a curious prediction of the attitude of the Spanish left in 1933–35. Finnish Socialist leaders talked of the "dictatorship of the proletariat," of "democracy," and of a "democratic majority" without being able to resolve the contradictions between the terms. Similarly, the draft constitution did not institute a socialist economy, but recognized the right of national and local government to "own property and set up or take part in economic enterprises" so as to "give the nation the opportunity to strive toward a socialist society."[33]

Schoolteachers and government employees went on strike en masse against the new regime, and most schools had to close. Most of industry had to shut down as well, as the new regime struggled to take control, often unsuccessfully, of key activities.

The Finnish Socialist Workers Republic applied less coercion than would be the case in subsequent revolutionary regimes, but on the local level rested on worker soviets (councils) and often was unable to control the Red Guards, so that a Finnish Red Terror developed. There were at least 1,649 political killings in Red territory, proportionate to the population a lower figure than

---

[33] The quotations are from Upton, *Finnish Revolution*, 391–93.

would later be registered in Russia, Spain, Yugoslavia, or Greece. Common victims were military volunteers seeking to flee to the White zone and White prisoners taken in combat, though the bulk were outright political executions, of which there were several hundred in the final days of Red power in the southeast. After some weeks there were more and more arrests of opposing leaders and of the social and economic elite, but these were not entirely systematic. Most members of the middle class suffered only limited harassment, and even though most cabinet ministers in the Finnish parliamentary government had gone into hiding in Red territory, not a single one was discovered or arrested. The century's first Red Terror by a revolutionary state was sporadic, not systematic. Revolutionary courts were instituted, but the Red Guards complained of their leniency. Socialist moderates protested the atrocities committed in the name of the revolution, and even formed a "Commission for the Investigation of Murder and Other Outrages Committed in Helsinki and Environs during the Revolution." It remained a dead letter, but constituted a more direct protest than would be found among the revolutionaries in Russia, Spain, or elsewhere. Ultimately, a few Socialist moderates even fled to the White zone.

The regular parliamentary government was reorganized in secure territory and recognized Gen. Carl-Gustaf Mannerheim, until recently a Finnish major general in the tsarist army, as commander-in-chief of its forces. Mannerheim came from Finland's Swedish-speaking elite. Fluent in Swedish, Russian, and German, he spoke only the most rudimentary Finnish and was resented by extreme nationalists as a "Russian," but proved an able and charismatic leader. He saw the initial problem to be clearing from Finland the thousands of Russian soldiers, whom he feared would constitute the military basis of Red power. On 27 January, just as the Socialists were seizing power in Helsinki, he launched his rag-tag units against Russian army barracks in western Finland. The mutinous Russian soldiers and sailors had little appetite for a civil war in Finland and surrendered with little fighting, which also provided more arms for the Whites. Within ten days Mannerheim gained control of central and northern Finland, which comprised the bulk of the national territory but contained scarcely more than half the population and none of the major economic centers.

At first neither Reds nor Whites were organized, trained, or equipped for serious combat and faced the customary problems of improvised armies in civil wars.[34] The Reds hoped for aid from the Russian Bolsheviks, but the latter had multiple emergencies of their own and, aside from the initial arms shipment, provided little direct support. Mannerheim obtained the assistance of eighty-four volunteer officers from the Swedish army, who formed his high command and supervised organization of a Finnish army. A new officer corps was composed mainly of 1,130 "Jaeger" volunteers, young Finns who had slipped off to Germany to be trained in the German army with the

[34] See K. Chorley, *Armies and the Art of Revolution* (Boston, 1973).

ultimate goal of fighting for Finnish independence, and had been sent back to Finland. The government instituted conscription, but the combat core of the new army was composed of volunteers, mainly from Lutheran family farmers. Then, in mid-February, the German government made an official decision to support the Whites and immediately dispatched a sizable shipment of arms.

The revolutionary regime had to organize an army of its own, a task for which the Red Guards were scarcely prepared. Over a period of four months, perhaps as many as 140,000 volunteers (a few thousand of whom were women) served in the Red forces, a force slightly larger than Mannerheim's army but inferior to them in combat quality. Though they developed the organizational structure of a regular army, the Red forces remained more or less a militia, lacking trained officers or firm discipline. They had featured a General Staff for several months prior to the revolution, but this was no more than a loose coordinating committee. Only a small number of Russian officers assisted. Moreover, at the beginning of March 1918 the peace treaty between Imperial Germany and the Bolshevik regime required that any remaining Russian forces be withdrawn from Finland. They were replaced by perhaps as many as 5,000 volunteer Russian Red Guards, who had no effect on the outcome.

Mannerheim devoted six weeks to organizing his army, remaining mostly on the defensive. He opposed the looming German intervention that had been negotiated by the Finnish government, believing that his own forces could decide the conflict and fearing that German intervention would lead to German domination. Mannerheim maintained his loyalty to the Entente, with whom he had fought for three years in the world war, and was convinced that Germany would eventually lose, realizing that the new arrangement might eventually prejudice Finland. Moreover, the ultimate enemy for Mannerheim was not the Finnish Reds but the Russian Bolsheviks, whose patron the Germans had now become. He therefore launched his first major offensive in mid-March to seize Tampere, Finland's second-largest city and the center of the Red position in the southwest. This operation was completed by 5 April, resulting in 2,000 combat deaths for the defenders and the capture of nearly 15,000 prisoners. It was a crucial victory. By this point it was clear that the Reds were incapable of successful offensive action, even when stiffened by Russian troops, and that their only hope was to defend the cities on the southern coast.

The German command had formed a special "Baltic Division" under Gen. Count Rudiger von der Goltz, amounting to some 12,000 men, including 600 Finnish volunteers. It landed on the Finnish coast on 3 April, just as Tampere was falling to Mannerheim, and the large Russian naval force on that coast, which still had not been withdrawn, quickly indicated that it would not cross swords with the smaller German unit. Within ten days the division had occupied Helsinki, against comparatively limited resistance.

The Red forces had been cut in two, and Mannerheim swiftly shifted the bulk of his troops to the southeast, where the strongest Red units were concentrated, to cut off retreat into Russia. He was determined to destroy and capture as much of the enemy forces as possible, to avoid the danger of a new Finnish Red Army on Soviet soil that might sustain a protracted and exhausting border conflict. In this he was largely successful, and by the first of May resistance in both southwestern and southeastern Finland had been crushed, with only small groups escaping to Russia. Victory was complete, and more than 80,000 prisoners taken. Foreign assistance to the two sides had been about equal in terms of men and supplies, though the intervention of the German Baltic Division had been much more effective than that of the scattered Russian forces. The Finnish government army had won the war substantially, though not entirely, on its own.

Mannerheim, however, was gone before the end of the month. He was increasingly opposed to the pro-German policy of the Finnish government, bent on establishing a regency that would make a German prince ruler of Finland. When he found that henceforth German advisors were to train and administer the Finnish army, he abruptly resigned and moved to Sweden. For Finland, it was a blessing in disguise; after the collapse of Germany six months later, a politically unsullied Mannerheim was able to return as Finland's new leader. His anti-German stance guaranteed him a strong reputation among the victorious Allies, with whom he was able to consolidate his nation's independence.

The victory of the Whites, fairly won by superior combat qualities, was marred by a severe repression, not dissimilar to that inflicted on the Communards in Paris in 1871. It has tended to be the winning side in revolutionary civil wars that enforces the greater repression, in large part simply because it is in a position to do so. The repression went through several phases. Like the Reds, the Whites had sometimes killed prisoners during the fighting, mainly in the earlier phases, and were particularly merciless with captured Russians, nearly all of whom were shot. These were illegal killings, since Mannerheim had decreed that the lives of prisoners be respected, but about 2,700 had been shot by 27 April, followed by another 4,745 in the following weeks. Altogether, such irregular executions totaled 8,380.

Of the 80,000 Red prisoners, 71,000 passed before newly created summary courts. About 67,000 were convicted, mostly to prison terms, but 555 death sentences were passed, of which 265 were executed. (This was roughly similar to Franco's commutation of about half the death sentences handed down on former Republicans in Spain in 1939–41, though there the total number of death sentences was much greater.) Nearly all the prisoners remained in special camps, where conditions were appalling. Finland was on the verge of famine in 1918, and the prisoners were fed little. Within four months 11,783 had died, mainly of malnutrition and dysentery.

In toto, within eight months nearly one percent of the total Finnish population of 3.2 million perished, amounting to about 31,000 deaths. Fewer than 10,000 of these died in combat on the two sides combined, but in one way or another the White repression took more than ten times as many

victims as the Red Terror.[35] Reasons for the ferocity of such repression have
been discussed in the Introduction and will not be repeated here. After those
first months, general conditions and the terms of the repression rapidly
improved. All remaining death sentences were commuted in May 1919, by
which time only a few more than 6,000 prisoners remained in confinement,
the final 200–300 prisoners from the civil war being released in 1927. It may
be observed that though Finland was ruled by a democratic parliamentary
government, the postwar repression of the left, in terms of proportionate
population, resulted in even more deaths than did that of the Franco regime
after the Spanish war.

Finland had clearly suffered contagion from Russian radicalization
between 1905 and 1918, yet the Socialists who launched the civil war were
not Bolsheviks, more nearly resembling the German Independent Socialists
(USPD). The genuinely moderate sector of their leaders reconstituted the
party in 1918–19 along the policy lines of the contemporary French Socialist
party, supportive of parliamentary democracy but refusing to participate in
"bourgeois" governments. The most radical minority formed the Finnish
Communist Party in Moscow in August 1919. The SDP was allowed to take
part in Finland's first postwar elections in 1919, in which it won eighty
seats, not a majority but still the largest faction. Nonetheless, since the
Communist Party was outlawed, an extremist sector broke off to create
the Finnish Socialist Workers Party. Urban workers benefited from relatively advanced legislation, but members of the regular Communist Party
remained subject to arrest, though de facto Communists led many of the
trade unions, which were affiliated with the Soviet Profintern rather than
with Western socialist trade unions. The SDP meanwhile moved slowly, if
uncertainly, toward the left center, changing its policy in order to participate in coalition governments, first in 1926 and next in 1937, eventually
winning as many as eighty-three seats in parliament. Finland achieved a
relative, if modest, prosperity during the interwar period, thanks to the
ingenuity and hard work of its people, recovering from the Depression
faster than the United States. Despite continued internal divisions, Finnish
patriotism proved stronger yet. When the Soviet Union invaded in 1939,
the Socialist foreign minister Vaino Tanner was one of the country's strongest leaders, and nearly all Finnish soldiers of Communist or revolutionary Socialist background fought patriotically for their country against the
Soviet colossus.[36]

Comparison of the history of Finland after the revolutionary insurrection
of 1918 to that of Spain after the revolutionary insurrection of 1934 reveals
striking differences. The repression in Spain, where the insurrection was less

---

[35] The definitive study is Jaakko Paavolainen, *Poliittiset väkivaltaisundet Suomessa 1918*
(Helsinki, 1967), 2 vols., which I was able to consult thanks to the assistance of my colleague
Prof. Pekka Hamalainen.
[36] For a brief history of twentieth-century Finland, see D. G. Kirby, *Finland in the Twentieth
Century* (Minneapolis, 1979).

powerful than in Finland, was much more limited. The more severe, if brutal, repression in Finland temporarily eliminated the revolutionary extreme left altogether, a situation that made it possible for the moderates to gain control of the SDP and convert it into a western European–type social democratic party, something that did not happen in Spain for many years. Finland sustained an effective and thriving parliamentary democracy that firmly rejected the fascist temptation during the 1930s.

2

The Russian Civil War, 1917–1922

The Russian civil war was the paradigmatic revolutionary civil war of the twentieth century, but the term is an oversimplification for the extensive series of military conflicts waged in the remnants of the tsarist empire between 1917 and 1922. "The wars of the tsarist succession" would be a more adequate description. There was indeed a massive civil war among Russians, but in addition both Russian sides sought to extend their control over all the non-Russian peoples of the former empire, among whom a lengthy and confusing series of campaigns were waged. One historian has counted eleven different armies that at one time or another fought in Ukraine. Independent rulers briefly emerged in remote areas, while criminal bands ravaged sizable districts. The major powers intervened militarily on the periphery, but without determination or effectiveness, except in the Baltic. Even before winning the civil war in Russia proper, the new Bolshevik dictatorship attempted to send its poorly organized forces into Europe, producing a major war with Poland in 1920 and, more successfully, carrying out the conquest of Mongolia in 1921, extending its control even beyond the former tsarist domains. All the while, the last phases of the intra-Russian civil war were being fought within ethnic Russia. This enormous series of struggles, which lasted for five years, produced immense collateral damage among civilians in terms of executions, famine, and mass epidemics, and cost nearly five times as many lives as were lost on the eastern front in World War I.

Though the Russian civil war was not the longest of the twentieth-century civil wars, it was the largest in geographic scope and the most important in its consequences for Russia and for much of the world in the years that followed. The Spanish war was better organized and militarily more sophisticated, in terms of both techniques and weaponry, and also mobilized a larger proportion of the population on both sides, while the Chinese and Vietnamese civil wars lasted longer, the Chinese conflict probably also mobilizing more total manpower. The Russian war, however, would be by far the most influential in world history, and would inaugurate the twentieth century's era of revolutionary civil wars, something that the Bolshevik victors hoped to spread around the world.

A precedent for pan-European politico-ideological civil war might be found to some extent in the wars of religion of the sixteenth and seventeenth centuries, which reached their climax in the devastating Thirty Years War (1618–48) that literally lay waste to Germany, in a fashion even more severe than the civil war's effect upon Russia, bringing vast destruction and a huge population decline. The political, ideological, and imperialist conflicts of the era of the French Revolution from 1792 to 1815 constituted a kind of second European civil war, no longer focused on religion and state, but rather on political, social, and ideological conflict and the struggle for empire. The initial conflict in France was universalized in an effort to export the revolution, promoting an international struggle that became geographically even more extensive than the wars of religion. Whereas the latter had proposed to change the religious structure and identity of government in various countries, the French Revolution and its heirs sought to transform much of Europe's cultural, political, and social order.

The protracted destruction wrought by World War I had profoundly negative domestic consequences, particularly on the powers with the weakest political and economic structures and on those who lost, all of which had been foreseen by those who unleashed the war.[1] The disastrous effect of a foreign conflict that went badly had been shown by the Russo-Japanese War of 1904–05, which served as the catalyst for the first Russian revolution that nearly toppled the tsarist regime. Subsequently, political councilors and even the imperial family's "special friend," Grigory Rasputin, had warned Tsar Nicholas that a major new European war would mean the end.

Tsarist Russia was never crushed militarily, and at the beginning of 1917 was in some respects stronger vis-à-vis Germany than at the beginning of the war. It still had the largest army in the world, better armed and equipped than ever. The revolution that occurred in March was not produced by the revolutionaries or political parties but by popular discontent and semi-spontaneous rioting, accompanied by a rapid breakdown of military discipline. It was the product neither of imminent military defeat nor of organized political revolt, but of social rebellion, especially in the capital, Petrograd.[2]

---

[1] Even as he prepared to request mobilization of the German army to launch the war, Gen. Helmuth von Moltke, chief of the general staff, sent a note on 28 July 1914 to the German chancellor, warning that the impending conflict was likely to be a new sort of "world war" that could produce the "mutual destruction of the European culture," leaving the "culture of all Europe" wrecked "for decades to come." S. Förster, "Der deutsche Generalstab und die Illusion des kurzen Krieges, 1871–1914," *Militärgeschichtliche Mitteilungen*, 54 (1995), 89, quoted in V. R. Berghahn, *Europe in the Era of Two World Wars: From Militarism and Genocide to Civil Society, 1900–1950* (Princeton, N.J., 2006), 37. That was about right, revealing that it was not just Austrians who were willing to run the risk of suicide in order to postpone their own death.

[2] After the war began, St. Petersburg was renamed Petrograd, in order to make the name sound more Russian. A decade later, after the death of Lenin, it became Leningrad, and then in 1991, after the demise of the Soviet Union, St. Petersburg once more.

The war had produced enormous social and economic dislocation. A total of 15.5 million men had been drafted, and several million more people had moved to the cities, while the army forced other millions to flee the western war zone, creating a dislocation of society without precedent. The social and economic experience was almost like Stalinism without Stalin or a police state. There had been an enormous expansion of the military and of heavy industry and military production, while consumer goods became scarce, prices shot up, and wages failed to keep pace. All the while peasants were expected to provide food in exchange for very little. The tax system weighed heavily on the common people, while distribution of goods was grossly unequal and credit disappeared. Every one of these features later reemerged under Lenin and Stalin, but Nicholas II did not operate a twentieth-century police state, and the populace rebelled, something they would not be at liberty to do under his successors.

The mood of rebelliousness passed from the urban population to the army. Norman Stone's quip that "the Russian Revolution was a huge mutiny"[3] is exaggerated, but makes a crucial point. The regime was not overthrown so much as it collapsed, showing once more that the beginning of a revolutionary process is often deceptively easy. The civil war was set off not by the revolution (though that was the beginning of much internal conflict), but by the Bolshevik coup d'etat that occurred seven months later.

In retrospect, it is clear that the democratic revolution of March–November 1917 represented the climax of the real revolutionary era in Russian history, the nearly six decades of reform, liberalization, and growing individual freedom inaugurated by the "Tsar Liberator," Alexander II, in 1861. This era, brought to a shuddering halt by the Bolshevik takeover, constitutes the only exception in Russian history, aside from the brief decade of the 1990s, to the historic Russian pattern of autocracy, state control, and limitation of individual freedom.

The liberal minority, which had been disproportionately vocal in politics, strongly supported the Entente and had seen the war as transformative, not in the revolutionary direction envisioned by radical nationalists in Italy, but rather with the calculation that alliance with Europe's most progressive countries, Britain and France, would liberalize Russia. At first they thought to see their dreams come true in 1917 with the inauguration of a parliamentary Provisional Government, which they briefly led. Their greatest mistake was then to continue Russia's participation in the war, which they saw as necessary to Russia's continued participation in progressive European civilization. Since the tsarist regime had collapsed in good measure because of its failure in state administration, the Provisional Government also sought to expand the administrative structure and create a new democratic "state consciousness," with broader capacity for social and economic penetration, but that capacity soon declined steadily.

[3] N. Stone, *World War One* (London, 2007), 170.

The Provisional Government's limited authority eroded in a situation of revolutionary dualism. The revolutionary movements reconstituted the "soviets" (councils), loose multiparty assemblies first organized in 1905 at a time when no parliament existed in Russia.[4] In this scheme of things, the Provisional Government, based on parliament, had nominal authority but little popular support and less power, while the soviets enjoyed much popular support but no official authority. Russia was the only country in Europe in which, because of the weakness of individualism and capitalist development and the delay in its political transformation, socialist movements enjoyed the great majority of whatever organized political support existed. This was totally different from the situation in any other country in the world.

The democratic revolution of the spring and summer of 1917 was nominally led by the small Russian middle classes, with the goal of making equal republican citizens of the Russian masses. This effort initially met with a limited positive response. Despite considerable anti-aristocratic and anti-"bourgeois" violence during the first phase, some urban workers showed interest in participating in a civic community of all social classes. At first there were a few signs of an attempt by workers to "level up," to improve their dress and acquire democratic respectability.[5]

Urban workers amounted to no more than 10 percent of the empire's population, but they were disproportionately concentrated in large cities, giving them special influence. Socialism was a powerful force in a society that had never known principled individualism. The most radical socialist party, Vladimir Lenin's Bolsheviks, was assisted by German money and strove mightily to replace any discourse of democratic citizenship with that of violent class conflict. After a few months, it achieved mounting success, especially in Petrograd, Moscow, and other principal cities, since Russian civil society was extremely weak.

The basis of society was a largely illiterate peasantry that constituted nearly 85 percent of the population. Peasants had little sense of nation or empire, much less of a responsible civil society, thinking primarily in terms of family and local interests, concerned above all with their own land and their autonomy over it. They distrusted all government and, once the tsar was gone, wished to forget the war, seize the 25 percent or so of the land – the best land – that was not in their possession, and ignore anything else.

In this climate more soldiers deserted, and state institutions began to wither. Mass demonstrations occurred in Petrograd in July, exploited by the Bolsheviks in an ambivalent threat of a coup d'etat, but this was poorly organized and failed, forcing Lenin and other leaders into hiding. As conditions steadily deteriorated, Gen. Lavr Kornilov moved troops to the capital to try to enforce greater discipline on the part of Alexander Kerensky, the prime minister, and his government.

---

[4] The best account of the growth of the "council" movement is O. Anweiler, *The Soviets: The Russian Workers Peasants and Soldiers Councils, 1905–1921* (New York, 1974).
[5] This is argued by O. Figes and B. Kolonitskii in their *Interpreting the Russian Revolution: The Language and Symbols of 1917* (New Haven, Conn., 1999).

The response of Kerensky revealed the fatal weakness of what would later be called "Kerenskyism" – a left-liberal government's attitude of *pas d'ennemis à gauche* (no enemies to the left), that the only serious enemies were on the right. Rather than accept the obvious need for greater law and order in an increasingly chaotic situation, which would have been in the interest of almost everyone, Kerensky turned to the extreme left in order to block Kornilov, a maneuver that succeeded but decisively shifted power to the extreme revolutionaries. (Thus in Spain in 1936 Manuel Azaña would be accused of "Kerenskyist" policies, and there is some analogy with the decision of the government of José Giral to arm the revolutionary movements).[6]

The Bolsheviks profited most from this situation, but Lenin realized that the radical mood in the cities might soon change and resolved to take advantage of it while it lasted. He drew inspiration not merely from breakdown in Russia but also from the mutiny in the French army some months earlier and the first major signs of war weariness and discord in Germany, particularly a sailors' strike in Kiel. Bolshevik insurrectionism was partially predicated on what was perceived as the imminent outbreak of international revolution on a grand scale.

In March 1917 there were only 24,000 members of the Bolshevik Party, but this had grown to more than 300,000 seven months later, though in an imperial population of 170 million it was proportionately smaller than the membership of the Spanish Communist Party in July 1936 or that of many other subsequent Communist parties. Lenin had for some time made it clear to his associates that power could be won only through coup d'etat or violent insurrection, but, even in revolutionary Russia, some form of legitimation was needed. The opportunity began to emerge when the Bolsheviks gained a majority in the soviet of the capital, Petrograd, at the beginning of October, the latter electing Leon Trotsky as chairman and making it possible for the Bolsheviks to fully reemerge from clandestinity as a major force. The Petrograd soviet set up a Military Revolutionary Committee to coordinate military garrisons on behalf of the revolution, together with the new Red Guards, which had been formed to follow the example of the Finnish Socialists in 1905.[7]

---

[6] Spain in 1936 was quite different from Russia nineteen years earlier, since Spain was a relatively stable country. The Popular Front nonetheless recreated some aspects of the situation in Russia by fostering a new form of governmental dualism, installing a weak minority left Republican government that, though not as feeble as that of Kerensky, suffered some of the same dysfunction, while embracing the violent revolutionary movements that pursued their own goals completely apart from the government. The Spanish prime minister, Santiago Casares Quiroga, was not unaware of the problem he faced, and is said to have declared privately that he would never play the part of a Kerensky. Thus he resigned power on the evening of 18 July 1936 rather than hand over arms to the revolutionary worker groups, even though the military rebellion in Spain was more formidable than the initiative of Kornilov in Russia. President Manuel Azaña and the new prime minister, José Giral, had no such compunctions but soon began to award arms and hence de facto power to the revolutionaries. They believed the latter to be the lesser evil, and have often been judged favorably by history, while the verdict on Kerensky has been almost uniformly harsh.

[7] R. Wade, *Red Guards and Workers' Militias in the Russian Revolution* (Stanford, Calif., 1984).

The timing of the coup was determined not so much by Lenin, who had been calling for an immediate insurrection for two months, but by Trotsky, who realized that violent action would need at least some pretense of legitimacy, for, as he wrote years later in his *History of the Russian Revolution*, "the attacking side is almost always interested in seeming on the defensive. A revolutionary party is interested in legal coverings."[8] The coup was thus postponed until November, when the Second All-Russian Congress of Soviets would meet in the capital. Thus, when the Bolsheviks carried out their coup d'etat against the Provisional Government, Lenin declared that power was being seized in the name of the soviets in order to guarantee that democratic elections to a Constituent Assembly, scheduled for several weeks later, would take place. This ruse, powered by the Red Guards, provided a thin veil of legitimacy for seizing power in nearly all the larger Russian cities, the Provisional Government being unable to defend itself.

The Bolshevik Party emphasized rigorous central organization combined with the use of paramilitary force, anticipating (and to some degree inspiring) the modus operandi of the fascist movements that would soon appear elsewhere. No other Russian party shared this combination of characteristics, and the other groups were totally unprepared to contest for political power by force. With the once massive tsarist army undergoing the greatest desertion in military history, the Bolsheviks won a limited central power almost by default. Serious fighting took place only in Moscow and a few other cities.

Before being dissolved by the new dictatorship, the municipal council of Petrograd denounced the coup as a "civil war initiated by the Bolsheviks." Lenin had always been more honest, at least in one respect, than Robespierre, St. Just, and some other revolutionaries, for he had always pointed out that the imposition of the dictatorship of the proletariat would require some degree of civil war. In practical terms, however, he sought to hide this behind a propaganda screen of soviet assemblies and democratic elections. It was a huge gamble, as coups d'etat or insurrections usually are, and at first even he was not sure that a comparatively small organization would be able to pull off so bold a stroke, but the complete unpreparedness of other forces for armed confrontation led him to hope that the Bolshevik takeover could be rapidly consolidated, perhaps avoiding the "inevitable" civil war. Only in the Cossack country of far southeastern Russia was there continuing armed resistance, and early in 1918 this was crushed by Red Guard and Latvian units sent from the larger cities.

Lenin at first won a degree of popular support on a platform of "land, peace, and bread." This meant that peasants could occupy all remaining land not under their control, that Russia would withdraw completely from the war, and that all the property of the middle and upper classes could be seized by workers and peasants. The Bolshevik slogan was "Loot the Loot," leading to

[8] L. Trotsky, *History of the Russian Revolution* (London, 1967), 3:259.

the greatest orgy of sacking and pillage in European history.[9] In urban factories the Bolsheviks at first accepted a nominal "worker control," but refused to allow worker committees to hold real power and soon moved to dominate labor more directly.

In the elections of December 1917, which were in large part free despite highly disturbed conditions, the Bolsheviks received 24 percent of the vote, mainly from the cities, while the Socialist Revolutionaries (SRs), a populist party that represented the peasantry, gained 40 percent and a majority of seats. In perfectly normal democratic conditions, the SR vote would probably have been even higher.[10]

When the Constituent Assembly – the first democratically elected parliament in Russian history – met in Petrograd in January 1918, it was prepared to vote the Bolshevik dictatorship out of power, something that Lenin and his associates prevented by dissolving the Assembly with armed force, shooting down workers and demonstrators in the streets. Heretofore the Bolsheviks had devoted their efforts to dissolving the last remnants of the old imperial army, but they now realized the need to create a new military force of their own, announcing on 15 January 1918 the beginning of a new Workers and Peasants Red Army. In this they were greatly assisted by the contribution of Latvia, at first the most revolutionary land in the former tsarist empire.

THE REVOLUTION IN LATVIA

The Baltic regions of Estonia and Latvia, forcibly incorporated into the empire two centuries earlier, were inhabited by an unusually enterprising and politically conscious peasantry that had been dominated for many generations by an aristocratic caste of Germanic landowners. Combining both social and nationalist rebellion, Latvia had been the most revolutionary part of the empire in 1905 and had suffered an especially severe repression. By 1917 part of Latvia was under German military occupation, and the war had uprooted much of the population. The unoccupied zone was the only region of the empire (as distinct from individual cities) in which the Bolsheviks came to power by democratic vote in the soviets in August 1917, after which they gained 72 percent of the Latvian vote to the Constituent Assembly.[11] The radicalization of opinion in Latvia, which would not long endure, apparently stemmed from three factors: a) the Latvian peasantry was largely literate and politically conscious, in

[9] This was later continued by the Bolsheviks in more organized form for quite some time. S. McMeekin, *History's Greatest Heist: The Looting of Russia by the Bolsheviks* (New Haven, Conn., 2009).

[10] O. H. Radkey, Jr., *The Election to the Russian Constituent Assembly of 1917* (Cambridge, Mass., 1950).

[11] This vote was admittedly somewhat ambiguous, because it went nominally to the Social Democratic Party, elsewhere divided between Bolsheviks and the more moderate Mensheviks. In Latvia the party was nominally united, though in fact the Bolsheviks predominated until the party officially divided in 1918.

a state of extreme rebellion against aristocratic landowners; b) Latvia and its capital, Riga, had a higher percentage of industrial workers than did most of the tsarist empire; and c) the war had disturbed social and economic conditions more severely in Latvia than anywhere else, with half the country under foreign occupation and a third of the population uprooted. By the autumn of 1917 the revolution was, for the moment, further advanced in Latvia than anywhere else, and the soviet government that had been set up in unoccupied Latvia in August took full power three months later. All estates had been seized, though Latvian society was becoming sharply divided between moderates and revolutionaries.

Latvia's unique contribution to the revolution was to become the first region in which the Bolsheviks created an organized and disciplined armed force, much more reliable than the Red Guard militia. This took the form of volunteer Latvian "Strelkii" (riflemen) regiments, stemming from elite Latvian regiments in the old army. The concept of organized armed force as the spearhead of the revolution – the "fascist" concept – is implied in various of Lenin's pre-revolutionary writings, but was nowhere explicitly outlined, and to that extent apparently constituted a unique contribution of Latvian Bolshevism. The Strelkii were not a militia but were formed under regular army standards, subject to tight military discipline. They did not elect their officers, as had become standard in revolutionized military units, but were controlled by a special political committee that supervised the officers, the predecessor of the Red Army's system of political commissars. In October the Latvian Bolsheviks urged Lenin to seize power, and the first Strelkii units arrived in Petrograd to provide armed support early in December.

For the next eight or nine months, until the new Red Army began to take full form, the Latvian regiments, which came to total more than 30,000 men, were crucial for the survival of the Bolshevik dictatorship. The remnants of the old army, undergoing final dissolution, were sometimes hostile to the new regime, and even the Red Guards could not always be counted on, whereas the Latvians were dedicated and disciplined revolutionaries, at first the only effective combat forces to be found. They made it possible for the Bolsheviks to cling to power, won the first significant combat in December 1917, suppressed the Constituent Assembly a month later, put down internal opposition during 1918, and fought effectively in the civil war that developed. Their senior officer, Col. Jukums Vacietis, became the first regular commander of the Red Army, and the Latvians provided the power base that made possible the development of the Cheka, the new Bolshevik police. Lenin esteemed the Latvians highly, characterizing Latvian Bolsheviks as more "mature revolutionaries" than their Russian counterparts. He formed his personal bodyguard and household staff in large measure of Latvians.[12]

---

[12] The principal accounts are those of A. Ezergailis, *The 1917 Revolution in Latvia* (New York, 1974) and *The Latvian Impact on the Bolshevik Revolution* (Boulder, Colo., 1983). The Strelkii units are treated in V. Mangulis, *Latvia in the Wars of the 20th Century* (Princeton Junction, N.J., 1983).

THE TREATY WITH GERMANY

Lenin promised to end Russia's participation in the world war, which he hoped to replace with pan-European civil war. The Germans and Austrians, however, demanded huge concessions and resumed their military advance in February 1918, declaring that they would "save Russia from Bolshevism." Against bitter opposition in his own party, Lenin persuaded his colleagues to agree to German terms, which were draconian. The Treaty of Brest-Litovsk, signed on 3 March 1918, deprived Russia of all the Baltic territories, Poland, Belarus, Ukraine, and the Caucasus. This amounted to 26 percent of the empire's former population and about a third of its economic resources. All these territories were, in effect, to be organized into client states of Germany. This new map of 1918, however, is essentially the same one found in eastern Europe since 1991, recognizing the principle of nationality and depriving the Russian empire of all non-Russian territories in the west and southwest.[13]

Lenin was already considered a German agent by many Russians, due to the subsidies he received. He argued that there was no alternative to coming to terms with Germany, which had gained the upper hand militarily and might even win the war, at least until revolution broke out internally. The peace treaty provided the Bolshevik regime with its first international recognition, enabling Lenin and his dictatorship to concentrate on consolidating power in a chaotic society. It also inaugurated the standard "two-track" system of Bolshevik foreign affairs, maintaining normal diplomatic relations, on the one hand, while fomenting revolution abroad on the other. Yet the most disastrous and humiliating peace treaty in Russian history also served as a kind of boomerang, since it greatly stimulated opposition to the dictatorship, even among some who had initially supported it. The new regime found itself facing a major civil war, with the counterrevolutionaries to some degree supported and assisted by the Western Allies, who sought to restore Russia to the anti-German alliance.

For imperial Germany, the treaty seemed to kill two birds with one stone. It made possible the liquidation of the eastern front, transferring many units for the decisive new offensives in the west. But it also made Germany totally dominant in eastern Europe, presenting a massive temptation that Berlin could not resist. Therefore, more than a million combat troops – who might have helped decide the war in the west – were kept in the east, to exploit Germany's new imperium. Some German officials argued that a force so subversive as Bolshevism should no longer be tolerated, and the kaiser agreed. The boundaries of the treaty were frequently violated as German forces advanced even farther east.

By the summer of 1918, the dictatorship's position had become desperate, beset by enemies on every side. Pursuing further the logic of Brest-Litovsk,

---

[13] J. W. Wheeler-Bennett, *Brest-Litovsk: The Forgotten Peace* (London, 1938); W. Baumgart, *Deutsche Ostpolitik 1918* (Vienna, 1966).

Western Russia.

Lenin turned to the Germans a second time, seeking a "final" peace treaty that would offer even greater concessions in return for an end to German pressure and for financial and military assistance in the civil war. After some hesitation, the German government overcame its revulsion, concluding that the Bolsheviks were offering too good a deal to resist. The "additional treaty" of 28 August 1918, sometimes overlooked by historians, was even more severe than Brest-Litovsk. Yet more territory was given up, and the dictatorship promised to pay a gigantic sum in reparations after the war was over, while making breathtaking concessions in return for future German investments, promising large shipments of foodstuffs and raw materials and one-third of all Russian petroleum production. A huge financial and industrial consortium was created in Berlin for the future exploitation of the Russian economy, while in return the German government pledged an immediate subsidy of nine million gold marks to shore up Bolshevik finances, while making rather vague promises of future military assistance. This treaty went much farther than the Nazi-Soviet Pact of 1939, but for the moment the Bolsheviks clung to it as a life preserver. Had Germany won the war on the western front, it would then have turned on Lenin as Hitler would later turn on Stalin, and could easily have liquidated the Bolsheviks at any time. Paradoxically, the latter were saved by the military triumph of the democratic capitalist Allies.[14] Lenin made his pact with the devil and won the gamble by the skin of his teeth. When Stalin followed the same path twenty years later, he would for a time not be so fortunate.

CIVIL WAR INTENSIFIES[15]

The Bolsheviks found it much easier to topple the Provisional Government than to build a new state and army, even though they inherited the apparatus of the old system and to some degree coerced it into working for them. Lenin's demagogy turned the economy into a shambles. Nationalization of the banks destroyed the credit system, and inflation, already very high, skyrocketed out of control. As industry produced less and less, the new state intervened

[14] B. Pearce, *How Haig Saved Lenin* (London, 1986). There is an excellent account of the relations between Bolsheviks and Germans in 1918 in R. Pipes, *The Russian Revolution* (New York, 1990), 569–624. See also G. Freund, *Unholy Alliance: Russian-German Relations from the Treaty of Brest-Litovsk to the Treaty of Berlin* (London, 1957). Page for page, however, the most incisive treatment will be found in the brief essay by S. Haffner, *Der Teufelspakt: Die deutsch-russische Beziehungen vom Ersten zum Zweiten Weltkrieg* (Zurich, 1989).

[15] There is of course an extensive literature on the Russian civil war. One of the best single books is V. Brovkin, *Behind the Front Lines of the Civil War: Political Parties and Social Movements in Russia, 1918–1922* (Princeton, N.J., 1994), which explains better than any other what really went on. The best one-volume military history is E. Mawdsley, *The Russian Civil War* (Boston, 1987). W. B. Lincoln, *Red Victory: A History of the Russian Civil War* (New York, 1989), is a well-written narrative. G. Swain, *The Origins of the Russian Civil War* (London, 1996), is helpful in separating the main factors and phases, while J.-J. Marie, *La guerre civile russe. Armées paysannes, rouges, blanches et vertes* (Paris, 2005), paints a

more and more, sometimes dismissing or arresting workers and initiating the nationalization of industry, to which the workers responded with slow-downs and strikes, as production continued to decline.[16] Offered very little in exchange, peasants increasingly withheld food from the cities, and in May 1918 the dictatorship first instituted the policy of *razverstka* – forced requisitions that seized food, sometimes all the available food, at gunpoint. This was continued for three more years, as peasant resistance mounted further, so that in one sense the most fundamental aspect of the civil war was the policy of coercion against the peasants.

In their naiveté, the peasants tended to find confusing the official change of name from Bolsheviks to Communist Party, and often concluded that the Bolshevik regime had been taken over by evil forces. It was sometimes said that the Bolsheviks were good, since they permitted peasants to hold almost all the land, but the Communists were bad, since they seized the production of the land at gunpoint.

Beginning in May 1918 the dictatorship's situation began to deteriorate, as opposition groups emerged in many parts of the former empire. Comparatively few volunteered for the new Red Army, so that for some months the Communist regime sought to recruit volunteers from political converts among the nearly two million prisoners of war, mostly from Austria-Hungary, still in Russia. Though only a fraction responded, the thousands of volunteers who came forward played a crucial role, together with the Latvians, in building the new army. Initially formed in "battalions of internationalists," they were precursors of the International Brigades later created by the Comintern in the Spanish war. Moreover, a limited number of German prisoners served in separate auxiliary detachments so long as the revolutionary regime was a quasi-ally of imperial Germany.[17]

A Czech Legion of nearly 50,000 former Czech prisoners presented a special problem because it had initially been formed to fight the Germans

---

broader canvas. Two of the best regional studies are O. Figes, *Peasant Russia, Civil War: The Volga Countryside in Revolution (1917–1921)* (Oxford, 1987), and D. J. Raleigh, *Experiencing Russia's Civil War: Politics, Society and Revolutionary Culture in Saratov, 1917–1922* (Princeton, N.J., 1992). The best account setting the civil war within the full context of Russian history and society will be found in O. Figes, *A People's Tragedy. The Russian Revolution: 1891–1924* (New York, 1996), but see also P. Holquist, *Making War, Forging Revolution: Russia's Continuum of Crisis, 1914–1921* (Cambridge, Mass., 2002).

[16] The theory and practice of labor policy are treated in F. I. Kaplan, *Bolshevik Ideology and the Ethics of Soviet Labor, 1917–1920* (New York, 1968).

[17] In Western accounts of the Russian war, there are only the most limited references to the recruitment of prisoners of war by the Red Army. See V. M. Fic, *The Bolsheviks and the Czechoslovak Legion: The Origins of Their Armed Conflict March–May 1918* (New Delhi, 1978), 126–57 and passim. More than 50,000 former prisoners may have joined the Red Army in 1918, while the Soviet historian V. M. Zharov, in his *Internatsionalnye chasti krasnoi armii v boiakh za vlast sovetov v gody innostrannoi interventsii i grazhdanskoi voiny* (Moscow, 1960), 51 (cited in Fic, *The Bolsheviks and the Czechoslovak Legion*, 129, 426), has calculated that in all units of the Red Army during the entire civil war approximately 150,000 foreigners were enrolled, the vast majority of them former prisoners of war.

and had been promised rail passage across Siberia with the aim of joining the Allies on the western front. Communist leaders hoped to recruit many of its members for the Red Army and then, when that proved impossible, tried to break up the Czech Legion in order to create labor battalions of ex-prisoners. After an armed altercation developed, the well-organized Czechs rose in revolt, seizing control of several towns. Their main goal was defensive, aimed at departure from Russia, rejecting what they saw as a new imprisonment by a pro-German regime. They became the first effective armed force to resist the Bolsheviks,[18] giving the anti-Communist opposition a strong foothold in the Urals region and western Siberia. Soon all of Siberia rose in rebellion, which spread farther into Russia proper. Then the Bolsheviks' only allies, the Left SRs (the most radical sector of the Socialist Revolutionaries), turned against them because of their pro-German policy, rose in revolt in Moscow, and almost overthrew the dictatorship. SR assassins murdered several officials and severely wounded Lenin.

The dictatorship responded by officially announcing a new policy of Red Terror that included mass arrests, the taking of hostages, and indiscriminate executions.[19] Prisons multiplied, and a system of concentration camps, forerunner of the later GULAG, was set up. Forced labor had been introduced earlier in the year. The other response was to accelerate creation of a mass Red Army. An initial goal had been to mobilize as many urban workers as possible, since peasants were distrusted, but it soon became clear that there were not enough workers. Hundreds of thousands of peasants were drafted, and large numbers of former tsarist officers agreed to serve for various reasons, whether patriotic or opportunistic, and their loyalty was enforced by development of a large cadre of "political commissars," Bolshevik political officers whose responsibility was to supervise regular officers, approve written orders, provide political instruction, and maintain morale. (The commissar system had already been attempted by Kerensky in a vain effort to hold the regular army together, and later would be copied by the Republican army, under the supervision of Soviet advisers, during the Spanish war.) During the next few years the army of the Russian government once more became the largest in the world, though its quality would leave much to be desired.[20]

[18] The Legion is treated in J. N. Bradley, *La Légion Tchécoslovaque en Russie 1914–1920* (Paris, 1965), and in two works by V. M. Fic, the previously cited *The Bolsheviks and the Czechoslovak Legion* and *Revolutionary War for Independence and the Russian Question: Czechoslovak Army in Russia 1914–1918* (New Delhi, 1977).

[19] The Red Terror was soon widely publicized abroad, acquiring a gory reputation and strongly influencing attitudes concerning the Communist regime. See L. D. Gerson, *The Secret Police in Lenin's Russia* (Philadelphia, 1976); K. Kautsky, *Terrorism and Communism* (New York, 1973); G. Leggett, *The Cheka: Lenin's Political Police* (Oxford, 1981); S. Melgunov, *The Red Terror in Russia* (Westport, Conn., 1974); and J. Baynac, ed., *La Terreur sous Lenine* (Paris, 1975).

[20] D. Fedotoff-White, *The Growth of the Red Army* (Princeton, N.J., 1944); F. Benvenuti, *The Bolsheviks and the Red Army, 1918–1922* (New York, 1988).

At the time of their initial takeover, the Bolsheviks had only asked neutrality of the anarchists, the other force of the extreme revolutionary left, whose competitive radicalism worried Lenin. Anarchists in the large cities were then suppressed by force in April–May 1918, many of them subsequently joining the Bolsheviks (many more, proportionately, than would later be the case in Spain).[21] The only two parties to enjoy very limited toleration were the Mensheviks (the Bolsheviks' more moderate Marxist rivals)[22] and the Socialist Revolutionaries. They were treated with the carrot and the stick, some of them occasionally arrested and then later released. A very limited degree of semipluralism was sometimes granted to them in elections to soviet assemblies, but the government remained exclusively in the power of the Communists. In 1922, at the end of the civil war, the other two parties would be completely suppressed.

An opposition government appeared on Russian soil for the first time in June 1918 after the SR underground in Samara in east Russia had prevailed on the Czech Legionnaires to overthrow Bolshevik rule in that city. SR leaders then organized a rival government in the name of the deposed Constituent Assembly, the "Committee of Members of the Constituent Assembly," colloquially known in Russian as "Komuch." "At its peak Komuch ... controlled Samara and Ufa provinces, and large parts of Saratov, Simbirsk, Kazan and Viatka,"[23] a region of more than ten million people. They proceeded to raise their own military force, the "People's Army" (which would be the official name of the Republican army in the Spanish war), composed of 10,000 volunteers and a somewhat larger number of draftees. Komuch was not a counterrevolutionary regime but an antidictatorial one, created in the name of the original democratic revolution. It proved, however, unable to achieve unity or much in the way of organization, roused only limited support, was gravely weakened by internal factionalism, and so became little more than a repetition of the Provisional Government. In a vast land with scant civic culture, similar weaknesses appeared in other anti-Communist forces. Though Bolshevik power had temporarily disappeared east of the Volga, during the late summer the new Red Army finally began to crystallize, and sizable Bolshevik units retook part of this region. To the east, in Siberia,

---

[21] Anarchists had been among the leading activists when the Petrograd soviet had first begun to form Red Guards at the beginning of August 1917, and seem to have played a disproportionate role in the fighting waged by the Red Guards in Moscow and elsewhere at the time of the coup in November. A few small urban groups remained in opposition during 1918 and 1919, carrying out violent actions until they were fully suppressed. Many anarchists, however, came to play major roles in the Cheka and the Red Army. See P. Avrich, *The Russian Anarchists* (Princeton, N.J., 1967); A. Skirda, *Les anarchistes russes, les soviets et la révolution de 1917* (Paris, 2000); and P. Avrich, ed., *The Anarchists in the Russian Revolution* (London, 1973).

[22] V. N. Brovkin, *The Mensheviks after October: Socialist Opposition and the Rise of the Bolshevik Dictatorship* (Ithaca, N.Y., 1987); V. Broido, *Lenin and the Mensheviks: The Persecution of Socialists under Bolshevism* (Aldershot, 1987); L. H. Haimson, *The Mensheviks: From the Revolution of 1917 to the Second World War* (Chicago, 1974).

[23] Mawdsley, *Civil War*, 63–64.

atamanshchina, or "warlordism," predominated, as a variety of tyrannical little fiefdoms sprang up.[24]

Western Siberia, however, came to be dominated by a new volunteer force led by former tsarist military leaders, a "White" counterrevolutionary movement that paralleled other volunteer forces that had rebelled far away in southeastern Russia. They adopted this color to symbolize purity and patriotism, in opposition to "Red" revolutionary internationalism. A Provisional Siberian Government took shape in Omsk, led by Admiral A. V. Kolchak, a former commander of the tsar's Black Sea Fleet. Unlike Komuch, it was rightist and counterrevolutionary, but a conference was held in Ufa, east of the Volga, in September 1918, resulting in the creation of the Provisional All-Russian Government, based on the democratic legitimacy of the Constituent Assembly. Meanwhile, Kolchak found it easier to recruit troops among the more individualistic Siberian peasantry and after some months had raised a sizable force. With the support of his new army and a group of right-wing civilians, Kolchak overthrew the All-Russian Government in November, installing himself as dictator of the White forces in Siberia and the Urals. He was recognized as "Supreme Ruler," a kind of regent or head of state, by the White military. The counterrevolution now had a single leader, but it would never be unified or capable of organizing much of an administrative apparatus, and found it impossible to overcome a high level of corruption in internal administration.[25]

THE REVOLUTION MOVES WEST

The Red Army had originally been planned as a screen against German militarism and then was developed to fight the civil war. During the late summer and early autumn of 1918 it rewon part of the territory east of the Volga, and the Whites seemed to have been checked, though not defeated. The first anniversary of the Bolshevik seizure of power fell on 7 November 1918, and four days later Germany admitted defeat, signing an armistice with the Allies. German power in the western territories crumbled, while the empire of Austria-Hungary underwent dissolution. All the while excitement increased in Moscow, for it seemed that international revolution was finally on the march. A new "Army of the West" was hastily thrown together, and Leon Trotsky, commissar-in-chief of the Red Army, announced that Communist forces would march to the liberation of workers abroad, Stalin writing on 17 November that "revolutions and Soviet government are matters of the very near future" in the western borderlands.[26] The concept was not that the Red army would

---

[24] J. Bisher, *White Terror: Cossack Warlords of the Trans-Siberian* (New York, 2005).

[25] For the White movement as a whole, see N. Katzer, *Die Weisse Bewegung in Russland: Herrschaftsbildung, praktische Politik und politische Programmatik im Bürgerkrieg* (Cologne, 1999), and G. A. Bordiugov et al., *Beloe delo: Ideologiya, osnovy rezhimy, vlasti* (Moscow, 1998).

[26] Quoted in C. J. Smith, *Finland and the Russian Revolution, 1917–1922* (Athens, Ga., 1958), 127.

necessarily conquer entire countries – though that was a possibility – but that military pressure would expedite internal rebellion abroad. In practice, however, the only new lands that would be revolutionized in Europe would be ones that the Red Army would conquer, either in 1919–21 or in 1939–45.[27]

One of the closest targets, and presumably the weakest, with a population of less than a million, was Estonia, now free of German occupation. Though Lenin had announced the independence of all the "mature" nationalities of the old empire, units of the Red Army quickly moved into Estonia, accompanied by (what would henceforth be standard procedure) a Russian-organized puppet government, the "Estonian Toilers' Commune." The Estonians, however, were one of the most advanced nationalities under the tsarist regime, and quickly formed in Tallinn their own center-left government, with a popular and democratic program. They also gained the support of Finnish and Swedish volunteers and anti-Bolshevik Russians, plus the assistance of British warships. The Red forces were thrown back, and although it tried to form an Estonian Red Army, the Toilers' Commune puppet administration was soon dissolved.

Latvia seemed more promising, because it had a radical tradition and showed popular support for Bolshevism. The Red Army arrived in Riga on 3 January 1919, and the first Communist regime outside Russia was set up as the Latvian Soviet Socialist Republic (SSR). Despite some initial popular backing, this government became increasingly unpopular because of its broad use of terror and extensive confiscation of property, together with the disastrous economic conditions that ensued. Latvia had been severely ravaged by the world war, and nearly 9,000 people died in Riga that winter. The victorious Allies permitted new ad hoc German units, organized as *Freikorps*, to operate in Lithuania and Latvia as a barrier against the Bolsheviks. The *Freikorps* attacked from the south and the new Estonian army from the north, assisted by Latvian volunteers and a British naval force. The Germans seized Riga in May, hoping to set up a new protectorate. They were soon forced out by the British in favor of an independent Latvian government, but not before they had executed more than 3,000 real or nominal Bolsheviks in a counter-revolutionary terror.[28]

Independent national governments had been formed in both Belarus and Lithuania during 1918, but the Red Army attempted to gain control of both countries. Local Bolsheviks seized power in Vilnius, Lithuania's largest city, and the Red Army occupied the eastern part of the new republic, as well as

[27] The partial exceptions were Yugoslavia and Albania in 1944–45, for the most part conquered by their own Communist Partisan forces, originally directed, of course, by the Soviet Union's Comintern.

[28] On the war in the Baltic region, see the previously cited works by Ezergailis and Mandulis, as well as G. von Rauch, *The Baltic States: The Years of Independence 1917–1922* (Berkeley, Calif., 1970), 49–75; S. W. Page, *The Formation of the Baltic States: A Study of the Effect of Great Power Politics upon the Emergence of Lithuania, Latvia and Estonia* (Cambridge, Mass., 1959); T. U. Raun, *Estonia and the Estonians* (Stanford, Calif., 1987); and A. Blondnieks, *The Undefeated Nation* (New York, 1960), 180.

Minsk, the capital of Belarus. In February 1919 Moscow proceeded to set up its own regime of a combined Lithuanian-Belarussian SSR ("Litbel"). This lasted until the newly independent government of Poland organized its own army, which, together with Lithuanian forces, chased the Bolsheviks out of Vilnius in April and later out of Minsk in August.

The Red Army was more successful in the south, where a major effort was made to conquer Ukraine. This invasion seized Kiev in February 1919, and a Ukrainian SSR was set up, though it held power for only a few months before being challenged by a major offensive from the White Volunteer Army, formed in southeastern Russia.

In March 1919 Moscow founded the Communist International (Comintern) as a revolutionary replacement for the old social democratic Second International, with the goal of forming and coordinating new Communist parties all over the world.[29] During the next two years there would be a flurry of activity to set up Communist parties in many countries, but the only new Communist regime established was the one that briefly held power in Hungary (and will be discussed in the next chapter).

ALLIED INTERVENTION

The Bolshevik regime was founded on the ideological basis of revolutionary internationalism, rejecting both tsarist imperialism and Russian nationalism. The latter was, in any event, weak, for patriotism in the old order had been directed to the *vserossiskii* ("all-Russian") empire, not to a Russian nation, which politically had never existed. Recognition of the nominal independence of nationalities was not intended to hinder their communization, for Lenin and his colleagues proposed to conquer as many nations as possible, all in the name, of course, of revolutionary internationalism, not of Russian imperialism.

During the civil war the regime made a strong appeal, nonetheless, to revolutionary patriotism and xenophobic anticapitalism because of limited intervention by the Allies on the periphery of the Russian empire. It is important to understand at the outset that the only intervention of any military or other importance was that of Germany, which the Bolsheviks accepted by treaty. Germany had employed a million or more troops to occupy a huge swathe of former imperial territory, while providing a crucial breathing space and other assistance to the new dictatorship. The Allied intervention of 1918–19, by contrast, always remained marginal, except for the assistance given to Baltic independence.

Allied intervention began in 1918 after the Bolsheviks had signed their separate peace with Germany, violating all the agreements of the tsarist government. Its goal was to force Russia back into a war that it looked at the time like Germany was winning, and later to prevent the latter from building

[29] J. W. Hulse, *The Forming of the Communist International* (Stanford, Calif., 1964).

an empire in the east that might compensate for its looming defeat in the west. After World War I ended, the Allies attempted to set up a meeting near Istanbul to mediate peace between the Bolsheviks and their foes, which came to nothing. The final and only major phase of Allied intervention (1919–20) then ensued as the Allies realized that Lenin was simultaneously asking for normal diplomatic relations and actively promoting revolution. Six months of Red Terror, following on the heels of the earlier genocide of the Armenians in Turkey, also constituted a humanitarian challenge. There ensued a half-hearted effort to assist the Russian foes of Bolshevism, which was deemed a menace to world peace and stability – a quarantine measure against the spread of Lenin's declared "world civil war."

The initial intervention involved a very small British force dispatched to the far northern coast of Russia in mid-1918. At that point the goal was as much or more to influence Lenin's regime as to overthrow it. The only military achievement of the handful of British troops was to assist the East Karelians and the latter's Red Finn allies in taking over East Karelia, the large, empty, mostly Finnish-inhabited region to the east of Finland (at that moment aligned with Germany). This was more antiliberation than liberation, for if Finland had been able to occupy the territory, it might have retained East Karelia, or at least part of it, in a postwar settlement.

The Japanese temporarily sent more than 70,000 troops, the only sizable foreign contingent, into eastern Siberia, but they did not advance very far and eventually were withdrawn. French and Greek forces very briefly landed on the Black Sea coast and almost as quickly withdrew, while small American contingents appeared in northern Russia and in Siberia. None of these initiatives had much military significance.[30]

Only Great Britain played a somewhat more important role through minor interventions in both northern and southern Russia, and also in the Caspian region. This helped to strengthen the Whites, while guaranteeing the independence of Finland and the Baltic states, defending the latter both from the Bolsheviks and from the new German *Freikorps*. Winston Churchill, the British secretary of state for war and air in 1919, was the chief promoter of this policy, for he saw the nascent Bolshevik regime as a menace to peace and civilization almost as great as the threat he would descry in Nazi Germany twenty years later. Churchill enjoyed little support, though he insisted that "after having defeated all the tigers and lions I don't like to be defeated by the baboons."[31] The rest of the government quickly tired of the enterprise; most of

[30] J. F. N. Bradley, *Allied Intervention in Russia* (London, 1968); M. J. Carley, *Revolution and Intervention: The French Government and the Russian Civil War 1917–1919* (Montreal, 1983); J. W. Morley, *The Japanese Thrust into Siberia, 1918* (New York, 1957); J. A. White, *The Siberian Intervention* (New York, 1969); W. S. Graves, *America's Siberian Adventure, 1918–1920* (New York, 1941).

[31] Mawdsley, *Civil War*, 130. See C. Kinvig, *Churchill's Crusade: The British Invasion of Russia 1918–1920* (London, 2006), and A. P. Schmid, *Churchills privater Krieg. Intervention und Konterrevolution im russischen Bürgerkrieg November 1918-März 1920* (Munich, 1994).

the small British units were withdrawn by the end of 1919, and the remainder three months later.[32] Aside from the achievements in the Baltic area,[33] the only consequence was to provide a certain amount of arms and equipment for the Whites.

THE WHITE OFFENSIVE, 1919

During the second half of 1918 two different White forces developed, the Siberian army of Kolchak and the "Volunteer Army" under Gen. Anton Denikin in the southeast. Kolchak initially organized larger forces and took the offensive just before the close of the year with his "Rossiskaya Armiya" (All-Russian Army). The previous Red Army advance had retaken nearly all the territory between the Volga and the Urals, but before the end of 1918 it had lost strength, while the Bolsheviks concentrated on their revolutionary advance into Europe and the south. Kolchak crossed the Urals and retook Perm in December, though the Red Army momentarily advanced further in the southern Urals region.

Kolchak's main offensive began in March 1919 and moved with surprising speed, about 400 kilometers in five weeks. Bolshevik forces in the area were worn down and the peasants disaffected after months of Communist rule. By the end of April the Whites were within seventy-five miles of the Volga, but they lacked the strength and organization to advance further, and were soon being driven back.

None of the White forces had serious infrastructure or logistical organization. Kolchak operated as a military dictator and failed to mobilize much political support, assuming that such a thing was possible. His main political advisors were from the centrist Constitutional Democrat Party, but he articulated no significant political message and was generally assumed, perhaps incorrectly, to be aiming at nothing more than restoring the old order. Despite the growing horrors of Bolshevism, the old order had only limited partisans. Moreover, there was no coordination whatsoever among the various White

Churchill's prescience and agility were amazing, if not always practical. He was the most serious leader of the struggle against Communist tyranny in 1918–20, as he would be the principal leader of the struggle against Nazi tyranny in 1938–41. At the close of World War II, he was the only major Western leader to contemplate serious action against the Soviet Union to roll back part of its domination of eastern Europe ("Operation Unthinkable"), but a decade later, after the death of Stalin, he would become the most important Western voice to press for détente with the new, more moderate Soviet chieftains.

[32] C. H. Ellis, *The British "Intervention" in Transcaspia: 1918–1919* (Berkeley, Calif., 1963); K. Jeffery, *The British Army and the Crisis of Empire 1918–22* (Manchester, 1984); R. H. Ullman, *Anglo-Soviet Relations, 1917–1921* (Princeton, N.J., 1968), 2 vols; M. Occleshaw, *Dances in Deep Shadows: The Clandestine War in Russia 1917–20* (New York, 2006). Official Soviet historiography for many years wrote the military history of the fighting in Russia in terms of the "Three Entente Offensives" (the White offensives of the spring of 1919, the autumn of 1919, and the summer of 1920), but the Allies had comparatively little to do with them.

[33] R. Jackson, *Battle of the Baltic* (Barnsley, UK, 2007).

forces across the vast Russian periphery, and Denikin would not begin to advance until May. Though Kolchak nominally mobilized 300–400,000 men, by far the largest of the anti-Bolshevik armies, he was never able to put more than one-fourth on the front line.

The Red Army, by contrast, mobilized much larger numbers and had improved in organization, logistics, political appeal, and combat quality. Though many of their recruits initially deserted, Soviet leaders eventually established greater discipline. They learned to develop more efficient cadres, with administrative control over more and more of their population, building effective personnel records, while creating a much more effective propaganda system than their adversaries. Red Army soldiers were provided with succulent carrots to accompany the stick of tighter discipline. They enjoyed significant perquisites in a society of increasing scarcity and penury, and their families received support as well. On this basis the Red Army began to be turned into a more effective military force.[34] Within a month it rewon most of the trans-Volga region and in July 1919 crossed the Urals, driving back Kolchak's army. Kolchak's one major counterattack in September failed, after which the Red Army advanced deeper into Siberia.[35]

The best of the White forces was Denikin's "Volunteer Army," which included many former tsarist officers and enjoyed significant support from the Don Cossacks, arguably the most anti-Bolshevik of all Russian-speaking regional populations. At the beginning of 1919 Red commanders had hoped to complete conquest of the entire southeast and even to occupy the Caucasus, committing 150,000 troops against 25,000 men in the Volunteer Army, but the latter were greatly superior in combat quality. Denikin's counteroffensive in January turned the Red Army's flank and rolled up its front, taking 50,000 prisoners.[36] Denikin was soon able to double his combat forces and, though the southeastern front had now become the top Red priority, fight off three Bolshevik counteroffensives in the Don region between March and May. Denikin's next advance cleared the southeast and broke into Ukraine, assisted by the usual strong reaction against Bolshevik rule exhibited by peasants who had lived under it. The Communist front virtually disappeared, and by July the Volunteer Army had occupied southeastern Ukraine and the lower Volga.

[34] See the analysis in J. A. Sanborn, *Drafting the Russian Nation: Military Conscription, Total War, and Mass Politics 1905–1925* (De Kalb, Ill., 2003), 40–55.

[35] Kolchak and the war in Siberia are treated in N. G. O. Pereira, *White Siberia: The Politics of Civil War* (Montreal, 1996); P. Dotsenko, *The Struggle for Democracy in Siberia, 1917–1920: Eyewitness Account of a Contemporary* (Stanford, Calif., 1983); and P. Fleming, *The Fate of Admiral Kolchak* (London, 1963).

[36] On Denikin and the Volunteer Army, see G. A. Brinkley, *The Volunteer Army and Allied Intervention in South Russia, 1917–1921: A Study in the Politics and Diplomacy of the Russian Civil War* (Notre Dame, Ind., 1966); P. Kenez, *Civil War in South Russia, 1918: The First Year of the Volunteer Army* (Berkeley, Calif., 1971) and *Civil War in South Russia, 1919–1920: The Defeat of the Whites* (Berkeley, Calif., 1977); D. V. Lehovich, *White against Red: The Life of General Anton Denikin* (New York, 1974); and R. Luckett, *The White Generals: An Account of the White Movement and the Russian Civil War* (Harlow, UK, 1971).

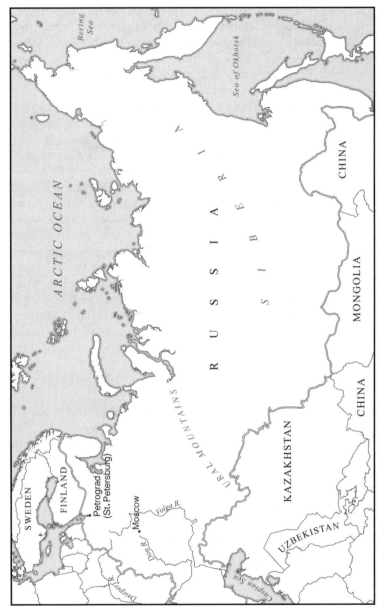

Eastern Russia.

During the spring, however, Kolchak had advanced too fast, and so Denikin paused to regroup.

The Communist regime at this point made its maximum military effort and by early autumn had mobilized, at least on paper, three million men. Nonetheless, its counterattacks against Denikin in August were ineffective, and he resumed his advance the following month, while another small White force threatened Petrograd far to the north. The Volunteer Army moved through Ukraine and by mid-October had taken Orel, less than 400 kilometers south of Moscow. This was high tide for the Whites.

Denikin at this point had well over 100,000 combat troops, but no organized base of operations and no logistical or supply network. His advance units depended on "self-supply" and soon found themselves hanging, as it were, in thin air. Most Ukrainian peasants supported neither Communism nor Ukrainian nationalism, but they did not support a restoration of the old order either. Peasant partisan bands that had once attacked the Bolsheviks now began to fracture Denikin's rear. Larger arms supplies began to arrive from Britain, but it was too late. The Volunteer Army was stretched too thin and could not resist the massive Red counteroffensive that began in mid-November, supported by large cavalry forces. Soon it began to retreat even more rapidly than it had advanced, and the entire position of the Whites in the south started to crumble. In the same month (November), the Red Army seized Kolchak's capital and moved deeper into Siberia. By the first part of 1920 the Volunteer Army had been compressed into a small area of southern Ukraine. The major phase of the civil war within Russia was in fact nearly over, but new imperial conquests awaited the Red Army.

THE RUSSO-POLISH WAR

Having gained apparent victory in the intra-Russian conflict, the Bolshevik regime prepared to reconquer as much former tsarist territory as possible. The Baltic republics were left to one side as particularly resistant and also as having Western support, so that attention focused on the third Communist drive to the south and west, following the earlier offensives of 1917–18 and 1919. The targets were Ukraine and Poland, whose occupation might also open doors to the Balkans and east central Europe, including Germany, always considered the key to world revolution.

The main obstacle was Poland, where both nationalism and internal organization were much stronger than in Ukraine. The military leader of the new Poland was Josef Pilsudski, a former socialist and one-time revolutionary associate of Lenin's older brother. The Polish government sought to restore as large a country as possible, creating a federation with Lithuania, Belarus, and Ukraine, which could form a sizable barrier to Russian expansionism, Communist or otherwise.[37] The nascent Polish army had driven Red forces out

---

[37] See M. K. Dziewanowski, *Pilsudski – A European Federalist* (Stanford, Calif., 1969).

of Vilnius and Minsk in 1919, signing a temporary truce with the Bolsheviks. The Soviet regime officially repudiated the eighteenth-century treaties that had partitioned Poland, a position which in theory would have recognized Polish sovereignty over the area west of the Dnieper River, but in practice Moscow had its own designs on the region. The Soviet Politburo approved a new plan for the invasion of Poland on 27 January 1920, though several key members were opposed. The decision to invade was reconfirmed shortly afterward, with the date set for April, but continuing resistance from the Whites in the south required postponement.

Since Polish cryptographers had broken the Soviet codes, Pilsudski soon learned of Lenin's plan and moved to thwart it. After the third Soviet occupation of the Ukraine some months earlier, Ukrainian nationalist forces had retreated into Poland, and in April Polish and Ukrainian troops seized the initiative, attacking the momentarily weak southwestern front of the Red Army. It collapsed, and Kiev was soon seized. Pilsudski's goal was to enable Simon Petlura, the Ukrainian leader, to develop rapidly a new Ukrainian state that, in association with Poland, might withstand the next Soviet invasion.

These complexities were too much for western European opinion, which saw Pilsudski's initiative as simply a Polish invasion of Ukraine, an interpretation still found in history textbooks.[38] Churchill, on the other hand, was annoyed that Pilsudski had not acted in the autumn of 1919, when, together with Denikin, he might have given the Soviet regime the coup de grace. The Polish leader had not done so because he regarded the Volunteer Army as the representative of classic Russian imperialism. Such absence of cooperation was a further indication of the political problems that crippled the White cause. By the end of May 1920, the Red Army fully dominated the southeastern front and was in a position to bring its principal weight to bear against Poland.

In the resulting campaign, the Soviet regime wore two hats – the world civil war, on the one hand, and aggrieved *rossiskii* patriotism on the other. Responding to the call of "Poland invading Russia" (though Pilsudski had only entered Ukraine, not Russia), thousands of Russians, including hundreds of ex-tsarist officers, volunteered for the Red Army. The first Russian offensive was stopped, but by mid-June a large Soviet force drove the Poles out of Kiev and into a seemingly endless retreat, which ended only when the Red Army was entering central Poland six weeks later.[39] This marked the fourth and definitive Soviet reconquest of the greater part of Ukraine.[40]

[38] For the full political background, see P. S. Wandycz, *Soviet-Polish Relations, 1917–1921* (Cambridge, Mass., 1969), and M. Palij, *The Ukrainian-Polish Defensive Alliance 1919– 1921* (Edmonton, 1995).

[39] The best military history in a Western language is N. Davies, *White Eagle, Red Star: The Polish-Soviet War, 1919–1920* (London, 1972).

[40] The civil war in Ukraine, with constant advances and retreats in a three-sided contest among Communists, Whites, and native Ukrainians, was the most complicated in any part of the former empire. See J. S. Reshetar, *The Ukrainian Revolution, 1917–1920: A Study in Nationalism* (New York, 1972); D. Dorosenko, *The Ukrainian Hetman State of 1918* (Winnipeg, 1973);

On 23 July the Bolsheviks created the usual puppet regime that they hoped to place in power, this time of Polish Communists, defining the invasion not as an international conflict but as "class war," a revolutionary civil war. The Soviet commander, Mikhail Tukhachevsky, announced to his troops that "the destiny of the World Revolution is being decided in the West. The path to World Conflagration passes over the corpse of White Poland: ... Forward!" Lenin wrote to Stalin, the chief commissar on the southern Polish front, to suggest the possibility of a further advance into Romania, Hungary, and possibly even Italy, to which the latter replied that "it would be a sin" not to attempt this.[41]

Soviet calculations relied especially on class conflict and civil uprising to advance the revolution across Europe, expecting in Poland the assistance of class-conscious workers and peasants. A little of this occurred, with numerous acts of arson by pro-Communists in Warsaw, where "entire working-class neighborhoods were temporarily cordoned off"[42] by the government, but in general Poles rallied strongly to the defense of their nation. Many volunteered, including several thousand women, organized as second-line defense forces. The usual atrocities accompanying the Red Army advance only spurred Polish determination.

The two invading Soviet armies diverged to north and south, with the latter lagging well behind. This made it possible for Pilsudski to throw his reserves into a well-designed counteroffensive that struck the northern army on its flank. Though the Russians were somewhat superior in numbers, they were caught off balance and forced into headlong retreat. The second phase of the counteroffensive began on 21 September and did not end until the middle of the following month, when Polish forces once more occupied Minsk. These operations merit a footnote in military history for having involved the last major cavalry battles in European history, won by the Poles. Ironically, only the day before Pilsudski's riposte began, Trotsky had ordered the preparation of revolutionary pamphlets in German to be used as soon as the triumphant Red Army advanced into Germany. The fighting came to an end in October 1920 and, when a final peace treaty was signed the following year, the new Poland included the western portions of Belarus and Ukraine. Though Pilsudski never attained his goal of a Ukraine in federation with Poland, the Soviet dream of a military advance to "world conflagration" was decisively disappointed. The only Red Army troops to reach Germany were the 40,000 or so who retreated into East Prussia to surrender.

T. Hunczak, ed., *The Ukraine, 1917–1921: A Study in Revolution* (Cambridge, Mass., 1977); A. E. Adams, *Bolsheviks in the Ukraine: The Second Campaign, 1918–1919* (New Haven, Conn., 1963); J. Borys, *The Sovietization of Ukraine 1917–1923: The Communist Doctrine and Practice of National Self-Determination* (Edmonton, 1980); and A. J. Motyl, *The Turn to the Right: The Ideological Origins and Development of Ukrainian Nationalism, 1919–1929* (Boulder, Colo., 1980).

[41] Quotations are from A. Zamoyski, *Varsovia 1920. El intento fallido de Lenin de conquistar Europa* (Madrid, 2008), 46, 60.

[42] D. Diner, *Cataclysms: A History of the Twentieth Century from Europe's Edge* (Madison, Wisc., 2008), 87.

In most historical accounts, considerable attention has been devoted to Stalin's role as chief commissar of the southwestern front, since he and the regional army commander allegedly failed to respond promptly to orders to break off their own advance and assist the conquest of Warsaw. Yet the orders were confused, not delivered in a timely fashion, and ignored major obstacles to their execution. There was not necessarily disobedience but general confusion. Still, the disaster seems to have rankled with Stalin during the next quarter of a century.

For some years the Polish victory was hailed as one of the "decisive battles of the Western world," though its results stood for no more than two decades. Nonetheless, it proved indispensable in consolidating the post–World War I settlement arranged at Versailles, temporarily helping to stabilize the new European order. The two decades that followed were important for Poland and other eastern European countries, making possible the fuller development of civil society and national culture, with concrete social and economic accomplishments, which enabled the country to endure the Nazi occupation, followed by the forty-five-year Soviet tyranny imposed in 1944, and later to reassert a more flourishing democratic society than anything found in post-Soviet Russia.

For Lenin, the invasion of Poland – "the only unredeemed military defeat in the Red Army's history"[43] – was not so much a military mistake as a political miscalculation, for no social revolt of any significance greeted it. This was not a civil war, for Polish Communism was not that strong, but it was not a normal international conflict either, for it was a highly ideological and revolutionary war aimed at revolution in east central and central Europe, which Lenin and his colleagues believed the key to worldwide revolution. The Soviet leaders did obtain indirect assistance from trade unions in Britain and France, which to some extent blocked arms shipments to Poland.[44] The Soviet government also saw to it that after 1921 the Soviet-Polish border would never be entirely quiet. Soviet agents would periodically conduct commando-style raids or other subversive operations across the frontier, seeking to rouse rebellion among the Ukrainian and Belarussian minorities.

Though he played the key role in defeating the Red Army, Pilsudski did not see the Soviet regime as the long-term menace that it turned out to be, and was determined not to cooperate with the remaining White forces in order to avoid recreating a stronger Russian state. Moscow was weakly defended in the autumn of 1920. Had the Polish army continued to advance, the White forces in the south might have made a major recovery.

As it was, the Polish campaign gave the remnants of the Volunteer Army a respite in which to reorganize. The new commander, Gen. Piotr Vrangel, was the only White general to show any political ability or imagination. He formed a new government that gestured toward democracy, instituted a land reform, and was willing to work with liberal and non-Russian interests. Yet

[43] Davies, *White Eagle*, 278.
[44] R. P. Arnot, *The Impact of the Russian Revolution in Britain* (London, 1967).

Vrangel could muster only about 30,000 front-line troops at a time when the Red Army – on paper, at least – numbered several million. After withstanding a limited assault in June 1920, in the summer the Volunteer Army struck once more into southern Ukraine, hoping vainly to link up with Pilsudski's forces. It maintained its position until October, when the end of the Polish war enabled the Red Army to mass huge numbers. Forced back into the Crimea, in November Vrangel, who had received very little foreign assistance, managed to evacuate 146,000 of his followers by ship – nearly half the number collected at Dunkirk in 1940.[45] Those who remained behind were subjected to the largest single mass slaughter of the entire civil war, with possibly as many as 40,000 executions. All significant White resistance had ended.

THE GREEN REVOLT

The civil war that the Soviets fought behind the front lines may have been more extensive than the one fought against the Whites. They had two major foes: the political opposition and the workers in the cities, to the extent that they challenged any of the policies of the dictatorship and, more importantly, the war against the peasants in the countryside. The peasants first began to rebel in the spring of 1918, and, with numerous ups and downs, this continued and also increased over the next three years. By and large, the peasants had been pleased with the Bolsheviks in 1917 because the latter offered them all the remaining land, but they were not pleased with what came afterward. That meant forced requisition of foodstuffs on a massive scale, few urban products in exchange, and the collapse of the economy, with more and more peasant workers moving from the cities back to the villages, so that more land failed to produce greater proportionate income. By 1918 the large Soviet zone lived under what became known as "War Communism," in which all industry and banking and nearly all commerce were taken over by the state, with the result that total production shrank steadily for three years. This was the second experience of "pre-Stalinism," a system in which, by 1920, the economy produced little more than military goods. The dictatorship responded with massive repression, relatively easy to accomplish in the cities but much harder to effect in the vast Russian countryside. By 1919 this repression enjoyed wide publicity, grisly accounts of the Red Terror appearing around the world.[46]

Vladimir Brovkin has observed that generally the peasants preferred whichever side in the civil war was not occupying their territory and abusing them at that particular moment. Under the Reds, they resisted and then encouraged the entry of the Whites, after which the opposite was true. The peasants

[45] L. M. Adramenko, *Poslednaya obitel: Krim, 1920–1921 gody* (Kiev, 2005), treats the final phase in the Crimea.
[46] Ernst Nolte has cited one publication typical of the genre: R. Nilostonski, *Der Blutrausch des Bolschewismus. Berichte eines Augenzeugen* (Berlin, 1920). Germans may have received even more reports than other western Europeans because of the suffering of the German minority in Russia.

remained a negative factor throughout the civil war – negative in that they failed to contribute consistently to any positive goal, negative in that they were always a political and economic problem for whoever occupied their territory. In general, the Bolsheviks handled the peasants more effectively, making a major effort – in part successfully – to divide them socially, and manipulating them with sufficient adroitness to win over at least some sectors. The Bolshevik system employed the carrot and stick: the carrot was made of propaganda, with the assurance that the new order promised the peasants all of the land; the stick was an apparatus of forced requisitions and repression much more ruthless than anything of which the Whites were capable.

In the short term, however, as the Reds occupied more and more territory and the general economy continued to deteriorate, peasant resentment and rebelliousness became harder and harder to control. Revolts were often simply *bunty*, that is, mere riots or "jacqueries," but eventually they began to assume a degree of organization.[47] In southern Ukraine, one manifestation was "peasant anarchism," particularly in the well-organized guerrilla band of Nestor Makhno, which was not broken up until 1921.[48]

In parts of Russia, particularly in Ukraine, Jews were frequent victims of the general resentment and suffering; through 1920 violent pogroms, sometimes on a large scale, were widespread. Almost all groups participated, especially local peasant bands, but also Ukrainian nationalists and White units, sometimes even sectors of the Red Army (though this was less common). The pogroms resulted in massive destruction, looting, rape, and murder. It is commonly calculated that at least 100,000 Jews perished.

The Communists' massive persecution of the Orthodox Church and clergy caused less of a backlash than might have been expected. Though the Whites emphasized restoring religious observance, the Russian civil war was much less a war of religion than the later war in Spain. This seems strange, since all the peasantry were formally Orthodox, and since ordinary Russian society was in some respects less secularized than would be the situation in Spain in 1936. One reason for the lesser salience of the religious issue in Russia was the character of Russian caesaropapism, which totally subordinated the ecclesiastical structure to the throne, and the primarily liturgical character of Orthodox religiosity, which produced a culture that was ritualistic. Peasant spirituality exhibited both a certain amount of genuine piety and considerable superstition, but this was not so closely associated with the church and the clergy as to motivate many to fight for them. As Orlando Figes has put it, "By all accounts

---

[47] T. Osipova, "Peasant Rebellions," in V. Brovkin, ed., *The Bolsheviks in Russian Society* (New Haven, Conn., 1997), 154–76.

[48] P. Arshinov, *History of the Makhnovist Movement (1918–1921)* (Detroit, 1974); M. Palij, *The Anarchism of Nestor Makhno, 1918–1921: An Aspect of the Ukrainian Revolution* (Seattle, 1976); M. Malet, *Nestor Makhno in the Russian Civil War* (London, 1982). As opposed to the tendency to romanticize anarchism, what this meant to ordinary people is chronicled in D. Navall, *A Russian Dance of Death: Revolution and Civil War in the Ukraine* (Winnipeg, 1977).

the peasants did not hold their priests in high esteem. When one compares this with the respect and deference shown by the peasants of Catholic Europe toward their priests then one begins to understand why peasant Russia had a revolution and, say, peasant Spain a counterrevolution."[49] Peasants were frequently in a state of rebellion against the exactions of Bolshevism, but essentially for the sake of their local and family interests, not on behalf of the church or any political project.

In the civil war the Bolsheviks developed the fundamental Leninist model that concentrated resources on military mobilization and the police apparatus more thoroughly than did any other system in modern history, later making possible Communist victory in World War II and in other regions as distant as Yugoslavia and Vietnam. Their initial economic policy was, conversely, a disaster. The longer Bolshevik rule and civil war continued, the more rebellious the peasants became, so that by 1920–21 hundreds of thousands had taken to resistance bands in the forests, mostly anti-Communist, though sometimes primarily given to banditry. Much of the countryside was in uproar. By 1920 the dictatorship was undertaking experiments in the "militarization of labor," and many units of the Red Army, once the latter achieved mass proportions, were converted temporarily into labor battalions. By the winter of 1921 even the revolutionary sailors at Kronstadt, the large naval base outside Petrograd, who four years earlier had been key supporters of Bolshevism, came out in armed revolt against a dictatorship that they declared to have betrayed the revolution. This was more serious than any of the numerous peasant revolts, and was suppressed only with difficulty.[50]

By 1921 the regime had won the civil war militarily but could not make the economy work or control the countryside and stimulate production. At that point Lenin offered the peasantry a truce, announcing the New Economic Policy (NEP), which abandoned "War Communism." Food requisitions were canceled, and the peasants would be left in peace, subject to a tax on production, selling part of their produce in a partially free market. Commerce and small industry reverted to private hands, the state maintaining nationalized ownership only of the "commanding heights" of large industry. This would also be the economic policy that the Communists proposed for the wartime Spanish republic in 1937.

Full economic communism would be introduced only at some undeclared point in the future. The Red Army would concentrate on reconquering all the old empire except for the western borderlands, renounced by international treaty. The NEP helped slowly to pacify the peasants. Those resistance bands that had not disbanded were finally crushed by the Red Army in 1922.

[49] Figes, *A People's Tragedy*, 67. Also of interest in this regard are the remarks of A. Besançon, *The Rise of the Gulag: Intellectual Origins of Leninism* (New York, 1981), 54–78.
[50] I. Getzler, *Kronstadt 1917–1921: The Fate of a Soviet Democracy* (Cambridge, UK, 1983); P. Avrich, *Kronstadt 1921* (Princeton, N.J., 1970).

CONQUEST OF THE NEW SOVIET EMPIRE

Once the Whites had finally been defeated, the Red Army was able to concentrate on the reconquest of all former imperial territory in the Caucasus and in Asia. Most of Ukraine and Belarus had been definitively reconquered in 1920, and during that year the Red Army reentered the Caucasus, occupying first oil-rich Azerbaidzhan in April and then Armenia in November, where to some extent the Red Army was welcomed as protection against further genocide from the Turks. Georgia, an independent state governed by a democratic Menshevik regime, was seized in February 1921. In all these regions there were soon major national revolts against Soviet imperialism, but control had been solidified by the end of 1924.

The only Soviet bastion in central Asia was Tashkent, the capital of Turkestan, where minority Russians in the city rallied to the coup d'etat in 1917 and managed with great difficulty to hold their position throughout the civil war, ruthlessly exploiting the largely apolitical Muslim majority. The rest of central Asia was reconquered with comparatively little difficulty by the Red Army in 1920 and, after Japanese troops finally withdrew, all of Siberia was occupied by 1922.[51]

Yet the comparatively large Muslim territories, though thoroughly dominated politically and economically, were never brought under police control as completely as other regions. So-called *basmachis* (Muslim "bandits" or, more properly, "maquis") continued to roam some parts of the countryside at least until 1936, and possibly even longer.

Reconquest made it possible to give definitive form to the new, nominally federated Communist empire, reorganized at the close of 1922 as the Union of Soviet Socialist Republics (USSR). The Soviet Union was composed of individual republics for the principal nationalities, these in turn containing smaller "autonomous republics" as well as numerous nominally autonomous districts, recognizing many but not all of the more than one hundred ethnic groups within the empire. It comprised the most complex state structure anywhere in the world.[52]

The only decisive advance beyond former tsarist territory came in 1921, when the Red Army invaded Outer Mongolia (a land nominally under Chinese sovereignty), ousting a White warlord who had temporarily seized the capital.[53]

[51] F. Kazemzadeh, *The Struggle for Transcaucasia (1917–1921)* (New York, 1951); C. F. Smith, *Vladivostok under Red and White Rule: Revolution and Counter-revolution in the Russian Far East, 1920–1922* (Seattle, 1975).

[52] R. Pipes, *The Formation of the Soviet Union: Communism and Nationalism: 1917–1923* (Cambridge, Mass., 1954).

[53] The Russo-Baltic nobleman Baron Roman von Ungern Sternberg was one of the most bizarre and psychopathic figures of the civil war. There is a growing literature; the best account is J. Palmer, *The Bloody White Baron: The Extraordinary Story of the Russian Nobleman Who Became the Last Khan of Mongolia* (New York, 2009).

Three years later, Outer Mongolia became the first Soviet-controlled "people's republic," inaugurating a new form created for the socialist development of new states that were not yet Communist but under Soviet control.[54] For two decades it would be the only such state, though Communist theorists defined a special "people's republic" status for the wartime Spanish republic. This would also be the formula applied to Soviet-dominated eastern Europe after 1945.

A notable outcome of World War I and of the Russian revolution and civil war was that to a large degree Russia and France reversed roles in the international order. For more than a century France had been the most "advanced" politically of all the larger continental countries, and the tsarist empire the most conservative. After the Treaty of Versailles, democratic France stepped forward as the chief guarantor of the status quo in Europe and the patron of a *"Cordon sanitaire"* against the expansion of Communism, while the Soviet Union was henceforth the revolutionary state, dedicated to subverting the status quo.

WHY DID THE BOLSHEVIKS WIN?

In the first weeks after the coup d'etat of 1917, again in the summer of 1918, and once more in the autumn of 1919, Communist power seemed to hang by a shoestring but eventually won a complete victory, with the exception of its partial inability to control the peasantry. For many Bolshevik leaders, uncertain in the early months as to whether they could retain power, it all seemed somewhat miraculous. The Communist victory was predicated on several factors: 1) From the beginning, they controlled nearly all the cities and the demographic heartland of Russia, an area of from sixty to eighty million people, depending on the extent of occupation in any given phase, giving them a much larger social, economic, and demographic base than their rivals, with the means to recruit and equip a very large army. 2) The Communists also controlled most of the arms depots of the old tsarist army, which had stocked a large array of weapons, munitions, and supplies, so that the Red Army to a large extent fought the civil war with captured tsarist weapons. 3) In a breathtaking move of *Realpolitik*, equally notable for its daring and its cynicism, Lenin turned the war with Germany to the advantage of the Bolsheviks, first as consummately effective propaganda and even more importantly through the Treaty of Brest-Litovsk and the additional agreement of August 1918, which achieved peace with Germany and even temporary German support, simplifying most of the new regime's problems, giving it a breathing space to mobilize the core Russian heartland for civil war. Thus, contrary to their propaganda and subsequent historiography,

---

[54] T. T. Hammond, "The Communist Takeover of Outer Mongolia: Model for Eastern Europe?," in Hammond, ed., *The Anatomy of Communist Takeovers* (New Haven, Conn., 1975), 107–44; G. G. S. Murphy, *Soviet Mongolia: A Study of the Oldest Soviet Satellite* (Berkeley, Calif., 1966).

the only decisive foreign intervention favored the Communists. 4) The Communists invented and imposed a new model of centralized totalitarian dictatorship that was turned into a unique "military-industrial mobilization agency,"[55] the likes of which had never been seen before. 5) They imposed a policy of absolute rigor and ruthlessness, equally revolutionary and unprecedented, even in Russia, that carried out systematic mass arrests, indiscriminate murder on a huge scale, and massive coercion in multiple forms. 6) They had the advantage of occupying interior lines and the center of the railroad network, making it easier to move a large volume of troops and supplies in various directions. 7) They recruited a new mass Red Army, greatly superior in numbers to its opponents, which combined enrollment of many thousands of former tsarist officers with a new system of political commissars. 8) They had superior economic and industrial resources, an advantage that was sustained, at least in military production, despite the fact that Bolshevik policies made a wreck of the urban economy. 9) There was profound disunity, mutual conflict, and internal contradictions among the opposing forces, which were divided by personality, ideology, party, faction, and ethnic identity. 10) There was a high level of corruption among the Whites, which greatly vitiated their potential. 11) The Bolsheviks had superiority in propaganda, which was extremely weak among the Whites. 12) Political consciousness was lacking among the peasantry, whose only goals were negative – to be left alone with the land – and who, with great difficulty, were thus divided and partially neutralized by the Bolsheviks.[56] 13) There was little tradition of or respect for the law in Russian society. 14) Russian nationalism was weak, the empire having always taken precedence. 15) The Orthodox Church played little role in society and politics, despite the religious affiliation of the great majority of Russians.[57]

If one compares these factors to those that existed in the Spanish war, for example, it immediately becomes clear that in the latter some of the key elements were reversed. In Spain, the advantages of unity and centralization would be enjoyed by the counterrevolutionaries, who were also supported by a much stronger sense of nationalism and, equally important, of religious motivation, while the Republicans became prey to some of the kinds of factionalism and disunity that afflicted the anti-Bolsheviks in Russia. In each

[55] Brovkin, *Behind the Front Lines*, 414. How the Bolshevik Party organization was adapted to this is explained in R. Service, *The Bolshevik Party in Revolution: A Study in Organisational Change 1917–1923* (London, 1979).

[56] "The key to the Bolshevik victory was not merely in the application of sheer force but in dividing the peasant community and inducing it, as a hostage, to participate in its own self-destruction." Brovkin, *Behind the Front Lines*, 420.

[57] For a somewhat different but broadly comparative analysis of such factors, see D. Wilkinson, *Revolutionary War: The Elements of Victory and Defeat* (Palo Alto, Calif., 1975). Needless to say, the standard Communist explanation was rather different, one of the last canonical expressions, prior to the demise of the Soviet Union, having been presented by Akademiya Obshchestvennykh Nauk in *Pochemu pobedili Bolsheviki. Otvet falsifikatoram istorii Velikogo Oktyabrya* (Moscow, 1987).

case, the winning side benefited from the more effective foreign intervention, though the character of that intervention was completely different in the two cases.

The nearest thing to a Lenin in the Spanish war was Franco, even though, unlike Lenin, he played little role in the origins of the conflict. He did not simply restore the old order – which in the Spanish case would have been a constitutional monarchy, or some sort of parliamentary government – but installed a radical new counterrevolutionary and semifascist regime that for some years liked to call its own project a "revolution." He was much more methodical and a much better organizer than any of the White generals, with infinitely better logistics and a much better organized and more secure rear guard.

There are also severe limits to comparison, because the society and culture of the two countries were so different. Russia still had a semitraditional society that was to some degree a caste society, modernized just enough to become profoundly destabilized but not enough to have gained many of the positive benefits of modernization. Spanish society was much more modern, despite being underdeveloped by comparison to northwestern Europe, and had a class society, not a semicaste society, in which, proportionately, the role of agriculture had been rapidly declining. Even the poorest and most benighted sector, the *jornaleros* (day laborers), were more modern in orientation than most Russian peasants. The level of political consciousness and mobilization was much higher in the more modern society of Spain, but that was a two-edged sword, and in the long run did not benefit the left as much as the latter thought. A decisive difference was that the minority of the population that directly supported counterrevolution was proportionately a great deal larger. Whereas the struggle in Russia has been described as essentially "a civil war within educated Russian society"[58] – no more than a small minority of the whole – proportionately much more of Spanish society was directly involved and committed.

Militarily, the Russian civil war was poorly organized and loosely conducted, with equipment dating from the nineteenth century, supplemented by a few of the innovations of World War I. The Red Army nominally mobilized nearly ten times as many men as the Whites, though a very large number either deserted or failed to report. To some extent the Bolsheviks got a taste of their own medicine. They had played the leading role in breaking up the old army, promoting in 1917 the largest military mass desertion in world history. When Red Army mobilization tried to move in the opposite direction, it struggled mightily, and seems to have suffered in 1918–19 the second largest mass desertion in world history, though during the course of 1919 the new regime was finally able to build a more coherent military organization.

No more than about 5 percent of the total population was ever mobilized, though that figure would not include the hundreds of thousands of peasants who rebelled in varying ways, on their own terms. In Spain, more than

[58] Brovkin, *Behind the Front Lines*, 406.

8 percent of the total population was mobilized by both sides combined, with virtual equality of numbers in the long run, something feasible only in a more modern society. In Russia, extensive social and institutional breakdown was a necessary prerequisite for the Bolshevik takeover, but, by the same token, the breakdown became hard for the Bolsheviks to overcome afterward. Spanish society and institutions, by comparison, were more effectively mobilized, and both sides developed more coherent armies.

Tanks and planes, though they had become quite important by the final phase of World War I, were rare in the Russian war, and, conversely, it was the last war in which cavalry played a major role, at least during 1919–20. In the broad expanses of Russia and Poland, where it was almost impossible to man continuous lines or strongly entrenched positions, the mobility of cavalry and their ability to turn the enemy's flank could become decisive, a little like the situation during the Mongol conquest seven centuries earlier. The Cossacks often fought well for the Whites, but the Reds eventually developed strong cavalry forces of their own, not merely militarily effective but capable of sowing panic because of their ruthless pillaging and widespread atrocities. Some of this is captured in Isaac Babel's classic memoir-novel *Red Cavalry*. The last major round, however, was won by the Poles in the summer of 1920.

In general, the armies followed the railroads as much as possible, and armored trains (and sometimes armored cars) played a significant role. Otherwise, logistics relied on peasant horse carts. One innovation was the *tachanka*, a horse cart with a machine-gun and its crew, which provided mobile firepower. Artillery, on the other hand, was usually but a faint shadow of the powerful forces engaged in World War I.

The human misery, destruction, and loss of life caused by the Russian war were beyond comparison to other European civil wars, the one in Yugoslavia during World War II occupying second place. There are no reliable statistics, all calculations being guesstimates. The world war had cost the tsarist army two million deaths, to which may be added an additional 1.5 million deaths of civilians in the western portions of the empire. According to the best calculation, the Red Army lost more than 1.2 million men in the civil war and the much smaller White forces only one-fourth to one-third of that number. Medical care and sanitary conditions were so poor that nearly half the deaths were from disease. In addition, it is estimated that more than half a million peasants died in the continuing and widespread peasant revolts. Estimates of the number of victims of the Red Terror and the continuing Bolshevik repression range up to 400,000. Victims of the Whites, though numerous, were considerably fewer, to which must be added 100,000 or more Jews killed in pogroms. The most severe destruction was inflicted on the Cossacks of southeast Russia, who proportionately had opposed the Bolsheviks more than any other regional group.[59] It has been calculated that the combination of military

---

[59] R. Karmann, *Der Freiheitskampf der Kosaken: Die weisse Armee in der Russischen Revolution 1917–1920* (Puchheim, 1985).

deaths, political executions, economic destruction, deportation, and famine
may have cost the lives of as many as 2 million of the 4.5 million Cossacks,
though such an estimate cannot be directly verified. Most lethal of all was
the great famine of 1921–22 and the huge wave of epidemics, in which from
eight to ten million perished. Finally, a considerable number permanently fled
the country; estimates range from 2 million to 3.5 million. Between 1914 and
1926, the total number of deaths in Russia in excess of the normal death rate
was in the neighborhood of sixteen million. As Mawdsley puts it, "The Civil
War unleashed by Lenin was the greatest national catastrophe Europe had yet
seen."[60] Never in history had a new regime been founded on the basis of so
much mass death and suffering.

   In the civil war the Bolshevik regime developed its fundamental style and
psychology, as well as its model of socialist "stratocracy," or military mobilization system. Stalin later perfected what had already become the language of
permanent war, to some extent coined by Lenin before 1917, full of "struggle,"
"offensives," "shock brigades," and "enemies." In its political and institutional development, this would become the first modern regime permanently
structured for war even in peacetime. The longest struggle, however, would be
the internal war within Soviet society, which would continue until the death
of Stalin.

CLIMAX OF THE INTERNAL WAR

Conventional accounts date the end of the civil war to no later than 1921–22,
when the last formal military operations took place. Though the Communist
regime won, it had also been forced to step backward in its social and economic policies, initiating the NEP in 1921, which awarded the rebellious and
hard-pressed peasantry a truce. Once the great famine of 1921–22 had been
overcome, the five years from 1922 to 1927 constituted a kind of golden age
for the Russian peasantry. Never before had they had control of so much of
the farmland – 90 percent or more – even though they continued to be significantly taxed and pressured and were never allowed the benefits of a full
market economy, facing highly discriminatory rates of exchange for industrial
products. Still, a new equilibrium was temporarily achieved, and the high
peasant birthrate made it possible to make good the population losses before
the end of the decade. The world's first socialist dictatorship nonetheless faced
a quandary because to a large extent it had been forced to abandon socialism.
The vast majority of the population was indifferent to the new system, and
potentially still an enemy of it. This was the situation addressed by the "Stalin
revolution" of the years 1927 to 1939, which asserted direct control over all

[60] E. Mawdsley, *Russian Civil War*, 287. His estimates for fatalities are given on pp. 285–87.
   See also J.-N. Biraben, "Révolution et démographie en Russie et l'URSS," in E. Vilquin,
   ed., *Révolution et population. Aspects démographiques des grandes révolutions politiques*
   (Louvain, 1990), 85–93.

society and institutions through the collectivization drive of 1928–34, tearing up peasant agriculture by the roots and herding many millions of peasants onto collective farms and state farms. In the process, millions were deported to central Asia and Siberia, with very high death rates, reaching a climax in the second great famine in Ukraine and southeastern Russia between 1932 and 1934. The most extreme suffering and loss was that of the Kazakhs in central Asia, as many as 40 percent of whom perished in a quasi-genocide. This "war against the people" was the most extreme internal war ever waged by a government against its own society, and resulted in another nine to ten million additional deaths, as Stalin admitted to Churchill during World War II. This was the Bolshevik revenge against the peasantry, achieving the total state socialist domination that had not been possible during and after the civil war itself.

The final round of internal war took place in Stalin's Great Terror and ethnic deportations of 1936–39, exactly contemporary with the Spanish war. This series of purges and ethnic cleansings was aimed primarily not at the Russian and other peasantries, as during the early 1930s, but at the Soviet elites and members of the Communist Party itself, and secondarily against the ethnic minorities in the western, southern, and eastern border territories of the Soviet Union. It was designed to achieve total domination, regimenting the elite, on the one hand, and the strategic minorities on the other. About 1.5 million people perished, nearly a million of them in direct executions, and many more were arrested and/or deported.[61] This was, of course, the same regime that intervened to defend "democracy" in Spain.

THE BOLSHEVIK MODEL AND ITS CONSEQUENCES

The Bolshevik leaders introduced a new concept of dictatorship as a permanent regime, whereas previously such a thing had been universally considered a transitory phenomenon restricted to emergencies. In the classical concept of politics, a temporary dictatorship could never change or introduce permanent laws. Lenin and his colleagues, by contrast, boasted of their lawlessness and freedom from all restraint. In the new era, the German theorist Carl Schmitt would distinguish between classic dictatorship and the new-style "sovereign dictatorship" – extralegal, a permanent state of exception that made up its own rules and policies as it went along, based not on legal arguments but on appeals to history and/or nature. In the same vein, the Bolshevik regime repeated and expanded the exterminationist rhetoric first essayed by the French Revolution in 1792–94, making state terror a permanent policy directed against entire

---

[61] Jorg Baberowski and Anselm Doering-Manteuffel assert that 70 percent of the large number of executions in 1938 were killings of members of the targeted nationalities. "Ethnic cleansing was not a marginal phenomenon of Stalin's terror. Rather, it was at the core." "The Quest for Order and the Pursuit of Terror," in M. Geyer and S. Fitzpatrick, eds., *Beyond Totalitarianism: Stalinism and Nazism Compared* (Cambridge, UK, 2009), 180–227.

groups, social classes, and, to some extent, ethnicities as well. Concentration camps and forced labor became permanent features.

Revolution inevitably stimulates counterrevolution. The reaction was too weak, divided, and contradictory to triumph in Russia, but the rejection of Communism in the rest of Europe was categorical and continuing. Soon a significant part of European politics functioned in the key of anti-Communism, a fundamental feature of the remainder of the century, but especially for the next two or three generations skewing politics to the right. In the democratic countries of northern and northwestern Europe, this had the effect of consolidating democracy, encouraging a broad moderate consensus, and isolating the extreme left. Later, however, in central, southern, and east central Europe, the consequence would be to encourage the emergence of rightist authoritarian regimes.

The effects would soon be felt in Germany and in Italy, strengthening the new fascist movements, key characteristics of which had first appeared in Bolshevism. Fascism was more than just another kind of communism, as some alleged, but it learned from and copied notable aspects of Leninism, as Russian Communists would themselves acknowledge in 1922–23.[62] Equally importantly, fascism would thrive on its opposition to socialism and communism, to such an extent that it is appropriate to inquire whether, in those cases where it gained power, fascism could have succeeded without the opportunity to play off that opposition. One aspect of Bolshevik propaganda was fully accurate, and that was the claim that Communism had inaugurated a new era in radical politics, one that would not play out for more than seven decades.

---

[62] I have discussed this in my article "Soviet Anti-Fascism: Theory and Practice, 1921–45," *Totalitarian Movements and Political Religions*, 4:2 (Autumn 2003), 1–62.

3

The Political and Social Crisis in Europe, 1918–1923

Revolutionaries were correct that the effects of the world war would be profoundly destabilizing, but in Europe as a whole the outcome was quite different from what they expected. Though the war destroyed the empires of central and eastern Europe, one of its major consequences was to exacerbate nationalism even more. The Balkanization of east central Europe made long-term international equilibrium more difficult to attain, for the new buffers between Germany and the Soviet Union were weak. Commerce had been severely disrupted and state control of production greatly expanded, with the result that a full international market could not be restored for decades, until well into the second half of the century. The war destroyed part of the fabric of European culture, seriously diminishing belief in common values and the nineteenth-century faith in progress, producing a brutalization of politics in central and eastern Europe, and to some extent in Spain as well. It introduced great social turmoil in eastern and central Europe, and to a lesser degree in the western European countries, though in central and eastern Europe the chief beneficiaries would be the new nationalist and fascist movements that crystallized out of the postwar crisis.

That, however, was scarcely to be seen in 1919, a year in large part dominated by the fear of leftist radicalization inspired by Bolshevism. There is no equivalent to this year either before or after in terms of worker militancy throughout Europe and the Western world, with large-scale strikes and also riots in many countries, in some cases continuing into 1920. Even in the United States, May Day in 1919 brought pitched battles in several cities, which later, in Boston, even spread into the police, producing the notorious Boston police strike, an event unique in American history. Strikes, disorder, and political violence, stemming from diverse causes and assuming multiple forms, stretched across the globe from Argentina to Egypt to India. There were a number of mutinies in both the French and British armies, which helped to put an end to Allied intervention in Russia.[1]

---

[1] The best account of all this is A. Read, *The World on Fire: 1919 and the Battle with Bolshevism* (London, 2008).

Radicalization was also encouraged by the basic demographics of European life during this era. From Russia to Portugal the younger generation was the largest in absolute numbers that had ever existed and, in proportionate terms, was larger than any that would ever exist again, as birth rates shrank. Anyone familiar with university campuses knows how prone very young people are to fads and extremism. The existence of large numbers of young males afflicted by social uncertainty and cultural dissonance provided fertile ground for political violence. This was evidenced in Russia in 1917 and in much of Europe during the two decades that followed, but the consequences would often be quite different from what the left expected. The growth in university enrollment in countries as diverse as Germany, Romania, and Spain would eventually produce, in somewhat different ratios, disproportionate support not for revolutionary socialism but for fascism.

THE "GERMAN CIVIL WAR," 1918–1923

The Bolshevik takeover in Russia was predicated, at least in part, on the outbreak of revolution in Germany. That is, in Marxist theory successful modern socialist revolution could not be led by a backward country like Russia, but would depend on success in the most modern and powerful country in Europe, the one with proportionately the largest working class and the largest socialist party, which for three decades had been the most powerful and influential in the world. At the end of January 1918 huge strikes broke out in Germany, accompanied by large demonstrations, denouncing the harsh imperialist peace being imposed on Russia. Though these were not officially led by the Socialist unions and were not revolutionary in character, martial law was imposed, and 50,000 participants were drafted into the army. Hope for a German revolution was a factor in delaying until March 1918 the Bolshevik acceptance of Germany's draconian peace terms, and afterward the new Soviet embassy in Berlin made little effort to disguise that one of its main goals was to promote revolution inside Germany. It provided advice and propaganda to some of the most extreme elements within the German labor movement, as well as a little money. A revolt was planned for mid-November, but plans were discovered by the Berlin authorities, who finally broke diplomatic relations with the Bolshevik regime on 5 November, closing the embassy and expelling its delegation. Within a week, however, the government was forced to accept military defeat in the war. A new democratic government had to be formed, and a genuine mood of popular revolution swept much of Germany during November and December of 1918. There was a very brief period at the end of World War I when it seemed as though Lenin's dream was about to come true.

The German Social Democrats (SPD) had split in 1917 over the issue of continuing to support the war effort. About 40 percent of the membership left the main party to form their own Independent Socialist Party (USPD),[2] but the established leadership and bureaucracy remained in control of the SPD and of the very large German trade unions. They all believed that the war had convulsed much of European society and would lead to decisive changes,[3] but theoretical and tactical concepts regarding the introduction of socialism varied widely.

As the armistice was announced, German workers and even some sectors of the middle classes, together with a number of units of soldiers and sailors, began to form their own revolutionary councils (*Räte*, in German), partially in imitation of the Russian soviets of 1905 and 1917.[4] Government leaders could conceive of no way to govern the country other than from the moderate democratic left, which alone would have the legitimacy and authority to satisfy both the Entente powers and the German masses. By 10 November, six Socialists (three from the SPD, three from the USPD), led by the SPD's extremely moderate secretary general, Friedrich Ebert, formed the new parliamentary government.

Totally apart from parliament, a general assembly of representatives of the workers and soldiers *Räte* of Berlin recognized the six Socialists as the government of a "Council of People's Commissars," or Provisional Government. Paradoxically, Ebert was both the legitimate and the revolutionary chancellor of Germany at the same time. The country was saturated with radical political meetings, demonstrations, and strikes. By the end of 1918 Germany seemed to resemble Russia fifteenth months earlier: it was governed by a Provisional Government, and there were revolutionary councils in many places (even in some military units), red flags, large demonstrations, and an army garrison of doubtful loyalty in the capital, flanked by a Council of Workers and Soldiers.[5]

Yet Germany and Russia were two very different countries. In Russia, Lenin faced a society with small elites and a very limited middle class – both generally demoralized – contrasted with radicalized workers and a vast majority of largely illiterate, totally disaffected peasants. In Germany the elites were chastened, apprehensive, and at first circumspect, but not demoralized. The middle classes were numerous and potentially very active. There were

---

[2] H. Krause, *USPD: Geschichte der Unabhängigen Sozialdemokratischen Partei Deutschlands* (Frankfurt am Main, 1975).

[3] P. Lensch, *Drei Jahre Weltrevolution* (Berlin, 1917).

[4] E. Kolb, *Die Arbeiterräte in der deutschen Innenpolitik* (Düsseldorf, 1962); P. von Oertzen, *Betriebsräte in der Novemberrevolution* (Düsseldorf, 1963); V. Arnold, *Rätebewegung und Rätetheorien in der Novemberrevolution. Räte als Organisationsformen des Kampfes und der Selbstbestimmung* (rev. ed., Hamburg, 1985).

[5] The chief general studies of the left during the German revolution are P. Broué, *The German Revolution 1917–1923* (Leiden, 2005), and H. A. Winkler, *Von der Revolution zur Stabilisierung: Arbeiter und Arbeiterbewegung in der Weimarer Republik 1918 bis 1924* (Berlin, 1984). For the first major phase, see U. Kluge, *Die deutsche Revolution 1918/1919* (Frankfurt am Main, 1985).

no illiterate peasant masses; the agrarian minority in Germany was basically conservative. The army did not desert, but came home in good order, and state institutions still functioned. Workers indeed were in a very radical mood, but were literate and accustomed to responsible political discipline and organization. The German equivalent of the Congress of Soviets had also accepted, at least for the time being, the new parliamentary government. Moreover, almost all sectors of society accepted the need for and legitimacy of a democratically elected national parliament to prepare a new republican constitution, as the only functional exit from Germany's national impasse. The mood of the councils in Germany was in many ways more populist than revolutionary, and when a National Congress of German Workers' and Soldiers' Councils met in Berlin in mid-December, it elected as leaders a Central Council of majority Socialists who supported the government.

There was no German Lenin, and though there were a certain number of extreme revolutionaries, only a very small number of them embraced a Bolshevik-style nihilism of power and violence. Few categorically rejected democracy. The National Congress of Councils in Berlin voted to demand that army officers be elected by their troops and that a national militia be formed alongside the army, but "provisionally" rejected a proposal to organize Red Guards. The most radical Socialists were the not-very-numerous activists of the Spartakist-Bund, led by Rosa Luxemburg and Karl Liebknecht. They were courageous revolutionaries who had stoutly resisted militarism throughout the war but equally rejected Bolshevik violence and terror. A week after the armistice, the Spartacists began to create a "League of Red Soldiers," but this remained exiguous. It was not a significant paramilitary organization and in no way comparable to the Soviet Red Guards.[6]

A German Communist Party (KPD) of determined revolutionaries, including the Spartacists, was organized at the close of December, with three clandestine representatives of Moscow participating. Karl Radek, the most important of the latter, declared that the Russians themselves would look at the great German proletariat as their "elder brothers" in the project of world revolution, but the nascent KPD was not yet a Bolshevik organization.[7] Its first meeting rejected the recommendation of its own leaders to participate in the forthcoming elections. Instead, the new party called for the organization of Red Guards, yet lacked the cadres to do so.

Between 1919 and 1923 there were several points of inflection. The first began in early January 1919 with a gigantic Berlin demonstration – perhaps 200,000 people – to protest the firing of the new Socialist chief of police,

[6] G. Badia, *Le Spartakisme, les dernières années de Rosa Luxemburg et de Karl Liebknecht, 1914–1919* (Paris, 1919).
[7] On the early KPD, see E. Weitz, *Creating German Communism, 1890–1990: From Popular Protests to Socialist State* (Princeton, N.J., 1997); H. Weber, *Kommunismus in Deutschland 1918–1945* (Darmstadt, 1983); and H. M. Bock, *Syndikalismus und Linkskommunismus von 1918 bis 1923* (Darmstadt, 1993).

whom the government thought unreliable. The demonstrators occupied and pillaged several key centers, and sporadic fighting went on for several days.[8] This was not a German "Red October,"[9] however, but a more extreme Berlin version of the July Days in Petrograd in 1917, a huge, angry demonstration turned into a chaotic quasi-insurrection without organization or clear goals. Even Lenin had blanched in Petrograd in July, and so did the Spartacist-KPD leaders in Berlin. They lacked any organized revolutionary military power, and, with democratic national elections soon to take place, Luxemburg and Liebknecht did not feel empowered to try to set up a dictatorship, nor did they wish to do so. They did sign a manifesto that the government should be over-thrown, but even that was not an immediate goal. The League of Red Soldiers called on the workers to assemble for combat, but lacked the means to form them into effective squads.

Nonetheless, insurrectionist workers were momentarily in control of sev-eral key sites in Berlin, and to that extent had gone further than their Russian counterparts of July 1917. The Russian analogy quickly passed from July to September, however, as what Ernst Nolte calls a "Kornilov Point" appeared, for there was plenty of armed force available to quench any revolution. A significant part of what was left of the German army was reliable, totally unlike the mutinous soldiers and sailors in Petrograd. In addition, the Socialist government encouraged the formation in several localities of a loyal militia, the *Volkswehr* (People's Army, the same name selected by the anti-Bolshevik Socialist Revolutionaries and liberals in Samara in 1918).

Equally or more decisive was the emergence of a new right-wing nation-alist militia, the *Freikorps* (Free Corps), all-volunteer units, mainly of army veterans, under military discipline, sworn to defend the nation and put down subversion. Chancellor Ebert and his defense minister, the Socialist Gustav Noske, were no Kerenskys, and they did not hesitate to call in the regular army and the *Freikorps* to repress quasi-insurgents ruthlessly. Ebert was the leader of the SPD organization, a staunch German patriot, and a firm believer in discipline and organization. Perhaps equally important was the fear that major disorder in Germany would be used as an excuse by the victorious Allies to impose even harsher peace terms. There would be no toleration of disorder. Repression in Berlin in January 1919 was categorical and brutal, and also not atypical of what happens when small disciplined armed groups deal with larger lightly armed or unarmed masses. At least 1,200 workers and leftists were killed. Luxemburg and Liebknecht were arrested and beaten up, then murdered. One KPD leader later spoke of precipitating "the most immense civil war in world history," and there was much talk and fear of civil war in the land, but genuine civil war never occurred. What took place instead

---

[8] There is a graphic description in H. Schulze, *Weimar. Deutschland 1917–1933* (Berlin, 1982), 179–81.

[9] Under the old Russian calendar, soon to be changed by the Bolsheviks, the latter's coup of November 1917 took place in October, hence the famous symbol of "Red October."

were cycles of disorder, violence, looting, and revolutionary activism, none of which seriously threatened to overthrow the government, followed in each case by rigorous repression.[10]

At the Paris peace conference, however, David Lloyd George, head of the British delegation, saw developments in central Europe in the direst terms:

> If Germany goes over to the Spartacists it is inevitable that she should throw her lot with the Russian Bolsheviks. Once that happens all Eastern Europe will be swept into the orbit of the Bolshevik revolution, and within a year we may witness the spectacle of 300 million people organized into a vast Red Army under German instructors and German generals, equipped with German cannon and German machine-guns and prepared for a renewal of the attack on Western Europe. The news which came from Hungary yesterday shows this is no mere fantasy.[11]

Despite the complete failure of the quasi-insurrection in Berlin, it was only the beginning, for economic conditions in Germany deteriorated further during the winter of 1919. The Allied blockade continued until the middle of the year, so that hunger grew yet more extreme, and with the end of the war unemployment mounted month by month. At the time of the Berlin insurrection, there were major demonstrations and minor forms of direct action and occupation of buildings in numerous cities all over Germany. These initiatives revealed the same confusion, lack of organization, and absence of concrete goals that had appeared in Berlin. In some areas lightly armed worker militias had been created, but they were militarily ineffective and never part of any major plan. The police and *Freikorps* repressed strikes and demonstrations in Dresden, Hamburg, Leipzig, Bremen, Düsseldorf, and elsewhere. Several hundred more workers were killed. If this was a civil war, the revolutionaries were losing. A general strike was called in the Ruhr mining basin, which was broken up by force. Socialization of the mines and certain other industries was proposed, and the government seemed willing at least to consider that. The *Räte* then called a general strike in central Germany, starting on 24 February, and the *Freikorps* swung into action once more. There were further arrests and killings. Nowhere were the workers or their militia (where it existed) in a position to resist for very long. Enthusiasm was great, but planning, coordination, and effective goals were nonexistent. Never was there ever in Europe so large and militant a labor movement with such ineffective leadership. The general strike spread on 3 March to Berlin, where another massacre took place. In Berlin and some other areas, the authorities decreed that anyone found with a gun on his person or premises would be shot. Noske later wrote that another 1,200

---

[10] For the history of political violence during this era, see W. von Schultzendorff, *Proletarier und Prätorianer: Bürgerkriegssituation aus der Frühzeit der Weimarer Republik* (Cologne, 1966); H. W. Koch, *Der deutsche Bürgerkrieg: eine Geschichte der deutschen und österreichischen Freikorps 1918–1923* (Berlin, 1978); D. Dreetz, K. Gessner, and H. Sperling, *Bewaffnete Kämpfe in Deutschland 1918–1923* (Berlin, 1988); D. Schumann, *Politische Gewalt in der Weimarer Republik 1918–1933. Kampf um die Strasse und Furcht vor dem Bürgerkrieg* (Essen, 2001); and E. J. Gumbel, *Vier Jahre politischer Mord* (Berlin, 1922).

[11] Quoted in Read, *World on Fire*, 160.

had been killed, though the revolutionaries said the total was two or three times that. The general strike in the Ruhr began once more, lasting until mid-April, when it was again broken by force. There were two weeks of fighting, and several hundred more people were killed.[12]

A local *Räterepublik* was declared in Munich on 7 April, led by a motley coalition of anarchists, independents, and Socialists. The KPD developed strength in the local trade unions, and the Communist Eugen Leviné took over the leadership of the self-styled republic, proposing to develop a local "Red Army." This petty Soviet state arrested several hundred hostages and executed at least ten people, while announcing revolutionary tribunals whose sentences would be carried out "in the act." The *Freikorps* soon fought their way in, using flamethrowers. Several hundred revolutionaries (including a few innocent bystanders) were killed and two or three hundred prisoners subsequently executed, including Leviné, who famously told his courtmartial: "We Communists are all dead men on suspended sentence!"[13] – a line subsequently much quoted by the KPD and others. Total fatalities numbered at least 600.

Worker councils were organized in much of central Europe during the first half of 1919, with Soviet republics briefly declared in Hungary and Slovakia. During the last phase of the war, there had been more worker unrest in Austria than in Germany, and in the spring of 1918 the Austrian ministry of war had kept seven divisions of troops at home to maintain order. In the new rump republic of Austria, however, the Socialist Party was proportionately stronger than anywhere else in Europe. Like their German counterparts, the Austrian Socialist leaders rejected revolution and firmly opted for following the road to socialism through social democracy. Though they refused to take as much responsibility for a parliamentary regime as their German counterparts, they saw to it that two Communist plans for insurrection failed completely.[14]

From his prison cell in Berlin, Karl Radek, the new Comintern's chief representative in Germany, summed up the differences between the situations in Russia and Germany:

1) Strong unions in Germany paradoxically restrained worker revolution; 2) The counterrevolution proved stronger at every level; 3) In Russia six months of confusion and institutional decay gave the Bolsheviks time to develop a potent organization; 4) The

---

[12] W. Hoegner, *Die verratene Republik. Geschichte der deutschen Gegenrevolution* (Munich, 1958); O. Hennicke, *Die Rote Ruhrarmee* (Berlin, 1957).

[13] In T. Dorst and H. Neubauer, *Die Münchner Räterepublik* (Frankfurt am Main, 1966), 167. See A. Mitchell, *Revolution in Bavaria 1918–1919* (Princeton, N.J., 1965); H. Hillmayr, *Roter und Weisser Terror in Bayern nach 1918* (Munich, 1974); and the anonymous *Die Münchner Tragödie: Entstehung, Verlauf und Zusammenbruch der Räterepublik München* (Berlin, 1919).

[14] There are two broader studies: F. L. Carsten, *Revolution in Central Europe 1918–1919* (Berkeley, Calif., 1972), and C. L. Bertrand, ed., *Situations révolutionnaires en Europe, 1917–1922: Allemagne, Italie, Autriche-Hongrie* (Montreal, 1977). Political violence in Austria has been carefully researched by G. Botz in his *Gewalt in der Politik: Attentäte, Zusammenstösse, Putschversuche, Unruhen in Österreich 1918 bis 1934* (2nd ed., Vienna, 1983).

military were much more thoroughly eroded in Russia; 5) The Ebert government, though itself a provisional government, was much firmer and stronger than the Provisional Government in Russia in 1917.[15]

He might have added a reference to the national elections of January 1919, which wisely were held much sooner than had been the case in Russia (or in Spain in 1930–31). In this contest the two German Socialist parties gained nearly 46 percent of the vote, establishing the democratic legitimacy of a coalition government led by the SPD.

Perhaps the greatest difference lay in the war itself. Despite all the tensions in Russian society, only the war had precipitated revolution. Conversely, despite all the revolutionary effervescence in German society, once the war was over it was not possible to fan such tensions into a genuine revolution. In 1917 it would have been perfectly possible for Russia to have continued the war, had there been the will do so. By comparison, in November 1918 Germany was more exhausted militarily, though not so totally disoriented politically. The Socialist leaders of the new German republic had not the slightest wish to continue the war, but accepted defeat, and after early 1919 the revolutionary tide steadily diminished.

During the second half of 1919, however, resentment against the terms of the recently signed Versailles Treaty continued to grow, and the *Freikorps* became a significant paramilitary force. In addition to helping repress the left, they had assisted in defending the eastern frontier and, most notably, had played a special role in the civil wars in Lithuania and Latvia. In the Baltic region, they had engaged in mass counterrevolutionary violence and major atrocities in dealing with an enemy whom they considered socially and racially inferior. They had experienced counterrevolution as a new and extreme form of nationalist revolution, and within Germany transmitted the attitudes and values of the Russian civil war, to which was added a kind of racial concept of revolution, together with special symbols, such as the swastika and the death's head.[16] Moreover, they were flanked by a growing number of patriotic militia groups, such as the more moderate *Einwohnerwehren* (Civil Guards) and the *Zeitfreiwilligenverbände* (Auxiliary Volunteer Units), the latter a paramilitary auxiliary to the *Freikorps*. All these groups together came to total perhaps a million men,[17] though of course the numbers of organized labor were much greater.

When it became known in March 1920 that the *Freikorps* planned a *putsch* (coup d'état), the commanders of the radically reduced German army (*Reichswehr*) made it clear they would not lift a finger to protect the government. In the face of a *Freikorps* revolt in Berlin, the government fled, replaced by a rightist insurgent executive, nominally led by the minor Prussian official

[15] In A. Paquet, *Der Geist der russischen Revolution* (Leipzig, 1919), vii–ix, quoted in Broué, *German Revolution*, 288.
[16] See R. G. L. Waite, *Vanguard of Nazism: The Free Corps Movement in Postwar Germany, 1918–1923* (Cambridge, Mass., 1952), and H. Schulze, *Freikorps und Republik, 1918–1920* (Boppard, 1969).
[17] J. M. Diehl, *Paramilitary Politics in Weimar Germany* (Bloomington, Ind., 1977).

Wolfgang Kapp. The response to the takeover in Berlin came from the trade unions, who declared a general strike that within forty-eight hours had shut down the capital. The government could not function, and the coup leaders had to flee after two more days.

The notion that worker militancy had declined was wrong, for, once the general strike began, hundreds of thousands of workers all over Germany refused to end it. In the Ruhr and in some other areas worker militias were formed, and the government, back in power, was willing to negotiate. Once more there was no organization or unity behind the worker militancy, and after a few more days the army, police, and *Freikorps* went into action. The new *Reichswehr* would not protect the government from the right but was eager to repress workers with great violence, even executing nurses, if found with arms. There were nearly two weeks of combat. As one nationalist volunteer put it, greater mercy was shown French soldiers during World War I than was accorded militant German workers.[18] Another "Kornilov point" had been reached, and in Germany once more the counterrevolutionaries had won, despite the failure of the rightist coup itself. In the new German elections the left-liberal coalition lost its majority, which it would never regain, though the USPD profited at the expense of the SPD, which it almost equaled in votes.

Responsible German politicians declared once more that Bolshevism was at the door, but in fact the KPD at first refused to lift a finger to oppose the Kapp Putsch, then was overwhelmed by a worker response that it had not organized. Moscow, however, interpreted news from Germany in a positive light, declaring that "civil war" was either present or latent in nearly all of Europe. The second congress of the Comintern in July 1920 defined the "Twenty-One Points" that communist parties must satisfy to qualify for membership in the organization, declaring that Europe was in a "period of acute civil war." At that point a number of the more radical Socialist parties were on the verge of affiliating, but the strict new conditions divided them, and in fact none of them ended in the ranks of the Comintern, though in Germany the left wing of the USPD split off to join the KPD, which now had slightly more members. All this had the long-term effect of merely increasing polarization in Germany, as the Comintern ordered each member party to create an illegal section with the responsibility of preparing for insurrection and civil war.

By the beginning of 1921, however, even some of the Comintern leaders began to realize that the situation was changing and that most European countries, at least for the moment, had become more stable. The invasion of Poland – whose ultimate objective had been Germany – had ended in complete defeat, and the new leftist front in Britain, the Council of Action, created to block shipments to Poland, proved to be totally ephemeral rather than a harbinger of new radicalization. Aggressive new strikes in Italy and Czechoslovakia that seemed to have revolutionary potential failed completely.

---

[18] Schulze, *Freikorps und Republik*, 315. See E. Lucas, *Märzrevolution im Ruhrgebiet. März/April 1920* (Frankfurt, 1970–78), 3 vols.

In January 1921 the Comintern central committee debated whether or not the emphasis on the revolutionary vanguard might have been misplaced, some now arguing that there was greater opportunity in backward southeastern areas such as Galician Poland, Romania, and Hungary, which could open the door to the Balkans.[19]

KPD leaders saw their chance in the increasing stringency of reparations payments demanded by the Allies. They hoped that this would lead to widespread protest and economic chaos, with the prospect of new international war, which they wished to encourage, for that might produce the breakdown for which they were working. A sudden opportunity emerged in March 1921, when a police crackdown took place in central Germany, where some of the militant workers had never been disarmed. This sparked large strikes in that region and in a number of other major cities. A splinter group, the German Communist Workers' Party (KAPD), which was more anarchosyndicalist in orientation, sought to fan this into insurgency, and the KPD then joined in, forming new worker militias, but within a matter of days this initiative ended in the usual repression.[20] The resulting disillusionment with this *Märzaktion* ("March action"), as it was called, drastically reduced the party's following.[21]

This coincided with the "two steps forward, one step back" reform of Soviet economics in Lenin's New Economic Policy. The focus was shifting from destabilizing Europe to achieving stabilization of the Soviet Union before its economy collapsed. In general, European opinion was extremely anti-Communist, and in most countries the postwar crisis was coming to an end. The social democrats had been weakened in some areas, but generally retained hegemony over industrial workers and the more leftist sectors of the lower middle classes. Though they rejected Soviet Communism, most social democratic parties, with the notable exception of those in Germany and several northern European countries, still sought to maintain an equivalent distance from direct collaboration with bourgeois politics.

The Soviet leaders did not believe that revolution would be long delayed, but accepted the need to concentrate first on winning allies and a broader base. They were also looking for a new international alignment that might strengthen a regime that no longer looked as strong as they had thought in 1920. If they could not revolutionize Germany immediately, or encourage a war between it and the Western powers, then a weakened Germany might be drawn into a new relationship with the Soviet Union.

Despite the violent battle against "Bolshevism" inside Germany, significant elites advocated a more friendly orientation toward the Soviet Union

---

[19] M. Drachkovich and B. Lazich, eds., *The Comintern: Historical Highlights* (Stanford, Calif., 1966), 285.

[20] S. Koch-Baumgarten, *Aufstand der Avantgarde. Die Märzaktion der KPD 1921* (Frankfurt am Main, 1986); S. Weber, *Ein kommunistischer Putsch? Märzaktion 1921 in Mitteldeutschland* (Berlin, 1991).

[21] On the KPD during this phase, see W. Angress, *The Stillborn Revolution: The Communist Bid for Power in Germany, 1921–1923* (Princeton, N.J., 1963).

itself. The new leadership of the *Reichswehr* was adamant about the need to overcome the foreign "encirclement" that had led the Germans to precipitate the war, and had also caused them to lose it. The major enemy of the Allied powers that had subjugated Germany was the Soviets, and German military leaders sought their own special relationship with Moscow. So did many economic luminaries, who believed that the large Soviet market might offer new opportunities to an economy oppressed by Versailles. Despite the opposition to Communism, the dominant emotion in Germany was resentment of the victorious Western powers.

In April 1922 the European governments convened a major international economic conference at Genoa to deal with the reconstruction of Europe. This was a much more inclusive conference than Versailles, involving representatives of both Germany and the Soviet Union, the most comprehensive European meeting since the Congress of Berlin in 1878. The British government sought to assist Germany, while creating a great international consortium to promote the recovery and development of the Soviet Union. Such a capitalist consortium the Communist leaders wanted to avoid at all costs, taking advantage of unusually slow and clumsy diplomacy by the Western powers.

The consequence was the Rapallo treaty of April 1922, the diplomatic bombshell of the postwar years, which established friendly relations between Berlin and Moscow, canceled mutual debts, created most-favored-nation terms between them, and soon led to the beginning of extensive secret military collaboration. The two major pariahs of Europe had begun to join hands, initiating a special relationship that would endure for more than a decade, until abruptly ended by Adolf Hitler.[22] German Communist leaders were surprised, but to Lenin and his associates this was a means of strengthening the Soviet Union, on the one hand, and of beginning to draw one of the most important capitalist countries away from the dominant bloc of the world bourgeoisie, on the other.

Within only a matter of months, such considerations began to pale, however, for the French and Belgian invasion of the Ruhr at the beginning of 1923, followed by hyperinflation and the incipient breakdown of the economy, once more threw Germany into turmoil. During the spring of 1923, the KPD fomented large strikes, disorder, and forced requisitioning of goods. A national militia (the "Proletarian Hundreds"), which included its own terror organization, was set up by districts, staffed by a cadre of Soviet military advisers headed by a Soviet general.[23] The possibility of collaboration with right-wing radical nationalists was also explored.

This redoubled Soviet attention on Germany, triggering concern that the French initiative to enforce payment of reparations might signal a new drive for even greater European dominance by the victorious Western capitalist

---

[22] L. Kochan, *Russia and the Weimar Republic* (Cambridge, UK, 1950).

[23] E. Wollenberg, *Der Apparat. Stalins Fünfte Kolonne* (Bonn, 1952), is a memoir by one of its German leaders.

powers, who might also try to punish the Soviet Union for its recent treaty with Germany. Conversely, an independent Germany might serve as a shield for the Soviet regime – even if in a different manner than in 1918 – while the right kind of nationalism in a humiliated and defeated power might be made to serve revolutionary interests. The paradox of Soviet policy was that it desired a Germany that was somehow both strong and weak at the same time, and had already initiated secret military collaboration that would last for more than a decade.[24] Nikolai Bukharin publicly, if ironically, thanked French president Raymond Poincaré for having disrupted an incipient European stability and in March announced to the Twelfth Party Congress that the national defense of Germany now had a completely different meaning than in 1914. Moscow discounted warnings by the KPD representative and others concerning what the latter termed the "fascist danger" in Germany.[25]

One consequence was Karl Radek's "Schlageter speech" to the Comintern executive Committee (ECCI), which declared that the "counterrevolutionary" Karl Schlageter, recently executed by the French for sabotage, should be considered at the same time a hero of the revolution, because supporting the nation in Germany should now be considered a "revolutionary act." Radical German nationalists should be seen by Communists as "erring brothers," not in the sense of political union but with the goal of attracting them to a pro-German Communism (the sort of thing briefly successful in Hungary), once they saw that only revolution would restore the nation. This, after all, was sound Leninist policy, since the now-stricken Soviet leader had always stressed the importance of the national question, which could be resolved only by revolution. Even though Hitler was viewed as a "caricature of Mussolini," many members of the Nazi Party (NSDAP) and other nationalist groups might be won over. Leaders of the KPD, who knew much better the temper and doctrine of German ultranationalists, were more skeptical. As it turned out, the debates with German nationalists that summer in the pages of the KPD's *Die Rote Fahne* did not feature any Nazi leaders, only a few theorists of the tiny "National Bolshevist" sector of German nationalists, as well as a few "conservative revolutionaries," though Communists addressed several Nazi meetings before Hitler broke off contact.[26] KPD leaders warned the Comintern that "German fascism" was preparing civil war, but the Comintern leaders feared premature action, despite the enormous unrest in the country.

---

[24] O. Groeler, *Selbst-mörderische Allianz: Deutsch-russische militärbeziehungen 1920–1941* (Berlin, 1992); Y. L. Djanov and T. S. Bushuyena. *The Red Army and the Wehrmacht* (Amherst, N.Y., 1995).

[25] P. Broué, *Histoire de l'Internationale Communiste 1919–1943* (Paris, 1997), 303–05.

[26] Some of the resulting material was published in *Schlageter. Eine Auseinandersetzung. Karl Radek / P. Frölich / Graf Ernst Reventlow / Moeller van den Bruck* (Berlin, 1923). See E. von Reventlow, *Völkisch-kommunistische Einigung* (Berlin, 1924); O-E. Schüddekopf, *Linke Leute von Rechts* (Stuttgart, 1960), 445–46; and K. Radek, *Der Kampf der Kommunistische Internationale gegen Versailles und gegen die Offensive des Kapitals* (Hamburg, 1923).

They, like Hitler, waited too long, for the process of stabilization began with the formation of a new government under Gustav Stresemann in September, and only after that did the Comintern decide to act. On 10 October *Die Rote Fahne* published a letter from Stalin to the KPD leadership which declared that the forthcoming German revolution would be the "most important world-historical event of our time," even more significant for Europe and the United States than the events in Russia in 1917. This would bring revolution to the most modern country in Europe with the largest proletariat, the quintessential Marxist revolution that Russia alone could not achieve, which would result in "the center of world revolution" moving from Moscow to Berlin.[27]

By October 1923 Soviet leaders speculated about the future policy of a new Communist Germany, which might begin with its own NEP, rather than arriving at it after four years, as had the Soviet Union. It would seek peace with the capitalist powers, but if the latter attacked, the Soviet Union would assist with large food shipments, while the new Communist regime would solve the problem of unemployment by creating a massive German Red Army. Even so, it might not have the strength to fight off all its enemies, and so might have to sign its own form of Brest-Litovsk treaty by temporarily handing over more territory to France.[28]

Nonetheless, Moscow never sent a clear signal for revolutionary insurrection, and so late in October the KPD leaders finally issued orders of their own, which were followed only in Hamburg. The attempted insurrection was an abortive fiasco that never got off the ground. By that time Germany had had an effective new government for more than a month, and the national crisis was already ending. Hitler's own "*Bierhallputsch*" came two weeks later, failing even more quickly and completely.

Thus the Weimar Republic survived five years of confusion and intermittent chaos, and for the remainder of the decade enjoyed relative stability and even prosperity. Did the period 1918–23 thus constitute a "German civil war," as some historians label it? Not really, but it was a more prolonged crisis, and for some years a more severe one, than that experienced by any country in central Europe other than Hungary. Some four to five thousand people perished in these strikes, demonstrations, insurgencies, and repressions, a total approximately equal to the proportion of the population killed in Italy during the four years 1919–22. A genuinely revolutionary mood had existed among many German workers, who constituted a much larger proportion of the population than in Russia, but in Germany revolutionaries lacked unity and were defeated by much stronger institutions and extremely militant, well-organized opposing groups, all of which had been lacking in Russia. Ultimately, the only

---

[27] Stalin apparently wrote this out of solidarity with the decision taken by the other leaders, since he had earlier observed that conditions in Germany did not at that time favor a new revolutionary initiative, as observed by R. Service in *Trotsky. A Biography* (London, 2009), 305–06.

[28] Broué, *German Revolution*, 779–89.

clear revolutionary leadership was that of the Comintern, which could never develop a single concerted plan of action, and the energies of worker radicalism were dissipated in multiple, disorganized efforts.

From the beginning the German republic was led by a legitimate democratic government that retained control of the nation's institutions and stood above the extreme right and extreme left, rejecting both alternatives, thus avoiding ultimate polarization. The new regime had created in 1919 a Commission for the Supervision of Public Order, which could invoke emergency powers, and developed a new form of "security state," establishing two new police corps, the "*Sicherheitspolizei*" ("Sipo," or security police) and the "*Schutzpolizei*" ("Schupo," or protective police), both mobile and well armed, to deal with disorders. These were supplemented by the "*Technische Nothilfe*," (TN, or technical emergency squads), a special riot police to put down major protests.[29] Neither Communists nor Nazis would be able to overthrow the German state. It could be conquered politically only from within, as Hitler would do in 1933. That Germany came through the long postwar crisis as a functioning democracy was a tribute to its leadership, the quality of its civil society, and the country's respect for law and order. It had survived a great ordeal, but ten years later would not be able to overcome the next sequence of multiple crises.

Sebastian Haffner has pointed out that three false legends have developed concerning the five years of intermittent revolutionary turmoil in Germany. The first is that there was really no serious revolution, whereas in fact much broader support for a worker revolution existed in Germany than in Russia, though this was held in check by the countervailing forces already detailed. The second is that revolutionary activism was primarily Communist. Though the KPD sometimes played an important role, the great majority of worker radicals in Germany were not organized by the Communists (and in that respect Germany during the period 1918–23 was rather more like Spain during the 1930s). The third legend is the nationalist "stab in the back" assertion, the idea that the revolution betrayed Germany by undermining its military in 1918. There was indeed a mass revolutionary upsurge, but it was not primarily led or organized by Communists, and it developed only after the military leaders had already conceded defeat.[30] The bottom line is that the German revolutionary tide was proportionately the broadest ever to have failed to develop into a full-scale revolution or civil war.

[29] See G. Jasper, *Der Schutz der Republik: Studien zur staatlichen Sicherung der Demokratie in der Weimarer Republik, 1922–1930* (Tübingen, 1963), and the discussion in Weitz, *Creating German Communism*, 101–02. This served as part of the inspiration for the initially vigorous approach to public order of the Spanish Republic, with its draconian legislation ("Ley para la Defensa de la República") and creation of a new urban riot police, the Guardias de Asalto. The very name of the latter, indicating that they would "assault," rather than merely control, disorder, was an indication of the militancy of this approach, though it ultimately failed, due to irresponsible leadership.

[30] S. Haffner, *Die deutsche Revolution* (Berlin, 1979), 214–23.

THE REVOLUTION IN HUNGARY

The only Communist regime established outside former tsarist territory was the short-lived Bela Kun government in Budapest, but it involved little in the way of civil war, being a by-product of the Hungarian collapse at the end of World War I, followed by the Carthaginian terms of the peace imposed by the Allies, far more severe than in the case of Germany. The Treaty of Trianon totally dismembered the kingdom of Hungary, not merely stripping it of territories inhabited by other nationalities, but also handing over land occupied by one-third of the ethnic Hungarian population, who were henceforth to live as minorities in the newly and artificially created multinational states of Yugoslavia and Czechoslovakia and in the bloated new Rumania, doubled in size as a reward for having blundered onto the winning side in the war and now favored due to its presumed utility as a bulwark against Bolshevism. Moreover, Hungary's resources were similarly divided, and the old economic configuration simply disappeared, adding to social dislocation.

In Budapest, as in Berlin and Vienna, the old regime was suddenly replaced by a much more liberal coalition government, headed by the aristocratic magnate Michael Karolyi, which also included representatives of the small Hungarian Socialist Party.

The Hungarian Socialist organization was modeled on that of Austria, exhibiting a similar moderation, but the situation changed rapidly when it became clear that the victorious Allies were determined that most of the kingdom of Hungary disappear from the map, an outcome totally discrediting both the conservatives and the governing liberals. In a move somewhat similar to events in Berlin and Vienna, power passed by default to the Socialists, but in Hungary they were only a small minority.

Being so much weaker than their German and Austrian counterparts, Hungarian Socialists feared trying to govern by themselves, and suddenly decided on a union with the newly founded Hungarian Communist Party. The latter had been created two weeks after the end of the war, when Lenin sent a number of recently Bolshevized Hungarian prisoners of war, led by Bela Kun, to Budapest. After a petty attempt at insurgency failed, the new Communist leaders were imprisoned, but their party grew rapidly, and in March 1919, thanks to the weakness of the Socialists, they suddenly found themselves transferred from jail to the seat of government. Whereas the German Socialists had done everything in their power to put down a massive worker insurgency, the Hungarian Socialists gratuitously handed over power to a small, totally unrepresentative group of Communists. Austrian Socialists referred to this as a "dictatorship of desperation." The resulting new political association was officially baptized in June as the Socialist-Communist Workers Party of Hungary.

The erstwhile Socialists held most of the seats in the new Revolutionary Governing Council of People's Commissars, but it was soon known as the Bela Kun regime, since, as foreign minister, the Communist leader became its most widely publicized member. It tried to move more rapidly than Lenin by proceeding to nationalize everything – all education, cultural life, industry, mines, transport, stores, hotels, service activities, urban housing, and nearly all farmland. State resources to administer all these sectors were lacking, but the government found time to issue orders about how to prepare lemonade in nationalized theaters. Perhaps the only noteworthy positive activity was a vigorous new policy in the arts.[31] The regime functioned as a strict dictatorship, permitting only a single party list in the national elections of April 1919. It banned the old flag and national anthem, terminated all traditional ceremonies, and sought to take over the churches. Kun proposed to maintain as much as possible of the old kingdom for the revolutionary regime, declaring a new system of autonomous federation for the former national minorities, a sort of Hungarian equivalent of the Soviet Union. The government sought to build a Hungarian Red Army to defend its borders from the occupying powers to the north, south, and southwest. Momentarily riding the crest of a wave of patriotism, it defeated the Czechs in the north and, hoping soon to make contact with revolutionary workers in Prague as well as to form a geographic link with Soviet Russia, helped to establish a Slovak Soviet Republic in June. The Hungarians, nonetheless, were hopelessly outnumbered and soon driven back. The revolutionary regime in Slovakia collapsed after the Czech army resumed its advance.

Meanwhile, the mindless radicalism of the Kun regime quickly alienated most of the population. Its massive statism ran roughshod over the interests of nearly all social sectors. The great majority of the population, composed of small farmers and farm laborers, opposed the confiscation of small properties and the insistence on reorganizing large estates as state farms – exactly the opposite of Lenin's initial policy in Russia.

Moreover, the revolutionary state was threatened by the advance of the Rumanian army – with the blessing of the western Allies – into what was left of southern Hungary. The regime reorganized its forces in mid-July for an offensive against the much stronger Rumanians, but this soon ended in collapse. On 1 August the revolutionary leaders abandoned power, taking the train to Vienna. Few mourned their departure, especially since in the final weeks they had conducted their own Red Terror, murdering approximately 500 people.[32] (Later, after returning to Russia, Kun was briefly placed in charge of the Crimea, where, at the close of 1920, he carried out the mass execution of thousands of White and anarchist prisoners of war, though they had been promised that their lives would spared. Even Lenin was said to be outraged by this "pre-Katyn.")

[31] Particularly notable in the nascent Hungarian film industry, some of whose luminaries went into permanent exile. These included Béla Lugosi, Mihály Kertész (who would be known in Hollywood as Michael Curtiz and go on to direct *Casablanca*), and Sándor Korda (later to become prominent in the British film industry as Sir Alexander Korda). B. Dent, *Budapest: A Cultural History* (Oxford, 2007), 97–99.

[32] On the regime, see R. Tökés, *Bela Kun and the Hungarian Soviet Republic* (New York, 1967), and I. Völgyes, ed., *Hungary in Revolution, 1918–19* (Lincoln, Nebr., 1971).

There had been two attempted revolts against the Kun regime; meanwhile, a volunteer White Army began to form in south Hungary.[33] When the Rumanians withdrew from Budapest in November, they handed over power to the counterrevolutionaries, who established a regency that governed rump Hungary for the next quarter-century under Admiral Miklos Horthy, reestablishing as much of the prewar system as possible. As is not infrequently the case with victorious counterrevolutions, the new repression proved to be more rigorous than the Red Terror of the Kun regime.[34] By 1922 the nationalist militia and paramilitary groups organized during the counterrevolution had largely been dissolved. The main effect of the Kun regime was to frighten much European opinion and skew Hungarian affairs strongly to the right for the next generation.

SOCIOPOLITICAL CONFLICT IN ITALY: THE EMERGENCE OF FASCISM

The situation of Italy immediately after the world war was perhaps the most paradoxical in Europe, for Italy, having entered the war in 1915, emerged on the winning side, yet the enormous cost, great losses, and very meager benefits made it seem to many Italians as though their country had lost. Moreover, there had been a special character to the Italian government's decision for war entry, since a secret "deal" had been negotiated in the Treaty of London (May 1915) that promised major territorial additions on the northeastern border with Austria, the eastern Adriatic, and even in Anatolia, treaty obligations that for the most part were never honored. Hence the outcry of "La vittoria mutilata" (the mutilated victory) – nearly 600,000 men killed, a huge outpouring of wealth, great social strain, and all for very little.

The Italian Socialists (PSI) had been one of only two major socialist parties – the other being the Russian Bolsheviks – not to support its nation's war effort. They were not directly subversive like the Bolsheviks, but studiously neutral, with the slogan "Né aderire, né sabbotare" (Neither support, nor sabotage), and Socialist workers continuing to toil in war industry.

The end of the war brought intense political conflict, economic dislocation, and social turmoil. The revolutionary faction of "Maximalists" (once led by Benito Mussolini) had gained control of the PSI in 1912, and in 1919 opened an offensive to achieve socialism in Italy. The next two and a half

---

[33] Arguably the most effective counterrevolutionary action was the raid by activists of the Hungarian Anti-Bolshevik Committee (ABC) on the Kun regime's embassy in Vienna in April 1919, in which they looted some 150 million crowns sent there to finance a Communist revolution in Austria. Nearly half this sum was said to have been confiscated by the Viennese police soon after, but most of the money then went to finance the Hungarian counterrevolution.

[34] Under Communism, Hungarian scholars calculated that as many as 5,000 people perished in the White Terror, doubtless an exaggeration. More recently this number has been reduced to no more than 1,500, and it has been pointed out that most of the Hungarian civilians slain at that time were victims of the invading Rumanian army. See the exchange between Balázs Ablonczy and Zsuzsanna Ozsvath, *American Historical Review* (December 2009 and February 2010), 340–41, 1567–68.

years were full of strikes, disorder, and a considerable amount of violence, with revolutionary land seizures in the south. Yet the Maximalists were not Bolsheviks, and they had no strategy for seizing power, eschewing a violent insurrection or coup d'etat. Instead, in August–September 1920 they followed the theory of the general strike – the attempt to achieve revolutionary power by economic action rather than political violence – through the direct occupation of factories in the industrial zone of northern Italy. Rather than attacking the occupiers with police violence, the government shrewdly isolated them physically and economically. After a short period, the Socialists realized that mere physical occupation of the factories did not permit them to dominate the economy and, after accepting a few face-saving concessions from employers, brought the occupation to an end. From that point the revolutionary left was increasingly on the defensive.

There was never any outright civil war in Italy, but there was a great deal of disorder and political and social conflict. At no point were the Socialists close to seizing power; their main achievement, instead, was to inspire great fear among the middle and upper classes, who thought for two years that there was indeed danger of civil war or a violent revolutionary takeover.

The new force that took advantage of this pre-revolutionary situation was the Fascist movement, officially organized as the Partito Nazionale Fascista in October 1921. Led by Mussolini, who had abandoned revolutionary socialism for nationalist revolution in 1915, the Fascists represented a new kind of radicalism, combining extreme nationalism with an appeal to modernization and social and economic well-being, uniting aspects of both the right and left. Fascism also preached a cultural revolution to produce a "new man" – an "anthropological" revolution more than a social revolution, based on the ideas of the vitalist cultural upsurge of the fin-de-siècle. It preached national unity to achieve a strong, dominant, modern new Italy – what, it said, the liberal governments of the era had failed to achieve.

Fascism reflected the experience of World War I, adopting tactics of direct action, embracing violence not as a necessary evil but as a positive good, not merely as a tactic but as a philosophical principle. The Italian new man would be daring and enamored of a salutary violence in the service of the nation, which he would lead to greatness both at home and abroad, and for which he would learn to excel in war. As much or more than Bolshevism, Italian Fascism represented the new militarization of politics, though it would never be able to build a structure of economic and military mobilization remotely equivalent to that of the Soviet Union. Whereas Latvian Bolsheviks had made the organization of regular political military units (*Strelkii*) a top priority, the Fascists went them one better in requiring all physically fit party members to be constituted as an active militia, a "party-army."[35] Whereas the German

---

[35] Perhaps the best study of the Fascist *squadre* is found in S. Reichardt, *Faschistische Kampfbünde. Gewalt und Gemeinschaft im italienischen Squadrismus und in der deutschen SA* (Cologne, 2002), which compares it to the Nazi SA.

Freikorps were formed as cadres for civil war but represented no fixed or final political purpose, Italian Fascists organized themselves politically and militarily to put an end to latent civil war before it had begun and to transform a newly united nation.

Fascism, founded in 1919, failed to gain support during its first year of existence, but the intensification of conflict during 1920 gave it the chance to break through. The Fascists presented themselves as bearers of a rival revolution and made Socialists and the small new Italian Communist party their targets, denouncing them not so much for their economic goals as for their social divisiveness, their internationalism and subversion of the Italian nation. They first gained broad support in the northern Italian countryside, where the Socialists had alienated even sharecroppers by their insistence on collectivizing land. During the latter part of 1921 the Fascists went on the offensive in many parts of northern Italy, attacking Socialists, closing down their centers, breaking their syndicates, and in 1922 beginning to take over local governments.

Moderates and conservatives tolerated Fascists because they repressed revolutionary socialism, but Mussolini insisted on political power. His tactics were more indirect but also more coherent than those of either the Socialists or the Communists or, for that matter, of Hitler in 1923. He appreciated the fact that Italy was not undergoing a genuine civil war, despite continuing violence, and that Italy was not Germany in 1919, much less Russia in 1917. Neither the Italian state nor the armed forces were undergoing dissolution, but retained the power to repress the 320,000-man Fascist Party at any moment.

Mussolini therefore inaugurated in 1922 a new tactic for seizing power, rejecting insurrection, coup d'etat, or pronunciamiento. He chose a largely legal route, based on political alliance and assisted by a certain amount of manipulation and direct action, foreshadowing Hitler in 1933 and the Comintern's subsequent adoption of the Popular Front, as well as the tactics of Latin American radicals in later years. The "March on Rome" by 50,000 Fascists in October 1922 represented not an effort to seize power by force, but rather a mass demonstration to pressure the king into appointing Mussolini the prime minister of a normal parliamentary coalition in which Fascists would originally hold only two of eleven cabinet portfolios. Only after more than two years as parliamentary prime minister did Mussolini move in January 1925 to convert a legal government into a political dictatorship, taking twenty-seven months to accomplish what Hitler would later achieve in less than two.

During the Italian crisis of 1918–22 there was never any genuine insurrectionism, as in Germany and some other countries, until Fascists began to seize control of a certain number of municipal governments in the summer of 1922. Mussolini's tactic was to combine legal political activity with considerable violence against targeted enemies – but never against the national state or its officials – assisted by a carefully controlled local militancy. Political violence had been initiated on a limited basis by Socialists and anarchists in strikes, demonstrations, and land seizures in 1919, the worst single incident being an anarchist bombing in Milan in which more than twenty people were killed. Between 1920 and 1922, Fascists and Socialists engaged in numerous affrays, usually but not in every case initiated by the Fascists, in which hundreds died. Fascists also played to the galleries by practicing *la beffa* (the "joke" or prank) – tactics such as forcing political enemies to drink a glass of castor oil in public. It became the practice for the police to stand aside to a greater extent than was ever to occur in Germany during the rise of Nazism, so that the Italian state did not ultimately retain the degree of control of public order exercised in Germany during the crisis of 1930–33. Total casualties for four years of political violence in Italy cannot be exactly determined, but are thought to have amounted to 2,000 deaths. In general, official statistics for those four years indicated an increase in violent deaths of 4,000 above prewar figures, but some of that may have been due to an increase in common crime. This is far below the proportionate figures for Russia and approximately the same, given the difference in population and the somewhat shorter timeline involved, as those for Germany from 1918 to 1923. It is of course much higher than the figures for Spain between 1917 and 1923, but in proportion to population lower than those for the Second Republic from 1931 to 1936.

Fascism presented itself as the "Italian national revolution," in contrast to the divisive doctrines of liberalism, socialism, and anarchism. It claimed to be morally and culturally superior to movements based on a narrow rationalism and materialism, insisting that Fascism incorporated a broader philosophy and more inclusive social concerns, and that it was ostensibly morally superior because it had overcome latent civil war and achieved power with only limited bloodshed, by contrast to the catastrophe in Russia, in which many millions perished. Mussolini also stressed that the nationalist corporatist economics of Fascism, which gave the state a special role but maintained private property, was superior to the economics of Communism in achieving greater production and well-being. Lenin presided over an economic disaster in Russia, while under Mussolini Italy rose to a new level of relative prosperity during the 1920s.

This latter point was correct, but overlooked the fact that the Communist system, whatever its limitation in overall productivity, had greater ability to concentrate state power and develop military resources. Fascism adopted the new term "totalitarianism" in 1925–26, but in Italy this initially meant the total concentration of political power and institutional coordination in the state, not total state control of society and ownership of virtually the entire economy. Thus Fascism would be unable to monopolize and control resources in the manner achieved in the Soviet Union by the "Stalin revolution" of agrarian collectivization and state-owned industry.[36]

---

[36] For references concerning the rise of Fascism, see my *A History of Fascism 1914–1945* (Madison, Wisc., 1995), Chapter 4.

SPAIN IN TURMOIL, 1917–1923

Spain did not undergo a true revolutionary crisis at the end of World War I, though there was much talk of revolution. The country maintained somewhat greater order than the other countries discussed in this chapter, primarily because it had remained neutral in the conflict. Nineteenth-century liberalism had finally achieved institutional stability after 1875, and neutrality in the war enabled the established elites, somewhat bolstered by continuing reform, to maintain power until 1923. The main challenge in public affairs was not social revolution but democratization. The only worker mass movement was the anarchosyndicalist National Confederation of Labor (CNT), which finally began to approach (but never reach) a million members in 1919–20.[37] By contrast, the Spanish Socialist Party (PSOE) and its trade union branch, the General Union of Labor (UGT), constituted the weakest socialist movement in any large European country.

Spain's two major crises, in 1917 and 1923, were for the most part political, not social, crises. The "Parliamentary Assembly" of July 1917 constituted a sort of peaceful parliamentary insurrection by a motley coalition of republicans, progressives, and Catalan autonomists, attempting to spark a national reform that would lead to democratization. It failed completely, both because of inadequate support and because the established regime remained strong. An attempted general strike by the CNT and UGT soon afterward also failed, costing about eighty lives.[38] The greatest division in the country in 1917–18 was the conflict between progressive liberals and the left, on the one hand, who wished to intervene in the war on the side of the Entente, and on the other the conservative elements, who tended to favor Germany but as a practical policy sought to maintain neutrality. The latter carried the day.[39]

Something of a postwar social crisis arose, without assuming revolutionary dimensions, with the CNT as the main actor. In the southern countryside this took the form of what became known with considerable exaggeration as the "Bolshevik triennium" of 1918–20, which was not Bolshevist and really lasted only about a year and a half. There was more than a little destruction of property but scant violence against owners, hardly comparable to what went on in some other countries.

The same might be said for the CNT's strikes and violence in Barcelona and several other large cities. Terrorism against industrialists began in 1917, to some extent stimulated by German agents as part of the German program

---

[37] The chief inspiration abroad for the CNT was French revolutionary syndicalism. See F. F. Ridley, *Revolutionary Syndicalism in France: The Direct Action of Its Time* (Cambridge, UK, 1970), and P. Stearns, *Revolutionary Syndicalism and French Labor* (New Brunswick, N.J., 1971).

[38] On the internal conflicts during 1917, see J. A. Lacomba Avellán, *La crisis española de 1917* (Málaga, 1970).

[39] The best study is J. Romero Salvadó, *Spain 1914–1918: Between War and Revolution* (London, 1999).

of revolutionary subversion abroad. The authorities responded with violent repression of their own. Over several years perhaps 300 people were killed, but again this cannot be compared to violence in some other countries.[40] The Russian revolution excited Spanish worker movements between 1917 and 1919, accompanied by much loose talk about Spain being the country of the "next revolution," the "most proletarian country" in Europe after Russia,[41] and so forth, but such talk was considerably exaggerated. Spanish society would remain relatively stable for another decade.

A more serious crisis developed in 1923. It had three dimensions: political, military-imperial, and social, of which the last was probably the least important. The political conflict stemmed from growing demands for reform and democratization in a system still under the domination of nineteenth-century middle- and upper-class elites. The military-imperial conflict was due to the failure of the army to occupy and pacify the new protectorate in northern Morocco, a venture that had led to military disaster and enjoyed very uncertain public support. The social conflict stemmed from the violent labor strife and *pistolerismo* ("gunmanism") that plagued Barcelona, Bilbao, and a few other centers. The two established political parties were divided and unable to come to grips with problems.[42]

In September 1923 Gen. Miguel Primo de Rivera imposed a dictatorship that declared that it would set matters right. With French assistance, it resolved the military-imperial conflict in Morocco,[43] while vigorous repression (though little bloodshed) for the time being ended the social conflict. Economic policy was at first extremely successful, presiding over the most rapid growth in all Spanish history, generating a new revolution of rising expectations that would prove very difficult to satisfy. The Achilles' heel of the regime, however, was

[40] On the problem of political violence in early twentieth-century Spain, see J. Avilés Farré and A. Herrerín, eds., *El nacimiento del terrorismo en Occidente: Anarquismo, nihilismo y violencia revolucionaria* (Madrid, 2008); R. Núñez Florencio, *El terrorismo anarquista, 1888–1909* (Madrid, 1983); J. M. Farré Moregó, *Los atentados sociales en España* (Madrid, 1922); F. de P. Calderón, *La verdad sobre el terrorismo* (Barcelona, 1932); A. Pestaña, *Terrorismo en Barcelona*, ed. J. Tusell (Barcelona, 1979); León-Ignacio, *Los años del pistolerismo: Ensayo para una guerra civil* (Barcelona, 1981); C. Winston, *Workers and the Right in Spain, 1900–1930* (Princeton, N.J., 1985); M. A. Serrano, *La ciudad de las bombas: Barcelona y los años trágicos del movimiento obrero* (Madrid, 1997); E. González Calleja, *El máuser y el sufragio: Orden público, subversión y violencia política en la crisis de la Restauración (1917–1931)* (Madrid, 1999); M. A. Pradas Baena, *L'anarquisme i les lluites socials a Barcelona 1918–1923* (Barcelona, 2003); and J. Aróstegui, ed., "Violencia y política en España," *Ayer*, 13 (1994).

[41] J. Avilés Farré, *La fe que vino de Rusia: La revolución bolchevique y los españoles (1917–1931)* (Madrid, 1999); G. Meaker, *The Revolutionary Left in Spain, 1914–1923* (Stanford, Calif., 1974).

[42] Of the two, the Liberal Party was the greater champion of reform, but lacked coherence. See T. G. Trice, *Spanish Liberalism in Crisis: A Study of the Liberal Party during Spain's Parliamentary Collapse, 1913–1923* (New York, 1991).

[43] S. E. Fleming, *Primo de Rivera and Abd el-Krim: The Struggle in Spanish Morocco, 1923–1927* (New York, 1991).

the failure to achieve political reform.[44] In the process, it ended the system of evolutionary parliamentary government that had ruled Spain since 1875, leaving nothing with which to replace it, creating the conditions for total regime change and the beginning of the most drastic revolutionary process in the country's history. Spanish history once more marched to its own rhythm, since the full Spanish equivalent of Europe's postwar crisis would not emerge until more than a decade later.

REGIME CHAOS AND BRIEF CIVIL WAR IN PORTUGAL

The severe political turmoil that developed in Portugal after 1910 differed from that of any other European country, for Portugal remained overwhelmingly agrarian and underdeveloped, its affairs dominated by middle-class elites. It had participated in the wave of radical agitation that swept the European periphery in the decade before World War I, as a violent republican movement assassinated the king and one of his sons in 1908 (the only act of regicide in Portuguese history), then overthrew the monarchy itself two years later. The republicans represented a nineteenth-century elite determined to create a progressive Portugal that would no longer be a "melancholy mass of poor people," as one of them put it, and that could maintain the country's imperial status, for in Africa it possessed one of the larger European colonial empires. The republic immediately emulated the recent French separation of church and state, moving rapidly to curtail Catholic property and rights, creating a major schism in society. Most Portuguese adults were illiterate, and the republicans, alleging that the peasants might support the church, reneged on their promises of democratization, restricting the suffrage to between 30 and 40 percent of adult males only – the ones most likely to vote republican.

The new regime consummated the radical liberal and anticlerical revolution of the nineteenth century, but had grave difficulty facing twentieth-century problems. It became the most unstable in Europe, surviving only because of limited support from its ally Great Britain, though many British diplomats found the new regime, as the ambassador in Lisbon put it, "detestable." Portuguese leaders compounded their mistakes in 1916 by insisting on entering World War I on the side of the Allies, in order to ensure the status of their empire. This produced economic misery and a fiscal crisis that could not be overcome.

The republican form of minority rule was more unstable than that of the monarchy, for Portuguese political forces were undergoing the fragmentation

---

[44] There is a considerable literature on the first Spanish dictatorship: S. Ben-Ami, *Fascism from Above: The Dictatorship of Primo de Rivera in Spain 1923–1930* (Oxford, 1983); J. Rial, *Revolution from Above: The Primo de Rivera Dictatorship in Spain, 1923–1930* (Fairfax, Va., 1986); J. L. Gómez Navarro, *El régimen de Primo de Rivera* (Madrid, 1991); E. González Calleja, *La España de Primo de Rivera: La modernización autoritaria 1923–1930* (Madrid, 2005); R. Tamames, *Ni Mussolini ni Franco: la dictadura de Primo de Rivera y su tiempo* (Barcelona, 2008); and others.

common to many countries. Organized labor was weak, and was sternly repressed in 1911–12, while two feeble efforts at monarchist insurrection, launched from Spanish sanctuary, failed completely, though other attempts were made. When the president named a general as prime minister in 1915, briefly moving Portugal toward neutrality, the dominant sector of republicans, known confusingly as Democrats, regained control through another violent insurrection. They in turn became increasingly unpopular because of the war policy they imposed, and were overturned by a more conservative insurrection at the close of 1917, which installed a presidentialist regime under Sidónio Pais, the short-lived "New Republic," which came to an abrupt end a year later when its leader was assassinated.[45]

In this state of semicontrolled chaos, the only true civil war broke out at the beginning of 1919. Participation in the war, coupled with political turmoil, had emboldened the military, which began to form local "military juntas," partly in imitation of a recent Spanish example. In Porto, the country's second city, the local junta declared for a constitutional monarchy, briefly seizing control of most of the northern half of Portugal for the so-called Monarchy of the North. The pretender to the throne, however, disowned this initiative, which did not enjoy support from either Britain or Spain, the two potential sources of foreign assistance. The republicans rallied their forces, together with loyal sectors of the military, and overwhelmed the monarchists in less than a month. It had been a civil war, but of scant duration and with few casualties.[46]

The restored "New Old Republic" then limped along for seven more years, hopelessly divided politically and administratively inept, unable to resolve crushing fiscal problems. Finally, in 1926, a large part of public opinion accepted with relief the imposition of a military government, leading to a moderate authoritarian regime that would remain in power, mutatis mutandis, until 1974 – the longest-lived non-Communist authoritarian system in twentieth-century Europe.

Some historians apply the concept of "ritualized aggression" to Portuguese affairs. Though the years 1910–26 were the most violent in modern Portuguese history (except for the brief liberal/traditionalist civil war of 1832–34), with possibly 2,000 or more killed, the losing side never fought to the bitter end in any of these confrontations, and reprisals by victors were limited. This was

---

[45] The only full account in English of the republican regime is D. Wheeler, *Republican Portugal: A Political History 1910–1926* (Madison, Wisc., 1978). The most extended treatments are those by A.-H. Oliveira Marques, "Portugal da Monarquia para a República," in Oliveira Marques and J. Serrao, eds., *Nova História de Portugal* (Lisbon, 1991), vol. 11, and by R. Ramos, "A segunda fundação," in J. Mattoso, ed., *História de Portugal* (Lisbon, 1994), vol. 6. See the commentary by L. Arranz, "Un hito en la historiografía portuguesa. El Portugal contemporáneo según Rui Ramos," *Historia y política*, 20 (July–December 2008), 315–58.

[46] The "monarchy of the north" has been treated in two master's theses: M. A. Dias Santos, "A contra-revolução monárquica – Do sidonismo à Monarquia do Norte" (Coimbra University, 1998), and A. Ferreira Coimbra, "Paiva Couceiro e a contra-revolução monárquica" (Braga University, 2000). (For these data I thank Prof. Maria Inácia Rezola.)

at least in part because Portuguese conflicts rarely exceeded the framework of radical nineteenth-century liberalism, the extremism of social revolution being absent in a still semitraditional agrarian society.

TENSIONS IN THE "GREEN EAST"

In eastern Europe, postwar democratization offered new political and social opportunities for the largest social class, the peasantry. With the exception of the industrialized western half of Czechoslovakia, all the new independent states were primarily agrarian, and the new conditions stimulated the rise of peasant parties in most of them. A few of these antedated the war; others were created immediately afterward. Agrarian conditions varied from country to country. In the north (Finland and the Baltic states) and in the Balkan south, smallholding was the rule, a situation that to some extent defused social tensions. Large estates existed, particularly in Hungary, but also in Poland and in some parts of Rumania. By far the largest agrarian proletariat – in proportionate terms distinctly larger than that of Spain – was that of Hungary, but there the counterrevolution placed power firmly in the hands of conservatives, and poor farm workers enjoyed little representation. Later in the 1930s, they would disproportionately support radical fascist-type movements. This was a political outcome exactly the opposite of what happened in most of Spain, and stemmed from the peculiar conditions of interwar Hungary – dominated on the one hand by one of the most intense nationalisms to be found in any European country, and on the other subject to nineteenth-century–type political restrictions.

Peasant parties were most important in Poland, Rumania, Yugoslavia, and Bulgaria. In general, they reinforced the parliamentary system and worked to improve social and economic conditions. During the immediate postwar crisis, agrarian tensions were particularly severe in Rumania, a sequel to the great peasant revolt of 1907 but also a consequence of wartime privations, followed by the new stresses and heightened expectations stimulated by the postwar crisis. This pressure was contained by a coalition government led by Gen. Alexandru Averescu (the "Rumanian Hindenburg") during 1920–21, which passed a moderate agrarian reform program and crushed an attempted Socialist general strike. This was much less than the reform sought by the Rumanian Peasant Party, but it succeeded in partially defusing the situation, though Averescu's new People's Party failed to establish itself as a populist alternative to the peasant movement. Agrarian poverty would remain the country's number one social and economic problem.

The majority of eastern European countries achieved little success during the interwar period in improving their agricultural economies.

A dramatic situation developed in Bulgaria, where the strongest of all the postwar peasant movements emerged in the Agrarian Union, led by Alexander Stamboliski, that governed from 1919 to 1923. This was the most progressive government in Bulgarian history, representing a strong reaction against the militarist and expansionist policy of the preceding decade, during which the "Prussia of the Balkans" had been almost continuously at war from 1912 to 1918 and had suffered two crushing defeats. The Stamboliski government promoted economic development and the interests of the peasantry, who constituted nearly 80 percent of the population, while encouraging peace and cooperation. The Agrarian Union also reflected the postwar militarization of politics, forming its own peasant militia, the Orange Shirts, and, like some other new parties in power, sometimes tended to ride roughshod over the opposition.

Stamboliski's government drew the ire of all the former established elites, in the cities, the bureaucracy, and the army. Conservatives formed their own White Guards, while urban politicians organized a new group early in 1922 called the National Alliance, which professed admiration for Italian Fascism. More violent was the terrorist IMRO (Internal Macedonian Revolutionary Organization), formed in 1897 to win Macedonia for Bulgaria. It had sparked armed insurrections in old Turkish Macedonia and threatened the same in the new Bulgaria, while actively engaging in political assassination.[47]

Despite growing strife, there was no danger of civil war because the Stamboliski government was too strong. Only the army had the power to overturn it, and the initiative was finally undertaken by the Military League, an association of army officers, who had come to form a virtual caste in a relatively undifferentiated society. Some sixty-five hundred officers had been permanently demobilized after the war, but many of them hoped to regain their positions, subdue the reformers, and reassert an expansionist policy. A conspiracy of Military League activists and IMRO terrorists carried out a coup d'etat in June 1923, overthrowing Stamboliski, who was tortured and summarily executed.[48] Since the military were both united and determined, there was no danger of civil war. The Agrarian Union was subdued and subsequently split. A Comintern attempt to take advantage of the situation through Communist insurrection failed completely. Though Bulgaria retained the form of a parliamentary monarchy, its affairs were henceforth dominated by King Boris, the military, and the successors of the old minority urban parties. As in Hungary and to some extent in Rumania, government in Bulgaria was patterned on prewar politics. The peasant breakthrough had failed.

As a defeated power with major international grievances and loss of territory, Bulgaria might have seemed a logical candidate to develop a significant fascist-type movement. Peasant smallholding provided considerable social stability, however, despite the prevailing poverty. Moreover, since the right had proven strong enough to subdue the left, there was little support for an alternative radical nationalism, and the army was strong enough to crush any

[47] D. M. Perry, *The Politics of Terror: The Macedonian Revolutionary Movements, 1893–1903* (Durham, N.C., 1988); J. Swire, *Bulgarian Conspiracy* (London, 1939).
[48] The key study is J. D. Bell, *Peasants in Power: Alexander Stamboliski and the Bulgarian Agrarian Union, 1899–1923* (Princeton, N.J., 1977).

challenge. Two small fascist-type movements did emerge, but failed to attract many followers.

END OF THE POSTWAR CRISIS

Between 1917 and 1923 Europe experienced a period of institutional crisis and social conflict without precedent. In the Russian lands, the increased death rate far surpassed anything since the time of the Thirty Years' War three centuries earlier. Sharply increased social and economic tensions affected all of Europe, but the advanced democracies of the northwest remained stable. This was not the case in eastern, central, and southern Europe, where the crisis continued in varying ways until 1923.

By 1924 general stability had finally been achieved, as even the Communist International had to admit. Most of the new political systems that emerged from the war had at least temporarily consolidated themselves. There were exceptions in eastern and southern Europe, as Italy and Spain fell under authoritarian rule, to be followed by Poland, Portugal, and Lithuania in 1926, but, outside of the USSR, parliamentary government would generally remain the norm. Most of Europe achieved relative prosperity during the mid and late 1920s, reducing social tensions for the time being.

Fascism remained a comparatively isolated Italian phenomenon, and the same might be said of Communism in the Soviet Union. The civil strife of the extremes appeared to have been overcome. The duration of the crisis had been extraordinary, but full civil war had developed only in the lands of the former tsarist empire.

4

Civil Strife and Dictatorship, 1930–1935

In 1924, Soviet policy recognized that prospects for "universal civil war" had vanished, at least for the time being. The Comintern announced the beginning of the "Second Period" in world revolution, recognizing that capitalism had achieved temporary stability, marking a temporary "transitional stage between revolutions."[1] Comintern leaders declared that promotion of violent revolution must be deferred in favor of building strength through the "united front from above," forming alliances with other worker groups.

As Iosif Stalin began to win the struggle for power after the death of Lenin, he developed his own revolutionary strategy, based on the slogan "Socialism in One Country." In 1928, he unveiled his twin strategies of immediate collectivization of agriculture and the ruthless prioritization of large-scale state industry in order to turn the Soviet Union into a major industrial and military power. This required renewal of internal conflict and repression. The Stalin-style creation of an eventual superpower was possible only in a country with the large population and abundant natural resources of the Soviet Union, for altogether it suffered nearly twenty-five million deaths as the direct and indirect results of state policy between 1917 and 1934.

It is still common for historians to cite Stalin's policy of "Socialism in One Country" as evidence that under his rule the Soviet Union had abandoned world revolution and adopted a strictly defensive policy, but that was far from the case. In 1928, as the internal Stalin revolution had begun to get under way, the Sixth Congress of the Comintern announced that a new "Third Period" had opened in the struggle for world revolution: a new crisis of capitalism. This had been predicted at the Seventh Plenum of the Executive Commission (ECCI) at the close of 1926, which had announced that the world revolution must inevitably proceed through three phases: first, the initial revolutionary upheavals of 1917 to 1923; second, a phase of temporary stabilization; and

---

[1] According to the Comintern Executive Commission (ECCI) in 1925, quoted in K. McDermott and J. Agnew, *The Comintern: A History of International Communism from Lenin to Stalin* (Houndsmill, Basingstoke, Hampshire, 1996), 52.

third, an inevitable new crisis of capitalist contradictions. The Sixth Congress in 1928 declared that the "Third Period" had begun, for a new crisis was at hand, one that would make the world situation "objectively revolutionary."[2] The only evidence that the leadership could point to, however, was a riot in Vienna the preceding year and moderate Communist gains in local elections in Germany and Poland. For Stalin, external crisis conditions constituted a necessary political and psychological counterpart to his "second revolution" at home, which he announced as indispensable to the survival of the Soviet Union in the "second imperialist war" that was to be unleashed by the new world crisis. The announcement of the "Third Period" was thus determined more by Soviet domestic policy than by any objective conditions abroad. Nonetheless, within two years a genuine crisis would begin to emerge, though its consequences in some respects would be quite different from what the Comintern had in mind.

The Comintern defined two paths to revolution: one was the direct Communist-led socialist revolution; the other and perhaps more common one would be a Communist-led bourgeois-democratic revolution, which would rapidly "grow over" into the socialist revolution. The first route was supposed to be feasible only in the most advanced countries. Heretofore there had been a Communist-led "bourgeois-democratic revolution," according to strict Marxist-Leninist definitions, only in relatively insignificant Outer Mongolia.

The 1928 theses involved the usual Communist carrot-and-stick approach, emphasizing the importance of peace proposals and disarmament. It was frankly stated, however, that this approach was not intended to disarm the proletariat, for generalized civil war in capitalist countries was inevitable. Disarmament proposals served two functions, one being to expose the true policy of capitalist powers, and the other in certain circumstances to provide a breathing space for the Soviet Union. Conversely, the official history of the Soviet party defined just wars as those for social revolution and national liberation. In a subsequent published letter to Maxim Gorky of 17 January 1930, Stalin wrote: "We are *for* a liberating, anti-imperialist, revolutionary war despite the fact such a war, as is known, not only is not free from 'the horrors of bloodshed' but abounds in them."[3]

The primary emphasis in the 1928 program was on the growth of conflict within capitalist societies and the development of "fascization," defined as the "terrorist dictatorship of big capital," as "direct dictatorship, ideologically masked by an 'all-national idea.'" Fascization employed social demagogy and might even appear to be temporarily anticapitalist, but was above all counterrevolutionary. "The chief task of fascism is the destruction of the revolutionary vanguard, i. e., the Communist strata of the proletariat and their cadres." This effort would only accelerate radicalization, as contradictions

[2] K. E. McKenzie, *Comintern and World Revolution, 1928–1943: The Shaping of Doctrine* (New York, 1964), 68–76.
[3] E. R. Goodman, *The Soviet Design for a World State* (New York, 1960), 292–93.

within capitalism intensified, sharpened the class struggle, and led inevitably to imperialist war.[4]

Fascism was now seen as a greater danger than before, all the more so because the new "Third Period" doctrine espoused a theory of "panfascism." In this connection, the recent congress of the Red International of Labor Unions (RILU) had labeled six countries as "fascist" – Italy, Spain, Portugal, Poland, Lithuania, and Bulgaria – all of them save Bulgaria being governed by varying forms of rightist or nationalist authoritarianism.

For the next six years, the practice would be to label all non-Communist forces as varying forms of hyphenate fascism, the number one enemy being the "social fascism" of social democratic parties, which must be thoroughly defeated in order to win the workers to revolution. During 1928–29, as he eliminated his last remaining rivals within the Soviet regime, Stalin identified himself ever more completely with the doctrine of the Third Period and of social democracy as social fascism, the latter formula being officially endorsed by the Tenth Plenum of the ECCI in 1929. The danger of a fascist takeover in Germany, for example, was now defined as stemming from the Social Democratic Party (SPD). The Comintern's tactic with regard to other worker parties during this period was the "united front from below," meaning a complete merger of organizations whereby the latter were progressively absorbed by Communist parties.

THE GERMAN CRISIS

Despite a lengthy succession of crises, Germany's Weimar Republic achieved temporary stability, but with respect to one crucial variable, attitudes in central Europe differed from those in the older democracies. Whereas the vast majority of voters in France, Britain, and Belgium were determined to avoid another war at almost any price, in Germany, Austria, and Hungary there remained great bitterness about defeat and the miseries that had followed, generating demands, at least by a minority, for a more militant national leadership. It was therefore no accident that during the crisis decade of the 1930s the new fascist movements developed their greatest support in precisely these countries.

Despite the relatively calm surface of affairs in Germany after 1923, the tendency toward the militarization of political activity continued. The various militia and volunteer associations transformed themselves into what the Germans called *"politische Kampfbünde,"* or "political combat leagues" (PCLs). These became a regular part of political life, imparting a style of "esthetic militarization," with mass marches, vehement demonstrations (the "demonstration march" becoming a specialty), and even regular participation in electoral activities.[5] Some parliamentary parties maintained

---

[4] McKenzie, *Comintern and World Revolution*, 120–22.
[5] T. S. Brown, *Weimar Radicals: Nazis and Communists between Authenticity and Performance* (Oxford, 2009).

uniformed youth organizations, with even the Social Democrats having their own militia, the *Reichsbanner*. Largest of the PCLs was the *"Stahlhelm"* (Steel Helmet) organization of more than two million military veterans. The *"Sturm-Abteilung"* (Storm Detachment – SA) party militia of Hitler's National Socialists were at first outnumbered by the *"Rote Frontkämpferbund"* (Red Front-Fighters League – RFB) of the Communists, whose uniforms were more completely military and who introduced in 1927 the clenched-fist revolutionary or "red front" salute that later became popular elsewhere, most notably in the Spanish Popular Front.[6] Historians have devoted their main attention to Nazi paramilitarism, but almost equally prominent was the "cult of violence on the left,"[7] where a not-so-dissimilar mystique of masculinity, "roughness," and violence would also be found among the Communists, who revealed pronounced "fascist" characteristics. As Eric Weitz has put it, "Male physical prowess came increasingly to define the KPD's model of revolutionary militancy."[8] Coercion was a regular feature of Communist strikes, the KPD developing a kind of "syndicalist" doctrine, seeking to build from more and more individual strikes to the revolutionary general strike and insurrection.

Even during the more peaceful years of the mid-1920s, major propaganda battles took place. The incitement to direct violence was stronger in the Communist than in the Nazi Party, for the KPD at that time was the larger organization. Prior to 1932, the main source of political violence in the larger cities was the RFB,[9] and German police focused more on the latter than on the SA, since the Communists tried to subvert all institutions, including the police themselves. The years of the Comintern "Second Period" (1924–28) were devoted to the full "Bolshevization of the KPD," which continued to proselytize civil war. In 1923 the KPD had begun to publish a magazine called *Vom Bürgerkrieg* (On Civil War) and later in 1928 brought out a book by a Soviet general, "A. Neuberg" (pseudonym of M. Tukhachevsky et al.) entitled *Der bewaffnete Aufstand* (Armed Rebellion), concerning the means of developing a successful armed insurrection.[10] In May 1929, months before the economic crisis began, an RFB riot produced a major street battle in Berlin that left thirty dead. Historiographic concentration on the subsequently massive crimes of the Nazis has obscured the fact that the main call to political violence inside Germany before 1932 came from the Communists, who

[6] K. G. F. Schuster, *Der Rote Frontkämpferbund, 1924–1929: Beiträge zur Geschichte und Organisation eines politischen Kampbündes* (Düsseldorf, 1975).

[7] E. D. Weitz, *Creating German Communism, 1890–1990: From Popular Protests to Socialist State* (Princeton, N.J., 1997), 62. Weitz notes the tendency among many historians to "underestimate the elements of coercion in the Revolution."

[8] Ibid., 187.

[9] See the data in S. Reichardt, *Faschistische Kampbünde. Gewalt und Gemeinschaft im italienischen Squadrismus und in der deutschen SA* (Cologne, 2002), 64–69.

[10] This Comintern manual was widely translated and, for example, later published in Spain in 1932. It played some role in the Socialist insurrection of 1934.

praised individual terror as well as "class terror" to "liquidate the leaders of the counterrevolution."[11]

In Germany, there was neither time nor adequate conditions to develop a stable national political community. A few years of relative prosperity were not enough. Each major political party came to represent a different ideological or economic interest group, and no broad consensus developed. When the Depression hit, the Socialists placed their priority on maintaining the economic benefits of their trade unions, a goal to which political cooperation became secondary, and thus no longer played the stabilizing role they had in 1918–20. The emphasis on maintaining what were at that time perhaps the highest "fringe benefits" in the world undoubtedly weakened German political and economic relations. The conservative parties, however, were even more myopic, and, as unemployment climbed to 30 percent, Hitler's National Socialists for the first time began to develop broad support as the only cross-class movement that stood for unity and the well-being of all social sectors. During major political campaigns the Nazis downplayed such themes as militarism, racism, and extreme anti-Semitism, emphasizing issues that could unite German society, while promising prosperity for all and the placing of common interests above individual or class interests.

The KPD became a mass party, stronger in most large cities than the Nazis. It was above all the party of the unemployed, not of organized labor, emphasizing the formation of "control committees" to carry out "control actions" and organized plundering of shops called "food requisitions." The possibility of civil war emerging from the German crisis of 1930–33 was, nonetheless, distinctly smaller than in the immediate postwar years, though it remained a concern for many Germans, who also worried about the prospect of collapse and/or foreign domination.

Throughout this period Germany remained the most important country for the Comintern, whose leaders decreed that their main foes were not fascists or rightist authoritarians but the Social Democrats, who enjoyed the support of the largest bloc of workers. The KPD's Twelfth Congress had declared categorically in June 1929 that "Social Democracy is preparing ... the establishment of the fascist dictatorship."[12] Social democrats were labeled "social fascists," a pejorative the more ironic since it was the Communist RFB, the "stormtroopers of the proletariat," whose highly militarized uniforms went one better than those of the fascist shirt movements and more closely approximated a complete soldierly appearance.

The Comintern judged the rapid rise of Nazism from mid-1930 as merely contributing to the weakening of the bourgeois system. Combating this was not a major priority. The KPD's new program for the "National and Social Liberation of the German People," issued in August 1930, followed the earlier

---

[11] E. Nolte, *Der europäische Bürgerkrieg 1917–1945: Nationalsozialismus und Bolschewismus* (Berlin, 1987), 166.
[12] McDermott and Agnew, *The Comintern*, 101.

"Schlageter line." A subsequent editorial in the official Soviet organ *Pravda* on 16 September declared that although the National Socialists represented "the bourgeoisie," they "had successfully used *anti-capitalist slogans*" and hence should be seen as "fighters for the social liberation of the masses, for the overthrow of the Versailles treaty and the Young Plan yoke," both also opposed by Communist policy.[13] The rise of Nazism was in this sense positive because it weakened the influence of France – one of the two dominant capitalist powers – and the possibility of any future Franco-German rapprochement. It was not so dangerous, since even if it represented "fascism," it constituted no more than the last gasp of the bourgeoisie and need not be feared nearly as much as the SPD's defense of "bourgeois democracy." Nazis and Communists sometimes made common cause against the Social Democrats and the democratic Republic.

Social democracy and the more liberal sectors of politics were indeed the major threat to Soviet policy in Germany, because they promoted greater democratization, rejection of militarism, and peaceful rapprochement with the Western capitalist powers. By contrast, under the Rapallo agreement, the Soviet Union enjoyed close economic and military relations with the more conservative and nationalist sectors of German affairs, and hence Stalin perceived little long-term danger stemming from the German right, whatever Hitler might have said about the Soviet Union in *Mein Kampf.*

Nonetheless, with each passing month the latent conflict between these two rival revolutionary movements increasingly came to the fore, so that most of the street violence in Germany during the Depression crisis involved battles between Nazis and Communists.[14] This did not prevent the Eleventh Plenum

---

[13] Quoted in J. Haslam, *Soviet Foreign Policy, 1930–1933: The Impact of the Depression* (New York, 1983), 61.

[14] During 1930–31, the SA carried out more assaults on the Socialist *Reichsbanner* than against the Communists, and in Germany as a whole made the latter their main target only in 1932. Within the state of Prussia (about two-thirds of Germany), which kept the most accurate statistics, SA attacks on the Communists came to outnumber those by the latter only in October 1932. Conversely, even though the KPD made the SPD its major political adversary and occasionally even collaborated with the Nazis, its RFB militia normally made the Nazis the major target of their physical assaults. Reichardt, *Faschistische Kampfbünde*, 63–69.

The extent of violence in Germany during 1930–33 has drawn many references in the historical literature, since it accompanied the rise of Nazism, but proportionately it was much less extensive than violence in Germany during 1918–20, in Hungary during 1919, in Italy during the rise of Fascism, or during the Second Republic in Spain. The Nazis claimed to have suffered seventeen fatalities in political combat during 1930, the Communists forty-four. These figures increased during the following year to forty-two for the Nazis and fifty-two for the Communists. For 1932 the respective claims were 84 Nazis and 75 Communists killed, exceeded in each year by more than a hundred times that number injured (2,500 injured Nazis in 1930, 9,715 in 1932). These street fights were usually more like barroom brawls than mortal contests. See E. Rosenhaft, *Beating the Fascists? The German Communists and Political Violence, 1929–1933* (New York, 1983). R. Bessel, in *Political Violence and the Rise of Nazism: The Storm Troopers in Eastern Germany, 1925–1934* (New Haven, Conn., 1974), 74–75, presents somewhat lower figures.

of the ECCI in March–April 1932 from reaffirming that the highest level of struggle against fascism was to combat the "cretinism" of parliamentary democracy. If street battles were mainly fought against Nazis, the principal political struggle was waged against the Social Democrats.

In the summer of that year the Comintern convened its International Congress against War and Fascism in Amsterdam. "Fascism" was understood in a very general way as referring especially to "the militarization of capitalist countries," so that the greatest danger of fascism was to be found in France and Britain. As Furet has paraphrased the Comintern line, "One of the great themes of Amsterdam was denunciation of 'Genevan pacifism' – in other words, the League of Nations. This ... was all the more urgent because the Congress declared that an anti-Soviet war was imminent."[15] Soviet publications during 1932 were dominated by war hysteria; the danger was said to stem from the crisis of capitalism and from Japanese imperialism. Neither Italy nor Germany, conversely, was of particular concern.

By the summer of 1932 German affairs had reached an impasse. A democratic government resting on a parliamentary majority had for some time been impossible because of the differences between the Socialists and the bourgeois parties, and, to make matters much worse, by 1932 parliament contained a "negative majority" in which the combined votes of the two antidemocratic revolutionary parties, Nazi and Communist, amounted to more than 50 percent.

Three types of alternatives were available. One was that of Hitler and the second that of the Comintern, which was the least likely of all. The third was a rightist authoritarian or "presidential authoritarian" government, based on the emergency powers under Article 48 of the constitution. Since mid-1930 the semisenile and octogenarian president, the former field marshal Paul von Hindenburg, had utilized the latter on a temporary basis to appoint governments vested with limited decree powers, but sectors of the extreme right had been scheming for some time to turn this into a more permanent rightist, non-Nazi authoritarian government.

After two years of decree-power government under Heinrich Brüning, in mid-1932 Hindenburg appointed a personal friend as chancellor, the aristocrat and former diplomat Franz von Papen. When Hitler refused to accept a subordinate position in Papen's government, the chancellor gained authorization for new elections, in which for the first time in four years the Nazi vote went down, declining nearly 20 percent, while the KPD's continued to rise. Papen's administration imposed a frankly reactionary policy, cutting unemployment benefits and talking of changes to the constitution that would give the executive permanent authoritarian power. To all the left, it looked like a return to the monarchy, producing an immediate polarization in which Papen was seen as a potential "civil war chancellor." Papen and his associates pondered

[15] F. Furet, *The Passing of an Illusion: The Idea of Communism in the Twentieth Century* (Chicago, 1999), 215.

the feasibility of imposing a pseudo-legal dictatorship of the extreme right in the autumn of 1932 but concluded that the extent of opposition made this impossible.

The aged Hindenburg lacked complete clarity of mind and was no particular friend of democracy, but he was a military man who respected law and order, and who doubted that nonparliamentary governments with decree powers could continue much longer. In December 1932 he appointed the third consecutive government with decree powers under Gen. Kurt von Schleicher, head of the political office of the German army, because Schleicher insisted that he had a plan to resolve the crisis. This consisted of a public works and economic stimulus program to revive the economy, as well as significant rearmament (by this time legal under international law) and a maneuver to split the Nazi party, bringing its more left-wing elements into a coalition government that would command a majority in parliament. The latter tactic failed miserably, and a year or more would have been needed to implement the new economic program. Yet something like the Schleicher alternative, a national coalition oriented toward the right and backed by presidential powers, was probably the best that Germany could do for the time being.

Schleicher, however, had ousted as chancellor Hindenburg's friend Franz von Papen, whose brief reactionary ultra-rightist government had been accused of fomenting civil war. Papen was determined to have revenge and, like most of the German elite, had a low opinion of Hitler. Despite the fact that the Nazi leader held firm to the position that he would enter no coalition government unless he himself were chancellor, Papen was convinced that he and his colleagues were clever enough to manage and manipulate the novice Hitler. He convinced Hindenburg that Schleicher's reforms were subverting the larger landowners and that there would soon be danger of civil war and of French or Polish intervention. Schleicher, meanwhile, found that he had no way to construct a majority and that he could not continue to govern without new elections, while in mid-January 1933, the police chief of Berlin filed a report that the radicalization of labor grew worse each day and that the KPD was confidently preparing for civil war.[16] Papen then successfully purveyed to Hindenburg the idea that a coalition government led by Hitler and himself, with the former as chancellor and Papen as vice chancellor, would eliminate these dangers and was the only way to command a parliamentary majority. From the viewpoint of the non-Nazi right, a majority was all the more vital because it provided the only route to a constitutional reform that would institute more authoritarian government.[17] Hitler himself would be "bound hand and foot" by his coalition allies, since there would be only two other Nazi

---

[16] Nolte, *Der europäische Bürgerkrieg*, 171.

[17] And that was the way it worked out, save that it would be Hitler's dictatorship and not the rule planned by the rightist parties. See H. Beck, *The Fateful Alliance: German Conservatives and Nazis in 1933; The "Machtergreifung" in a New Light* (New York, 2008).

cabinet ministers. At first it was not clear whether Papen or Hitler would end up as chancellor, and at that point democratic opinion was particularly concerned to avoid the return of Papen, who seemed to be seeking an extreme right-wing authoritarian state. Initially, Hitler as chancellor was not seen as the gravest danger.

A paradox of the German crisis was that after nearly three years of governments ruling by decree, Hitler's accession to power was expedited by a strong concern in some quarters for a return to legality. In November 1932 the Nazi vote had suddenly begun to decline, and it was thought that the danger of a genuine Nazi takeover had receded. The Nazis held only a third of the seats in parliament; the party was financially bankrupt, and among many Nazi leaders there was a mood of desperation. The greatest danger to parliamentary government was deemed to stem from the authoritarian and reactionary Papen, who had no popular support whatsoever, and from the "militarist" Schleicher. It was known that Hindenburg disliked Hitler and was probably not likely to give him power to rule by decree. A further paradox was that there were signs that Germany had passed the trough of the economic Depression, the first limited indications of recovery beginning to appear in the autumn of 1932. The "Hitler recovery" later noticeable in the spring of 1933 was not completely new but resulted from the continuation of these limited trends. Finally, if Hitler were to overstep the bounds as chancellor, Papen insisted that a parliamentary majority could vote him out.

This was the basis on which Hitler legally became constitutional and parliamentary chancellor of Germany on 30 January 1933. Just when the Nazis seemed finally to have lost, Hitler began to win. Hermann Göring told fellow Nazis that a "miracle" had occurred. As chancellor, Hitler immediately reneged on his promises, subverted the possibility of any majority in the present parliament, and insisted on convening new elections, the third in eight months. Hindenburg and Papen had maneuvered themselves into a corner, and the feeble old president was convinced that any alternative ran the risk of civil war or political breakdown. The elections of March 1933 were accompanied by Nazi street terror, but the votes seem to have been accurately counted. The Nazis gained nearly 44 percent of the ballots, and Hitler then browbeat the other nonleftist parties into passing the Enabling Act that permitted him to govern legally as dictator for the next four years. Again, Hitler could use the threat of civil war to overcome opposition. The Nazi dictatorship had begun, and the next twelve years would be the most destructive in history.

Given the multitude of problems and crises besetting Germany, the failure of democracy was not surprising. The most reasonable outcome, however, would have been a longer quasi-dictatorship by the relatively moderate Schleicher. That the alternative assumed the disastrous form of Hitler was due in considerable measure to the stubbornness and guile of Hitler himself. His refusal to compromise even after Nazism seemed irremediably in decline was fanatical and irrational, but it happened to work, a big gamble that succeeded.[18] Ever afterward, all the way to the end in 1945, Hitler would justify his greater and greater gambles, and his refusal to compromise or cut his losses, with reference to his "miraculous" breakthrough in 1933.

The suicidal character of Comintern policy in the German crisis has generated considerable debate.[19] Beginning in 1931 there was occasional speculation among Communists in Moscow and Berlin about the possibility of a short-term Hitler government (though not a Nazi regime) whose quick collapse might open the way for the Communists. Comintern doctrine was that "pure fascism" could take major form only in less developed countries, and was thus not conceivable as a serious alternative in Germany. From this perspective, Germany featured mass Socialist and Communist movements, as well as a powerful bourgeoisie, none of which had equivalents in Italy in 1922. The German bourgeoisie would have no long-term need for a "carica-ture of Mussolini." With an Italian-style compromise neither necessary nor feasible, Hitler could come to power only through another *putsch*, like the one attempted in 1923, which the Communists correctly judged could never suc-ceed. Such an analysis seemed confirmed by the elections of November 1932, in which the Nazis declined while the KPD, the largest Communist party west of Russia, rose further. Germany, it was calculated, continued to be gravely weakened and could not recover for years. Were the temporary outcome a new rightist authoritarian government, this must, according to the Soviet cal-culation, continue to find itself at odds with the dominant Western powers. A weak ministry led by a Hitler or a Papen would result and would generate such discontent that a popular revolutionary uprising would be inevitable.[20]

Even when this analysis proved incorrect, the initial development of the Hitler government was received calmly. As in the case of the first Mussolini government, it was held to be inevitably transitory; at the worst, the KPD could continue to operate as a clandestine party, just as Communists had done under other contemporary dictatorships, including that of Mussolini. When

---

[18] There are many accounts of Hitler's triumph and the downfall of German democracy, but one of the best discussions may be found in D. Diner, *Cataclysms. A History of the Twentieth Century from Europe's Edge* (Madison, Wisc., 2008), 106–52.

[19] Two examples are C. Fischer, *The German Communists and the Rise of Fascism* (London, 1991), and K.-H. Niclauss, *Die Sowjetunion und Hitlers Machtergreifung* (Bonn, 1966). R. C. Tucker, in *Stalin in Power: The Revolution from Above, 1928–1941* (New York, 1992) and "The Emergence of Stalin's Foreign Policy," *Slavic Review*, 36 (1977), 563–89, argues that Stalin followed a Machiavellian policy of encouraging the Nazis to make trouble in western Europe, hoping that such conflict would not involve the Soviet Union, which might then derive revolutionary advantages. T. Weingartner, in *Stalin und der Aufstieg Hitlers: Die Deutschlandpolitik der Sowjetunion und der Kommunistischen Internationale 1929–1934* (Berlin, 1970), takes an opposing approach. He argues that Soviet policy never consciously sought to abet the Nazis, and that Stalin never really anticipated any revolution in Germany at that time, but sought to maintain friendly relations with a Germany in which he expected the nationalist right, not the Nazis, to come out on top. The latter interpretation is the more convincing of the two, but neither may be altogether correct.

[20] This follows the analysis in L. Luks, *Entstehung der kommunistischen Faschismustheorie* (Stuttgart, 1984), 156–58.

only a few months revealed this was not the case, there was neither time nor imagination for any alternative policy. The old KPD died not with a bang but a whimper. Muscovite analysis continued to place the principal blame on the Social Democrats and their "social fascist" policies, correct analysis of which showed that they inevitably led to "pure fascism," which hopefully would be no worse in Germany than the "pure fascism" of Mussolini in Italy, all of it merely the mask of finance capital and the grand bourgeoisie. Although during the course of 1933 Communist parties in several countries began to place more emphasis on serious antifascism, in Moscow the ECCI continued to reiterate that the policy of concentrating against "social fascism" had been the only correct one.

During 1933, nonetheless, the concept of fascism among Comintern leaders had to be altered, insofar as the Thirteenth Plenum of the ECCI in November recognized the fallacy of the earlier notion that fascism could triumph only in underdeveloped lands. The hope still was that the stabilization achieved by the Italian regime would not be repeated in Germany, which was more advanced and had a larger, better organized, "undefeated" proletariat. The basic Communist contention about the historical role of fascism – that it represented the final throes of a doomed capitalism – could be demonstrated by a revolutionary worker overthrow of the National Socialist regime. A purely transitory triumph of fascism would merely expedite the world revolutionary process, or, in the KPD slogan, "After Hitler, Our Turn!" To some extent it would work out that way, but only in the long run, not at all as Communist theorists projected, and only after unimaginable danger and destruction in a world war.

As Soviet relations with Germany deteriorated, the relatively amicable relations between Rome and Moscow became more important to the latter, so that by 1934, when denouncing "fascism," Moscow stressed that it was referring to Germany, not to Italy. For the moment, Italian Fascism was evidently not part of what Soviet spokesmen called "pure fascism." The most hopeful Fascist theoretical approach toward domestic policies in the Soviet Union was made by the Fascist journalist Renzo Bertoni in his books *Il trionfo del fascismo nell'URSS* (1934) and *Russia: Trionfo del fascismo* (1937), which asserted that the Soviet emphasis on domestic development and massive state capitalism, combined with the renewal of traditional patriotic themes in Soviet culture,[21] meant that the Soviet Union was now on a course to converge with Fascism, and would itself become "fascist."

The importance of stable relations with Rome was one argument used by Stalin and other Soviet leaders to support their contention during 1933 and 1934 that the existence of the Hitler regime should not in any way disturb the

---

[21] In May 1934 the newspaper *Pravda* for the the first time revived usage of such terms as *rodina* (native land) and *otechestvo* (fatherland). The turn toward Russo-Soviet patriotism is studied in D. Brandenberger, *National Bolshevism: Stalinist Mass Culture and the Formation of Modern Russian National Identity, 1931–1956* (Cambridge, Mass., 2002).

special relationship that Moscow had enjoyed with Berlin since 1922. Soviet leaders hoped that military collaboration would continue, as indeed it did temporarily, though in ever-diminishing volume, until Hitler terminated it in November 1933. The Soviet military attaché, Levichev, was in the meantime astonished at the similarity of the mass revolutionary liturgy now being practiced in Germany to its counterpart in the Soviet Union, but "consoled himself with the thought that Nazism could hold onto power 'only by draping socialist slogans and words around itself'."[22] The complete absence of any positive response to Soviet blandishments had become increasingly troubling by the last months of 1933. Although the Red Army command would continue efforts to promote further collaboration on into 1934, some Soviet leaders began to feel that Soviet policy should become broader and more flexible in order to counter Nazism, and should seek to improve relations with France and other capitalist states. Accordingly, a number of new gestures were made in that direction.

Nonetheless, at the Seventeenth Party Congress held in February 1934 – the "Congress of Victors," highlighting the success of collectivization, the Five Year Plans, and the new militarization – Stalin took unusual care in his discussion of what he called "the German type of fascism." He declared once more that "the most careful analysis cannot uncover a single atom of socialism" in National Socialism, yet insisted that "what counts here is not fascism," since relations with Fascist Italy had always been good.[23] Public and private statements of Soviet policy reiterated the desire to maintain the best possible relations with Germany, together with more proposals to renew military cooperation. At the same time, Soviet representatives stated that they were seeking to develop closer ties to other powers because they could not afford to become isolated, but that they would relax such efforts if relations with Germany improved. Hitler dictated a cool, correct policy toward Moscow, but there would be no restoration of military ties, even though commerce continued normally and a new commercial agreement was signed in 1934. Hitler wanted no trouble with the Soviet Union while Germany struggled to recover from the Depression and begin rearmament, but there was no positive response to Soviet overtures, either. Relations continued to deteriorate.

THE EXPANSION OF FASCISM AND AUTHORITARIAN RULE

Though the establishment of the Mussolini government had inspired several efforts to create imitation fascist movements in other countries (even as far distant as Argentina), it had not inaugurated any new general trend, much less an "era of fascism," for it soon coincided with the stabilization and relative prosperity of the mid-1920s. A temporary mild and nonfascist dictatorship

---

[22] A. M. Nekrich, *Pariahs, Partners, Predators: German-Soviet Relations, 1922–1941* (New York, 1966), 66.
[23] Ibid., 71–72.

was imposed in Spain in 1923, and three years later relatively moderate but, as it turned out, more permanent systems of authoritarianism were introduced in Poland, Portugal, and Lithuania, followed by the royalist dictatorship in Yugoslavia in 1929. These all emerged in less developed countries on the periphery of Europe, seeming to confirm the Comintern's thesis that such overt breakdowns were typical only of more backward lands. In 1927, Mussolini himself had announced that Fascism was uniquely Italian and "not export merchandise," as he put it.

Coming amid the general crisis of the Great Depression, inauguration of the Third Reich had much greater impact, since Germany was still considered potentially the most powerful European country. Fascist-type movements proliferated and expanded in many places, though they reached the dimension of mass movements only in Austria, Hungary, and later Rumania. To that extent Nazi Germany initiated an "era of fascism," even though fascist-type parties in most countries were unsuccessful.

A particularly conflictive situation developed across Germany's southern border in Austria. Most Austrian citizens would have preferred to unite the two countries in 1919, but that was expressly forbidden by the peace treaties. Political representation in the rump Austrian republic was triangulated among the Social Democrats, the Catholic Christian Social Party, and right authoritarian pan-Germanists. The Social Democrats helped to consolidate a democratic republic but then withdrew from participation in a "bourgeois" government, which was usually led by the Christian Socials. The depression of 1930 was even more severe in Austria than in Germany, and, three years later, Hitler's victory across the border gave a tremendous boost to the Austrian Nazis, who gained much popular support and launched a campaign of terrorism to undermine the government. Engelbert Dollfuss, the Christian Social chancellor, sought a broader coalition against the Nazis, but the Socialists (paralleling Comintern policy in Germany) refused, confident that they would gain control of Austria themselves. After a momentary procedural crisis brought the resignation of the chief officers of parliament in March 1933, creating a brief void in the legal succession of authority, Dollfuss assumed full power, forming a coalition with the right-radical *Heimwehr* (Home Army) that he called the Fatherland Front. The two principal internal enemies, the Nazis and the Socialists, were both outlawed, and when the Socialists responded with an abortive insurrection in February 1934, they were suppressed.[24] The Austrian Nazis made a bid for power five months later, assassinating the chancellor, but were even more easily put down. About 500 were killed in these failed insurrections. For the next four years the new Christian Social leader, Kurt Schuschnigg, governed as quasi-dictator, presiding over the second republic to install a corporative constitution (after Portugal),[25] but Hitler's pressure

---

[24] A. G. Rabinbach, *The Crisis of Austrian Socialism, 1927–1934* (Ithaca, N.Y., 1983).
[25] For a recent evaluation, see G. Bischof et al., eds., "The Dollfuss/Schuschnigg Era in Austria: A Reassessment," *Contemporary Austrian Studies*, 11 (2003).

grew stronger and stronger, until he occupied Austria militarily in March 1938, sweeping away the anti-Nazi Schuschnigg regime and incorporating the country into the Third Reich.

The drastic changes in Austria in 1933–34 were part of the transition to authoritarian rightist and nationalist government throughout most of central, eastern, and southern Europe. Only the established democracies of the north and west, together with Switzerland, Czechoslovakia, and Finland, resisted this trend. The new authoritarian regimes were generally not fascist, though they adopted some of the trappings of fascism. In Austria, Latvia, and Estonia they were imposed in good measure to avoid fascist radicalization, while the regimes in Hungary, Portugal, Rumania, and Yugoslavia all moved to repress fascist movements within their borders. They developed strongly nationalist programs to defend their economies and to buttress their regimes politically, so that, in general, this became an era of nationalist authoritarianism more than an era of fascism. By 1939 over half the countries in Europe had abandoned parliamentary government. Early in 1937, Gen. Francisco Franco, leader of the new insurgent regime in Spain, thought to join the trend by developing his own form of one-party nationalist authoritarian state (here combined, as in some other cases, with neotraditionalist culture), for that, more than Communism, seemed to be the "revolution of the twentieth century."

THE POPULAR FRONT

By 1934 the Soviet government was revising its foreign policy, and in September of that year the USSR joined the League of Nations. A rapprochement with "fascist Poland," with whom Hitler signed a ten-year nonaggression pact that year, was not a possibility, owing more to Polish than to Soviet resistance, but mutual defense pacts were signed with both France and Czechoslovakia in May 1935, though arrangements for practical implementation proved much harder to work out.

Germany remained the primary concern, though events elsewhere played a role. Political riots in Paris in February 1934, primarily initiated by the leagues of the radical right, raised the specter of "fascism on the march" in France, which assumed a new importance in Soviet policy, even though as recently as 1930 Stalin had publicly ranted that France was "the most aggressive and militarist of all aggressive and militarist countries in the world."[26] In Paris there was growing restiveness with the Comintern's Third Period policy of revolutionary extremism and isolation in domestic affairs. Not merely did French Socialists raise the question of leftist unity in the face of fascism, more and more Communists, particularly in the French and Czech parties, were raising the same issue. Most insistent was Jacques Doriot, the mayor of the Paris industrial suburb of St. Denis and a rising star of the French Communist Party (PCF). Doriot demanded a Communist policy in the interests of the French,

[26] J. V. Stalin, *Works* (Moscow, 1955), 12:263.

not the Soviet, left and a new program that would border on nationalism. By March 1934 the Comintern had expelled him from the French party, sending him on the journey that would eventually bring him to his own style of fascistic national socialism. At the same time, the Moscow bosses moved to satisfy some of these demands, authorizing a unity-of-action pact against fascism between French Communists and Socialists, signed in July 1934.[27] This was the first major alteration of Comintern Third Period policy, a policy that within a year would be discarded altogether.

In April 1934, Stalin appointed the Bulgarian Georgi Dimitrov secretary of the Comintern. Though he continued to reiterate from time to time the standard line that social democrats were "social fascists," Dimitrov and his lieutenants were allowed to work further with French Socialists and before the end of the year even to approach the liberal democratic French Radical Party. By October Stalin had authorized initial planning for a Comintern congress that would quietly bury the Third Period strategy and inaugurate a new policy, which would become known as the Popular Front.

The German espionage service provided Berlin with versions of transcripts of a series of Soviet Politburo meetings and other Soviet documents between 1931 and 1935. The source of this material, captured by United States occupation forces in 1945, was not revealed, and there has ensued a considerable controversy over its authenticity, but the reports clearly predicted the course of Soviet policy between 1934 and 1941.

According to these data, in May 1934 Stalin informed the Politburo that, given the major changes in European affairs, Soviet policy could not follow classic Communist precepts but must adopt a program of total pragmatism. This did not involve jettisoning the Comintern, but was a matter of adjusting its policy. "The world Communist movement must remain ideologically ... intact, ... remaining an enormous reservoir for the future decisive offensive against world capital." Later Politburo resolutions in the first half of 1935 concluded that amid the growing conflict and realignment of European powers, "the Soviet government must do everything possible to find a place for itself in the camp of powers which forms the strongest coalition," so as to remove conflict "as far as possible from the borders of the Soviet Union." This last point was not new, but merely updated the thesis regarding a future major war that Stalin had originally formulated in 1925. Though it would be possible to postpone war for a time, the latter remained ultimately "almost unavoidable," so that the goal must be "to aim, persistently and systematically, for an

---

[27] Some top French Socialist leaders remained very wary of the Communists. Paul Faure, general secretary of the French Socialist Party from 1920 to 1940, detested the Communists, whom he considered barbaric, un-French, and "agents of Moscow." He informed the press on 13 November 1934 that in France "the fascist peril is perhaps not so real.... Fascism in France is in retreat." N. Greene, *Crisis and Decline: The French Socialist Party in the Popular Front Era* (Ithaca, N.Y., 1969), 39. Faure's judgment was of course correct, since there was only one tiny fascist party in France at that time, though there were all manner of rightist groups, from the most moderate to the most radical.

outbreak of the world war in a form which is most favorable for the USSR." This would presumably require restoration of the pre-1917 military alliance with France.[28]

Soviet doctrine had long held that another major war would be the "ice-breaker" for the expansion of Communism, but at the same time stressed that Soviet policy would never be so cynical as to encourage a war for that reason. On 9 March 1935 the official Nazi newspaper *Völkische Beobachter* purported to cite Soviet documents revealing that "the Politburo is firmly convinced that a new world war is absolutely inevitable, but it is at the same time the absolute prerequisite for the world revolution."[29] Soviet spokesmen vehemently denied the authenticity of the quotation, but the latter in fact did no more than to restate the standard Soviet and Comintern position of the past decade.

The Politburo meeting of October 1934 concluded that Soviet policy should seek to act as a peaceful intermediary in central European affairs, aiming toward a broad defensive alliance but, at the same time, always being prepared to respond positively should there be improvement in relations with Germany. In turn, this would require a more moderate Soviet domestic policy to rally popular support, while making maximal use of the Comintern in opposition to "fascism and reaction." Soviet policy should seek greater security not only in Europe, but also vis-à-vis Japan in the Far East, though Japan's policy must lead very soon to a war that Moscow should seek to deflect in the direction of other East Asian powers and the United States.[30]

At the same time, Soviet Foreign Minister Maxim Litvinov was reprimanded for not always bearing in mind the distinction between current tactics and long-term strategy. Rapprochement with the capitalist powers during this period of crisis was no more than "a tactical step and is not a basic line of foreign policy," "no more than a transition stage, … a preparatory maneuver for a communist offensive against international capitalism." This essentially foreshadowed the distinction that would be drawn at the Comintern congress nine months later. The Politburo nonetheless saw that it might be necessary in pursuit of the "peace policy" to distance the Soviet Union from the Comintern. It repeated that "the inevitable result of the present political situation will be a world war" initiated by Germany and Japan, and the fundamental goal remained that of deflecting this away from the Soviet Union.[31]

A Politburo resolution of February 1935 reiterated a paranoid conclusion expressed earlier, that there existed a secret anti-Soviet entente between Germany, Poland, and Japan. Given the inevitability of war and its importance as "the obvious prerequisite for the world revolution," the Soviet Union must

---

[28] Quoted in M. Loventhal and J. McDowell, "The Stalin Resolutions and the Road to World War II (I)," *San Jose Studies*, 7.1 (November 1980), 78–104. (My thanks to Milton Loventhal and Jennifer McDowell for drawing my attention to this material.)

[29] Ibid.

[30] M. Loventhal and J. McDowell, "The Stalin Resolutions and the Road to World War II (II)," *San Jose Studies*, 7.1 (February 1981), 1–24.

[31] Ibid.

strengthen its position militarily and politically, distancing itself as much as possible from Communist revolutionism, which as an official policy would for the moment be disastrously counterproductive. Future resolutions repeated the same line: the Soviet Union must pursue international security arrangements and avoid entanglement in the forthcoming war, which "can prove to be, under certain conditions, the first stage in the reactivation of the revolutionary world movement under the banner of the III International." A resolution in April reaffirmed the goal of a broad international security arrangement "which essentially would allow the USSR to provoke artificially an armed conflict among the individual powers or groups of powers at a moment most favorable to the Soviet Union." It also endorsed "the simultaneous seeking out of ways for a direct understanding with Germany and Japan, in order to turn their expansion in the direction of a conflict with states which are not directly bound up with the Soviet Union by obligations of mutual assistance,"[32] a prediction of the goals of the eventual Nazi-Soviet Pact of 1939.

Initial conclusion of the French-Soviet defensive alliance in May 1935 produced a mood of optimism in the Politburo, which concluded that the "almost inevitable war in Europe" would lead to the dismemberment of both Germany and Poland, with the USSR absorbing the Baltic states and much of Poland. By 8 August 1935 the mood was more somber, however, and Soviet policy emphasized more strongly than ever that Germany was the major enemy and that it was vital to maintain peace at the present time, even if that strengthened Britain and France, for continued peace would allow time for internal conditions in the fascist powers to grow more contradictory, inevitably weakening them. Thus a policy of rapprochement with the Western capitalist powers remained "revolutionary and proletarian" and should be supported by all revolutionary worker groups.[33]

The Seventh Congress of the Comintern convened in Moscow on 25 July 1935, lasting nearly four weeks. Dimitrov announced the need for "a broad people's antifascist front," and presented a new definition of fascism as "the open terrorist dictatorship of the most reactionary, chauvinistic and most imperialist elements of finance capital." Fascism was no longer the same as liberal democracy, which had been the Comintern's previous position, but now was declared to be much worse, all the more so because of fascism's ability to generate mass support from broad sectors of the petite bourgeoisie, and even from some workers. Countries identified as "fascist" were Germany, Italy, Japan, Poland, and Hungary.

To combat this scourge, "a broad people's anti-fascist front" was needed, even though Dimitrov declared that the new tactic required no change in fundamental Comintern strategy. The basis of any alliance would still be "the proletarian united front," which must be adjusted to conditions in any given country. Language remained ambiguous, but pointed toward a Popular Front

[32] Ibid.
[33] Ibid.

that would be broader than a workers united front, for it would seek to unite all worker and/or democratic antifascist elements, even strictly petit bourgeois groups, in electoral coalitions. If successful, this would logically lead to Popular Front coalition governments, but these would not necessarily include representatives of the Communist Party, at least at first. Dimitrov strongly emphasized that all this involved only a change in tactics, not a change in strategy. Both Mussolini and Hitler had gained power on the basis of a coalition, and the Popular Front tactic adjusted such an approach for the use of the left. Italian Fascists had to some extent copied Bolshevik tactics in 1920, and in 1935 Communists would adopt the fascist approach to gaining political power, using democratic elections and parliamentary processes to advance Comintern policy, which would initially be defensive and then, if successful, might take a more aggressive turn.

Had Dimitrov foreseen the virtual unanimity with which Western historians would write for the next three generations that the Popular Front tactic was based on "renunciation of revolution," he would doubtless have been delighted, but he emphasized to the faithful at the Seventh Congress that this was not at all the case. Dimitrov stressed that a Popular Front coalition government, as "a special democratic intermediate stage lying between the dictatorship of the bourgeoisie and the dictatorship of the proletariat" was not at all intended to delay transition to the latter. It could be no more than temporary, a tactic for the defeat of fascism that would also have the advantage of advancing "the revolutionary training of the masses."

A full Popular Front government would be "a democracy of a new type" that went beyond bourgeois democracy and pointed toward soviet democracy. It would not be a standard Western liberal democracy, for, under the banner of antifascism, such a "new type democracy" would begin the nationalization of parts of the economy and distribute land to poor peasants. It was a type of government that would be formed "on the eve of and before the victory of the proletariat," and was "in no way" to restrict Communist activities. Even after formation of a Popular Front government, the ultimate goal would remain the insurrectionary seizure of power and the dictatorship of the proletariat. Dimitrov emphasized: "We state frankly to the masses: Final salvation this government [of the Popular Front] cannot bring.... Consequently it is necessary to prepare for the socialist revolution! Soviet power and only soviet power can bring such salvation!"[34]

For the next four years, until the signing of the Nazi-Soviet Pact, the Comintern would proceed on a two-track strategy that for Communists had the advantage of confusing many political commentators at the time and has often confounded historians ever since. The ultimate strategy would be the same at the end of both tracks, but this has simply been too complicated for most analysts. The united front under Communist direction was the basic

---

[34] The foregoing quotations of Dimitrov are all from McDermott and Agnew, *The Comintern*, 130–32, 155–59.

revolutionary tactic vis-à-vis other worker parties, such as the Socialists, though for the moment its functioning must be subordinated to the broader tactic of the Popular Front. The latter was the broader macropolitical tactic to combat fascism. Whereas the former dealt with the current dynamics of revolutionary worker politics, the Popular Front concerned national elections and potential government coalitions. As Furet says, "The dictatorship of the proletariat and the overthrow of the bourgeoisie were still the ultimate goal; the prescribed path, however, was different."[35] Moreover, in countries where popular fronts were not possible, more typical Third Period tactics would continue, as in the Brazilian insurrection of 1935 and the Greek general strike of 1936.

Neither collective security nor Popular Front policy necessarily implied rigid hostility in direct Soviet relations with the two regimes of "open fascism." Further economic negotiations between Moscow and Berlin expanded mutual trade, although Hitler saw to it that arms exports were excluded. Throughout the decade about half of all metal-processing machinery imported by the Soviet Union came from Germany, while the latter depended on Moscow for much of its petroleum and grain. The Soviet trade representative was used repeatedly as a liaison to explore improvement of relations in other areas.[36] The Italian invasion of Ethiopia in 1935 provoked sharp Soviet denunciation and the League of Nations imposed economic sanctions, yet the restrictions in Italo-Soviet trade never went beyond the official embargo list. Compared to the decline in British and French commerce with Italy, Soviet trade dropped only a little, while Soviet oil exports increased significantly, fueling the Fascist war machine. The Kremlin took more seriously Hitler's remilitarization of the Rhineland in March 1936, though it also responded with another feeler to Germany for improved relations. Soviet policy would remain bimodal for the next three years, pursuing collective security against Germany as the main goal, while quietly exploring any possibility of a rapprochement with Hitler.

---

[35] Furet, *The Passing*, 222. In France during 1936–38 and in Chile in 1938, Popular Front coalitions were primarily defensive, undertaking only a certain number of new initiatives before breaking down altogether. Only in Spain during the revolutionary conditions of the civil war could the Soviets announce the beginning of the "democracy of a new type," using the same term announced by Dimitrov in 1935.

[36] Semicontinuous overtures to Hitler by Stalin during the years of the collective security policy have been most thoroughly chronicled by J. Hochman, *The Soviet Union and the Failure of Collective Security, 1934–1938* (Ithaca, N.Y., 1984).

PART TWO

THE CONFLICT IN SPAIN, 1931–1939

5

The Revolutionary Process in Spain

The last revolutionary process of the era, and the only one initiated in the middle of the interwar period, opened in Spain in 1931. It was unique in not having been stimulated or catalyzed by major war; it was almost exclusively the product of endogenous factors, which to that extent makes it the most singular of all the European cases under consideration. This was all the more extraordinary in that Spain had an entire century of parliamentary government behind it, even with all the limitations involved in early parliamentary development. For the second half of that period, stable and reformist constitutional monarchy had prevailed, free from any significant foreign or military pressures in Europe, complicated only toward the end by the establishment of the Spanish Protectorate in northern Morocco in 1913.

On the other hand, innovation and precocity had been features of Spanish political life for more than a century, ever since 1810; rapid transition to a new regime had multiple precedents. Moreover, in 1931 it was by no means clear that a revolutionary process, as distinct from another regime change, was beginning. Thanks largely to its neutrality, Spain had been spared the full effects of the post–World War I crisis, even though it experienced some of the same stresses as other countries. The parliamentary system finally broke down in 1923, under the weight of demands for reform and democratization, violent social conflict in the industrial centers, and a bloody military stalemate in the effort to consolidate control of the Moroccan Protectorate, where the Riffi leader Abdul Karim led the most powerful native insurgency in any part of Africa or Asia at the time. Even many liberals welcomed the imposition of a reformist military dictatorship under Lt. Gen. Miguel Primo de Rivera. In conjunction with France, this regime put down the Moroccan insurgency and presided for five years over the greatest economic expansion in Spanish history. It was one of the mildest dictatorships in any land during the twentieth century, but, rather than reforming the parliamentary system, it simply terminated parliamentary government without being able to replace it. When temporary dictatorships or military-led governments ended between 1918 and 1934 in other southern European countries such as Portugal, Bulgaria,

Greece, Rumania, and Yugoslavia, they were replaced by a return to the old parliamentary system.

Why was Spain different? There are several possible answers. Portugal remained a backward agrarian country that still excluded political democracy, and, after the overthrow of Stamboliski, the same was true, to some extent, of Bulgaria. In Greece the dictatorship of 1926 was so short-lived that it failed to fully replace the parliamentary system, and the same might be said for the quasi-parliamentary government of Gen. Averescu in Rumania. In both Rumania and Yugoslavia the systems were reinforced by the major gains accruing from World War I, and by strong support from nationalism (Serbian nationalism, in the case of Yugoslavia). The six and a half years of the Spanish dictatorship lasted long enough to obliterate the old parliamentary system, and upon its downfall the monarchy – which had originally consented to the dictatorship in 1923 – was not reinforced by strong sentiments of tradition, conservative nationalism, or imperialism, sentiments shared only by small minorities. Added to this was the singular ineptitude of conservative leadership, whether on the part of the king or the old political elites. A generational change had set in, spurred by the extremely rapid transformation of Spanish society and culture in recent years, with neither youth nor energy at the service of the monarchy. Finally, new elections were delayed for fifteen months, even longer than in Russia, whereas in Germany in 1919 they had wisely been convened in only ten weeks. Though monarchists won a majority of seats in the municipal elections of 12 April 1931, their defeat in all the larger cities generated an enormous surge of confidence and ambition on the part of a new coalition of republican parties. Elderly monarchist politicians completely lost their nerve, while military leaders made it clear they would not impose any repression in order to save the monarchy. Within forty-eight hours, large crowds, summoned by the republican leaders, took to the streets in Madrid and several other cities in a "peaceful pronunciamiento" to demand an immediate change of regime. This direct action was completely successful. On 14 April, Alfonso XIII left the country, and the republican leaders occupied the seat of government, proclaiming the inauguration of Spain's Second Republic.[1]

Events in Spain once more showed that revolutionary processes are sometimes initiated rapidly and peacefully, and with comparatively little effort – sometimes almost none at all – by the revolutionaries. This generalization obviously does not always hold, but it describes the situation in France in 1789, in Russia in March 1917, and in Spain in 1931. A revolutionary process initiated with little conflict usually evolves through a series of phases or sequences, the first of which are also comparatively moderate, and this once more describes the situation in Spain, for the new regime took the form of a democratic republic, at first based on the existing social and economic systems.

[1] The first republican regime, the Federal Republic of 1873–74, had quickly dissolved into chaos, anarchy, and civil war, not an encouraging precedent.

One of its initial Socialist ministers, Francisco Largo Caballero, declared that in Spain what he termed "extremism" could have no future, because of the evident success of peaceful reformism. Ironically, three years later he would become the chief revolutionary leader to take up "extremism" as an indispensable tactic.

Events in Spain were not as telescoped as those in Russia in 1917, for Spain was a stable country, completely at peace, not immediately subject to any radical pressures, domestic or foreign. The chronology of events was more similar to that of France in the 1790s. The mistake by one of the republican leaders in 1931, when he contrasted his country's seemingly peaceful democratization with the violence and bloodshed of revolutionary France, was to compare Spain in 1931 to France in 1793, whereas the comparison should have been to France in 1789. Spain would experience increasing violence soon enough. Moreover, this comment overlooked the fact that the republicans had initially attempted to introduce their regime by military revolt in December 1930. Though on that occasion they had failed completely, some of them would soon show little reluctance to return to illicit or violent tactics.

During the next few years Spain would reveal the most completely pluralist political society of all the countries that experienced a revolutionary process in early twentieth-century Europe, offering the widest variety of alternatives, and the most rapid shifts in political orientation, with a broad variety of totally different options briefly having an opportunity to establish themselves. In different phases such diverse regime projects as liberal democracy (1931–32, 1933–34), the "Jacobin" exclusivist all-left republic (1932–33, 1936), Catholic corporatism (1934–35), revolutionary socialism and anarcho-syndicalism (1936–37), a "new type" of people's republic (1937–39), military dictatorship (1936–37), and a kind of semifascism (1937–39) had their day in the sun, with this last finally winning by force of arms. No other country experienced such a kaleidoscope or underwent such an extremely variegated revolutionary process.

Fundamental to initiating the process in Spain was that most basic of all revolutions, the psychological revolution of rising expectations, which took place during the generation of World War I. This had grown stronger not so much because of political development as because of the rapid social and economic transformation of the 1920s, for several years achieving one of the highest rates of growth in the world, producing a "takeoff" of modernization that was brutally truncated, but not fully reversed, by the Great Depression. By 1930 employment in the primary sector had dropped to less than half the labor force, and accelerating modernization sparked increasing demands for greater political expression and major social and institutional reforms. The initial effects of the Depression were proportionately milder in Spain than in many other countries, but the frustrations that they imposed nonetheless helped to encourage a radicalization that pushed reformist demands toward revolutionary goals in a classic demonstration of the basic theory of revolution discussed in the Introduction.

This was not apparent in 1931, for there appeared to be general, though never complete, agreement on something like a liberal democracy as the political structure of the new regime. Yet of the three main sectors of the governing coalition – the centrist (and misnamed) Radical Party, the middle-class left republican groups, and the Socialists – only the Radicals fully accepted a liberal democracy, played according to the rules of the constitutional game, with fixed rules and uncertain outcomes. The left republicans, led by Manuel Azaña, at first rejected socialism but identified the new Republic exclusively with a radical reform project based on anti-Catholicism and the permanent exclusion of all conservative interests from political power. The Socialists at first accepted the democratic Republic as opening an inevitable path to full socialism, but would soon begin to reject it when they saw it failing to follow this course.

The product of these divergent forces would be a highly ambiguous new regime that began in some respects to curb civil rights, producing a system that the historian Javier Tusell succinctly defined as "una democracia poco democrática" (a not very democratic democracy), the best brief description of the Second Republic ever coined. This first became apparent in the religious sphere, with the semitoleration of the widespread "quema de conventos," or church burnings, that took place on 12–13 May 1931, the violent expression of a mood that had been building for more than a generation, capped by complete rejection of the principle of a free church in a free state and the constitutional curbing of religious rights, with plans to end most religious education.[2] All this was the Spanish variant of the sharp and illiberal restrictions placed on the church by anticlericals in some other Catholic countries during the early twentieth century, beginning with France in 1905 and followed by the radically anticlerical republics in Portugal and Mexico, the latter having tried to bring the clergy completely under state control in 1926, a policy revived and implemented for a time in 1935. This provoked a major guerrilla war from 1926 to 1929, followed by a government policy of targeted assassination of Catholic lay leaders.[3] The left republican program of 1931–32 was only

---

[2] V. M. Arbeloa, *La Iglesia que buscó la Concordia (1931–1936)* (Madrid, 2008), offers a brief survey of church and state under the Republic. See also M. Alvarez Tardío, *Anticlericalismo y libertad de conciencia* (Madrid, 2002), and J. Vara Martín, *Un episodio en la historia de España: La lealtad de los católicos al poder* (Valencia, 2004). For the reaction of the papacy, see V. Cárcel Ortí, *Pío XI entre la República y Franco* (Madrid, 2008).

[3] In Mexico this incited a new phase of insurgent civil war after the end of the years of fighting brought about by the revolution of 1910. The tyrannical Mexican state was unable to suppress the new "Cristero" volunteer movement of peasants and had to offer a compromise in 1929, which it then implemented with the targeted assassination of hundreds of Cristero leaders. Tens of thousands were killed in this nasty second civil war brought on by the religious persecution imposed by the revolutionary regime, which was renewed with greater intensity in 1935, when religious services were temporarily almost abolished. Full religious freedom did not come to Mexico until after the beginning of the presidency of Manuel Avila Camacho in 1940. The best account is by the French scholar J. Meyer, *La cristiada* (Mexico City, 1973), 3 vols., now in its twentieth printing; see also Meyer, *El sinarquismo, el cardenismo y la*

the beginning in Spain; by June 1936 religious services would be completely suppressed in some districts, and after the civil war began the mass murder of Catholics and clergy would follow, far beyond anything seen in Mexico.

During 1932, as reforms moved to labor affairs, the army, and the granting of Catalan autonomy, opinion polarized further. The political center – the Radicals – dropped out of the governing coalition because of their opposition to the Socialists. By September 1933 the alliance between the Socialists and the left republicans had broken down as well, setting the stage for new elections in November 1933.

The first groups to reject the new regime in favor of violent revolution were the anarcho-syndicalists of the FAI-CNT (Iberian Anarchist Confederation–National Confederation of Labor) and the very small Spanish Communist Party (PCE). Activists of the FAI-CNT used the freedom of the new regime to wreak vengeance on their enemies, committing twenty-three political assassinations in Barcelona during the first days, and initiating violent strikes. Subsequently they launched three successive revolutionary insurrections in January 1932, January 1933, and December 1933. They did not consider these outbursts as civil war per se, but as the beginning of what they hoped would be a nationwide uprising against the capitalist system. Though each insurrection extended across half a dozen or more provinces, each was poorly organized and none threatened in any way to destabilize the country, despite acts of terrorism and the deaths of several hundred people.[4] Only part of the movement participated in these outbursts, but the broad repression that followed recognized few distinctions. The PCE followed the Comintern's Third Period strategy of seeking to promote insurrection and revolution, rejecting the Republic as the "beginning of Spanish fascism," but was too weak to accomplish anything. In addition, small sectors of the radical right organized an attempted military revolt in September 1932, which gained almost no support at all, but cost the lives of ten people.

During 1932 conservative forces finally began to organize themselves, primarily in the form of the Spanish Confederation of Autonomous Rightist Groups (CEDA), henceforth the largest single political party in the country. The size and strength of this Catholic and conservative resurgence came as a shock to the left, who had been convinced that historical change had thoroughly eroded Spanish conservatism.

Iglesia, 1937–1947 (Mexico City, 2003); A. Azkue, *La cristiada: Los cristeros mexicanos (1926–1941)* (Barcelona, 2000); and L. López Beltrán, *La persecución religiosa en México* (Mexico City, 1987). From a different perspective, see H. G. Campbell, "The Radical Right in Mexico, 1929–1949" (Ph.D. diss., UCLA, 1968).

[4] The principal historian of Spanish anarchism is Julián Casanova. See his *Anarchism, the Republic and Civil War in Spain: 1931–1939* (London, 2004) and *Anarquismo y violencia política en la España del siglo XX* (Zaragoza, 2007), and J. Brademas, *Anarquismo y revolución en España (1930–1937)* (Barcelona, 1934). The best review of anarcho-syndicalist doctrine is J. Paniagua Fuentes, *La larga marcha hacia la anarquía. Pensamiento y acción del movimiento libertario* (Madrid, 2008).

The elections of 1933 produced results almost diametrically opposed to those of the first republican elections two years earlier, the CEDA winning a plurality though not a majority of the seats. For the time being the Radicals, as the number two party, led a minority government that was supported by the CEDA. Leaders of the left republicans and the Socialists responded with demands that the president of the Republic, Niceto Alcalá Zamora, cancel the electoral results and permit them to change the rules for new elections in a way that would guarantee victory for a reunited left. They did not charge that the balloting had been unfair, for in fact these had been the first fully democratic elections in Spanish history,[5] but simply protested the fact that victory had gone to the center and right. Their position was that the Republic could never achieve the strongly reformist goals that they espoused unless it was permanently dominated by the left. They did not propose dictatorship but something more like a Turkish or Latin American "guided democracy," semipluralist in nature but not a full electoral democracy, which was an unprecedented position for the left in any Western European democracy during these years.

In November 1933, President Alcalá Zamora, a Catholic liberal, rejected four different requests from left republicans and Socialists to cancel the electoral results and change the rules ex post facto. At that point, he insisted on fixed rules and uncertain outcomes.[6] Nonetheless, the fact that most of the Republic's founders rejected electoral democracy as soon as they lost an election meant that prospects for democracy, as distinct from a revolutionary outcome, were at best uncertain.

The radicalization of Spanish Socialism (the Spanish Socialist Workers Party – PSOE) and of its affiliated labor movement, the UGT (General Union of Labor), puzzled observers and commentators, because it seemed to go counter to the trend of all other major Western European socialist or social democratic parties. The chief issue for Spanish Socialists was at first not revolution but simply political power, which they had lost with the breakup of the leftist coalition government in September 1933. This was followed by decisive defeat in the elections of November, in which the electoral law of heavily weighted disproportionate representation (ironically engineered by the left themselves to favor their own interests) had a disastrous effect on the now disunited left. From that point the revolutionary process began to accelerate, despite the complete failure of the isolated anarcho-syndicalist insurrection of December 1933. The most extreme Socialist leaders declared that the party must undergo "Bolshevization," though it was not becoming truly Leninist so much as it tended now to reflect the position of the "Second and a half International," led by the vigorous Austrian Socialists, who refused all collaboration with

---

[5] R. Villa García, *La República en las urnas: El despertar de la democracia en España* (Madrid, 2011), presents a detailed, exhaustive, and definitive study of these elections.

[6] On the role of Alcalá Zamora, see A. Alcalá Galve, *Alcalá-Zamora y la agonía de la República* (Seville, 2002).

other forces (though the latter also rejected violence so long as the Austrian Republic remained a democracy).

The Socialists' turn toward violence was exhibited during the electoral campaign, when they were responsible for the majority of incidents, which resulted in at least twenty-six deaths. In January 1934 a Revolutionary Committee was set up and prepared a program that called for the nationalization of land (though not of industry), dissolution of all religious orders, and dissolution of the army and civil guard. It also called for a democratically elected parliament to ratify all these changes, once the revolutionaries had seized power, but such language was evidently Aesopian, since a truly democratically elected parliament could not be expected to ratify the Socialist takeover.[7] The committee's instructions declared that the insurrection must have "all the characteristics of civil war" and be organized on a fully national level.[8] Though these ambitions were never completely realized, the eventual Socialist revolt was the most broadly organized insurrection to occur in interwar Europe.

Meanwhile, Manuel Azaña and other left republican leaders developed the politics of tactical ambiguity that would characterize their behavior during the next three years, maneuvering between legality and revolution without ever directly endorsing the latter. Between April and July 1934 they engaged in a lengthy series of initiatives that insisted on the "hyperlegitimacy" of an exclusively leftist government, irrespective of elections. On the one hand, they sought to encourage, or force, President Alcalá Zamora to appoint a minority government of the left, despite the absence of support in parliament. If he would not agree, the alternative was to force the president's hand with a sort of "peaceful pronunciamiento," based on an alliance of the left republicans, the left Catalan nationalists (Esquerra), and the Socialists. This could form an alternative government in Barcelona, supported by a Socialist general strike, which might convince the president that it must be allowed to take office. The left republicans were probably influenced by the trend in Europe during the previous four years toward "presidential," at least partially extra-parliamentary, governments, though in Germany this had ended in disaster. Nonetheless, the maneuver proved impossible, because the Socialists, fixed on revolution, refused any collaboration with "bourgeois" parties, however leftist.

If Alcalá Zamora refused to allow the left to form an extra-parliamentary government, the latter hoped that he would preserve the existing formula of a minority government led by Alejandro Lerroux and his centrist Radicals,

---

[7] J. Avilés Farré, "Los socialistas y la insurrección socialista de 1934," in Avilés Farré, ed., "Violencia y política en España, 1875–1936," *Espacio, Tiempo y Forma*, Serie V – Historia Contemporánea, t. 20 (2008), 129–57, is a good recent analysis of the Socialists' goals.

[8] From the text of the instructions in S. Juliá, ed., *Largo Caballero: Escritos de la República*, quoted in P. Moa, *Los orígenes de la Guerra Civil Española* (Madrid, 1999), 404–14. For facsimiles of some of the numerous incendiary announcements of the Socialists during 1933–34, see the second part of Moa's *1934: Comienza la Guerra Civil. El PSOE y la Esquerra emprenden la contienda* (Madrid, 2004). Moa's writings on the insurrection of 1934 have been widely denounced, but none of the data he has presented has been disproven.

forever denying the CEDA any opportunity to participate. Yet the latter's chief, José María Gil Robles, announced prior to the reopening of parliament on 1 October that his party would demand several seats in a new coalition that would give the Republic its first normal majority government in a year. Alcalá Zamora could have resisted this demand only at the price of new elections, which he realized were unjustified.

Entry of three *cedistas* into a center-right coalition government dominated by Lerroux and the Radicals then became the nominal justification for the revolutionary insurrection launched by the Socialists and their new Worker Alliance, together with the Catalan Esquerra, on 4 October. The left's argument was that both Mussolini and Hitler had legally taken power with only a minority of seats in a coalition government. Such a rationale hinged on categorizing the CEDA as "fascist," even though the new Catholic party had scrupulously observed legality and, unlike the Socialists, had carefully eschewed violence, even though a number of its militants had been murdered by the left. As Trotsky emphasized in his own writings during this period, even violent and aggressive revolutionaries seek some form of legitimacy and prefer to present their actions as defensive. The Bolsheviks claimed to be seizing power for the soviets and guaranteeing democratic elections; the Spanish Socialists claimed that they had to act to defend the Republic from "fascism." By this point, however, the PSOE had more characteristics of a fascist organization than did the CEDA, as the veteran Socialist leader Julián Besteiro publicly pointed out. The insurrection also assumed that it was in the interest of Spain – or at least of the left – to abandon parliamentary government, though such a position was dubious in the extreme.

Though the insurrection broke out in fifteen provinces, its only success was achieved in Asturias, where it seized the province's entire mining basin and most of its capital, Oviedo. Units of the army had to engage in two weeks of combat before the revolt was quelled. The revolutionaries committed numerous atrocities, murdering more than fifty priests and civilians, carrying out widespread destruction and arson, and looting at least fifteen million *pesetas* from banks, most of which was never recovered. In putting down the insurrection, the military engaged in a number of summary executions, estimates of which range from a low of 19 to a high of 100 or more. Altogether, nearly 1,400 people were killed, the majority of them revolutionaries. Some 15,000 were arrested, and during the weeks that followed there was mistreatment of prisoners.[9]

Insurrection against parliamentary governments was hardly unprecedented in postwar Europe, the first, as we have seen, having been launched by Finnish Socialists in 1918. In Germany, there had been confused efforts by the Spartaists in 1919, by the Communists in 1921, and then separate efforts by

[9] There is a lengthy literature on this traumatic and polarizing event. The most detailed account is P. I. Taibo II, *Asturias 1934* (Gijón, 1984), 2 vols., which is favorable to the revolutionaries. See, in addition to those works previously cited, F. Aguado Sánchez, *La revolución de octubre de 1934* (Madrid, 1972); B. Díaz Nosty, *La comuna asturiana* (Madrid, 1974); and A. del Rosal, *1934: el movimiento revolucionario de octubre* (Madrid, 1983).

the Communists and Nazis in 1923. Only the civil war in Finland had equaled or exceeded the scale of the Spanish insurrection of 1934. From this time forward the possibility of future civil war began to hang like a pall over Spanish affairs, yet the insurrection had been completely defeated, and the possibility remained of consolidating a parliamentary regime.

The centrist government of 1934 led by Lerroux had been the fairest and most balanced that the Republic had experienced. The pendulum moved toward the right in the center-right governments that followed in 1934–35, yet, rather than opening the door to "fascism," they scrupulously maintained constitutional government, while using it to reverse several of the earlier republican reforms. Indeed, with the revolutionaries defeated, the next fifteen months would be the most peaceful in the brief history of the Republic, with comparatively few acts of political violence.

Beyond changes in policy, the other great drama of 1935 was the campaign about the repression. Spain was full of atrocity stories, the right recounting and embellishing the atrocities of the revolutionaries, the left launching a gigantic propaganda campaign (supported by Comintern funds and the European left generally) exaggerating the extent and brutality of the repression and portraying the revolutionary perpetrators as victims.[10]

The most notable aspect of the repression of 1935, however, was its comparative leniency. Hundreds of revolutionaries were prosecuted by military court-martial, but only two were executed, one of these clearly convicted of multiple murders, the other a military mutineer. The Socialist Party was never outlawed; some of its centers remained open throughout; and after the first weeks the leading prisoners enjoyed special privileges. An international investigative commission was permitted to visit them, and in little more than a year the revolutionaries would be allowed to participate in new elections to regain peacefully the power they had attempted to win by violence. The repression by the Spanish Republic was historically unprecedented in its leniency, and did not bear the slightest comparison to the infinitely more brutal policies followed in roughly similar circumstances by the Third Republic in France (1871), the Weimar Republic in Germany (1918–23), the parliamentary regime in Italy (1920–22), and in a number of other countries.

The repression in fact fell between two stools. It was enough to infuriate the perpetrators and provide them with their chief propaganda theme, but in general was so limited that it failed altogether to repress them in any lasting manner, serving only to stimulate the recovery of the left. Since the government failed to effect genuine repression, it might have been better advised to follow a policy of conciliation. Conversely, however, the case can be made that the repression, initially severe in the mining basin, should have been applied more, not less, rigorously. As it was, it failed to uphold constitutional law and to punish those who had so egregiously violated it. The eventual policy of

---

[10] B. D. Bunk, *Ghosts of Passion: Martyrdom, Gender, and the Origins of the Spanish Civil War* (Durham, N.C., 2007), studies the propaganda campaign, its images and influence.

total amnesty, which was the way things worked out in 1936, with the perpetrators subsequently empowered to prosecute their victims, was a travesty that scarcely served the cause of democracy or constitutional government.

The center-right maintained uninterrupted democratic government; support for fascism was almost nonexistent and did not increase; and many civil liberties were soon restored, followed by total restitution after little more than a year. A more genuine repression might have been the only way to check the revolutionary process and save parliamentary government and democratic elections, just as would have been the case in Weimar Germany in 1932–33. In both countries, indulgent policies toward extremists opened the door to disaster.

The argument used by the left, that the CEDA was "fascist," soon fell by its own weight. Had that been the case, a failed insurrection, which for the time being gravely weakened the left, would have only increased the danger, but in fact almost the opposite occurred. The CEDA's youth movement often employed extremist language, but never moved to extremist action, and in practice the party restricted itself to parliamentary initiatives.

Much more negative, however, was the fact that the CEDA concentrated more on undoing aspects of the leftist reforms than on developing a positive program. If it expected to play a greater role, it needed to come fully to terms with republican democracy not merely in practice, but also in theory. The CEDA's great limitation was that the Christian democrats in its ranks remained a minority, so that, like the moderate left, it practiced a politics of long-term ambiguity, a major obstacle to the consolidation of democracy. If the moderate left insisted on a sort of guided democracy, the moderate right aimed ultimately for a basic constitutional change that would have made the Spanish system more corporate and authoritarian. Even more than the conflict between extremes, this basic tension between moderate left and moderate right made democratic consolidation very difficult, if not impossible. Even so, it need not have condemned the country to civil war.

When the governing coalition broke down in September 1935 as the result of two petty financial scandals that eroded the strength of the Radicals,[11] Gil Robles logically expected to become prime minister of a CEDA-led coalition. Instead, President Alcalá Zamora abused his constitutional prerogative by arbitrarily handing power to an independent centrist prime minister who had no significant support, his administration lasting barely three months. The republican president then refused to follow normal constitutional practice. On the grounds that the CEDA was too rightist, he appointed as prime minister a personal crony, Manuel Portela Valladares, who did not even have a seat in parliament. Lacking support, Portela would have no alternative but to ask the president for new elections, even though the existing chamber still had nearly two years of its mandate remaining. Alcalá Zamora's manipulation

---

[11] J. C. García Rodríguez, *El caso Strauss: el escándalo que precipitó el final de la II República* (León, 2008).

and restriction of parliament, though technically legal, may be compared to the three years of presidential government authorized by Hindenburg in Germany, the difference being that Hindenburg had little alternative, whereas a parliamentary majority was readily available in Spain.

The decision to move toward premature elections was his greatest mistake of all, for his scheme to have Portela Valladares create a new center coalition from the seat of government was a stratagem of the old regime that was doomed to failure under the politically mobilized Republic. His connivance in undercutting the Radical Party (his own great rival) succeeded, but at the cost of destroying the main bulwark of liberal democracy. As a result, he set the stage for an election that was neither necessary nor, under existing conditions, a routine test of opinion, but rather a polarized and plebiscitary contest, with both left and right inflamed, each determined to impose an alternative system.

For the elections of 16 February 1936, the left remedied its preceding error by forming a great coalition that included all the left republicans and all the Marxist parties, one that also enjoyed a certain amount of support from the anarcho-syndicalists. Though the Communists remained of scant importance, the coalition agreed to adopt the Comintern's new term of Popular Front, even though that was distasteful to some of the more moderate left republicans. By comparison, the center found itself isolated, and the right formed a competing alliance that was considerably less inclusive.

The elections of 16 February 1936 were generally free and fair, though the process was less complete and orderly than the elections of 1933, with early returns showing a slight margin in favor of the left. On the night of the elections and for several days following, the left then repeated its tactics of 13–14 April 1931, with large crowds taking to the streets and sometimes occupying public buildings, though violence was limited. The Portela Valladares government completely lost its nerve and refused to apply martial law, fearing another insurrection. It resigned within forty-eight hours, ignoring its constitutional responsibility to record the election results accurately, and a new left republican government under Manuel Azaña took office on 19 February. This was technically a minority administration, since the Socialists refused to enter a "bourgeois" coalition, but was supported by the majority vote of the other Popular Front parties in parliament.

With the exception of a very few districts, the balloting had been orderly, though the right (and, later, President Alcalá Zamora) would charge that in some districts illegal leftist takeovers had falsified the returns. At any rate, the Popular Front was the recognized victor, though its margin in popular votes was scarcely more than one percent.[12] The left then dominated the second round, exercising such coercion that the right withdrew from participation, and when the parliament's Electoral Commission met on 24 March to verify

---

[12] J. Tusell et al., *Las elecciones del Frente Popular* (Madrid, 1971), 2 vols.; J. J. Linz and J. de Miguel, "Hacia un análisis de las elecciones de 1936 en España," *Revista Española de Opinión Pública*, 48 (April–June 1977), 27–67.

the results, the Popular Front used its majority to invalidate a large number of victories by the right, arbitrarily changing the results for thirty-two seats, all of them taken from the center and right. Once all these manipulations were complete, the Popular Front held two-thirds of the seats in parliament. Worse was yet to come, for in the provinces of Cuenca and Granada completely new elections were ordered for 5 May. Extreme physical coercion was employed to exclude the right from participating, and two provinces that normally voted for the right were swept by the left.[13] Democratic elections had apparently come to an end in Spain; the balloting in the German elections of March 1933 had been more honest, despite Nazi terror in the streets, a sad commentary on the political decay of the Second Republic and the advance of the revolutionary process. This gives the lie to the left's oft-repeated contention that the military revolt of 18 July overthrew democracy. The military rebels would have no intention of restoring democracy, but they cannot fairly be accused of destroying it, because electoral democracy had ceased to exist in Spain.

By the late winter there had developed what most historians, following Gabriel Jackson,[14] call a "pre-revolutionary situation." Conditions in Spain clearly matched those posited by the Tocquevillian or behaviorist theory of revolution – that revolutionary situations do not normally develop in times of intense misery and oppression, but rather amid conditions of greater well-being and freedom. Major new frustrations occurring in such circumstances – in this case, the Depression, the left's loss of power in 1933, the reversal of several reforms by the right in 1935, and the defeat in four consecutive revolutionary insurrections, followed by repression, however limited – produced intense radicalization.

A key factor was the role of the moderate left. In France, the Radical Party and most of the Socialists eschewed extremism in 1936, but Azaña and the Spanish left republicans had no interest in a consensual democracy with equal rights for all. They had insisted since the beginning of the Republic on alliance with the revolutionaries as the only means of achieving a complete leftist majority that could permanently exclude the center and right. The Republic's first historian, the noted Catalan journalist Josep Pla, termed this Azaña's "ideological Kerenskyism."[15] Allying with the center would have required democratic moderation and compromise, something that was anathema to the left republicans, who were certain, like Kerensky, that they knew how to deal with revolutionaries.

The descent into civil war began with the elections, and later many Spaniards would conclude that civil war became inevitable, but such a conclusion is doubtful, for there are few inevitable outcomes in history. The tendency that had existed on the part of leftist and reformist orators for the previous

[13] R. Villa García, "The Failure of Electoral Modernization: The Elections of May 1936 in Granada," *Journal of Contemporary History*, 44:3 (July 2009), 401–29.

[14] G. Jackson, *The Spanish Republic and Civil War 1931–1939* (Princeton, N.J., 1965), 194.

[15] J. Pla, *Historia de la Segunda República española* (Barcelona, 1940), 4 vols., passim.

generation to invoke the need for civil war as a way of effecting a clean break with the past merely constituted a rhetorical trope, not a design for action. The civil war became inevitable only in mid-July, in the very final days, and even then most sectors of both the left and the right did not seek a genuine civil war, raising the question – did anyone other than the rebellious military really desire a civil war?

The answer is not the left or the right in general, but the more dedicated revolutionaries on the left and the hard core of the extreme right. It should be understood that most proponents of collective violence in Spain did not think in terms of a long, highly destructive civil war, just as in 1860–61 very few Americans believed that any armed conflict between the states would last four years and claim nearly 700,000 lives (nearly 2.5 percent of the entire population, or twice the proportionate death toll in Spain). On both the revolutionary left and the extreme right the idea was that a short, sharp conflict would be resolved within at most a few weeks, not in months or years.

At its national reunification congress in Zaragoza in May 1936, the anarcho-syndicalists of the FAI-CNT reaffirmed their goal of using "the path of insurrection" to achieve power, just as they had attempted three times in recent years. Their leaders made it clear, however, that the time had not come for another such effort at what the anarchists called "revolutionary gymnastics," and at no time prior to the eighteenth of July did they formulate any such plan,[16] though their followers engaged in numerous strikes and acts of disorder and violence.

Revolutionary Marxists more directly embraced the concept of civil war as a necessary step in consolidating the dictatorship of the proletariat – indeed, as indispensable. This had been the position of the Communists prior to August 1935 and remained that of the "*caballeristas*," the main sector of revolutionary socialists who followed Largo Caballero. Luis Araquistain, their chief theoretician, avowed this explicitly,[17] as did Joaquín Maurín, the leader of the new Leninist revolutionary Worker Party of Marxist Unification (POUM).[18] The civil war concepts of Araquistain and Maurín were similar – a revolutionary civil war was inevitable but would be brief, since the left would win quickly. They held that the long, enormously destructive Russian civil war would not have to be repeated, since the revolutionary left was proportionately stronger in Spain, while the danger of counterrevolutionary foreign intervention was smaller. This was, supposedly, due to the fact that by 1935–36 European relations were becoming so tense that potential counterrevolutionary states would lack the freedom of initiative to intervene, or so the Marxist-Leninist theorists thought. And should foreign intervention take place, both theorists

---

[16] J. Getman-Eraso, "'Cease Fire, Comrades!' Anarcho-Syndicalist Revolutionary Prophecy, Anti-Fascism and the Origins of the Spanish Civil War," *Totalitarian Movements and Political Religions*, 9:1 (March 2008), 93–114.

[17] In his writings in his monthly *Leviatán* and in the new *caballerista* newspaper *Claridad* (Madrid).

[18] In his book *Hacia la segunda revolución* (Barcelona, 1935) and elsewhere.

were convinced that they could depend on the Soviet Union to thwart it. (This overlooked the fact that the biggest difference in Spain, as compared to Russia, was that the right was not so moribund and was capable of a much stronger, more organized reaction than the center and right in Russia, and represented a much larger proportion of the population. The calculation regarding foreign intervention was equally disastrously mistaken, but then revolutionary theorists are normally wrong. It is, so to speak, an occupational hazard.)

Such concepts, however, were not the official policy of either the Socialist or the Communist Party. The *caballeristas* had no clear strategy of civil war, but planned to continue a pre-revolutionary offensive of strikes, property seizures, violence, and other acts of disorder in order to goad the military into a counterrevolutionary revolt, which was confidently expected to be a feeble effort easily overcome by a revolutionary general strike. This was supposed to clear the way for *caballerista* leadership of a revolutionary government. As will be seen, to some extent that was the way it worked out, the miscalculation being that the military revolt was more powerful than anticipated.

The Communist Party was growing rapidly but remained much smaller, and Comintern planning had changed drastically under the Popular Front tactic. Moreover, electoral victory had given the left complete power over both government and parliament – something totally unprecedented outside Germany and Scandinavia – with the ability to initiate the first phases of a revolutionary process by nominally legal means. Hence the Communists discouraged any notion of civil war, which could only render problematic an otherwise guaranteed political outcome. Only Santiago Carrillo and other very young leaders of the newly Communist-dominated Unified Socialist Youth (JSU) momentarily presented a different analysis. In one speech that spring, Carrillo declared that the inevitable civil war would create a powerful new revolutionary army, as in the Soviet Union, which would be the instrument for the completion of the revolution, but this sort of talk was promptly discouraged by the party leadership.

For Azaña and Santiago Casares Quiroga, the two minority left republican prime ministers in the final five months, the top priority was to maintain the Popular Front alliance with the revolutionary parties. This meant indulging their extended campaign of pre-revolutionary disorder and violence, hoping that somehow it would subside. To have taken vigorous action against the revolutionaries would have required not merely a police crackdown, possibly imposing martial law, but also coming to terms more broadly with the center and moderate right, an unthinkable alternative for the left republican leaders, at least until it was too late. Thus the government also eventually began to assume the inevitability of a military revolt, though here its calculation was different. After replacing Azaña as prime minister in May,[19] Casares Quiroga

---

[19] For more than two years, the chief demand of the left had been the convening of new elections that would make possible defeat of the right. Once Alcalá Zamora did so (arbitrarily and prematurely), making possible a leftist victory, the left promptly impeached him for not having done it even earlier, using as justification an extremely dubious interpretation of the constitution. Elevation of Azaña to the presidency of the Republic in May 1936 virtually completed the leftist domination of civic institutions.

would count on being able easily to defeat a weak military rebellion, the result of which would give the left republican government, not the revolutionaries, greater strength and authority. The fundamental mistake of nearly everyone on the left was their complete scorn and disdain for the right, whom they judged to have been rendered impotent by historical change.

During the final months there were several proposals for a new government. The most widely discussed involved a much broader coalition under the semi-moderate Socialist leader Indalecio Prieto, the chief rival of Largo Caballero. Prieto indicated his intention to repress violence firmly, achieving what he called "the disarming of Spain," satisfying the demands of the worker groups by accelerating social and economic reforms (as distinct from tolerating the growing strike wave with its often exorbitant demands and numerous illegal seizures of property), and eliminating the danger of civil war by undertaking the drastic political purge of the military from which Azaña and Casares Quiroga shrank. All such plans, however, foundered on the refusal of the majoritarian Largo Caballero sector of Socialists to permit any Socialist participation in a "bourgeois" coalition. Azaña may have been a Kerenskyist, but Largo Caballero was not a collaborating reformist. There were other proposals for a temporary Republican "constitutional dictatorship" to restore law and order, as well as a carefully thought out proposal by Felipe Sánchez Román of the minuscule National Republican Party for a broader left-center coalition that would impose law and order and enforce strictly constitutional government, which the Socialists might join when and if they were willing to accept such a program. These last proposals were rejected by the left republican government as too far-reaching and requiring the dismantling of the Popular Front.

The broader fantasy was the dream of Azaña and most of the left republicans that by means of some political magic the moderate left could dominate an only semidemocratic leftist Republic that would exclude both the center and the right, while somehow restraining the revolutionaries. These were the illusions of petit bourgeois dilettante radicals that ignored the reality that by 1936 only three kinds of government were possible in Spain – a broad republican coalition that might bring together most of the left-center, center, and moderate right; a revolutionary dictatorship; or an authoritarian regime of the right. Once the first alternative had been rejected by the government, the stage was set for an all-out conflict between the other two. Thus, though neither Azaña nor Casares desired civil war (and would even have regarded such a prospect with horror), their policies had the effect of encouraging, rather than restraining, such an outcome. The irony of their situation was that it might be conjectured that a more firm, prudent, and orderly government that applied the law and maintained better order might have gone on, at least temporarily, to consolidate its own version of an all-left Republic (since the right had been rendered impotent), had it done so in a more legalistic, coherently administered manner, but that would have required the full cooperation of the Socialists, which was not forthcoming. As it was, under its existing policy the government could not restrain the revolutionaries, a fundamental contradiction that merely points up the fact that the left republican policy represented an impossible attempt to square the circle.

In France, the Popular Front also won a narrow but decisive electoral victory at the end of May, which led the following month to an enormous strike wave that was larger in both absolute and proportionate terms than the massive strike wave in Spain. The difference was that the mood of French militants was more pragmatic than revolutionary and produced little violence, while the new government in Paris acted promptly and resolutely to arbitrate an end to the conflict, on terms favorable to labor. The divided Spanish labor movements were more chaotic and harder to deal with, and the Spanish government was irresolute, making many concessions but unable to articulate a decisive policy.

Critics of the situation in Spain during June and July spoke in terms of chaos, anarchy, and preparation for revolution. As early as April the foreign diplomatic corps in Madrid consulted among themselves concerning how to react if and when violent revolution broke out. This prompts the question – how great was the danger? The lengthy series of abuses, assaults on property, and political violence in Spain during the spring and early summer of 1936 was without precedent for a modern European country not undergoing total revolution. These included a massive, violent, and destructive strike wave, large-scale illegal seizures of farmland in the south, a wave of arson and destruction of property, arbitrary closure of Catholic schools, seizure of churches and church properties in some areas, broad extension of censorship, thousands of arbitrary arrests, impunity of criminal action for thousands of members of Popular Front parties, manipulation and politicization of justice, arbitrary dissolution of rightist organizations, completely coercive by-elections in Cuenca and Granada that excluded all opposition, subversion of the security forces, and a great growth in political violence, resulting in 300 or more deaths.[20] Moreover, the takeover of local and provincial governments, decreed by Azaña in a large part of the country, created conditions of coercive local administration somewhat similar to those produced by the Italian Fascist takeover of local governments in northern Italy during the summer of 1922, yet as of early July the right remained divided and impotent. There had been no revolt against oppressive conditions so extreme that they would already have provoked rebellion in some other countries.

Several historians have recognized that a kind of pre-revolutionary situation had developed but that it was doubtful that a successful collectivist revolution could ever have been carried out because of the extreme division among the left, a problem that also concerned some of the revolutionary leaders themselves. Even if the revolutionaries managed to seize power, the result might logically have been an intra-revolutionary civil war, as developed twice in the republican zone during the conflict that ensued. The question is a valid

---

[20] The most exhaustive study, J. Blázquez Miguel, "Conflictividad en la España del Frente Popular (febrero–julio de 1936)," *Historia 16*, 328 (August, 2003), 76–86, presents a total of 444 killings, but the methodology involved is uncertain.

one, but there is no doubt that there existed a pre-revolutionary climate of lawlessness, coercion, and increasing violence that would have been intolerable in any country.[21] Many major rebellions and civil wars have been initiated with less direct provocation.[22]

The rightist political forces were divided and virtually impotent, having completely lost any institutional power. Elements of the military began to conspire soon after the Popular Front victory, but the army officer corps was also divided and very reluctant to act. Two years earlier, on 31 March 1934, two ultra-rightist monarchist groups had signed an agreement with the Mussolini government in Rome that would have provided Italian financial support, military training facilities, and a limited amount of arms to assist a revolt, but the monarchists lacked support within Spain, and this agreement had become a dead letter.[23] The small fascist movement, Falange Española, had been outlawed in March but fought back against the revolutionaries and also targeted several government officials, adding to the mayhem and violence, but this underground movement had no capacity to produce an insurrection.[24]

A catalyst for explosion erupted in the early hours of 13 July, when the monarchist leader José Calvo Sotelo, who had become the leading opposition spokesman in parliament,[25] was kidnapped from his home and murdered. The immediate incentive stemmed from the street killing of the Socialist police officer José del Castillo, slain a few hours before, apparently by Falangists. The death of Calvo Sotelo created a sensation not merely because it had happened,

---

[21] The most direct contrast with Spain in 1936 was Sweden, another country late to industrialize and one where universal male suffrage was introduced later (1907) than in Spain. Moreover, according to one analysis, Sweden had lost more industrial workdays to strikes than any other country between 1890 and 1936. Violence was also sometimes present in Sweden, where as late as 1931 five strikers were shot down by state forces. Nonetheless, in Sweden a general framework of mutual recognition and arbitration was signed between organized labor and employers in 1936, opening the way to the corporative welfare state.

In their unpublished paper "Civil War Spain versus Swedish Harmony: The Quality of Government Factor," Victor Lapuente and Bo Rothstein argue that a major difference stemmed from the separation of politics and administration in Sweden, which developed much greater state capacity for honest administration not subject to political manipulation or the spoils system, convincing Social Democrats that they could work within the system.

[22] To take the American examples, the great war of the American Revolution was sparked by a modest tax increase. The lives and property of the colonists were never threatened. The movement of secession in the South in 1861 was a response not to any intervention in the lives and property of the Southerners, but to a longer-term political fear in the face of Lincoln's election, spurning a constitutional amendment that would have permanently guaranteed slavery in the states where it existed. On neither occasion was there a breakdown of law and order that directly threatened lives or interests. Many other examples might be found.

[23] F. Olaya Morales, *La conspiración contra la República* (Barcelona, 1979); J. Gil Pecharromán, *Conservadores subversivos: La derecha autoritaria alfonsina (1913–1936)* (Madrid, 1994); M. Blinkhorn, *Carlism and Crisis in Spain 1931–1939* (Cambridge, 1975); I. Saz, *Mussolini contra II República (1931–1936)* (Valencia, 1986).

[24] The role of the Falange is summarized in my *Fascism in Spain 1923–1977* (Madison, Wisc., 1999), 185–208.

[25] A. Bullón de Mendoza, *José Calvo Sotelo* (Barcelona, 2004).

but even more because of the way it had happened. He was not shot down on a street corner like Castillo and so many others, but illegally arrested and murdered by a detachment of state police. Moreover, the detachment was totally irregular in composition, made up of leftist police, on- and off-duty, combined with Socialist revolutionaries, reflecting a policy by which the left republican government had sometimes mixed regular police and revolutionary militants, in a manner slightly reminiscent of the Hitler regime's use of SA and SS troopers as *Hilfspolizei* in its first weeks. For very much of conservative opinion, all this represented the climax of the left republican government's partisanship and toleration or encouragement of pre-revolutionary activity. Even though the government's claim that the murderers had acted strictly on their own was probably correct and was to some extent accepted by conservative leaders, this made little difference to the latter because there was no sign of change in a state policy that had gone from bad to worse and, it was now thought, could no longer be trusted in any way.

On 13 July the Azaña/Casares Quiroga government faced the last chance of averting civil war. Casares Quiroga should immediately have been replaced by a firm moderate who would initiate a policy of conciliation accompanied by the strict imposition of law and order, for which means were readily at hand. There was no need to fear the response of the revolutionaries, since the army would have almost unanimously supported such a program. Instead, the government proceeded in the opposite direction, merely redoubling its existing policy. Hundreds of rightists were arrested, as if they had been responsible for killing one of their own leaders, extending the standard policy of blaming the victim, and the monarchist center in Madrid was closed down. There was no review of police policy, only an abortive investigation of the crime, and the authors of the deed soon came out of hiding (carefully protected by the Socialist leaders, since most were Socialists) to receive promotions as soon as the civil war began.

It has been said that the magnicide was virtually irrelevant, since minority sectors of the military were already planning to rebel against the government in a matter of days. That was their intention, but the dramatic killing had an electric effect on opponents of the government and greatly expanded support for the insurrection, transforming a weak and limping effort into a revolt that gained the support of more than half the army, creating conditions of genuine civil war. The best example was that of Gen. Francisco Franco, the most prominent of all the younger generals, formerly chief of staff and currently military commander of the Canary Islands. As recently as 12 July he had told the conspirators that he thought there was still a chance that the government could rectify the situation, but as soon as he learned of the way in which Calvo Sotelo had been kidnapped and murdered, he informed the conspirators of his complete commitment, and from that moment, so far as anyone knows, never looked back.

The revolt has often been described as a military coup, but this is inaccurate. A coup d'etat requires centralized organization and execution, seizing the seat of government almost immediately, as in Greece in 1967 or Chile in 1973. Brig. Gen. Emilio Mola, director of the conspiracy, always lacked the means for such a mission. He recognized that the revolt would doubtless fail in Madrid and several other large cities, and that it must rely on the veteran combat units in the Moroccan Protectorate, as well as on inexperienced troops in barracks in the conservative districts of northern Spain. There could be no coup in Madrid; instead, it would be necessary to organize columns of troops in other districts to seize the capital and several other large cities, where revolutionary workers were strong. This was a chancy scheme, but the only hope that the conspirators had, and, if successful, would require a kind of mini–civil war that would probably last at least a few weeks.

The plan was poorly coordinated, calling for military rebels to declare martial law in various parts of the country in a series of echelons from south to north over three days. This was more like a nineteenth-century pronunciamiento than a twentieth-century coup d'etat, and very nearly failed altogether. The revolt began prematurely in Spanish Morocco about 5 P.M. on Friday, 17 July, and spread into parts of southern Spain the following day, with the first rebel units in the north beginning their revolt later that evening, and the insurrection becoming generalized on the nineteenth. This created a state of confusion on both sides.

For some time the Casares Quiroga government had accepted the fact that some military men were likely to rebel, but it knew that most were not eager to do so. Hence it was confident that only isolated units would be involved, and that the easy suppression of the revolt would only strengthen the government, both with regard to the right and to the revolutionary left. By the evening of 18 July, however, as more and more units joined the rebellion, Casares Quiroga grasped that it was mushrooming out of control and hastily resigned as prime minister.

That night, for the first and only time, President Azaña took decisive action to avoid civil war, but by this point he had delayed too long. He appointed as new prime minister Diego Martínez Barrio, the most moderate of the major Popular Front leaders, with the task of forming a broader new left-center coalition that would move at least some distance to the right in an effort to conciliate the rebels. This may have involved an attempt to strike a direct deal with Mola and even to offer him a place in the new government, though the evidence is uncertain. The whole initiative represented a salutary effort at compromise, and coming a few weeks earlier might have succeeded, but now was too little, too late. Mola refused any kind of compromise, while the Socialists and even some left republicans announced their unremitting opposition to the new government. Martínez Barrio resigned about 7 A.M. on the nineteenth.

At this point Azaña and the left republicans who controlled state institutions could respond in one of three ways: 1) surrender power to the rebels, as was done by Alfonso XIII in 1931 and as had been done by a number of other Spanish governments facing pronunciamientos or revolts in earlier generations; 2) proceed as in 1932, 1933, and 1934, using state institutions and the remaining security forces to try to put down the revolt in a return to law and order; 3) give way to the revolutionaries and engage in what was euphemistically termed "arming the people," that is, distributing weapons en masse to the revolutionary groups, who would be asked to play a major role in defeating the military. Given the degree of mobilization and radicalization that existed, option one was not very feasible. The rebels hardly had the strength to seize most of the large cities immediately, while the revolutionary organizations would never have accepted surrender and would have provided as much resistance as they could. Even had the government sought to avoid fighting, there would have been armed conflict, as the revolutionary leaders made clear very early on the nineteenth, though they lacked the arms and military organization to have won the contest by themselves.

Instead, Azaña and a new minority left republican government led by José Giral tried to follow options two and three simultaneously. They prepared to resist by mobilizing loyal military and security units, but doubted that enough of these were left to guarantee victory, and so within a few hours began the distribution of arms en masse to the revolutionaries (a small number of whom had already armed, or were arming, themselves). This was the consummation of Azaña's "Kerenskyist" policy; though it guaranteed a broader counter-mobilization to wage a real civil war, it had the effect of handing power in large measure to the revolutionary groups, who began to take control of most local districts and regions in what would henceforth be known as the "Republican zone," now dominated by the revolution often feared and long predicted. Azaña and Giral, reduced to a mere vestige of power, claimed that it was all the fault of the military rebels, who had rendered them helpless, though this was obviously not the full truth. To the rebels, the government action was the logical consummation of what they regarded as a pro-revolutionary policy, though that was also an oversimplification. These conditions – slightly over half the army in rebellion and facing some loyal units, much of the national police, and a large number of revolutionary militia – guaranteed that there would be real civil war, though of what duration and intensity remained uncertain.

In this manner, complex interaction between fragmentation on the one hand and polarization on the other created a crisis totally different from anything else seen in Europe between 1923 and 1936. No hegemonic force, whether democratic or authoritarian, had emerged in Spain, but instead conditions similar to those found in some countries at the end of World War I had reemerged, though in quite different form. After 1919 every attempt at insurrection and direct revolution elsewhere in Europe had failed, but in Spain full civil war erupted, combined with an explosive revolution in the leftist zone that in some ways was more extensive, and mobilized proportionately more workers and farm laborers, than anything seen during the civil war in Russia.

6

Revolution and Civil War, 1936–1939

Civil war implies some degree of equivalence of force, even if the two sides are far from equal. A unique feature of the Spanish case was the extent of the division within the armed forces. Had they been united on one side or the other, there would not have been much of a war. The Popular Front government had refrained from purging the army, for two reasons. One was the calculation that most of the military was reliable, and the other was that if the Popular Front should break down or there should be another anarchist insurrection, the full strength of the army and security forces might be needed. The government had not erred with regard to the generals in command. Very few of them joined the revolt, which in many garrisons depended primarily on middle-rank and junior officers.

Units in the peninsula, numbering less than 90,000 men, were severely divided, less than half joining the revolt, but the most crucial elements were the approximately 25,000 men in the elite, veteran combat units of the Legion and the Moroccan Regulares in the Protectorate.[1] Early on their participation became problematic, because, in this thinly organized revolt, two-thirds of the navy, including all the ships in the Mediterranean, remained loyal to the leftist government. Another special feature was the importance in Spain, where most of the army was a weak force of short-term recruits, of the approximately 65,000 men in the security forces (civil guards, assault guards, and *carabineros*, these last border and customs police), who, though lacking heavy weapons, had more carefully selected personnel and sometimes better discipline. The left retained the support of more than half of these security forces, who, even more than armed worker revolutionaries, sometimes played the key role in crushing the revolt in the larger cities, most notably in Barcelona. Moreover, financially, the Republicans (as the Popular Front forces quickly came to be called) held a huge advantage, possessing five of the seven largest cities and nearly all the modern industry, capped by

---

[1] There are a number of accounts of the revolt in the Protectorate, the most recent being J. Gil Honduvilla, *Marruecos !17 a las 17!* (Seville, 2009).

the gold and silver reserves of the Bank of Spain, the fourth largest in the world.

The gravest handicap of the Popular Front was the revolutionary explosion set off by the arming of the trade union and leftist groups, which shattered much of the government's authority. The situation in the Republican zone was a little like that in Russia in 1917, except that in the first months of the revolution the Provisional Government in Petrograd actually had somewhat more authority than the government in Madrid. For some time effective power mostly lay in the hands of the local and regional revolutionary coalitions, or what Carlos M. Rama called the "revolutionary Republican confederation of 1936–37."[2]

That half the military units in the peninsula had not rebelled was partially neutralized by the fact that the new Giral government officially dissolved all units in the insurrection, the only effect being to loosen bonds within those that had remained loyal. Moreover, the revolutionary groups distrusted all the military, so that soon not more than 10–15,000 regularly organized troops remained with the Popular Front. In the first weeks, the Republicans organized mixed columns of remnants of army units, of the civil and/or assault guards, and of the new revolutionary militia. At a wage of ten *pesetas* a day, these nominally constituted the most highly paid troops in the world, but their military effectiveness was in inverse proportion to their pay, for they lacked leadership, training, or discipline. Probably their major achievement was to play the major role in stopping the small insurgent columns in the mountains north of Madrid, temporarily safeguarding the capital. In general, however, if rebel resistance was weak, certain districts were reconquered, but wherever the rebels possessed any strength, the Republicans were stymied or fell back.

The Nationalists,[3] as the insurgents soon came to be called, also relied on mixed columns, but theirs contained more regular army units and, in the northeast, made very effective use of the Carlist Requetés, volunteers from this monarchist traditionalist movement being generally more disciplined and determined, as well as having larger numbers of Falangists. The military quality of these columns was also limited. They were able to occupy a large sector of northern Spain, where the left was weak, but had difficulty advancing into other regions, so that after some days, General Mola, the commander in the north, showed signs of discouragement.

The prospects of the Nationalists would therefore rise or fall with the elite veteran units in Morocco. Republican warships controlled all the Mediterranean coastline and blockaded Morocco, frustrating the efforts of General Franco, who had taken command of the forces in the Protectorate

---

[2] C. M. Rama, *La crisis española del siglo XX* (Mexico City, 1960), 3.

[3] The term in Spanish was "*Nacionales*," not Nationalists, but the latter became the common term abroad and nowadays is sometimes even used (incorrectly) by Spanish historians. In American English, "Nationals" is simply the name of a baseball team.

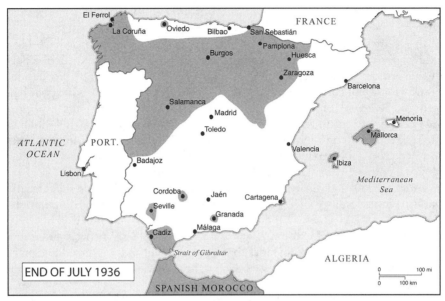

Spain, end of July 1936.

(the "Army of Africa"), to move troops to the peninsula. Possibly as many as 700 were transported by ship before the blockade became effective. Franco then showed resourcefulness in beginning the first major airlift in military history, but was severely handicapped by the fact that there were only a few small planes in Spanish Morocco. Once Hitler and Mussolini had decided to provide assistance, nine Italian medium bombers became available by the end of July, followed by a squadron of German Junkers 52 transport planes, which also doubled as improvised bombers. During the first two weeks of the airlift, possibly as many as 1,500 troops, with some equipment, were flown across, and on 5 August a small convoy ran the blockade, with crucial Italian air support. This moved another 2,500 troops, with vital equipment, in a daring operation that, according to all odds, should have been smashed by the Republican fleet. This was the sole occasion during the entire war on which Franco took a big risk, feeling at that moment that he had no choice. He got away with it, but never did anything like that again. Though the Republican fleet had proven feeble and inept, in the following days it managed to tighten the blockade. The airlift then accelerated, so that by the end of September, when the blockade was finally broken, Franco had moved a total of 16,000 troops, the remainder crossing during October.

   This was an extremely slow buildup, so slow that it would have failed completely had it not been for the disorganization of the Republicans. At the beginning of August, Franco moved his headquarters to Seville, where, in the revolt's most crucial and audacious operation, the retired Gen. Gonzalo Queipo de Llano had seized control of the nerve center of southern Spain with a small number of troops.[4] As Queipo consolidated the insurgent position in western Andalusia, Franco initiated his drive to the north on 2 August.

In recent years the military leadership and strategy of Franco have been extensively criticized for slowness and lack of imagination.[5] No doubt part of this criticism is justified, but Franco and Mola faced a complex situation. Franco could not concentrate exclusively on the drive toward Madrid, but had to organize an infrastructure and logistical base from scratch, and also provide crucial aid to other regions where the Nationalists were barely holding their own under considerable pressure. He moved first toward the northwest to Cáceres, to link up with Mola, who was almost out of ammunition. Then he briefly moved west to secure the border with Portugal, seizing Badajoz on 14 August. Throughout the war Franco would err on the side of carefully building logistics, as well as shoring up secondary fronts, succeeding impressively in an area in which all the White Russian generals had failed. It has been said that "amateurs do strategy, while professionals do logistics." Franco, a professional, certainly did logistics, but he also sometimes dispersed his forces and operations at the expense of strategic imagination and concentration of strength, his two great weaknesses as a commander.

In the main drive on Madrid, Franco calculated that he could rely on his elite units, marginally supplemented by other forces. Despite their limited numbers, they defeated larger militia columns by fixing the latter with the threat of frontal attack, then carrying out flanking maneuvers to force the militia into panicked retreats. Nonetheless, as the Nationalists neared the capital, resistance increased.

A month of successive defeats finally concentrated the minds of the revolutionary leaders, who formed a unified all–Popular Front government under Largo Caballero in Madrid on 5 September. This was the first full government of the revolution, faced with the need to build a new set of institutions, a process that would take months. On 27 September it initiated formation of a new regular "Ejército Popular" (People's Army), with regular discipline and a completely new unit structure. With the red star as official insignia, the German Communist *Rote Front* clenched-fist salute, and on 16 October the installation by decree of a system of political commissars alongside regular officers, this quickly became an attempted Spanish variant of the Red Army.[6] The first six

[4] N. Salas, *La guerra civil en Sevilla* (Seville, 2009); J. Ortiz Villalba, *Del golpe militar a la guerra civil: Sevilla 1936* (Seville, 2006). The memoirs of Queipo de Llano, recently edited by J. Fernández-Coppel, *Queipo de Llano. Memorias de la guerra civil* (Madrid, 2008), 11–111, are not altogether reliable.

[5] See C. Blanco Escolá, *La incompetencia militar de Franco* (Madrid, 2000); J. A. Vaca de Osma, *La larga guerra de Francisco Franco* (Madrid, 1991); and J. Semprún, *El genio militar de Franco* (Madrid, 2000), which defends him. The most balanced treatment is J. Blázquez Miguel, *Auténtico Franco: Trayectoria militar, 1907–1939* (Madrid, 2009).

[6] Principal histories are R. Salas Larrazábal, *El Ejército Popular de la República* (Madrid, 1973), 4 vols.; M. Alpert, *El Ejército Popular de la República 1936–1939* (Barcelona, 2007); and C. Engel, *Historia de las Brigadas Mixtas del Ejército Popular de la República, 1936–1939* (Madrid, 1999).

mixed brigades, the basic units of the new army, were ready by the beginning of November, abetted by the first two of the international brigades being organized by the Comintern. The first Soviet arms had arrived shortly before, the nine-ton Soviet T-26 tanks and late-model Soviet planes completely outclassing weapons employed by Franco's forces.[7]

Franco's assault on Madrid began on 6 November, at first utilizing only about 22,000 troops against a larger number of entrenched defenders, who had superior weaponry.[8] This was quite different from combat in open country, and the attackers quickly lost their advantage, gaining only a narrow foothold on the western edge of the city. A series of subsequent operations toward the northwest in December and January similarly resulted in only marginal advances. Failure of this assault marked a turning point, for it was the end of the original insurgent design of a relatively quick victory. The conflict would henceforth turn into a long war of attrition, as both sides concentrated on raising mass armies. At first the People's Army grew more quickly, though it also provided poorer training, and was assisted by an eventual total of 42,000 volunteers in the International Brigades.[9] Franco's forces were augmented by extensive recruiting in Morocco and the arrival of nearly 50,000 Italian troops early in 1937, though almost half the latter force was soon withdrawn. In February 1937 the city of Málaga on the southern coast, its defenses in total disarray, fell quickly to a combined Spanish-Italian offensive, but for two more months Franco's attention was focused on attempts to capture Madrid.

The largest operation to that point took place in mid-February, as Franco launched an expanded assault through the Jarama River valley to outflank the capital from the south and east. For the first time, full-sized regular units of both sides met in open-field combat. Though the Nationalists gained ground, they could not achieve a breakthrough.[10] The final attempt to outflank the capital was the Guadalajara offensive in March, in which the main effort was made by the newly constituted Italian Corpo di Truppe Volontarie (Corps of Volunteer Troops – CTV). Despite an initial breakthrough, the advance was halted by the mixed brigades, assisted by Soviet tanks and control of the air. Though their offensive ended with a small net gain in territory, the Italian units precipitously abandoned their farthest line of advance, losing prisoners and providing the Republicans with a major propaganda victory (hailed as

[7] On initial Soviet support, see Y. Rybalkin, *Stalin y España* (Madrid, 2007); D. Kowalsky, *La Unión Soviética y la guerra civil española. Una revisión crítica* (Barcelona, 2003); and also A. Viñas, *El escudo de la República: El oro de España, la apuesta soviética y los hechos de mayo de 1937* (Barcelona, 2007).

[8] Franco's troops, who had only small Italian and German tankettes of their own, responded to the Soviet tanks by creating an improvised device (a bottle filled with gasoline or another flammable liquid) that three years later the Finnish army, using the same technique against the Soviets, dubbed the "Molotov cocktail" (with satirical reference to Stalin's foreign minister).

[9] C. Vidal, *Las Brigadas Internacionales* (Madrid, 2006); R. Skoutelsky, *Novedad en el frente: Las Brigadas Internacionales en la guerra civil* (Madrid, 2006).

[10] L. Díez, *La batalla del Jarama* (Madrid, 2005).

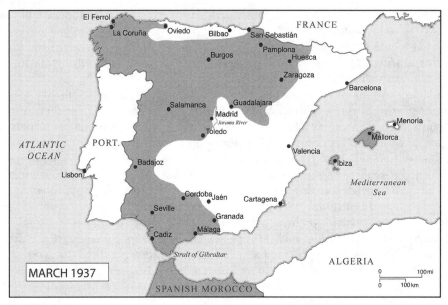

Spain, March 1937.

"the first defeat of Fascism"). The outcome was complete stalemate on the Madrid front. The defense of the capital between November 1936 and March 1937 was the most notable accomplishment of the People's Army, a defensive victory that would never be repeated. At that point, Franco accepted the advice of his military staff to concentrate instead on the internally divided northern Republican zone, whose conquest could alter the balance of power in his favor.

THE REVOLUTION

The revolution that took place in the Republican zone during the weeks following the arming of the worker movements on 19–20 July was the most extensive, and also most nearly spontaneous, worker revolution in a European country, Russia not excepted. The revolution of March 1917 in Russia had not been specifically a worker revolution (though workers figured prominently in it), but a general revolt against the autocracy in which various social sectors participated, giving rise to a sort of anarchic democracy and a temporary system of dual government. The Bolshevik coup d'etat seven months later was supported by many, but not all, workers and involved the agrarian majority very little.

The arming of the worker movements in Spain enabled them to seize control of most of the public power and the economic institutions of the Republican zone, which went far beyond anything initially seen in Russia. Moreover, the Spanish revolution also involved many agrarian workers, organized by the revolutionary syndicates, which also went far beyond Russia or Hungary. The nearest parallel, even if quite incomplete, may have been, at least momentarily, unoccupied Latvia in 1917.

The military revolt had been designed as a preemptive insurrection against the left republican government in particular and the revolutionary process in general. Given its failure in two-thirds of Spain, however, it unleashed the full force of the process that it sought to avoid, initially worsening rather than improving the situation of the counterrevolutionaries. From the viewpoint of the revolutionary leaders – with the exception of the Communists – it merely played into their hands, since none of them had a clear strategy for winning power, the *caballeristas* simply counting on the reaction to the military revolt that they were seeking to provoke.

Cynics and counterrevolutionaries alike would argue that all this was the logical culmination of the left republican abandonment of constitutionalism under the Popular Front. For Azaña and Giral, however, the arming of the revolutionaries was a panic response stemming from their anxiety about how to deal with the military insurgency. Yet, like most of their other policies, this initiative was also a partial failure, helping only to suppress the rebellion where it was comparatively weak, which might have been done in many cases without the worker militia. The revolutionaries devoted most of their energy to revolutionary activities, involving pillage, arson, and massive violence against civilians. While thousands of workers volunteered and fought bravely – though often with little skill – only a minority were willing to devote themselves to the military effort. After the first week or so, a military standoff developed that was altered only by the slow march of Franco's Army of Africa. Meanwhile, the social and economic revolution of worker control and collectivization expanded. All the leftist groups in the Republican zone grew rapidly, led by the two principal union movements, the CNT and UGT, each of which claimed to have two million affiliates by the end of 1936.

The government of Catalonia, the Generalitat, installed a system of revolutionary dualism on 22 July, when its president, Lluis Companys, formally recognized alongside his own administration the new CNT-led Central Committee of Antifascist Militia, deferring to it in many matters.[11] The committee, whose leadership included representatives of the Esquerra (left Catalan nationalists) and the smaller revolutionary parties, mobilized 40,000 men, many of them not dedicated to the military struggle. For the first weeks it controlled most affairs in Catalonia, but strong antagonism and revolutionary rivalry developed between the CNT and the new Catalan Communist party,

---

[11] On Catalonia in the civil war, see J. M. Solé Sabaté and J. Villarroya, eds., *Breu història de la Guerra Civil a Catalunya* (Barcelona, 2005); Solé Sabaté, *La Guerra Civil a Catalunya* (Barcelona, 2004); E. Ucelay da Cal, *La Catalunya populista: Imatge, cultura i política en l'etapa republicana (1931–1939)* (Barcelona, 1982); M. Cruells, *El separatismo català durant la guerra civil* (Barcelona, 1975); V. Castells, *Nacionalisme català i guerra civil a Catalunya* (Barcelona, 1989); and P. Moa, *Una historia chocante: Los nacionalismos catalán y vasco en la historia contemporánea de España* (Madrid, 2004), 337–438.

the Partit Socialist Unificat de Catalunya (PSUC).[12] This was Spain's third Marxist-Leninist party (not counting the majority sector of the Socialists) and had been formed in the first week of the civil war by the merger of four small Catalan revolutionary groups (chief of which were the Catalan Socialists and Communists).

CNT leaders declared that their organization was perfectly capable of taking over all the affairs of Catalonia, but that they accepted the continuation of a limited Catalan Generalitat for the duration of the military crisis in order not to frighten foreign powers. The CNT's chief ally was the minuscule Leninist (but anti-Stalinist) POUM, from the beginning even more committed to revolution *à l'outrance*, demonstrating fanatical determination to copy Lenin in 1917–18 (at least as the POUM understood it). Companys's official *Butlletí de la Generalitat* announced that real power lay in the hands of the Militia Committee, which had established a revolutionary new order that all parties must respect. As in nearly all violent revolutions, the new order was thoroughly authoritarian. Horacio Prieto, the secretary of the CNT's national committee, was later explicit: "We went directly to dictatorship. Even the Bolsheviks ... were not as fast in establishing absolute power as the anarchists in Spain."[13]

Other multiparty committees sprang up in towns, provinces, and sometimes in regions throughout the Republican zone. They represented the revolutionary forces strongest in each district, formed as broad alliances of the leftist parties. The left republicans, who had served as sorcerer's apprentices throughout, accepted subordination. Their younger and more radical members often joined the revolutionaries, while older and more moderate sectors were simply bypassed. Yet, with the exception of the POUM, most of the revolutionaries agreed that it was still best to maintain the shell, however hollow, of a Republican and parliamentary government, if only for purposes of propaganda and foreign relations.

This new configuration of power quickly produced social and economic revolution throughout the Republican zone and even, though in a much more limited fashion, in the new Basque nationalist regime in the province of Vizcaya. In industry and much of agriculture, as well as to some extent in services, this took the form first of worker control and then of collectivization. The Comintern official André Marty reported on 16 October that in the Republican zone 18,000 enterprises had been "taken in hand.... The

[12] J. Almendros, *Situaciones españolas 1936/39: el PSUC en la guerra civil* (Barcelona, 1976); R. Casteras, *Las Juventudes Socialistas Unificadas de Cataluña y la revolución* (Barcelona, 1982).

[13] H. Prieto, *El anarquismo español en la lucha política* (Paris, 1946), 7. This statement, though technically correct, requires some qualification. The anarchists soon began to accept greater semipluralism, while the Bolsheviks moved subsequently to introduce totalitarianism.

    There is a sizable literature on anarcho-syndicalism during the Spanish war. The most systematic and objective treatment is R. J. Alexander, *The Anarchists in the Spanish Civil War* (London, 1999), 2 vols.

great bulk of Spanish industry is now controlled by the workers."[14] No formal collectivization was announced; the trade unions simply took control. Only in Catalonia, where Companys sought to channel the revolution, was a legal structure developed. The CNT entered the Catalan government in September (the first time that anarchists, as such, had ever entered a government), and on 24 October the CNT councilor of economics, Juan Fábregas, issued a decree formalizing collectivization of all factories employing more than 100 workers and providing for collectivization of those employing between 50 and 100 workers, provided that 75 percent of the workers in a given enterprise approved.

Smaller units could be collectivized only with the consent of the owner – if still alive and present – but otherwise de facto worker control would reign. By contrast, state nationalization was rejected as contrary to anarcho-syndicalist doctrine. In addition, smaller firms and shops were included in larger "groupings" (*agrupaciones*) or "concentrations" that served as an intermediate form of coordination.[15] The revolutionary movements generally did not approve confiscation of very small properties, unless the owners were obviously pro-insurgent. In Asturias, mining and industrial firms were not formally collectivized but brought under complete control of the trade unions.

The CNT's grand design to achieve "libertarian communism" took the form of what it termed "socialization" (as distinct from state nationalization) of entire branches of production under the unions. The idea was that socialization would guarantee representation and autonomy while avoiding state domination. This did not conform to Socialist notions, however, and in urban industry the UGT frequently would not collaborate. Socialization, in fact, never went beyond a single entire industry in any given city.

CNT leaders were aware that collectivization was only a first step, and that they faced the challenge of modernization and increasing production. When possible, new equipment was purchased, but under wartime conditions this rarely occurred. There was no overall plan. Factories often continued to produce only civilian goods, which were easier to make or more profitable, and collectivized enterprises would later be charged with "trade union capitalism" and "egotism" in Barcelona. Financial support services were totally inadequate, and on the shop level there was a lessening of work discipline, increased absenteeism, and occasionally even sabotage.[16]

[14] Quoted in C. Serrano, *L'Enjeu espagnol: PCF et la guerre d'Espagne* (Paris, 1987), 65.

[15] Collectivization in Catalonia is treated in A. Pérez-Baró, *Treinta meses de colectivismo en Cataluña, 1936–1939* (Barcelona, 1974); A. Castells Durán, *Les collectivitzacions a Barcelona, 1936–1939* (Barcelona, 1993); J. M. Bricall, *Política económica de la Generalitat, 1936–1939* (Barcelona, 1970); and P. Pagès, *La Guerra Civil espanyola a Catalunya (1936–1939)* (Barcelona, 1997).

[16] The only good social history of the war that treats ordinary people is M. Seidman, *Republic of Egos: A Social History of the Spanish Civil War* (Madison, Wisc., 2002). For an approach to the revolutionary experience from the viewpoint of workers rather than revolutionary organizations, see his *Workers against Work: Labor in Paris and Barcelona during the Popular Fronts* (Berkeley, Calif., 1991), as well as his articles "Work and Revolution: Workers' Control

Collectives were most widespread in agriculture. Though smallholdings were usually respected, this was not always the case. CNT and UGT agrarian unions occupied all the large and many of the medium-sized properties. Edward Malefakis, the author of the principal study of the prewar agrarian reform, has concluded that in the fourteen provinces that made up the core of the Republican zone, 41 percent of all the land was expropriated. This amounted to well over half of all arable land, and of that amount, approximately 54 percent was organized into collectives, with the remainder reassigned for individual farming.[17]

This constituted a marked contrast with the first two phases of the Bolshevik regime, or, at the other extreme, with Communist Hungary in 1919. Malefakis has pointed out that proportionately more than twice as much land was expropriated in Republican Spain as during the first decade of the Bolshevik regime, and very much more was organized into collectives. In Russia, from 75 to 80 percent of farmland was already owned by the peasantry, and Lenin permitted them to take over nearly all the remaining 20 percent, which tended to be the best and most productive land. There was very little revolutionary collectivization or nationalization of land by the new Bolshevik state in the early years. Expropriated property was mostly incorporated into the traditional peasant commune system (*mir*), until Stalin began collectivization ten years later. The situation in Hungary was somewhat more similar to that of Republican Spain. More of the land was held in larger estates than in Spain, and all that was confiscated under the Bela Kun regime, but the government retained the land for nationalized state collective farms, angering the peasants. In neither Russia nor Hungary was there anything equivalent to the CNT and UGT farm worker unions, though in Hungary there were proportionately even more landless laborers, while in Russia there were proportionately far fewer.

Purely CNT collectives tended to be the most radical, featuring total social inclusion, family salaries, and a number of attempts to ban the use of money. Some UGT collectives were more moderate, functioning more as cooperatives. Blessed by favorable weather, production increased slightly in some areas in 1937, only to fall disastrously, together with that of industry, in 1938.

in Barcelona in the Spanish Civil War, 1936–38," *Journal of Contemporary History*, 17 (July 1982), 409–33; "Towards a History of Workers' Resistance to Work: Paris and Barcelona during the French Popular Front and the Spanish Revolution (1936–1938)," *Journal of Contemporary History*, 23:2 (April 1988), 193–219; "The Unorwellian Barcelona," *European History Quarterly*, 8.1 (March 1990), 163–80; and "Individualisms in Madrid during the Spanish Civil War," *Journal of Modern History*, 20:1 (March 1996), 63–82.

[17] E. Malefakis, "La revolución social," in E. Malefakis, ed., *La Guerra de España, 1936–1939* (Madrid, 1996), 319–54. Ramón Tamames earlier calculated that the land expropriated in the Republican zone comprised 60 percent of all "land sown": R. Tamames, *La República. La era de Franco* (Historia de España Alfaguara VII) (Madrid, 1975), 332. Regional variations were considerable. In the Valencian region, for example, only a little more than 14 percent of arable land was expropriated, according to A. Bosch Sánchez, *Ugetistas y libertarios: Guerra civil en el País Valenciano 1936–1939* (Valencia, 1983), 372.

It will never be possible to say how many agrarian collectives were formed. During the latter part of the civil war, after many anarchist collectives had been broken up, the government's Institute of Agrarian Reform (IRA) recognized 2,213 collectives, a figure that did not include Catalonia, Aragon, or the Valencian region. Of this official total, 823 had been formed by the UGT, 284 by the CNT, and 1,106 by the two together. The CNT claimed that they alone had formed more than 3,000 collectives, the bulk of which had never been recognized by the Communist-led IRA. The CNT's figure is almost undoubtedly an exaggeration, and may have been made up by counting each semiautonomous collective subsection as a collective in itself. One of the few attempts at a comprehensive study has suggested that even the IRA engaged in this practice, so that the total number of agrarian collectives may not in fact have been greatly in excess of 1,500.[18]

For spokesmen of the extreme revolutionary left, the uprising of organized workers in the Republican zone constituted a proletarian revolution more profound, authentic, and spontaneous than that of Russia. Thus Andreu Nin, acting leader of the POUM, declared that what was happening in Spain was "a more profound proletarian revolution than the Russian revolution itself," declaring with typical POUMist hyperbole on 1 August that "the government does not exist." On 7 September he announced that the dictatorship of the proletariat already existed in Catalonia, and the POUM's youth organization (JCI) called for the formation of revolutionary soviets throughout the Republican zone. Despite these exaggerations, there is little doubt that there was more semi-spontaneous and also organized revolutionary activity by genuine workers in the more advanced and politically conscious Spanish society of 1936 (even though little more than half the country was involved) than in the more backward Russia of 1917, and in the countryside the difference was greater yet. Not only was proportionately more land seized in Spain than in Russia, but the rural population (more precisely, a significant part thereof) was itself much more consciously revolutionary in a political sense. Russian peasants wanted more land, but had little interest in any broader revolutionary project.

Nonetheless, in the comparative histories of modern revolutions one often cannot find a chapter devoted to the Spanish revolution.[19] Why has so extensive a revolution been overlooked? There seem to be three reasons. One is that history likes winners, and the Spanish revolution was soon defeated. A second

---

[18] L. Garrido González, F. Quilis Tauriz, N. Rodrigo González, and J. M. Santacréu Soler, "Las colectivizaciones en la Guerra Civil," in J. Aróstegui, ed., *Historia y memoria de la Guerra Civil* (Valladolid, 1988), 2:63–124. The most inclusive study is W. L. Bernecker, *Colectivizaciones y revolución social: El anarquismo en la guerra civil española, 1936–1939* (Barcelona, 1982), which, as the title indicates, is devoted to the CNT. For a briefer and more general survey, see Bernecker's chapter, "La revolución social," in S. G. Payne and J. Tusell, eds., *La Guerra Civil: Una nueva vision del conflicto que dividió España* (Madrid, 1996), 485–533. There are numerous monographs on collectivization in individual districts.

[19] P. A. Jureidini et al., *Casebook on Insurgency and Revolutionary Warfare: 23 Summary Accounts* (Washington, D.C., 1962), 547–74, treats the Nationalists as the "revolutionary movement," since they rebelled against the existing government.

is that nominal worker revolutions in the twentieth century have usually been Communist revolutions, and the Spanish revolution was not a Communist revolution. Even more, the Spanish revolution cannot be defined or described according to any simple or single model. Its precise character and also degree varied from city to city, district to district, and province to province, ranging from informal worker control to *"incautaciones"* (takeover or seizure, but without clear new ownership or juridical status) to official collectivization, but with state *"intervenciones"* and even occasional nationalization taking place in certain industries. Similarly, the extent and pattern of land expropriation and collectivization varied from province to province. Any simple chart or map of the Spanish revolution would be impossible.

The third reason for the uncertain historiographic status of the Spanish revolution stems from systematic Republican denial. The massive violence against civilians that accompanied the revolution quickly gained the wartime Republic a negative reputation, and some of the more moderate Republican leaders, on the one hand, and Soviet and Comintern bosses, on the other soon, grasped that the most useful strategy would be to deny that the revolution even existed. Assistance from the Western democracies would be more likely to arrive if the wartime Republic could be presented as simply a parliamentary democracy based on private property, similar to France or the United States. This produced what Burnett Bolloten called "the grand camouflage"[20] – the basic denial that the revolution even existed, a staple of Republican and Comintern propaganda throughout the conflict. The Spanish revolution became the revolution that dare not speak its name.

This propaganda was not particularly successful while the war lasted, since the British government, arguably its main single target, knew better, but, curiously, has been more effective afterward among historians who should have known better. It subsequently became the official line among the Spanish left generally, "democracy" being a more useful code for their cause than violent revolution. Then, in the twenty-first century, with the discrediting of socialism and collectivism, the dogma of "Republican democracy" under the Popular Front regime has been made the official fiction not only of the Spanish left in general but also of the Socialist government of José Luis Rodríguez Zapatero in particular, which has codified it as a law (2007).[21]

TERROR AND REPRESSION

To understand the savage repression that marked the Spanish war, the specific nature of such a conflict must be kept in mind. Revolutionary civil wars of the first half of the twentieth century were conflicts of the transition to "classical modernity," a process involving drastic social and cultural transformation,

---

[20] B. Bolloten, *The Grand Camouflage: The Spanish Civil War and Revolution 1936–1939* (New York, 1961) [*El gran engaño* (Barcelona, 1961)].

[21] What is commonly termed the "Law of Historical Memory" was approved by the Spanish parliament in October 2007.

generating unprecedented tensions and hatreds. The only direct precursors would be found in the great French Revolution and in the Paris Commune of 1871. Murderous repression, first using the modern term "terror," was a major feature of those conflicts, and it reappeared in all the revolutionary civil wars of the first half of the twentieth century, first in Finland, then in Russia and elsewhere. During the 1940s such repression would reappear in the civil wars in Yugoslavia and Greece.

The blood lust in revolutionary civil wars stems from the apocalyptic nature of such contests, specifically the attempt on each side to create a new society, not merely a separate political order, purged of antagonistic elements. In these conflicts the enemy is perceived not just as an ordinary opponent but as a metaphysical incarnation of evil that must be eradicated before he imposes the same terror against one's own side. A revolutionary civil war is not merely a political conflict but a contest of ultimates about society, religion, and culture, demanding a total and uncompromising solution.

During the war both sides widely publicized (and in fact greatly exaggerated) the atrocities of their opponents, using the most inflated statistics, sometimes claiming up to half a million killings by the other side,[22] an exaggeration of somewhere between 500 and 800 percent. Subsequent studies would indicate a total of perhaps 130,000 executions during the war by both sides combined – slightly more than one-half of one percent of the total population, a horrifically high figure. It was probably proportionately greater than the equivalent figure for the civil war in Russia, though exceeded by the proportionate statistic for Finland, where a three-month civil war and its aftermath produced more than 20,000 victims of repression by both sides combined, a figure amounting to about two-thirds of one percent of the small Finnish population. The composition of these statistics is, nonetheless, dissimilar, since so many of the victims in Finland died of malnutrition and disease. If one adds to the Spanish total the approximately 30,000 executions carried out by the Franco regime during 1939–42, the disproportion begins to narrow, but the Finnish total still remains proportionately higher, and it was the product of only about eight months and not six years, as in the Spanish case.

Mass executions began almost immediately, much sooner than was the case in Russia. There were many random murders in Russia from the beginning of the revolution in March 1917, but organized mass killings began only in mid-1918, when the Red Terror was officially initiated. The immediacy of large-scale executions in Spain stemmed from several factors, two of them general and the third specific to Spain. The Spanish conflict was the last European revolutionary civil war of its generation, feeding on the propaganda, fears, and hatreds aroused by its predecessors. Associated with this was the fact that the 1930s was a time of growing tension during which the earlier example of

---

[22] And repeated by the World War II–era newsreel *Inside Fascist Spain* (1943), produced in the United States.

Bolshevism was followed by the rise of fascism – a deadly combination that evoked increasingly widespread fear and enmity. More specific to Spain was the long run-up to the revolution, with increasing political violence beginning in 1931, and a total of more than 2,500 deaths due to political violence in slightly more than five years. Even the Russian revolution of 1917 did not have such a prelude, a decade having passed since the great violence of 1905–08. In Spain there had been a lengthy period of growing tensions, multiple attempts at revolutionary insurrection, and the most virulent forms of mass propaganda, instigated especially by the hate movements of the revolutionary left, which talked of "extermination" and the liquidation of the bourgeoisie, accompanied by a discourse of both left and right that sought to dehumanize and demonize the adversary.

Moreover, media coverage had expanded greatly between 1917 and 1936. During the first months of the war, the eyes of foreign correspondents, cameramen, and news services were fixed particularly on the large cities of the Republican zone, which generated the greater share of the atrocity stories sent abroad. As Ernst Nolte has written, "What an unsympathetic external world saw in Red Spain was above all Bolshevik terror and chaos: poorly dressed masses armed with rifles filling the streets, death squads executing enemies, undisciplined mobs of anarchists, mummies of nuns taken from their tombs and placed on exhibit in the streets, violent expropriation, forced collectivizations."[23] Later, the weight of publicity shifted, and by 1937 the Republican zone was receiving a better press abroad, but in the early months its image was frequently negative.[24]

The first recorded executions in the peninsula took place in Madrid on 19 July, with many more to follow the next day, while executions were also beginning in the areas dominated by the insurgents. On both sides these rapidly grew in volume, the largest number in most regions taking place during August and September, though continuing at a high rate through the autumn.

Apologists for the left have always sought to distinguish between the two terrors, arguing that repression by the left was decentralized, "spontaneous," and subject to little organization, while holding that repression by the right was more planned, centralized, and implacable. There is a small degree of truth in this distinction, though it has been exaggerated. There was nothing spontaneous about the revolutionary terror, for violent revolution had been planned and publicized by the revolutionary groups for years. In general, however, it was not centrally planned as in Russia, since there was no single hegemonic force in the Republican zone.

There was, nonetheless, considerable organization of the repression in the Republican cities, where the leftist parties formed numerous death squads and

[23] E. Nolte, *Der europäische Bürgerkrieg, 1917–1945: Nationalsozialismus und Bolschewismus* (Berlin, 1991), 228, and *La Guerra civil europea, 1917–1945: Nacionalsocialismo y bolchevismo* (Mexico City, 1994), 239.

[24] For the British media, which the Republicans particularly wanted to impress, this can be tracked in D. Deacon, *British News Media and the Spanish Civil War* (Edinburgh, 2008).

set up special facilities to accommodate them. Left republicans and members of the Catalan Esquerra also participated, though less prominently than did the members of the revolutionary parties. In Barcelona, Esquerra members were regular activists of the "control patrols" that carried out the second phase of the repression. The notorious *"checas"* of Madrid were organized death squads, deriving their name from the original acronym of the repressive state apparatus in the Soviet Union (CHEKA), and in some cases were specifically authorized by Republican government authorities, such as Manuel Muñoz, the director general of security, and Angel Galarza, the minister of the interior in September 1936. Regular Republican police and security forces sometimes participated, and the work of the *checas* was publicly praised by Republican newspapers.[25] Moreover, Republican government authorities coordinated much of the large-scale looting and pillaging that took place, building a sizable treasure in stolen valuables.[26] In Madrid, the most independent *checas* were those of the FAI-CNT, which operated for months, whereas in Barcelona the system of revolutionary dualism to some extent channeled the repression by the anarchists.

In the insurgent zone, the repression was controlled and directed by the military. In some areas Falangists, particularly, or other civilian auxiliaries enjoyed a very limited autonomy to engage in repressive acts, but such autonomy never went any further than local military commanders approved. Before long, it became a matter of convenience to blame most of the repression in the insurgent zone on the Falangists, but they were always subordinates. In the great majority of cases, Falangist squads acted at the behest of military authorities. The repression by the insurgents was more thorough and effective than that of the left, and more practical in its modus operandi. As David Wilkinson observed, "Nationalist repression, besides being more thorough and continuous, was more carefully targeted at political activists, rather than at symbolic class enemies."[27]

Leaders in the Republican zone began to control and moderate the repression somewhat earlier than Franco did. A new kind of revolutionary court

---

[25] C. Vidal, *Checas de Madrid* (Barcelona, 2003); J. Ruiz, *The Red Terror in Madrid* (forthcoming).

[26] Most of this was carted off to France. There is no reliable or thorough study of the systematic looting, for records have not survived. Much of what is known is summarized in J. A. Sánchez Asiaín, "Recursos económicos y organización territorial en la República de la Guerra Civil," *Anales de la Real Academia de Ciencias Morales y Políticas*, 85 (2008), 516–21. Various data are presented in F. Olaya Morales, *El expolio de la República* (Barcelona, 2004), dealing mainly with the Socialists. For an account by an anarchist participant, see M. Mir, *Diario de un pistolero anarquista* (Barcelona, 2006). The most public controversy had to do with the quarrel between the Socialist leaders Indalecio Prieto and Juan Negrín over the disposition of one major portion of the loot after the war was over. See A. Herrerín, *El dinero del exilio: Indalecio Prieto y las pugnas de posguerra (1939–1947)* (Madrid, 2007). For comparison, the looting of Russia by the Bolsheviks is described in S. McMeekin, *History's Greatest Heist: The Looting of Russia by the Bolsheviks* (New Haven, Conn., 2009).

[27] D. Wilkinson, *Revolutionary War: The Elements of Victory and Defeat* (Palo Alto, Calif., 1975), 59.

system, the "popular tribunals," was announced on 23 August and then slowly implemented through most of the Republican zone. These new courts were highly politicized but also followed a legal procedure, intended not to end repression but to channel and regularize it, bringing some degree of judicial control.[28] During the first months they decreed hundreds of death sentences, and during the autumn thousands of killings were still being carried out by *checas* and other death squads, while the largest single round of killings during the entire war was ordered by the Junta de Defensa de Madrid during November and December.[29] By the close of the year, however, the reorganized Republican authorities had achieved greater control, and the rate of executions dropped sharply.

An equivalent change was adopted by Franco only some two months later, when the system of military tribunals in the insurgent zone was both expanded and regularized, bringing greater formality and considerably reducing the number of victims, at least until after the end of the civil war.

The largest number of killings, in both absolute and proportionate numbers, took place in and around the largest cities, though in some rural areas the proportion of victims was also high. During recent decades a growing number of monographic studies have attempted to record and measure the incidence of repression in many provinces and regions, though this research remains incomplete. Moreover, the methodology, quality, and reliability of such studies vary considerably, ranging from the careful and exacting work carried out for Catalonia and the Valencian region by Josep María Solé Sabaté, Joan Villarroya, and Vicent Gabarda Cebellán[30] to accounts that are sometimes careless and less exacting.

[28] G. Sánchez Recio, *Justicia y guerra en España: Los Tribunales Populares (1936–1939)* (Alicante, 1991).

[29] C. Vidal, *Paracuellos-Katyn: un ensayo sobre el genocidio de la izquierda* (Madrid, 2005); C. Fernández, *Paracuellos del Jarama: Carrillo culpable* (Barcelona, 1983); I. Gibson, *Paracuellos: cómo fue* (Barcelona, 1983); J. Reverte, *La batalla de Madrid* (Madrid, 2004), 577–81; A. Viñas, *El escudo de la República: El oro de España, la apuesta soviética y los hechos de mayo de 1937* (Barcelona, 2007), 35–87.

[30] J. M. Solé Sabaté, *La repressió franquista a Catalunya (1938–1953)* (Barcelona, 1985); Solé Sabaté and J. Villarroya i Font, *La repressió a la reraguarda de Catalunya (1936–1939)* (Barcelona, 1989–90), 2 vols.; V. Gabarda Cebellán, *Els afusellaments al País Valencià (1938–1956)* (Valencia, 1993) and *La represión en la retaguardia republicana: País Valenciano, 1936–1939* (Valencia, 1996).

J. Ruiz, "Seventy Years On: Historians and Repression during and after the Spanish Civil War," *Journal of Contemporary History*, 44:3 (July 2009), 449–72, provides an excellent account of the evolution of the literature on the repression. Principal general accounts are R. Salas Larrazábal, *Pérdidas de la guerra* (Barcelona, 1977); S. Juliá, ed., *Víctimas de la guerra civil* (Madrid, 1999); and A. D. Martín Rubio, *Los mitos de la represión en la guerra civil* (Madrid, 2005). The more important studies include F. Alía Miranda, *La guerra civil en retaguardia: Conflicto y revolución en la provincia de Ciudad Real, 1936–1939* (Ciudad Real, 1994); J. Casanova et al., *El pasado oculto: Fascismo y violencia en Aragón* (Madrid, 1992); R. Casas de la Vega, *El terror: Madrid 1936* (Madrid, 1994); J. Cifuentes Chueca and P. Maluenda Pons, *El asalto a la República: Los orígenes del franquismo en Zaragoza (1936–1939)* (Zaragoza, 1995); F. Espinosa Maestre, *La justicia de Queipo (Violencia selectiva y*

If the Republican repression in Madrid claimed the greatest volume of victims in absolute numbers, the most severe repression in proportion to population took place in Zaragoza, where the insurgents executed nearly 6,000 people, if postwar figures are included. The absolute number of executions by Republicans in Barcelona was high – nearly 5,700 – but in proportion only two-thirds that of Madrid.

Political executions continued on both sides throughout the war, but at a diminished rate. During 1937–38 a new form of repression emerged in the Republican zone – the repression imposed on the extreme revolutionary left, spurred on by the Soviet NKVD. As many as 2,000 militants of the POUM and FAI-CNT were arrested in Catalonia alone, and anarchist sources assert that several hundred were executed, though the number remains uncertain.[31]

The final phase of the civil war repression was carried out by the military tribunals of Franco's triumphant regime, which handed down approximately 50,000 death sentences. Forty percent may have been commuted, but at least 30,000 executions were carried out.[32] It may be noted that the death rate after the end of fighting was proportionately even higher in the Third Republic's repression of the Paris commune, in the case of Finland, and also in the case of Tito's summary mass executions in Yugoslavia in 1945.

A WAR OF RELIGION

Various commentators have pointed out that, in some sense, most wars are deemed "holy wars,"[33] and this was certainly the case with twentieth-century revolutionary civil wars. The Bolsheviks saw the Orthodox Church as a prime enemy, while their White opponents emphasized the restoration of traditional religion. The White troops in Finland were mainly Lutheran farmers, for whom the religious difference with their enemy was fundamental. In Hungary, the Bela Kun regime went further than the Bolsheviks in religious matters, as in other things, and sought to nationalize the churches directly,

---

terror fascista en la II División de 1936) (Montilla, 2000) and *La columna de la muerte (El avance del ejército franquista de Sevilla a Badajoz)* (Barcelona, 2003); A. D. Martín Rubio, *La represión roja en Badajoz* (Oviedo, 1995); F. Moreno Gómez, *1936: el genocidio franquista en Córdoba* (Barcelona, 2008); M. Núñez Díaz-Balart, ed., *La gran represión* (Barcelona, 2009); J. Rodrigo, *Hasta la raíz: violencia durante la Guerra Civil y la dictadura franquista* (Madrid, 2008); N. Salas, *La guerra civil en Sevilla* (Seville, 2009); E. Silva, *Las fosas de Franco* (Madrid, 2003); and F. de A. Vega Gonzalo, *Aniquilar la Falange: Cronología persecutoria del Nacionalsindicalismo* (Barcelona, 2005).

[31] F. Godicheau, *La Guerre d'Espagne: République et révolution en Catalogne (1936–1939)* (Paris, 2004), 174–328.

[32] The best study of any aspect is the work of Julius Ruiz on Madrid, which concludes that the total number of executions after the civil war may have been higher than that: *Franco's Justice: Repression in Madrid after the Spanish Civil War* (Oxford, 2005). See also M. Núñez Díaz Balart et al., eds., *La gran represión* (Barcelona, 2009).

[33] Cf. J. Flori, *La Guerra santa: La formación de la idea de cruzada en el Occidente cristiano* (Madrid, 2003), and A. Becker, *War and Faith: The Religious Imagination in France, 1914–18* (Oxford, 1998).

something too radical even for Lenin. With all these precedents, however, religion defined the conflict in Spain in ways that went beyond any other revolutionary civil war.

In recent decades an attempt has been made to study Spanish anticlericalism[34] and to try to understand why it sometimes took the form of such extreme violence. Most of these studies do little more than repeat the arguments of the anticlericals themselves: that the church held tyrannical power, that it wielded economic dominion, that priests were abusive and hypocritical. Such arguments held little validity, however, in 1936: church and state had been separate for five years; the church in Spain had long since lost most of its economic possessions; and whether priests were hypocrites or not should scarcely have mattered to anticlericals. The left's hatred of religion was essentially motivated by the same feelings that motivated revolutionaries in France in 1792 and throughout the century that followed: the church was the cultural and spiritual bulwark of the old order, which the left was determined to destroy, and of which its clergy and properties were both tangible and symbolic representatives, even more than were members of "bourgeois" centrist and conservative political groups. The motivation, in other words, was itself religious or, at least, ideological, and since the revolutionary credo emphasized violence, massive violence was employed. Despite all the rhetoric about "extermination" in the left-wing victimist culture in Spain during recent years, the only social sector marked out for "extermination" by either side was the clergy in the Republican zone.

At times there have been widespread persecutions – though more commonly, severe restrictions – of Christians in Islamic societies, but these have not been applied to the clergy alone. Ethnic cleansing of Armenians and Assyrians by the Turks in 1915–16 was aimed at eliminating entire Christian peoples, not just their clergy. The same may be said of the slaughter of Christians in the later Persian empire, or of Catholics in seventeenth-century Japan. In Spain, of course, the revolutionaries intended to repress Catholics in general, not just the clergy, and many thousands of lay Catholics were killed, sometimes because of their religion alone, but there was never any intention to exterminate Catholics generally.

The slaughter of the clergy should thus be examined from the perspective of modern revolutions generally and of early twentieth-century radical anti-Catholic regimes specifically. The Jacobin phase of the French Revolution slew about 2,000 members of the clergy. This was less than one-third of the number killed in Spain, and so, since the total of the two clergies was not greatly different, the ferocity of the Spanish revolutionaries was evidently greater. It is absurd to think that the power of the church was greater in Republican Spain than in the France of the Old Regime; the principal difference must have lain in the Spanish revolutionary culture. The total killed in Russia probably

---

[34] The most recent effort is E. A. Sanabria, *Republicanism and Anticlerical Nationalism in Spain* (New York, 2009).

exceeded the total in Spain, but Russia was a much larger country with a much more numerous clergy. The killing in Mexico was directed more at Catholic laymen than at the clergy, so that the slaughter of nearly 7,000 clergy,[35] mostly within a few months, probably stands as proportionately the most extended and most concentrated massacre of Catholic clergy of which we have historical record.

The anticlerical terror has naturally been understood as the expression of violent opposition to Catholic religion, but it was also the expression of radically rival new secular religions – Jacobin, anarchist, and Marxist-Leninist.[36] Bruce Lincoln has called the phenomenon "millennial antinomianism," expressing the revolutionaries' sense of complete freedom from all rules or law as they uprooted the old order in the process of establishing their new millennial utopia. This was even more evident in the manner of the killings. Most victims in the civil war were not tortured, though when torture occurred, the revolutionaries, more often than not, were the torturers. Members of the clergy were particularly singled out for rites of humiliation and torture. Julio de la Cueva has observed that while most were killed with firearms (the common method on both sides),

Others were hanged, drowned, suffocated, burned to death or buried alive. On many occasions, victims were tortured, at times in shockingly sophisticated ways. Mockery, insults, blasphemy and coercion to blasphemy were very likely parts of the torture, which could also include forcing the victims to strip naked, beating, cutting, skinning and mutilation. In the cases of mutilation, there was a morbid fixation on genitalia.... All these 'rites of violence' performed on the clergy further contributed to dehumanizing people whose humanity had long ago been denied by anti-clerical discourse, and, at the same time, facilitating 'conditions for guilt-free massacre.' The combination of cultural and sexual references, ritualized violence and humiliation of the victim – who was no longer a human being but an animal – reached its most exact expression in instances of being treated like pigs at the slaughterhouse or bulls in the bullring. Finally, irrespective of the death they suffered, the corpses of the clerics were likely to be dragged through the streets, exposed in public places or desecrated in many other ways.[37]

The similarity to the most extreme forms of anti-Jewish pogroms is striking.

---

[35] The largely definitive study is A. Montero Moreno, *Historia de la persecución religiosa en España, 1936–1939* (Madrid, 1961). See also V. Cárcel Ortí, *La gran persecución: España, 1931–1939* (Barcelona, 2000) and *Caídos, víctimas y mártires: La Iglesia y la hecatombe de 1936* (Madrid, 2008), and J. Albertí, *La Iglesia en llamas: La persecución religiosa en España durante la guerra civil* (Barcelona, 2008).

[36] I have addressed the issue of so-called political religion in my essay "On the Heuristic Value of the Concept of Political Religion and Its Application," in R. Griffin, R. Mallett, and J. Tortorice, eds., *The Sacred in Twentieth-Century Politics: Essays in Honour of Professor Stanley G. Payne* (Houndsmills/New York, 2008), 21–35.

[37] J. de la Cueva, "Religious Persecution, Anticlerical Tradition and Revolution: On Atrocities against the Clergy during the Spanish Civil War," *Journal of Contemporary History*, 33:3 (1998), 355–69.

An enormous wave of vandalism and destruction of churches and religious properties also took place.[38] This resulted in the disappearance of many priceless historic works of art, whose value was incalculable, art that was not merely the patrimony of the church but the cultural heritage of all Spain. This was only the most visible part of the great volume of pillaging and looting that went on in most parts of the Republican zone, a common feature of violent revolutions.

The left later reproached the leaders of the church for strongly supporting Franco, since the church hierarchy was unable to maintain irenic equanimity in the face of such ferocious persecution. Hardly surprisingly, the leadership soon committed itself more and more to the side that affirmed and protected the church. The bishops were not saints – though perhaps they should have been – but more practical leaders, and they did comparatively little to mitigate the ferocity of the insurgents.[39]

Mola's original plan had been to maintain a republic, though not a democratic one, that would continue the separation of church and state. In nearly all of the insurgent zone, this was the scheme with which the revolt began, but the tone changed quickly. It soon became clear that the dividing line in the civil war was religious even more than political, and the military authorities became increasingly deferential to the church and to the expression of Catholic sentiment. By mid-September 1936, Bishop Marcelino Olaechea in Pamplona, where support for the insurgents was the most intense and also ultra-Catholic, would be the first to proclaim that the conflict was a "crusade," language that later became official, not in the church but in the Franco regime. Finally, in July 1937, all but five of the surviving members of the church hierarchy who had escaped the revolutionaries formally endorsed the cause of the new Franco regime in their *Collective Letter* to the "Bishops of the Whole World." It denied that Catholics were engaged in a "crusade," pointing out that the church had always obeyed the laws of the Republic, laws that the erstwhile Republicans themselves did not obey. In view of the great violence and destruction unleashed by the left, the church leaders declared their support for the faithful in the insurgent cause, whom they held were waging a just war.[40]

---

[38] For the destruction in Catalonia, see J. Bassegoda Nonell, *La arquitectura profanada: La destrucción sistemática del patrimonio arquitectónico religioso catalán (1936–1939)* (Barcelona, 1989).

[39] The principal studies of the church leadership and the civil war are G. Redondo, *Historia de la Iglesia en España 1931–1939* (Madrid, 1993), vol. 2, "La Guerra Civil (1936–1939)"; A. Alvarez Bolado, *Para ganar la guerra, para ganar la paz: Iglesia y guerra civil, 1936–1939* (Madrid, 1995); H. Raguer, *La pólvora y el incienso: La Iglesia y la guerra civil española* (Barcelona, 2001); R. Comas, *Isidro Gomá Francesc Vidal i Barraquer: Dos visiones antagónicas de la Iglesia española en 1939* (Salamanca, 1977); R. Muntanyola, *Vidal i Barraquer, cardenal de la pau* (Montserrat, 1976); and M. L. Rodríguez Aisa, *El cardenal Gomá y la guerra de España* (Madrid, 1981).

[40] The extreme violence practiced by the insurgents, particularly the mass execution of civilians, was hardly in accord with traditional Catholic principles of just war.

The Vatican would have preferred a more neutral stance, for Pope Pius XI, having already burnt his fingers in relations with Hitler, showed caution regarding Franco's regime.[41] The impact of the *Collective Letter* was considerable, nonetheless, and in September 1937 the Vatican named a representative (apostolic delegate) to Franco's government, though not an official nuncio.

For the majority of Spanish Catholics, there is no doubt that the civil war turned into a war of religion.[42] Such commitment, involving spiritual, emotional, and also personal dimensions, became the strongest single force behind Franco's cause. It became so powerful that even the fascistic Falangists had to redouble their efforts to define their own Catholic identity. This was arguably the most important factor in the morale and cohesion of Franco's forces.

For most of the left, it was also to some extent a war of religion, but having unleashed that aspect of the conflict, the revolutionaries could not respond with the same unity and clarity. Extreme anti-Catholicism was fundamental to their cause, but could not provide a positive ideal equal to that of the revolution or the all-left Republic. Civil war as crusade, by contrast, was very effective for Franco in public relations abroad, rallying many millions of Catholics and other conservatives throughout Europe and the Western world.[43] As a result, Catholic Ireland became the only Western democracy to support Franco's cause. This put the left on the defensive and constituted one of its greatest weaknesses in the struggle for world opinion. Altogether, the religious persecution became a boomerang for the left, strengthening their enemies more than it did their own cause, but then that was probably true of the revolution in general.

The civil war thus did great damage to the church, on the one hand, while also sparking the beginning of a major Catholic revival, on the other. By 1939 the church had been restored to a position in some respects more favored than its position under Alfonso XIII. The blood of the martyrs[44] became the seed of the church, which, during the following generation of the 1940s and 50s, underwent the most extensive revival of traditional Christianity in any Western country during the twentieth century.

INTERVENTION AND NONINTERVENTION

For several years European observers had taken notice of the convulsive politics of the Spanish Republic, and diplomats in Madrid had been bracing

[41] V. Cárcel Ortí, *Pio XI entre la República y Franco: Angustia del Papa ante la tragedia española* (Madrid, 2008), 159–370; A. Marquina Barrio, *La diplomacia vaticana y la España de Franco (1936–1945)* (Madrid, 1983), 13–153.

[42] The best brief analysis is M. Vincent, "La Guerra Civil Española como Guerra de Religión," *Alcores*, 4 (2007), 57–73.

[43] J. Tusell and G. García Queipo de Llano, *El catolicismo mundial y la guerra de España* (Madrid, 1993).

[44] In October 1987 the Roman Catholic Church beatified 489 martyrs of the Spanish civil war, the largest single beatification in church history.

themselves for a possible major revolutionary outburst. Of the major Western European capitals, the only one that looked favorably on the left republican government was Paris, where a new Popular Front government had just taken power, though the political character of the French Popular Front was more moderate than that of Spain. Thus when the Giral government asked Paris to send arms, particularly planes, to be used in putting down the revolt, the initial French response was positive.

By 1936, however, the principal concern of Paris was Nazi Germany, and in that regard it was becoming increasingly dependent on its ally Great Britain.[45] The Conservatives in power in London viewed the outbreak of the Spanish conflict, accompanied by full-scale revolution in the Republican zone, with a very jaundiced eye. They informed Paris that Britain would have nothing to do with this conflict, and urged the French not to become involved, suggesting that this might compromise relations between Paris and London. Thus, after an initial shipment of arms, the French government drew back.

When Franco arrived in Spanish Morocco on 19 July, he found the situation of the insurgents militarily desperate, and soon sent requests to the Italian and German governments, the most likely sources of assistance, for weapons and ammunition, particularly airplanes. These initial requests were brushed off, for the Germans had little interest in or contact with Spain, and Mussolini, who had burnt his fingers in an earlier attempt to assist monarchist conspirators, was informed by his ambassador that there was nothing to be done, since the rebellion was apparently failing.

Franco was persistent, however, and dispatched personal delegations to both Rome and Berlin. Hitler met with his envoys on the night of 25/26 July and, after a lengthy conversation, agreed to send a small shipment of arms, accompanied by a limited number of personnel. A day later, Mussolini decided to change his position and, completely independently of Hitler's decision, agreed to do the same thing. Airplanes began to reach Franco before the end of the month, stiffening his forces.[46]

The French Popular Front government of Léon Blum, alarmed at the prospect of German and Italian intervention, proposed an international agreement of nonintervention in the Spanish war. The thinking in Paris was that

---

[45] M. Thomas, *Britain, France and Appeasement: Anglo-French Relations in the Popular Front Era* (Oxford, 1996).

[46] German intervention is treated in A. Viñas, *Franco, Hitler y el estallido de la Guerra Civil: Antecedentes y consecuencias* (Madrid, 2001); M. Merkes, *Die deutsche Politik gegenüber dem spanischen Bürgerkrieg 1936–1939* (rev. ed., Bonn, 1969); H.-H. Abendroth, *Hitler in der spanischen Arena: Die deutsch-spanischen Beziehungen im Spannungsfeld der europäischen Interessen Politik vom Ausbruch des Bürgerkrieges bis zum Ausbruch des Weltkrieges 1936–1939* (Paderborn, 1973); and R. H. Whealey, *Hitler and Spain: The Nazi Role in the Spanish Civil War* (Lexington, Ky., 1989). For that of Italy, see J. F. Coverdale, *Italian Intervention in the Spanish Civil War* (Princeton, N.J., 1975); A. Rovighi and F. Stefani, *La partecipazione italiana alla Guerra civile spagnuola* (Rome, 1992), 2 vols.; and M. Heiberg, *Emperadores del Mediterráneo: Franco, Mussolini y la guerra civil española* (Barcelona, 2003).

if all other countries would stay out of the war, the Spanish Popular Front, having greater resources, would win. All the major European governments agreed to the French proposal, and on 15 September representatives met in London to form an International Non-Intervention Committee to monitor the agreement.

Neither Hitler nor Mussolini had any intention of abiding by the agreement, but hoped to assist the insurgents to a quick victory. Both were motivated primarily by geostrategic conditions, Hitler concerned to weaken the strategic position of France, Mussolini to develop a new client state in the Mediterranean.

The Giral government first approached its Soviet counterpart on 25 July. To that point the Comintern had been delighted by developments in Spain, and had discouraged revolutionary excess to the extent that it could. It had understandably sought to avoid any sort of explosion, since the existing situation, which permitted all manner of radical changes under the cover of parliamentary government, was optimal. Once fighting began, it insisted that the PCE leaders concentrate on organized military resistance and immediate victory. The war presented Stalin and the Soviet Politburo with both a political and a military-strategic dilemma. On the one hand, they desired the victory of the left; on the other, they were not clear how the Soviet Union might assist in practical terms, even though world radical opinion as well as certain figures in the Soviet government expected the world's only revolutionary state to assist the only ongoing leftist-collectivist revolution, even though not a Communist revolution, anywhere in the world.

The Soviet decision to intervene was incremental and proceeded through several steps. The first arrangements were for financial assistance and civilian supplies, followed by the establishment of normal diplomatic relations for the first time and the arrival of Soviet diplomats late in August. These were followed early the next month by a small number of Soviet aviators disguised as tourists. Only in mid-September, once the Popular Front government was being reorganized and planning to develop a regular army, did Stalin and his associates make a firm decision to intervene. Supplies began to arrive before the close of October and helped to make possible the defense of Madrid. Late-model Soviet planes and tanks, manned by Soviet crews, outclassed the more obsolescent equipment originally supplied by Germany and Italy. Meanwhile, payment was guaranteed in October by the shipment to Moscow of most of the sizable Spanish gold reserve (the fourth largest in the world), worth about $530 million, for safekeeping.

Rather than accepting stalemate or defeat, however, Hitler and Mussolini chose escalation. By November Germany had dispatched the "Condor Legion" of ninety planes and crewmen, accompanied by a small number of other arms, while Mussolini decided to send full units of Italian volunteers and troops, amounting to nearly 50,000 men. Of the three dictators, Mussolini became the most committed to sustaining large-scale intervention, judging the outcome in Spain fundamental for the broader policy of Italy in the Mediterranean. Both

Italy and Germany continued to supply Franco with sizable shipments of arms on easy terms of credit,[47] though in 1938 Hitler did force the Spanish dictator to allow Germany to control a series of mining and other raw materials companies that would guarantee exports to Germany.[48]

The country whose domestic politics were most affected by the Spanish war was France, whose political system was more similar to that of the Second Republic than was any other. French conservatives vehemently opposed the Spanish left and any support for them, charging that this would bring civil war to France. Part of the French left wished to assist the Spanish Republic (as did a very few conservatives, strictly for military and geostrategic reasons), but the government did not wish any conflict with Britain, while some of the more moderate sectors of the left were strongly anti-Communist and suspected that Soviet policy sought indirectly to involve France in a war with Germany.[49]

The British government never varied its policy, taking a disdainful view of both sides in Spain, viewing the Spanish revolution as nothing but destruction and trouble for Western Europe. If this meant that Franco and the rightists won the war, London was willing to accept such a result, judging that Franco would govern in the interests of Spain as an independent dictator who would not become a pawn of Hitler.[50]

SOVIET POLICY

Of the three intervening powers, the Soviet Union differed from Italy and Germany in that it had maintained its own political party in Spain since 1920, though for the first fifteen years quite ineffectually. The Spanish Communist

[47] The role of the Italian military is examined in E. Chiappa, *Il Corpo di Truppe Volontarie durante la Guerra Civile spagnuola 1936–1939* (Milan, 1999); F. Pedriali, *Guerra di Spagna e aviazione italiana* (Rome, 1992); F. Bargoni, *L'impegno navale italiano durante la Guerra civile spagnuola (1936–1939)* (Rome, 1992); and in the excellent summary by G. Rochat, *Le guerre italiane, 1935–1943: Dall'impero di Etiopia alla disfatta* (Turin, 2005), 98–141.

[48] See G. T. Harper, *German Economic Policy in Spain during the Spanish Civil War, 1936–1939* (The Hague, 1967), and, more broadly, C. Leitz, *Economic Relations between Nazi Germany and Franco's Spain 1936–1945* (Oxford, 1996).

[49] For French policy, see J. Borrás Llop, *Francia ante la guerra civil española: Burguesía, interés nacional e interés de clase* (Madrid, 1981); J. Martínez Parrilla, *Las fuerzas armadas francesas ante la guerra civil española (1936–1939)* (Madrid, 1987); and P. Jackson, "French Strategy in the Spanish Civil War," in C. Leitz and J. Dunthorn, eds., *Spain in an International Context, 1936–1959* (New York, 1999), 55–79.

[50] See J. Edwards, *The British Government and the Spanish Civil War* (London, 1979); T. Buchanan, *Britain and the Spanish Civil War* (Cambridge, UK, 1997); E. Moradiellos, *La perfidia de Albión: El gobierno británico y la Guerra Civil española* (Madrid, 1996); W. L. Kleine-Ahlbrandt, *The Policy of Simmering: A Study of British Policy during the Spanish Civil War* (The Hague, 1962); J. Avilés Farré, *Pasión y farsa: Franceses y británicos ante la guerra civil española* (Madrid, 1994); and, more broadly, E. Moradiellos, *El reñidero de Europa: Las dimensiones internacionales de la guerra civil española* (Barcelona, 2001), and M. Alpert, *A New International History of the Spanish Civil War* (Houndsmills/New York, 1997).

Party had preached revolutionary insurrection and the formation of soviets almost uninterruptedly, but had changed its line in accordance with the new Popular Front policy late in 1935, which enabled it to increase its parliamentary representation from one to sixteen in the elections of 1936. It still remained a small party, but expanded to at least 50,000 members (official propaganda claiming twice as many). Concentrating major activities and marches in Madrid, it succeeded in giving frightened conservatives and moderates an exaggerated notion of Communist power, thought erroneously by some to be manipulating the entire Popular Front.

Spain provided the first opportunity to implement the Comintern's new strategy of using electoral coalitions to inaugurate the new kind of coalition, a "people's republic," by nominally legal and parliamentary means, and thus the PCE took the most advanced position of any of the leftist parties during the final months before the war in promoting radical legislation. Its position was not "moderate," as sometimes alleged, except insofar as it discouraged random violence and destructive strikes, setting itself firmly against any form of insurrectionary provocation. The political situation was too promising to weaken with any threat of civil war.[51]

The outbreak of the civil war therefore posed a major dilemma. The Comintern had preached revolution uninterruptedly between 1919 and 1935, but had never sparked a single successful revolution. In 1936, such a revolution took over most of the Republican zone in Spain, but it was primarily an anarchist and socialist, not a communist, revolution, and it was taking place amid a desperate civil war in which Italy and Germany were clearly intervening on behalf of the counterrevolutionary forces. The extreme left in the Soviet Union and around the world expected the Soviet government to support the revolution, communist or not, but only a year earlier Stalin had adopted a new policy of collective security, which aimed at rapprochement with Britain and France against Nazi Germany. This required downplaying the subversive and revolutionary aspects of Soviet policy, which, conversely, direct intervention on behalf of the Spanish revolution would only reemphasize.

After two months of dithering, Stalin sought to square the circle, sending sufficient military support to give the revolutionaries a chance to win, while directing Communists inside the Republican zone to ally with the more moderate forces in order to channel and control the revolution. Strategically, this would also function as antifascist policy, though Maxim Litvinov, the foreign minister, warned Stalin that it might frighten London and Paris, undercutting the policy of collective security. The military intervention was to be kept as secret as possible, but its dimensions soon became well enough

---

[51] Comintern strategy in Spain is treated in A. Elorza and M. Bizcarrondo, *Queridos camaradas: La Internacional Comunista y España, 1919–1939* (Barcelona, 1999), and S. G. Payne, *The Spanish Civil War, the Soviet Union, and Communism* (New Haven, Conn., 2004). See also R. Cruz, *El Partido Comunista de España en la II República* (Madrid, 1987).

known, and often were even exaggerated in news reports and enemy propaganda alike.[52]

A major collateral benefit would be the strengthening of Spanish Communism. As Georgi Dimitrov, the secretary of the Comintern, and Palmiro Togliatti, the head of its Western European section, made clear in their internal memoranda and publications, the goal was not restoration of liberal democracy – merely a propaganda line – but to make possible an increasingly influential role for the Communists in achieving the "new style" "people's democracy." This would not be a Communist regime, but a new kind of exclusively leftist republic in which all conservative interests had been eliminated, with an economic program similar to the New Economic Policy introduced by Lenin in the Soviet Union in 1921.[53]

From September 1936 the Soviet regime became committed to a four-track approach to the war: 1) major direct military participation in the form of Red Army weapons and personnel; 2) major internal political participation through the Comintern and the PCE; 3) major collateral political, propaganda, and material assistance to the Republic, through the Comintern, its parties, and its front organizations, as well as through the provision of food and other nonmilitary supplies from the Soviet Union, along with other Soviet collateral assistance from a variety of international dummy companies; and 4) active diplomatic support for the Republic, particularly in the Non-Intervention Committee in London, as well as in bilateral diplomacy. The military cost of this was slight. The assistance was paid for by the $530 million in gold shipped to Moscow, and few more than 200 Soviet military personnel died in Spain – in terms of Stalinist expenditure of human life, the merest drop in the bucket.

The strategic situation became more complicated in the summer of 1937, for two reasons. One was the new offensive by Franco's navy in the Mediterranean, abetted by pirate attacks by Mussolini's submarines against shipping bound for the Republic. This greatly increased the risks, leading Stalin to close the direct Mediterranean route for Soviet arms. Henceforth all supplies would move from northern Soviet ports to France, to be transshipped at considerable expense.

---

[52] There is a growing literature on the Soviet role. In addition to the works previously cited, see R. Radosh, M. Habeck, and G. Sevostianov, *Spain Betrayed: The Soviet Union in the Spanish Civil War* (New Haven, Conn., 2001); D. Kowalsky, *La Unión Soviética y la guerra civil española: Una revisión crítica* (Barcelona, 2003); F. Schauff, *La victoria frustrada: La Unión Soviética, la Internacional Comunista y la guerra civil española* (Barcelona, 2008); the several books by Angel Viñas, *El oro de Moscú* (Madrid, 1979), *La soledad de la República* (Barcelona, 2006), *El escudo de la República* (Barcelona, 2007), *El honor de la República* (Barcelona, 2009), and *El desplome de la República* (Barcelona, 2009), and the exposition catalog of the Fundación Pablo Iglesias, *Los rusos en la guerra de España 1936–1939* (Madrid, 2009).

[53] As presented in Togliatti's article in *International Press Correspondence*, 16:48 (24 October 1936), 1292–95; in Dimitrov's remarks as quoted in Elorza and Bizcarrondo, *Queridos camaradas*, 321; and in A. I. Sobolev et al., *Outline History of the Communist International* (Moscow, 1971), 416–17, 436.

The second development was Japan's invasion of China in July 1937. A two-front war was the Soviet strategic nightmare, and Stalin considered it vital to maintain Chinese resistance, even though the Chinese government was a political foe. Soon he was sending as much or more assistance to China as had been sent earlier to Republican Spain, so that supplies for the latter diminished in the second half of 1937 and in 1938, though they never stopped altogether. Meanwhile, as the situation in Europe grew more dangerous, Stalin virtually gave up on the possibility of a Republican victory and searched for an exit strategy. In mid-1938 Soviet representatives mentioned the possibility of withdrawal, even without a clear-cut leftist victory, if Hitler and Mussolini would terminate their own intervention. They would not, and Stalin found no alternative to continuing Soviet support for the Republic, albeit at a much diminished rate, sending the final shipment of Soviet arms at the close of 1938.

FRANCO'S COUNTERREVOLUTION

Franco has been called the leader of the most successful counterrevolutionary movement of the twentieth century.[54] This seems a valid conclusion, all the more ironic in that Franco had no such ambition as late as 12 July 1936, or even afterward when he arrived in Spanish Morocco to take command of what would be called the Army of Africa. He had always been a conservative, but also a strict professional who kept out of politics, and under the Republic at first a relatively moderate conservative who, at the beginning of the rebellion, showed no disagreement with Mola's "open" project that provisionally retained the republican form of government, with separation of church and state, and a referendum and/or constituent parliament to determine the character of the new regime. Franco and nearly all other district commanders began the rebellion under the slogan "!Viva España! !Viva la República!"

The issue of supreme military leadership nonetheless soon became an open question after the nominal commander-in-chief, Gen. José Sanjurjo, was killed in a plane crash on the third day of the conflict. From that point Franco began to step forward ever more prominently. The Junta de Defensa Nacional, formed by Mola in Burgos on 23 July 1936, was a standard interim military junta. Its head, Gen. Miguel Cabanellas, nominally presiding as the most senior general, ultimately became something of an embarrassment insofar as he was a Mason, a moderate liberal, and a former candidate of the Radical Party. Its first two months were a time of prolonged military emergency, punctuated in the rear guard by mass atrocities against the left.

The war entered its second phase in September with the formation of the first coherent Popular Front government under Largo Caballero, just as

---

[54] By Michael Seidman, in *The Victorious Counterrevolution* (Madison, Wisc., 2011), a study not of politics but of the surprisingly efficient internal mobilization of the insurgent zone, which made military victory possible.

Franco was marshaling his forces for the final drive on Madrid. At that point the insurgent commanders were expecting victory within no more than a few months.

From the beginning Franco stood out as the most important rebel general. He already enjoyed greater prestige than any of his colleagues, and he led the only high-quality combat force on either side, one on which the whole conflict apparently turned. Moreover, he was the only general who had begun to develop an international profile, for it was his representatives who had negotiated the crucial assistance of Hitler and Mussolini. By September he clearly stood head and shoulders above his fellow commanders.[55]

The idea of establishing a *mando único* – commander-in-chief – stemmed from two sources: the minority of monarchist senior commanders and the members of Franco's own entourage, made up of several officers of slightly lower rank and a few key associates, such as his older brother Nicolás. Once the appointment of a *generalissimo* was agreed upon at the junta's meeting on 21 September, Franco was the leading candidate, though there are no reliable documents on exactly how the meeting developed. It apparently ended with all the junta members except Cabanellas voting for Franco.[56]

The other principal issue has to do with precisely what the members of the junta thought they were voting for. Electing Franco *generalissimo* gave him full power, since the junta operated a strictly military government, but for how long, with what political title, and with what ultimate objective? There is no evidence that these issues were ever thoroughly discussed. When Franco was officially invested with authority in a ceremony on 1 October 1936, it was announced that he assumed the authority of "chief of state," without the slightest indication of any time limit. And that was the way Franco would govern ever afterward.

In his classic *On War*, Carl von Clausewitz wrote of the effect in wars of what he called *Wechselwirkung*, unforeseen changes wrought by the reciprocal interaction of the combatants, resulting in new tactics or policies, and sometimes in mutual radicalization. Something of that sort seems to have happened with Franco during the first months of the conflict. He began the war apparently in consonance with Mola's "open project," which would bring decisive change, but also to some extent potentially limit such change.

There is no indication that he schemed originally to become *generalissimo*, but once the role of commander-in-chief became vacant on 20 July, he showed increasing initiative. Monarchist commanders, definitely in a minority,

[55] For biographical accounts, see P. Preston, *Franco: A Biography* (London, 1993); J. P. Fusi, *Franco: Autoritarismo y poder personal* (Madrid, 1985); and J. Palacios and S. G. Payne, *Franco, mi padre* (Madrid, 2008).

[56] There are two informed accounts of this meeting. Gen. Alfredo Kindelán presents his version in his *Mis cuadernos de guerra* (Barcelona, 1982), 103–04, and Félix Maíz, Mola's civilian aide, a different one in his posthumous *Mola frente a Franco. Guerra y muerte del general Mola* (Pamplona, 2007), 287–89. Maíz was not present but claimed to have had access to the notes prepared by Col. Federico Montaner, who acted as secretary.

encouraged his election because they judged that Franco would both provide firm leadership for victory and prepare for a monarchist restoration. He eventually would, yet that would take nearly forty years. He had been a loyal monarchist until 1931, but afterward had refused to conspire on behalf of the monarchy and, once he assumed full power, would for some time show little inclination to steer the new regime toward a restoration. Moreover, in his first official remarks as *generalissimo* he gave no indication of planning a brief interim government, but rather talked of restoring Spain to greatness, which implied a lengthy agenda.

By that point he seems to have given up any idea of a reformed republic, even an authoritarian and corporative republic. Franco's new perspective was that Europe had entered the age of dictators, who provided a more advanced form of strong and unified government – exactly what Spain needed. Italian authorities discreetly suggested Fascist Italy as a model, but when the first German ambassador exceeded instructions and tried to involve himself in domestic politics, Franco had him recalled. It is doubtful that Franco ever read Joseph de Maistre, the Savoyan political theorist of the early nineteenth century, but he implicitly accepted De Maistre's dictum, "The counterrevolution is not the opposite of a revolution, but rather is an opposing revolution." To deal with a country broken in two and to overcome the effects of the revolution in the Republican zone, Spain needed a strong, even radical, new kind of modern regime, authoritarian and socially mobilized, a one-party regime that would also be a Catholic regime.[57]

All this was easier said than done and did not begin to take form until Franco formed by fiat his new state party, Falange Española Tradicionalista de las JONS (FET) in April 1937, merging the fascist Falange with the Carlist Traditionalists. The Falange had no strong leaders but had swelled in numbers as the radical nationalist party most able to mobilize for civil war.[58] Merger with the Carlists brought together the two main sources of paramilitary volunteers, but the goal of unifying the most right-wing, Catholic, and completely traditionalist movement in western Europe with a fascist party created cognitive dissonance from the beginning, and implied the subordination of the Carlists, who were given lesser parcels of influence.[59]

Internal division within the army was one of the major factors that resulted in civil war rather than a coup d'etat, but the new regime of Franco provided firm direction and achieved unity. This was totally different from the situation of the anti-Bolsheviks in Russia or the counterrevolutionaries in some other conflicts. In Russia, Leninism had been a strength of the Bolsheviks,

[57] The best account of Franco's political leadership during the conflict is J. Tusell, *Franco en la guerra civil* (Barcelona, 1992).
[58] The history of the Falange is treated in J. M. Thomàs, *Lo que fue la Falange* (Barcelona, 1999); J. L. Rodriguez Jiménez, *Historia de Falange Española de las JONS* (Madrid, 2000); and S. G. Payne, *Fascism in Spain, 1923–1977* (Madison, Wisc., 1999).
[59] On the political role of Carlism during the conflict, see J. C. Peñas Bernaldo de Quirós, *El carlismo, la República y la Guerra Civil* (Madrid, 1996).

but in Spain the nearest equivalent of a Lenin was the counterrevolutionary Franco, a major advantage of the insurgents that proved indispensable to their victory.

Franco achieved political unity by proscribing politics, naming himself "national chief" of the FET, abolishing other parties (the other rightist parties accepting dissolution, having already initiated it themselves), and requiring that all energies be concentrated on the military struggle. This was accepted with little murmur, for everyone knew that too much was at stake. It was true that by the winter of 1937, Mola, Queipo de Llano, and a number of other military commanders had grown unhappy with the overweening style of personal dictatorship that Franco was developing, even though he was relatively discreet with his fellow generals, but Mola insisted to his colleagues that any question of demanding changes from Franco be postponed until the hour of victory. By June 1937 Mola himself was dead in a plane crash, and none of the others had the prestige to question the *generalissimo*.

Franco saw his new regime as eclectic and uniquely Spanish, which to a large extent was indeed the case, though it adopted the standard new form of the one-party nationalist authoritarian regimes already in vogue in central and east central Europe. In the early months Franco had made a few references to the Portuguese model of authoritarian and corporative republic, which may also have been what Mola had in mind, but Salazar's system in Lisbon was soon rejected as too moderate, a partial compromise with parliamentarianism. By accepting the Twenty-Six Points of the Falange as official doctrine, Franco adopted a fascistic credo, but he insisted on its eclecticism and willingness to incorporate changes. A one-party regime with an ideology, even though one not fully developed in every respect, was something that he considered crucial to avoid repeating the "Primo de Rivera mistake," the "hollow" dictatorship of the 1920s.

During the civil war, the FET apparatus devoted itself primarily to propaganda and to military mobilization.[60] For the duration of the conflict, there was only limited development of the institutions of the new state, though a regular government of ministers, most of them civilians, was established at the close of January 1938.[61]

The military were more important than the party, and when Franco's brother-in-law and minister of the interior Ramón Serrano Suñer led a "victory visit" to Rome in June 1939, one of the generals accompanying him explained to a high Fascist official that the difference between Fascist Italy and Franco's Spain was that the role played in the former by the Fascist Party was played

[60] On the party's evolution, see J. M. Thomàs, *La Falange de Franco. Fascismo y fascistización en el regimen franquista (1937–1945)* (Barcelona, 2001).

[61] The development of the new state is treated in J. L. Orella, *La formación del Estado Nacional durante la Guerra Civil española* (Madrid, 2001), and in S. G. Payne, *The Franco Regime 1936–1975* (Madison, Wisc., 1987), 87–230 [*El régimen de Franco 1936–1975* (Madrid, 1987), 91–241]. The most detailed history of the regime is L. Suárez Fernández, *Francisco Franco y su tiempo* (Madrid, 1984), 8 vols.

in the latter by the army. That, however, was something of an exaggeration. Franco knew that a merely military dictatorship would be doomed to fail. He appointed a considerable number of army and navy officers to important government positions, especially during the decade 1936–45, but only as individual state appointees, not as corporate representatives of the armed forces.

Franco was well aware that he led a semipluralist and diverse "National Movement," as the entire insurgent effort was often called. From the beginning, he gave limited representation to the military, the monarchists, Falangists, Carlists, and so-called political Catholics within his state apparatus, to which he also appointed a certain number of relatively apolitical technical specialists.

Once the conflict assumed the dimensions of a war of religion, support for the church became fundamental, and the idea of maintaining separation of church and state was forgotten. Nonetheless, there existed considerable contradiction between the fascistic doctrines of the Falange and the church, though the former made a special effort to emphasize its Catholic identity.[62] The Vatican remained wary, and even after Franco had won the war, negotiations for an official concordat moved very slowly. Later, by 1945, Franco's regime presented itself as the most Catholic in the world, though the papacy did not necessarily agree. A concordat was signed only much later, in 1953, after the regime had become more moderate and had gained a degree of international rehabilitation thanks to the Cold War.

The war effort of the insurgent zone was more effectively organized than that of its adversary in almost every respect. Initially, the territory held by the insurgents was severely handicapped industrially, financially, and commercially, enjoying only one economic advantage – nearly 70 percent of the country's agricultural production. It nonetheless quickly came to enjoy a key economic advantage: completely unified policy and regulation. All financial and industrial activities were regulated by a series of national and provincial boards, and all foreign exchange was controlled by the state, as were exports and precious metals. In some cases major export items were taken over directly, and in key areas of agriculture, such as wheat and almonds, "national services" were established for finance and marketing. Economic regulations were not merely comprehensive but generally coherent and effective, encouraging sustained production and consumption while maximizing the export potential, especially in minerals. When the Republican northern zone was conquered in 1937, metallurgical and coal production received special attention and soon exceeded prewar norms. Martial law guaranteed labor discipline, wage levels generally being rolled back to those of February 1936. The banking system was coordinated, and banks in the insurgent zone generally turned a profit during the war, while inflation remained moderate.[63]

[62] This dissonance is especially emphasized in A. Lazo, *Una familia mal avenida: Falange, Iglesia y Ejército* (Madrid, 2008).

[63] The best study of Franco's social and economic mobilization is presented by Seidman, *Victorious Counterrevolution*. Key economic studies will be found in J. A. Sánchez Asiaín, *Economía y finanzas en la Guerra Civil española (1936–1939)* (Madrid, 1999) and *La banca*

Franco's forces also carried the economic war directly to the enemy, harassing Republican shipping relentlessly, making energetic efforts to handicap Republican financial activity abroad, and later, in 1938, flooding the international market with millions of captured Republican *pesetas* so as to eliminate most of the latter's purchasing power. In September 1937 the Republican *peseta* was still worth nearly 60 percent of the "*peseta nacional*" but declined precipitously in the final year, as inflation in the Republican zone reached more than 1,500 percent.

Franco was able to wage a large part of the war on foreign credit, something denied to the revolutionary regime. Altogether, Mussolini and Hitler provided about $600 million of war materiel, primarily, though not exclusively, on credit. The insurgent zone maintained production and consumption, a stable *peseta*, adequate imports, and only a moderate inflation of little more than 10 percent a year. Economic success was essential to Franco's victory. His economic results were in every respect superior to those of the victorious Bolsheviks in Russia.

Exactly the opposite was true of the Republican zone, whose political divisions generated territorial, administrative, and economic divisions. During the first year, it contained six different regional governments – the ones in Madrid and Barcelona, the anarchist Council of Aragon, and three different governments in the northern zone. In addition, any number of local revolutionary councils issued their own money or script, so that "by the end of 1937 more than two thousand different organizations had issued in the Republican zone approximately 10,000 kinds of paper bills and 50 metallic coins.... Of 1075 municipalities in Catalonia, 687 issued money."[64] In addition, each distinct government on the coastline controlled its own foreign trade and financial exchange, at least during the first year, and maintained its own customs duties, sometimes even with regard to other Republican regions.

Much the same happened with the Republic's extensive financial resources. During the early months multiple purchasing commissions were established in a chaotic and wasteful manner, amateur operations often swindled by foreign suppliers and occasionally looted by their own administrators. Placing most of the capital in Soviet hands at least achieved a degree of coordination. The same chaos reappeared at the close of the war, as remaining financial resources, and especially the gold, silver, and jewels obtained from the large-scale looting, were mostly sent abroad, though in a disorderly fashion. The two main Socialist factions came off with the greater share,[65] while a small part was recovered by Franco.

---

española en la guerra civil 1936–1939 (Madrid, 1992), and P. Martín Aceña and E. Martínez Ruiz, eds., *La economía de la guerra civil* (Madrid, 2006).

[64] J. A. Sánchez Asiaín, "Recursos económicos y organización territorial en la República de la Guerra Civil," *Anales de la Real Academia de Ciencias Morales y Políticas*, 60:85 (2008), 523–24.

[65] The principal denunciation of the disposal of the loot is presented from an anarchist point of view, which ignores the role of the FAI-CNT, in the two books by F. Olaya Morales,

Though certain sectors of Republican agricultural production increased with good weather during 1937, industrial production declined. From October to March 1938, it stabilized at about 55 to 60 percent of prewar output, but then, with the sources of Barcelona's electric power occupied by Franco's advance, dropped off sharply. Even worse was the disastrous decline in food production and supplies. The Republican zone suffered severe malnutrition during the last year of the war and was on the verge of starvation when the conflict ended.[66]

So far as can be determined, the economic performance of the Franco regime during the Spanish conflict was in a class by itself for the European civil wars of the era. Though Spain was coming out of a depression (in its case, perhaps more a severe recession than a great depression), the economy had not been disrupted by a major war, as was true in every other case. The Bolsheviks won their struggle, but only at the cost of oppressive totalitarian policies that left the economic structure gutted, as Lenin had to admit. In the case of relatively more advanced Finland, the economic dearth resulting from World War I heightened the paranoia of Finnish Socialists, already subject to the propaganda of the Bolsheviks, and was a factor in their initiation of civil war. Later, in Yugoslavia and Greece, the economic disruption brought by World War II would be fundamental. By contrast with Franco's territory, the economic disaster of the Republican zone was striking, a graphic expression of the internal divisions and incoherence of the Spanish left, and a major factor in the latter's defeat.

A SECOND COUNTERREVOLUTION?

Beginning in 1937, the extreme revolutionary left charged the Communists and their moderate allies (mainly left Republicans and non-*caballerista* Socialists) with imposing a counterrevolution in the Republican zone, a thesis later repeated by quite a few historians. The charge always infuriated the Communists, since they claimed to be the only serious revolutionaries, the only ones who had experience in carrying out a successful revolution. They insisted that they simply wished to apply revolutionary discipline, indispensable to the revolution's long-term success.

The growth in the numbers and power of Spanish Communism can be traced to three factors: the centralized discipline of the party structure, which gave it greater unity, cohesiveness, flexibility, and efficiency than any of the other leftist parties; its emphasis on centralized military power, for which it

La gran estafa: Negrín, Prieto y el patrimonio nacional (Barcelona, 1996) and *El expolio de la República* (Barcelona, 2004).
[66] In addition to the work edited by Martín Aceña and Martínez Ruiz, see J. M. Bricall, *Política económica de la Generalitat* (Barcelona, 1979), 2 vols., and "La economía española (1936–1939)," in M. Tuñón de Lara, ed., *La guerra civil española 50 años después* (Barcelona, 1985), 359–417; and J. Palafox, "La economía," in S. Payne and J. Tusell, eds., *La Guerra Civil: Una nueva visión del conflicto que dividió España* (Madrid, 1996), 195–265.

was better prepared than any other party; and the support of the Comintern and the Soviet regime, which gave it greater resources. The Soviets insisted on building a new regular army, the People's Army, by analogy with the Red Army, but also on waging the war under the banner of the "democratic republic," a war between "democracy and fascism." They held this to be indispensable for two reasons: first, it would facilitate mobilizing the more liberal sectors of the lower middle class, and, second, it might more readily attract Britain and France, in order not merely to assist the left in Spain but also to endorse the Soviet strategy of collective security.

Though the Soviet and Comintern leaders thought in terms of analogy to the Russian civil war, they also emphasized significant differences. In Russia, the Bolsheviks occupied the space of the extreme revolutionary left, co-opting, crowding out, or coercing the anarchists and left SRs. Though they took a more moderate line vis-à-vis the peasantry, they soon nationalized most of the urban economy. By comparison, the struggle in Spain was in some ways even more complex. In 1936 it was more important to win the battle of foreign opinion, which required a more moderate line; at the same time, the Spanish independent extreme revolutionary left was stronger than its Russian counterparts. The extreme left policy of "total revolution now" had to be combated, for three reasons: first and foremost, it concentrated resources on social and economic revolution to the detriment of the military effort; second, it narrowed the base of support by alienating the lower middle class: third, it frightened opinion in France and Britain. Moreover, unlike the earlier situation in Russia, the left had to strongly wave the banner of patriotism, insisting that they were defending Spanish independence from invasion by Italy and Germany.[67]

For the Comintern, the situation had become paradoxical in the extreme. For fifteen years it had sought desperately to promote revolutionary insurrections and civil wars, always without success. After the disastrous failure in Germany provoked the change to the Popular Front tactic, the revolutionary process in Spain developed rapidly, positioning the bulk of the worker left to the left of the PCE. But since the Popular Front also controlled what was left of Republican institutions, the Comintern stressed use of the latter under the flag of democracy and legitimacy, so as to maximize support at home and abroad. This required a two-level policy of international propaganda and diplomacy to emphasize democracy, while within the Republican zone the revolution had to be channeled on behalf of the war effort and the "democratic republic of a new type."

The Spanish Communist Party grew first as a party of revolution but second as a party of order, drawing many members of the lower middle class. Its numbers had swelled to nearly 250,000 by March 1937, and to a purported

---

[67] Both sides stressed that they were waging a war of national independence. X. M. Núñez Seixas, *!Fuera el invasor! Nacionalismos y movilización bélica durante la guerra civil española (1936–1939)* (Madrid, 2006).

370,000 eighteen months later, gaining influence particularly among the Republican military.

From the autumn of 1936 the state apparatus was steadily expanded under the Largo Caballero government, which sought to reassert authority throughout the Republican zone, and the Communists hoped to make use of this to channel the revolution. Particular targets were the anarcho-syndicalists of the FAI-CNT, as well as the much smaller rival communist party, the POUM, which was charged with being "Trotskyist," though its leaders had broken with Trotsky in 1934. The POUM was actually an independent anti-Stalinist Marxist-Leninist party, which demanded that total revolutionary socialism be imposed immediately, a process that, it claimed, would inevitably bring military victory in its wake.

Stalin took the unusual step of writing a personal letter to Largo Caballero in December 1936, emphasizing that the course of "the Spanish revolution" was different from that of Russia and should emphasize "the parliamentary path" while striving to attract the lower middle class and making greater use of the more moderate left Republicans, who could provide a valuable smoke screen. The Republican prime minister replied that he took Stalin's point, but that among the Spanish left "parliamentary institutions ... have few enthusiasts," while the left Republicans seemed to show little interest in leading the revolution.[68]

In a public polemic against the anarchists in March 1937, *Mundo Obrero*, the official Communist daily, insisted that the extreme revolutionary left had no reason to doubt the meaning of the kind of "democratic republic," a republic "of a new type," that was needed to win the war. This had nothing to do with a "classic democratic republic," as in France or the United States, but was a special transition regime in which the left had a monopoly on armed force, having replaced the old army with a People's Army, and in which the peasants held most of the land, worker control and/or nationalization reigned in industry, large-scale expropriation of property had taken place, conservative forces and large-scale capitalism had ceased to exist, and the government was led primarily by the working class. This was repeated ad infinitum by the leadership and the Communist media.

Beginning in September 1936 Prime Minister Largo Caballero also served as war minister, but both Communists and the more moderate left charged him with ineptitude, and with privileging revolution more than war. In May 1937 he was abruptly replaced by the Socialist Juan Negrín, a follower of Prieto and the candidate of the more moderate Socialists, as well as of President Azaña. Negrín subsequently became the most controversial figure of the civil war, the only major leader not merely hated by the other side but, by the end of the conflict, scorned by most of those on his own side as well. Contrary to what was often said, he was not selected by the Soviets, but he was fully acceptable to them because he was a professor of physiology with impeccable professional

---

[68] The original French text first appeared in S. de Madariaga, *Spain: A Modern History* (New York, 1958), 672–74.

credentials, a serious, practical, and determined administrator who had never been an extreme revolutionary.

Formation of the first Negrín government represented a major victory in the struggle to restore state authority, though it still had far to go. It was a product of the "May Days," a three-day revolt of the extreme revolutionary left in Barcelona from 3 to 6 May 1937, in which possibly as many as 400 people were killed. This ended in defeat for the extreme left, who grudgingly accepted the need for greater cooperation with a central government.

Negrín became the principal war leader of the Republic. He reduced the council of ministers from eighteen to nine, excluded the FAI-CNT, handed a new unified Ministry of National Defense to Prieto, and cooperated closely with Soviet advisors and the Communists in military affairs, where they shared the same priorities. Many anarchist agricultural collectives were broken up, and on 16 June the POUM was outlawed and all its top leaders arrested, under the indirect supervision of the Soviet NKVD. Andreu Nin, the party's political secretary, was tortured and secretly murdered, as in the Soviet Union, though his disappearance and the fate of the POUM became the principal cause célèbre of the Republican side during the war. Later, during 1938, the other top POUM leaders were officially prosecuted, convicted of hindering the war effort, and sentenced to prison terms.

Amid growing military frustration, a serious rupture developed between Negrín and Prieto, the latter resenting the growth of Soviet and Communist influence, and concluding that defeat was inevitable. A second Negrín government was formed in April 1938 without Prieto, marking the apex of the prime minister's leadership, as he personally took over the Defense Ministry. Even more Communists were appointed to top posts in the army, the police, and intelligence.

By that point Negrín had become indispensable to the Republican resistance. It is clear from the evaluations in Comintern reports that the Communists, grateful for his close collaboration, did not consider him either an agent or a crypto-Communist, but rather a pro-Soviet Socialist who retained an independent identity. He did not give them everything they wanted and refused to do certain things they desired, particularly in domestic political and economic affairs. Though a faction of *"negrinistas"* emerged in 1937–38 as a result of his leadership, he had no genuine base within the Socialist Party, but retained power because none of the other leaders had the courage to try to replace him.

What were Negrín's personal goals and ideals? Since he wrote almost nothing, this is hard to determine. By his own standards, Negrín – unlike much of the left – was not merely a Spanish patriot but even something of a Spanish nationalist. Like all the left, he was a strong sectarian, believing that rightist rule would utterly ruin Spain. He was not an extreme revolutionary, but neither was he a democrat, believing that the salvation of the country lay in a strong authoritarian leftist state, with a statist economy based on extensive nationalization but not on extreme revolutionary collectivism, an approach that happened to coincide up to a point with Communist policy. He did not, however, seek a Communist regime, though for the time being he could find no alternative to large-scale support from the Soviets. Negrín believed his own propaganda, convinced that in fighting Franco he was preventing Hitler and Mussolini from taking over Spain. During the spring and summer of 1938, he worked wonders in reviving Republican military strength, but by the close of that year had come to the conclusion that the war must be prolonged primarily for the purpose of gaining more acceptable terms of surrender.

TWO WAR EFFORTS

The Spanish civil war was the most broadly mobilized and militarily innovative of all the civil wars of the era, and was fought on the largest scale. In toto the Russian conflict lasted longer, was fought over a much greater geographic expanse and at one time or another involved many more men (and women), but, despite calling up more than five million men, it is doubtful that at any time the Red Army had many more than a fraction of these fully mobilized and ready for combat, at least until the final phase. By the end of 1937 both armies in Spain were proportionately larger, organized with greater sophistication, and also better armed.[69]

Nonetheless, neither army in Spain could remotely be compared to that of a major power. Altogether, more than two million men were called up on both sides combined, which, proportionate to population, constituted even more extensive recruitment than that of the Bolsheviks, but there were severe limits to training, organization, and leadership. Though front lines were very long, they were also generally quiescent, offensive operations being narrowly focused. Overall, the Spanish struggle was a low-intensity conflict punctuated by a number of high-intensity battles. Despite sophisticated new arms, firepower in general was limited, which explains why overall casualties were not higher. Few more than 150,000 men on both sides combined were killed (some

---

[69] Attention to the Spanish war has focused on political, propagandistic, and international issues to the neglect of military history. The first serious studies were the Monografías de la Guerra de España, prepared by the Servicio Histórico Militar under the direction of Gen. J. M. Martínez Bande. These were, not surprisingly, written from the viewpoint of the victorious army. The most thorough and detailed military history, and one of the most impartial, is J. Blázquez Miguel, *Historia militar de la guerra civil española* (Madrid, 2004–08), 6 vols. The best military treatment in a one-volume general history of war will be found in R. and J. M. Salas Larrazábal, *Historia general de la Guerra de España* (Madrid, 1986). Other principal accounts include R. Salas Larrazábal, *Historia del Ejército Popular de la República* (Madrid, 1973), 4 vols.; J. Semprún, *Del Hacho al Pirineo: El Ejército Nacional en la Guerra de España* (Madrid, 2004); G. Cardona, *Historia militar de una guerra civil. Estrategia y táctica de la guerra de España* (Barcelona, 2006); C. Vidal, *La guerra que ganó Franco. Historia militar de la guerra civil española* (Barcelona, 2006); M. Alpert, *El Ejército Popular de la República, 1936–1939* (Barcelona, 2007); C. Engel, *Estrategia y táctica en la guerra de España 1936–1939* (Madrid, 2008); and J. M. Reverte, *El arte de matar: Cómo se hizo la Guerra Civil Española* (Barcelona, 2009). The best military account in English will be found in A. Beevor, *The Battle for Spain: The Spanish Civil War 1936–1939* (London, 2006).

20,000 of them not Spanish), which represented not much more than six percent of all those mobilized. Militarily, the Russian war was of even lower intensity, though the overall death totals in the population were enormous, due to famine and epidemics. By contrast, in Spain both sides maintained decent standards of public health.

Every major revolution faces the problem of creating an effective new army. This was the case in England in 1642, in the North American colonies in 1775–76, in France in 1792–93, in Russia in 1918, and in China after 1927. In each case, the revolutionaries moved to create a "new model" army (though perhaps least so in the American case, which was also in some respects the least revolutionary) that nonetheless had the structure of a regular army. That the Spanish revolutionaries at first resisted this was not surprising, for, to some extent, it had first been resisted in the other cases. The founding of the People's Army did not settle the problem, for the Spanish revolution was unique in its semipluralism. Political conflict about the army persisted, particularly in the northern Republican zone, where there were three separate military administrations, plus a fourth in Catalonia.

Leadership would always be the Achilles' heel. There were about 10,000 officers from the old regular army in the Republican zone, but only about 3,500 ever served in the People's Army. These provided most of the senior commanders, however, together with the top Communist militia leaders, plus a number from other political groups. Communist commanders soon predominated on the key central front, where they also provided most of the political commissars, and also spread into other regions. The most important single figure, however, was Col. Vicente Rojo, a military academy professor and a practicing Catholic, who in 1937 became chief of the Republican general staff and was promoted to general.

Beginning in the autumn of 1936 the two opposing regimes increasingly devoted themselves to building mass armies. In general, the insurgents did a better job of it. Their entire command was more professional, and the German instructors who arrived in 1937 proved more proficient than the smaller number of Soviet officers who assisted the Republicans. At the end of 1937 Franco's army had achieved numerical parity, with nearly 700,000 troops on each side. One of the most crucial differences was that the 30,000 or so new "provisional lieutenants" in Franco's forces, plus the new noncommissioned officers, were better trained and generally functioned better in combat. Neither army ever became very proficient in complex new-style combined arms operations, but Franco's army, enjoying key advantages, was somewhat better. As one of his commanders wrote in his diary, "It's a good thing that the Reds are worse!"

As in some other civil wars, desertion was a problem for both sides.[70] Many draftees were at best what was termed "geographically loyal," men trapped in one zone who might have preferred the other side. Since the insurgents won most of the battles, they captured many more prisoners. They did one of the

[70] P. Corral, *Desertores: La Guerra Civil que nadie quiere contar* (Barcelona, 2006).

best jobs of incorporating former enemy soldiers found in any of the revolutionary civil wars.[71]

The German[72] and Italian commanders always criticized Franco for being slow and unimaginative, since his operations were ponderous and usually fairly obvious. Franco was careful and conservative, refused to be hurried, and was reluctant to accept advice. He seems to have believed that a methodical war, even if slow, was best militarily and also politically, consolidating each new position and also building his political strength in each captured province. After the failure of his operations against Madrid in the autumn and winter of 1936–37 (his only failure of the entire war), he accepted the advice of staff officers and German commanders to concentrate on conquest of the northern Republican zone. It was small but industrially potent and severely divided internally.

The offensive against the northern zone began on 31 March 1937 and ended with complete success nearly seven months later. It eliminated the newly autonomous Basque government in Vizcaya, greatly improved the economic strength of the insurgent zone, and captured at least 200,000 of the best Republican troops. These could never be fully replaced, and about half were then incorporated into Franco's own forces. By the end of October 1937, the balance of power had clearly swung in favor of Franco, and discouragement mounted among some of the key Republican leaders.

The northern campaign developed what would be the standard procedure of Franco's offensives for the remainder of the war, relying on the air-to-ground support of the German Condor Legion and the Italian and Spanish sectors of his air force, accompanied by heavy artillery bombardment. This was the first fully developed use of the combined arms approach, initially essayed in 1918 and soon to become a standard feature of World War II. Heavy use of sometimes sophisticated firepower was crucial in softening Republican positions for Franco's infantry.

The principal military *cause célèbre* of the war took place on 26 April 1937, when the small town of Guernica (pop. 5,000), a traditional site of Basque political ceremonies, was bombed by Franco's forces. A total of twenty-two German and three Italian medium bombers dropped about twenty-five tons of bombs. The town was not far from the front lines, constituted the main escape route for the Basque Republican forces, featured a key bridge, and contained arms factories. Incendiary bombs ignited major fires that eventually consumed more than half the town, and altogether perhaps 200 people died.[73] This soon became a major news story, the Republicans claiming that the town had no military significance and was the target of a new kind of terror bombing.

[71] The only study is J. Mathews, " 'Our Red Soldiers': The Nationalist Army's Management of Its Left-wing Conscripts in the Spanish Civil War 1936–1939," *Journal of Contemporary History*, 45:2 (April 2010).

[72] But not Hitler, who preferred – and got – a long war in Spain that helped to divide France and to distract international attention from his own buildup in central Europe.

[73] Principal studies are K. A. Maier, *Guernica 26-4-37* (Madrid, 1976), and J. Salas Larrazábal, *Guernica* (Madrid, 1987).

Claims about casualties were greatly inflated, a standard practice on both sides, and the whole thing soon became a major embarrassment for Franco's government, which sought to deny responsibility, blaming it on anarchists, who had already set fire to one Basque town as they retreated.

Republican propaganda by this time made enemy air attacks against civilian centers one of its major themes, gaining considerable attention abroad. In fact, air and naval bombardment of civilian targets had been standard Republican procedures from the first days of the war, a practice that the Republicans continued throughout, though typically to very little effect. The only thing that could be called terror attacks on cities were a series of assaults by Franco's planes on Madrid in November 1936 that killed several hundred people and, more especially, three days of deliberate attacks on Barcelona by Italian planes from the Balearics ordered by Mussolini in March 1938, killing about a thousand people. Franco mostly avoided the practice, the only continued assaults on cities by his planes being the attacks on Republican Mediterranean ports in 1938–39, where the targets were the docks and shipping, not civilian districts.[74] Strategic terror bombing was not a common feature of the Spanish war, since neither side had the equipment for it. The Luftwaffe, which never operated more than ninety planes at a time in Spain, made few preparations for such things, emphasizing tactical bombing in support of ground operations, which to a large extent explains its later failure in the Battle of Britain.

The Republican People's Army first developed the cohesion to begin major offensive operations in mid-1937, launching its largest initiative to that point in the district of Brunete, immediately northwest of Madrid, on 6 July. This was designed to relieve the pressure on the northern zone and, if all went well, cut Franco's territory in half. It became the prototype for all the Republican offensives of 1937–38, achieving complete surprise and an initial breakthrough. On each occasion of this sort, however, Franco's troops resisted stubbornly in key positions, and the Republicans lacked the leadership and coordination to bypass them and press on. Franco moved in major reinforcements and rapidly regained the ground lost.

In the autumn of 1937 the focus of the war shifted to the northeast, where it would remain for the rest of the conflict, a decision made by Gen. Rojo and the Negrín government, which had moved the government to Barcelona in October 1937.[75] The insurgents held a tenuous defensive front in neighboring

---

[74] Like many, the Republicans often believed their own propaganda, and so early in 1938 asked the League of Nations to send a commission of inquiry to the Republican zone in order to report objectively on Franco's "terror raids." The League did so, but the resulting conclusions accurately reported finding no particular evidence of any such activity, since the raids involved few planes and the bombing patterns clearly targeted bridges, railway stations, docks, and shipping, rather than civilian districts. "Commission chargée de l'enquête sur les bombardements aériens en Espagne," *Société des Nations. Journal Officiel*, 19–20 (1938–39). This report, long overlooked by historians, was brought to light by the German military historian Hermann Hagena in his *Jagdflieger Werner Mölders* (Aachen, 2008), 78–79.

[75] The government had first moved to Valencia in November 1936, when Madrid seemed on the verge of falling to the insurgents.

Spain, October 1937.

Aragon, while the Republican leaders intended to develop firm control of the northeast, where anarchists were numerous. After a small attack had failed in August, a major offensive was launched in Aragon in October 1937, the "Belchite offensive," named for the small town that became its focus. This merely repeated the experience of Brunete, as the initial breakthrough could not be followed up.

When intelligence revealed that Franco was planning a major offensive at the end of the year to outflank Madrid from the northeast, the Republican command attempted preemptive action. In December 1937 it launched an offensive to seize the provincial capital of Teruel, which occupied an exposed salient in southern Aragon. Though Teruel fell, Franco canceled his own plans, shifted his major forces east, and shattered the Republican units that had taken the city. In March 1938 he then opened a major offensive of his own in southern Aragon that rapidly drove to the Mediterranean, cutting the remaining Republican zone in half, as morale collapsed in some units of the People's Army.

There followed Franco's most controversial decision of the war. Catalonia, the most important Republican region, lay defenseless, but, rather than seizing it as he might easily have, Franco turned his forces south, through difficult hilly terrain and along a narrow coastal road, toward Valencia, the center of Republican communications. Franco never adequately explained this decision, which baffled his subordinates. There is speculation that he feared provoking French intervention if he moved immediately through Catalonia to the Pyrenees, but confirmation is lacking. After the sudden breakthrough to the sea, his troops encountered slow going between March and July, though they moved steadily nearer Valencia.

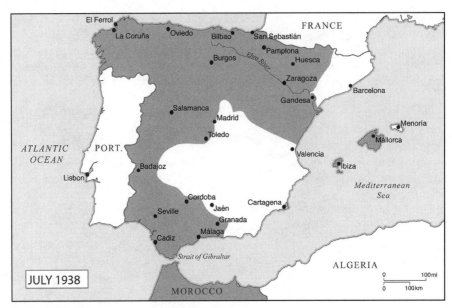

Spain, July 1938.

Once again Franco was surprised by a sudden Republican offensive toward his rear, beginning on 25 July with an amphibious crossing of the Ebro River, the most impressive operation ever conducted by the People's Army. Negrín and Rojo had worked wonders with the respite provided to Catalonia, training a new army corps there in part by calling up teenagers and older men, scraping the bottom of the manpower barrel. The offensive succeeded in occupying a hilly bulge in the Ebro valley before being sealed off, and once again Franco canceled his own operations to respond to a Republican initiative.

During 1938 the Nationalists enjoyed an increasing advantage in planes and artillery, as few Soviet supplies reached the Republicans. The Battle of the Ebro was the longest single engagement of the war, lasting until November, as Franco slowly rewon lost terrain hill by hill, relying on decisive superiority in firepower. Once this was over, however, the best remaining sector of the People's Army had been destroyed, and morale hit rock bottom. Franco finally launched an offensive into Catalonia in the final days of the year, occupying the entire region and the whole Pyrenean frontier by February 1939.

By that time Franco had won the war at sea. Though the Republic initially retained control of two-thirds of Spain's warships, the revolution touched off widespread mutiny in the navy, and many officers were either murdered outright or arrested and executed later. Though order of sorts was restored, the leadership and combat performance of the Republican ships were generally poor, and, though outnumbered, Franco's warships soon seized the initiative. The Republican naval command abandoned the blockade of Morocco at the close of September 1936 in an attempt to attack the small insurgent navy on the northern coast, but this failed completely. In 1937 Franco began to seize the initiative in the Mediterranean and, though the Republican forces did sink one of the two best insurgent warships, they remained largely on the defensive for most of the war, trying to protect Republican supplies at sea, with ever-diminishing success.

Whereas the moderates in the Republican government hoped desperately for international arbitration, early despairing of military victory, Basque and Catalan nationalists intrigued with foreign powers to bring about the partition of Spain, with equal futility. The Negrín government did not assume that it could win a clear-cut military victory, but during 1938 hoped for a change in the international situation that might produce an Anglo-French antifascist initiative that could assist the Republic. The outcome of the Munich conference in September 1938 largely ended such hopes.

By the close of 1938, Republican morale was near collapse. Even the Spanish Communist Party was weakening, having lost many members in battle, and opportunistic supporters began to drop out. All the other leftist parties began to turn against the Communists, accusing them of seeking dictatorship under Negrín and trying to prolong the war irrationally. Popular Front unity started to collapse, while the FAI-CNT began to plot the overthrow of Negrín.

After the occupation of Catalonia, the Republican zone was reduced to the southeastern quarter of Spain. Though there were still more than half a million men under arms, weapons and supplies were limited, and the food shortage was producing near-famine conditions. President Azaña and many other key personnel who had crossed into France refused to return. Negrín hoped to resist long enough to find a way to end the war with dignity and some measure of protection for the many leftists who would remain under Franco's rule, but was unable to communicate clearly this desperate rationale.

To most of the left, the situation seemed hopeless. Col. Segismundo Casado, a professional (and non-Communist) officer who commanded the Republican central front in Madrid, conspired with the other leftist parties to overthrow Negrín and end the war almost immediately. Casado believed, or was led to believe by representatives of Franco, that a completely non-Communist military-led government could negotiate more lenient terms, though Franco made no official promise other than a pledge not to arrest leftists not guilty of crimes. (In fact, the new Law of Political Responsibilities his government promulgated in February 1939 made any sort of initiative on behalf of leftist parties since October 1934 a punishable crime.)

At midnight on 5 March, Casado's Committee of National Defense, comprised of all the leftist parties except the Communists, rose in revolt. Casado refused to accept Negrín's resignation but insisted on expelling him. Negrín and most Communist leaders fled abroad by airplane, though Communist military units in Madrid engaged the rebels in violent combat for several days until a truce was arranged. The Spanish revolution had come full circle, and when Franco launched his final "Victory Offensive" on 26 March, there was virtually no resistance. On the first of April he announced that the civil war had ended. His new regime had gained full power, and the era of Franco had begun.

Thus the Spanish Civil War ended the way it began, with a military-led national defense junta rebelling against the existing Republican government on the grounds that it was tyrannical, violated the rights of others, and was increasingly dominated by Communists who planned to establish their own dictatorship. "Civil war within the Civil War" has become a cliché about the revolutionary Republic. The conflicts of May 1937 in Barcelona and March 1939 in Madrid were not, of course, full-scale civil wars, but they were violent confrontations of significant proportions. In both cases days of combat occurred, with hundreds killed, entire brigades of the People's Army fighting each other in 1939.

The Spanish Republic was always prone to severe internal conflict. Violent insurgency antedated the start of the regime in the attempted military pronunciamiento of December 1930, which took place, symptomatically, not during the dictatorship but during the period when the monarchy was moving, however slowly, toward open elections. There followed the four revolutionary insurrections of 1932–34. For the Republicans, as Edward Malefakis has written, the civil war was less the morality play that Republican propaganda has always striven to present than it was "Greek tragedy or modern drama, with their portrayal of the protagonist as his own chief enemy, unable to triumph because he is unable to gain ascendancy over himself."[76] Juan Negrín seems to have agreed with this assessment.[77] Even when they were able to exclude all the rest of Spanish society, the revolutionary movements differed violently among themselves, which had led *El Socialista* to ask rhetorically, in the spring of 1936, how a single victorious revolution could ever be possible. The left in Spain was so much more diverse and mobilized than its Russian counterparts that the development of a single hegemonic force like the Bolsheviks was not possible, despite the strength of the Communists in 1937–38. "The tragedy of Republican Spain, in short, was that a civil war of its own always lurked within its ranks as it fought the greater Civil War against the Nationalists."[78]

Conversely, the great historical responsibility of the Spanish right was their inability to find ways of coping with or exploiting these differences, short of grappling with them in mortal conflict. The Spanish Republic was indeed a morality play, but not of the kind narrated by either left or right.

---

[76] E. E. Malefakis, in R. Higham, ed., *Civil Wars in the 20th Century* (Lexington, Ky., 1972), 97.

[77] See Negrín's letter to Herbert L. Matthews, cited in the latter's *Half of Spain Died* (New York, 1973), 231.

[78] Higham, *Civil Wars*, 111. Malefakis further points out that the term "Loyalist" (still sometimes used in the English-language literature to refer to the left) was developed primarily for propaganda purposes abroad. Within Spain, the revolutionaries did not term themselves "*lealistas*," since they were loyal only to their own several radical and revolutionary projects.

7

Significance and Consequences

The Spanish war was Europe's most important conflict of the 1930s prior to the expansion of Nazi Germany. It produced the last of the collectivist revolutions in the sequence that had begun in 1917, but in Spain the revolution became partially subordinated to a military struggle that could not be entirely separated from quite different issues, some of them to be involved in World War II. Thus the right has seen the war as stemming from the upsurge in revolutionism that followed World War I, sustained by the Comintern and other revolutionary forces, while the left has preferred to ignore the revolution and the causes of the war in order to connect it, not with its causes and origins, but with its aftermath in other countries, as the "opening round" or "first battle" of World War II. There is some merit to both arguments, though somewhat more to the first than to the second.

All five of the major European powers responded to the war in different ways. British policy was the simplest, a hands-off approach except for intermittent humanitarian activities and attempts to maintain the freedom of the seas. It viewed Spanish politics as an unstable, amoral contest of extremes – an accurate evaluation, as far as it went. There was never any question of London supporting a violent revolution. Should Franco win, that could be accepted on the grounds that he would likely be an independent Spanish dictator with whom one could do business. And such, indeed, was eventually the way it worked out, though British policy overlooked the developing relationship between Franco and Hitler, which might have produced a different result.[1]

France was the country whose political system and internal rivalries most closely resembled those of the Spanish Republic, and it was the country whose domestic politics were most seriously impacted by the civil war, which further deepened the divisions between the left and the right. Nearly all the French right, and also part of the French left, saw Soviet intervention in Spain as

---

[1] This relationship is examined in my *Franco and Hitler: Spain, Germany, and World War II* (New Haven, Conn., 2008).

part of a design to involve France in a war with Germany to the benefit of the Soviets.

Hitler was almost totally ignorant of Spain, and to some degree deceived by Franco's initial representatives into thinking that he was helping to thwart an imminent Communist plot to seize power in Madrid. As the civil war developed, however, Hitler was not at all displeased with it, because he saw a chance to gain a friend in southwestern Europe, and to divide and disarm France internally, while distracting international attention from his own rearmament and expansion. He refused to increase German assistance much beyond the level of November 1936, letting Italy carry a greater burden, because Spain lay more within the Italian sphere and a long war was more useful as a diversion in the greater Hitlerian scheme of things.

Mussolini became more deeply involved than either Hitler or Stalin, even though, unlike the latter, he did not have his own political party in Spain. After several months, he came to see a victory for Franco as indispensable to the Fascist goal of *"mare nostrum,"* so that by early 1937 Mussolini had converted it into a "Fascist war," a conflict to which he was committed until final victory. It also became a "Fascist war" in a different sense, in that it catapulted Spain's Falangist party into becoming a mass movement and, in modified form, the new party of the Spanish state, the latter at least a "fascistized," or "semifascist," regime, though not a genuine satellite or necessarily even an ally of Italy or Germany. (To that extent the British gamble held.)

The Spanish war was not the basic cause that drew Rome and Berlin together, but it was the immediate catalyst. There had been considerable tension between semiuniversalist Fascism and racist National Socialism in 1934, but Germany had been the only power to support Italy's invasion of Ethiopia the following year. Though Hitler and Mussolini made separate and independent decisions to intervene in Spain, once they found that they were on the same side they drew closer yet, signing the agreement that Mussolini preferred to call the "Rome-Berlin Axis" in October 1936. Though he still regarded Hitler with a mixture of fear and envy, Mussolini continued to tighten relations with Berlin. He and Hitler did not synchronize their policies with regard to Spain any more than they synchronized anything else in their "brutal friendship," and Mussolini rather resented that Hitler left him with the greater burden, but he committed all of Italy's prestige to Franco's victory, and in a completely asymmetric way it became the first "Axis war."

Stalin's policy was different from that of either of the other two dictators, more committed than that of Hitler but less heavily involved than that of Mussolini. In 1936–37 he hoped for leftist victory, but by mid-1938 was searching for an exit strategy that he was unable to find. As Foreign Minister Maxim Litvinov warned, Soviet policy became contradictory, for the intervention on behalf of the revolution in Spain was not seen in London and Paris as the antifascist crusade painted by Comintern propaganda. It had the effect of undermining collective security policy against Germany, though it is doubtful that London and Paris would have made a truly effective defensive alliance with Moscow unless absolutely forced to do so by Hitler.

After 1945 Communist propaganda hailed the third or revolutionary Spanish Republic as the first "people's republic," a precursor of the new Communist regimes in Eastern Europe, but this was another exaggeration. The wartime republic fit the Comintern formula insofar as it was an exclusively all-left, pseudodemocratic system in which all centrist and conservative groups had been suppressed by revolutionary terror, and in which economic collectivization and, to some degree, nationalization had been established. But the Spanish Republic never developed the concrete Communist hegemony required by the Soviet formula, ever though it advanced further in that regard than any other system in Western Europe. Though they became a central influence, the Communists remained a minority force, however powerful, and were never in a position simply to take over. Moreover, they made themselves so hated by their leftist allies that the Spanish left became much more anti-Communist than their counterparts anywhere else in the world. That was the only thing that the Spanish left and right could agree on by 1939. Had Franco been more imaginative and generous, he might to some extent have made it a basis for national reconciliation.

Of the three intervening powers, the Soviets made the greatest effort to learn from the war militarily, convinced that it accurately represented the conditions of a future conflict in Europe. Every aspect was studied carefully by the Red Army, though a major mistake was made in drawing conclusions from the ineffectiveness of Republican armored operations. Late in 1939, the Red Army broke up its *Blitzkrieg*-style armored corps, only to begin to reassemble them a year later after the success of German panzer divisions in France. In other ways, however, the Red Army learned a great deal.

The German attitude was more pragmatic, focusing mainly on the small *Luftwaffe* unit in Spain and the development of combined arms and tactical air support. The superiority of Soviet armor was not taken as seriously as it ought to have been. The Italian forces generally performed adequately, except at the Battle of Guadalajara, with Italian planes and artillery playing a major role in Franco's offensives. Italian specialists pointed out serious problems that needed correction, but ultimate victory and the peculiar limitations of Italian military culture prevented them from being taken very seriously. Most Italian weapons sent to Spain remained there afterward, and their supply was never entirely made good before Italy entered World War II. Though Italian troops and arms made a major contribution to Franco's victory, the overall consequence may have weakened the Italian military, as well as badly skewing Mussolini's policy, with regard to the broader conflict that followed.

Almost from the beginning, Republicans declared that their war was part of a broader struggle against fascism, which might well become a great war in

the future. Only five months after the end of the civil war, the German invasion of Poland touched off the European conflict, and the Republicans insisted
that the Spanish struggle had constituted a "prelude" to it. This also became
the theme of certain scholarly studies, beginning with Patricia van der Esch's
Prelude to War: The International Repercussions of the Spanish Civil War
(1951).

In this regard it is important to distinguish among the various dimensions
of the conflict. Within Spain, it was a clear-cut revolutionary/counterrevo-
lutionary contest, with the fascist totalitarian powers supporting the right
and the Soviet totalitarian power supporting the left. World War II, by contrast, began in Europe only when a pan-totalitarian entente was formed by
the Nazi-Soviet Pact, with the aim of allowing the Soviet Union to conquer
a sizable swathe of Eastern Europe while Germany was left free to conquer
as much of the rest of the continent as it could. This was a complete reversal
of the terms of the Spanish conflict. Only later, after Hitler turned on Stalin,
did the roster of the two sides begin to resemble the alliances in Spain, but
even then it was considerably different. The "grand alliance" against Hitler of
1941–45 was not a leftist Popular Front, but an extremely broad international
coalition that stretched from the extreme left to, in some cases, the extreme
right, not at all the same sort of thing as the "new type" all-left revolutionary Republic. The most prominent figure in the resistance against Hitler was
a conservative, Winston Churchill, who said that if he had been a citizen of
Spain he would have supported Franco.

The proposition might be reversed, with the conclusion that the Spanish
revolution and civil war constituted the last of the revolutionary crises stemming from the era of World War I, just as the initial Republican democracy
had constituted the most belated phase of the wave of democratization that
had swept Europe in 1919. In Germany, the counterrevolutionary moderation
of the Socialists had guaranteed the provisional consolidation of democracy,
as had the leadership of the moderates in France in 1871, while leftist radicalism brought revolution and civil war to Spain.

Just as the weaponry and characteristics of much of the conflict resembled those of World War I as much or more than those of World War II, the
Spanish situation had more characteristics of a post–World War I revolutionary crisis than of an internal conflict of the World War II era. Among these
were 1) the almost complete breakdown of domestic institutions, as distinct
from the coups d'etat and semilegal impositions of authoritarianism more typical of the World War II era; 2) the development of a full-scale revolutionary/
counterrevolutionary civil war, a more common phenomenon at the close of
World War I than during World War II; 3) creation of a typical post–World
War I "Red Army" in the form of the People'sArmy; 4) the extreme exacerba-
tion of nationalism in the insurgent zone and among some political sectors of
Catalonia and the Basque Country, also more typical of World War I and its
aftermath; 5) the frequent use of World War I–style military materiel and concepts; and 6) the fact that in its origins it was not the result of any plan by the

major powers, and thus more similar to post–World War I crises. Similarly, the extreme revolutionary left inside and outside Spain hailed the Spanish revolution as the latest and perhaps the greatest of the revolutionary upsurges of the post–World War I era.

Both sides developed a strongly patriotic discourse that defined their struggle as a battle against a foreign invader. Each developed a myth of the supposedly exogenous origins of the conflict, both myths being equally false. Republicans created the notion that a conspiracy by Hitler and Mussolini was behind the war, using the military insurgency as their cat's paw, and saw their intervention as the first phase of a plan to occupy all Spain. Spokesmen for the Nationalists, in turn, propagated the idea that Soviet Communism was responsible for originating the conflict, that the rebellion of 18 July had been necessary to preempt a Communist and Soviet takeover planned for a month later, and that the subsequent Soviet intervention was part of a strategy to take complete control of Spain.

International considerations became increasingly important for both sides. Franco feared, while Negrín hoped for, the sharpening of European tensions to the point of French military intervention. Both the Negrín government and the Soviet leadership in Moscow were convinced that a change in policy by the Western democracies held the key to a leftist victory.

Even though the Spanish war was no mere "prelude to" or "opening round" of World War II, it contributed significantly to the way in which the European war developed. Without directly linking the Spanish conflict and World War II, historians often advance the argument that the diplomacy surrounding the Spanish war contributed more than a little to the perceptions and psychology that precipitated the greater conflict. Thus it has been contended that the behavior of Britain and France vis-à-vis the Spanish war encouraged Hitler and Mussolini to believe that the democracies lacked the will to face a challenge and would not contest further initiatives by the fascist powers. According to this interpretation, the Spanish war was not a unique prelude but simply the longest in a series of crises in which the fascist powers acted aggressively and the democracies passively: Ethiopia (1935–36), the Rhineland (1936), Spain (1936–39), Austria (1938), and the Sudetenland (1938).

Hitler's policy of prolonging the Spanish conflict in order to distract attention from his own expansion in central Europe was generally successful. On the one hand, he used the complications arising from it as an excuse to avoid reaching any broader understanding with Britain and France. On the other, he calculated correctly that continuation of the war would further divide France internally, distracting it from focusing on Germany during the period (1936–38) when German rearmament had still not achieved parity.

The Spanish war also provided incentive for the beginning of the Italo-German entente that Hitler had always sought. Mussolini became fully committed to the Spanish struggle, making it a semiofficial "Fascist war," which increasingly deprived Italian policy of freedom to maneuver, tying it to a Germany that became the dominant partner. Italy's realignment made it possible for Hitler to incorporate Austria as early as March 1938, enabling him then to move more rapidly against Czechoslovakia.

From this perspective, it was not that Britain and France ignored the Spanish war but that they sometimes dedicated more attention to it than to Austria and Czechoslovakia, though without taking decisive action. As Willard Frank has observed, "Even in 1938, the year of Munich, British MPs asked almost half again as many parliamentary questions about Spain and the Mediterranean as about Germany and central Europe. ... The French Chamber of Deputies had to suspend its deliberations twice in one day for fear of a free-for-all fight over the Spanish question."[2] The Spanish issue severely divided France internally, while complicating and disorienting its broader policies.

Italian and German intervention elicited a Soviet counter-intervention that Stalin would not expand sufficiently to assure Republican victory (assuming that this was possible), for fear of the international consequences and also because of the objective limitations of Soviet power. Even so, the fact that there was a significant Soviet intervention had the benefit for Germany of intensifying the democracies' suspicion of and alienation from the Soviet Union. To the French military command, this only confirmed the conviction that the real Soviet goal was to provoke war among the Western powers. The more the Soviet Union intervened in Spain, and the more aggressive the Soviet representative in the Non-Intervention Committee became, the less likely was any genuine defensive undertaking by Paris and Moscow against Berlin. Soviet policy proved counterproductive, except for the gains in espionage, and the Soviet Union was more isolated in April 1939 than in July 1936. Hitler largely outsmarted Stalin, as he would do the second time during 1939–41, until he made the absurdly fatal mistake of making war on the two largest powers in the world at the same time.

British policy was motivated not only by aversion to the Spanish revolution, though that was genuine, but also by the growing appeasement policy toward Germany and the concern to avoid war in Western Europe. This was accompanied by the hope for better relations with Rome that might detach the latter from the Rome-Berlin Axis, though this ploy failed completely. The outcome of the Spanish war, then, had the effect of making Spain a further counterweight against any understanding with Moscow, so that

in May 1939 the chief of staff in London had to decide on "the balance of strategic value in war as between Spain as an enemy and Russia as an ally." Chamberlain had already made up his mind: "If an alliance which is unable to give much effective aid [to Poland] were to alienate Spain or drive her into the Axis camp we should lose far more in the west than we could ever hope to gain in the east."[3]

Once more the situation was not so much underestimated as overvalued.

[2] W. C. Frank, Jr., "The Spanish Civil War and the Coming of the World War," *The International History Review*, 9:3 (August 1987), 368–409.
[3] J. Edwards, *The British Government and the Spanish Civil War* (London, 1979), 213; M. J. Carley, *1939: The Alliance That Never Was and the Coming of World War II* (Chicago,

The outbreak of the European war did not depend on the Spanish conflict and would undoubtedly have taken place in one form or another even if there had been no war in Spain. Even had the civil war dragged on into the autumn of 1939, it is doubtful that this would have deterred Hitler in Eastern Europe, but, however that may be, the Spanish war's ramifications to some extent determined the pace and timing of broader affairs. Without the complications arising from it, the Western democracies might have taken a stronger stand against Hitler, and conceivably Mussolini might have delayed or even avoided an entente with him, despite the seeming logic that brought the two dictators together. Similarly, without these distractions and developments, Hitler probably would not have been able to move as rapidly as he did in 1938.

The British government very early came to the conclusion that a Spain dominated by the Franco regime would be independent of Germany and would not threaten British interests. In the very long run, that is more or less how things worked out, but, as Wellington said of the Battle of Waterloo, it "was a very near-run thing." The extensive collaboration between Madrid and Berlin, together with Franco's interest in entering the European conflict so long as he could get the right terms, raised the possibility that London's calculations might end in disaster. It was too close for comfort.

Even some French rightists, such as Admiral Darlan, the commander of the navy, and Lt. Col. Louis-Henri Morel, a French military attaché with the Republican government, both believed that, strictly for geostrategic reasons, France should hold its nose at the politics of the Spanish left and provide arms to the Republic, even carrying out a limited military intervention. The goal was not so much to defeat Franco (though such a policy would have had that effect) as to thwart any geopolitical expansion of Germany and Italy.

Churchill thought much the same. No one detested Communism or any form of leftist revolution more than he, and Churchill readily admitted that had he been a Spanish citizen he would have supported Franco. His official position was neutrality, but one that tilted increasingly toward the Republic, for Churchill also said that as a Briton he supported those forces opposed to the expansion of German and Italian power. By 1938 he believed the policy of the British government toward Spain to be cavalier and irresponsible, not so much with regard to the domestic issues in Spain, but with regard to its effects on the international situation.[4] This is a serious issue that cannot be dismissed, for the outcome of the Spanish war created a potentially dangerous

1999), 144, quoted in D. Tierney, *FDR and the Spanish Civil War: Neutrality and Commitment in the Struggle That Divided America* (Durham, N.C., 2007), 136.

[4] Amid the mound of Churchilliana, there seems to be no complete study of his position on the Spanish war, though E. J. Sanchez, "Churchill and Franco: 1936–1955" (M. Phil. thesis, Cambridge University, n. d.), helps to point the way. At first Churchill perceived Spain as a hopeless mess that would only confound the necessary defensive relations between Britain and France, writing in August 1936 that "this Spanish welter is not the business of either of

situation in the western Mediterranean, held in check only by a complex series of developments that might well have turned out differently.

The transformation of Franco into Caudillo during the civil war created a new political personality, arrogant and overweening, and one determined to make Spain a major power. New plans of June 1938 and April 1939 proposed a gigantic naval construction program, officially approved in September 1939, that proposed for the next decade the expenditure of 5.5 million pesetas to build a fleet of four new battleships, fourteen cruisers, and many other warships, which was to be accompanied by creation of a large new air force. The naval plan presumed that Spain would eventually join the "autarchic group" (that is, the Axis), though with complete "liberty" and "independence." It proposed that Spain enter a future war only at the most opportune moment in order to "break the equilibrium," thus making of Spain "the key to the situation" and the "arbiter of the two blocs,"[5] though Franco was never able to act on such a design.

Spain's logical position in both world wars was neutrality. The country held importance only for a peripheral, not a core, strategy. Stalin had been temporarily interested in Spain as part of a highly complex, multidimensioned grand strategy that did not seek to impose a Communist regime at that time and that turned out to be too complex and contradictory to pull off. Hitler's interest was also broadly strategic, and secondary rather than intrinsic, until the problem of mounting greater pressure against Great Britain suddenly achieved prime importance in the late summer of 1940. Even then, Spanish participation in the war was not such a primary objective that he was willing to meet Franco's high price. After that he grew increasingly disgusted with

us. Neither of these Spanish factions expresses our conception of civilization" (Sanchez, 16). Moreover, in October he reflected the common perception that revolutionary violence was more wanton and indiscriminate than what he called the "grim retaliation" of the insurgents (Sanchez, 18). As early as February 1937, however, he began to tilt somewhat toward the Republic, in a personal letter to finance minister Juan Negrín offering advice on where to purchase planes for the Republican air force (Churchill to Negrín, 22 February 1937, Archivo de la Fundación Nacional Francisco Franco, 33:57). Conversely, two months later he said in the House of Commons, "I will not pretend that if I had to choose between Communism and Nazism, I would choose Communism" (quoted in D. Reynolds, *In Command of History: Churchill Fighting and Writing the Second World War* [London, 2004], 102). Thus during 1937 his opinions were in flux, but they began to crystallize in 1938, especially after Munich. In a letter to the *Daily Telegraph* (30 December 1938), he urged mediation of an end to the war that would permit the Republic in some fashion to survive, both for reasons of British imperial strategy and security and also because of the perceived moderation of the Negrín government, which would offer Spaniards a less vengeful and more hopeful future. (Thanks to Paul Preston for this reference.)

When he became prime minister in 1940, Churchill was forced to return to Chamberlain's policy regarding Spain, the dire circumstances of that moment permitting no alternative. By 1944, however, as the general circumstances of Europe began to change drastically, Churchill embraced that policy not out of opportunism but out of conviction. An adjustment was also made by the Labourite government that succeeded him.

[5] This is best presented and analyzed by M. Ros Agudo, *La guerra secreta de Franco (1939–1945)* (Barcelona, 2002), xxiii–xxv and 44–55.

Franco, declaring him shockingly ungrateful for German assistance in the civil war and hopelessly shortsighted in thinking that his regime could ever survive a German defeat. Hitler professed to be profoundly disillusioned with Franco, whom he came to view as a unprincipled opportunist, later opining that "during the civil war, the idealism was not on Franco's side; it was to be found among the Reds." Like many observers, he thought Franco incompetent, believing that his "reactionary" government would inevitably fail. When that hour came, the *Fuehrer* said, the next time he would support the Spanish "Reds."[6]

During the last two years of World War II, both sides asked the same thing of the Spanish government: that it remain neutral and not favor the other side. By the time that the Allies had gained the upper hand at the beginning of 1944, Washington began to pressure the Spanish regime more than Berlin ever had. This was possible because the Spanish economy depended much more on commerce with the Allies than with Germany. Franco reluctantly made the concessions needed to survive, but never went further than he was forced to. By the time the war ended, he had formulated a new political strategy that would enable his regime to survive, and for some time to prosper, in a postfascist world.

The myth of the "Spanish-national revolutionary war," the official Communist and Soviet label for the conflict, would later play a minor role in the establishment of the Communist people's republics in Eastern Europe. It served as a beacon for the possibilities of "revolutionary antifascism" in the West, and veterans of the International Brigades played important roles in developing several of the new totalitarian regimes, particularly in military and security affairs. The myth achieved special importance in the German Democratic Republic.[7]

In their own terms, however, the myths of the civil war could never be resolved, because for both sides these admitted only the complete elimination of the enemy. Such terms were finally transcended only by the Spanish democratization of 1976–78, which rejected both sets of myths. The creation of a new democracy did not represent a return to July 1936, or even to 1931, but a new departure in modern Spanish regime building based on broad democratic consensus and equal rights for all. To the extent that it may have been a vindication of any of the political forces of the 1930s, those forces would have been Lerroux's Radicals and the small liberal-democratic center parties, neither the right nor the left.

---

[6] *Hitler's Table Talk, 1941–1944: His Private Conversations*, trans. N. Cameron and R. H. Stevens (New York, 2000), 569–70.

[7] J. McLellan, *Antifascism and Memory in East Germany: Remembering the International Brigades* (October, 2004); A. Krammer, "The Cult of the Spanish Civil War in East Germany," *Journal of Contemporary History*, 39:4 (October 2004), 531–60.

PART THREE

CIVIL WAR AND INTERNAL VIOLENCE IN THE ERA OF WORLD WAR II

8

The Multiple Wars of Europe, 1939–1945

The idea of a universal civil war would never regain the prominence that it had briefly possessed in the years after 1917, yet this sense lingered into the 1930s, when it was exploited by Hitler as a kind of smoke screen to cloud German expansion, and was also developed in quite a different way by the Republicans in Spain, which eventually began to influence the thinking of Franklin Roosevelt. In a diffuse manner, a sense developed among more than a few that, whereas in 1914 there had been a great conflict between nation-states and empires, a new international struggle would be more a war for or against ideas – such as race, revolution, fascism, and antifascism – both because of the ideological character of the new dictatorships and because of the stimulation of political consciousness that they had provoked. Col. Amedeo Mecozzi, an Italian air force commander, wrote in 1937 "that the next European war will have the character of a civil war.... It will perhaps not be a war between countries but a war of ideals (which everyone claims to be his own position) against [false] ideologies, which everyone claims to be the other side's."[1]

Certainly all modern wars have invoked ideals, but in reality the war that began in 1939 was a conflict of nations and empires, even though ideas played a more important role than in 1914. The fact that both sides immediately claimed the moral high ground was, of course, no novelty, and citizens of nearly all political persuasions supported their own countries. Communists at first were the principal exceptions, but in most countries fascists were not, for in Poland and France domestic fascists initially fought against Hitler.

During World War II and for years afterward, there was a tendency among the victorious great powers, whether the Western democracies or the Soviet state and its satellites, to treat the war as a kind of simple morality tale, of good versus evil, with very clear demarcations. Definitions differed, since in the West this was presented as a war of democracy versus fascism and in the East as a Soviet and communist struggle against fascism, yet both versions

---

[1] Quoted in J. Gooch, *Mussolini and His Generals: The Armed Forces and Fascist Foreign Policy, 1922–1940* (Cambridge, UK, 2007), 382.

were simplistic and unidimensional. Afterward, with the onset of the Cold War, the picture became more complicated, but even so the basic myths of the "good war" remained unaltered. Only with the passage of years did historians begin to discover a more complex pattern.[2]

There was one predominant struggle, the enormous war between Nazi Germany and its enemies, the latter made up of both the countries Germany attacked or declared war on and those who declared war on Germany. This conflict was fundamental, but the war against Germany involved different kinds of war efforts and goals. Moreover, the central struggle was accompanied by a variety of "parallel wars" and civil wars and insurgencies. Many of these were aligned with the central struggle, but others were separate from it. A full taxonomy of the wars and conflicts of Europe between 1939 and 1945 must distinguish among 1) the war between the great powers, 2) the parallel wars, 3) the national liberation struggles, and 4) the civil wars.

The war of the great powers included three different undertakings: a) Hitler's war, b) the Soviet war, and c) the Anglo-American war (more broadly, the war of the Western democracies). Hitler planned to launch a war for *Lebensraum* in the East that would lay the basis for Germany's world dominion. Before he could do that, he had to dominate Central Europe, something largely accomplished in 1938, and secondly to align and subordinate Poland. Since the Polish government resisted this, Hitler determined to invade and destroy Poland, which in turn required a temporary agreement with the Soviet Union. Hitler's war suddenly became much more complex when Britain and France declared war on Germany to protest the invasion of Poland.

Hitler thus found himself in a contest of dimensions he had not foreseen, involving war with France and Britain and the progressive conquest and/or subordination of the lesser powers. All this, save the defeat of Britain, had been completed by April 1941, opening the way for his ultimate European campaign, the invasion of the Soviet Union, in June 1941. In Hitler's thinking, his wars were divided into two categories, which may, for the sake of convenience, be called his western and his eastern wars. The western wars were fought at least partly according to conventional norms concerning the treatment of soldiers and civilians, even though the goal in the West was to subject all the conquered areas to increasingly stringent terms of German rule. The eastern war was conceived in different terms as a race war, requiring not merely the Final Solution for the extermination of Jews but also, even more ambitiously, the greatest program of ethnic cleansing in world history, involving the elimination through starvation, mistreatment and deportation of at least thirty million inhabitants – perhaps more – of Poland and the western territories of the Soviet Union, to open the way for millions of new German

---

[2] Arguably, the best recent "revisionist" scholarly history of the war in a single volume is N. Davies, *Europe at War 1939–1945: No Simple Victory* (London, 2006). See also L. Rees, *World War II behind Closed Doors: Stalin, the Nazis and the West* (New York, 2008).

colonists. In the eastern war, military prisoners and civilians alike would be treated with the utmost brutality.[3]

During the course of the war a discourse developed that labeled it a "European civil war." This was a distortion, though there were aspects of civil war accompanying the struggle, completely of a secondary nature. The principal war was the opposite of a civil war, insofar as it represented something in the nature of an interruption of, or a truce in, the civil war between revolution and counterrevolution that had been waged intermittently since 1917. In several countries that struggle nonetheless continued during the new war, and after it was over the truce soon ended altogether, resulting in the new conflict that became known as the Cold War.

Though the Axis powers made some efforts to incite rebellion against the Allies among the Islamic peoples of North Africa and the Middle East,[4] they failed to develop a program of subversion and revolution abroad equivalent to that of imperial Germany in World War I, despite all the talk about the supposed "Axis fifth column." This was no doubt due in part to the dramatic successes of the early years of Axis military expansion, as well as to the Nazi racial obsession, so that Germany and Italy failed to make a major effort to capitalize on their momentary role as the major new revolutionary factor in European affairs. By comparison, the Japanese were more active and imaginative in East Asia.

In 1941, with nearly all continental Europe either occupied by Germany or in some fashion allied with it,[5] and the invasion of the Soviet Union under way, the Hitler regime began to unfurl the banner of "Europe," with Germany the leader of a pan-European New Order, and even the defender of European civilization against Bolshevist barbarism. During the remainder of the war, this was increasingly employed as a mobilizational device, and, though it never attracted more than a small minority, it did gain a certain following under

[3] A. J. Kay, "Germany's Staatssekretäre, Mass Starvation and the Meeting of 2 May 1941," *Journal of Contemporary History*, 41 (2006), 685–700, treats the initial planning. On repression in the occupied Soviet Union, see B. Shepherd, *War in the Wild East: The German Army and Soviet Partisans* (Cambridge, Mass., 2004). The massive bloodletting in Eastern Europe during these years is treated in harrowing detail in T. Snyder, *Bloodlands: Europe between Hitler and Stalin* (New York, 2010).
[4] J. Herf, *Nazi Propaganda for the Arab World* (New Haven, Conn., 2010). German military recruitment of Arabs is treated in C. Caballero Jurado, *La espada del Islam. Voluntarios árabes en el Ejército alemán 1941–1945* (Alicante, 1990). For years, Fascist Italy had been preparing its own appeal to the Islamic world. See R. De Felice, *Il fascismo e l'Oriente. Arabi, ebrei e indiani nella politica di Mussolini* (Bologna, 1988); E. Galoppini, *Il fascismo e l'Islam* (Parma, 2001); and R. L. Melka, "The Axis and the Arab Middle East: 1930–1945" (Ph.D. diss., University of Minnesota, 1966). On sequelae among the Arabs, see P. Wien, *Iraqi Arab Nationalism: Authoritarian, Totalitarian and Pro-fascist Inclinations, 1933–1941* (London, 2006); I. Gershoni and J. Jankowski, *Confronting Fascism in Egypt: Dictatorship versus Democracy in the 1930s* (Stanford, Calif., 20010): and M. Küntzel, *Jihad and Jew-Hatred: Islamism, Nazism, and the Roots of 9/11* (New York, 2009).
[5] The nearest thing to a true neutral on the continent was Portugal. Both Sweden and Switzerland collaborated extensively with Germany, though not as much as did Spain.

the banner of anti-Sovietism. It has subsequently been presented as a form of European civil war, and to a degree such a thing did exist, but the concept is easily exaggerated.

The Germans mobilized their own international brigades in the form of the Waffen SS, which recruited 300,000 non-Germans.[6] In addition, on the eastern front Hitler was supported by entire army corps from Italy, Romania, and Hungary; two divisions from Slovakia; and one very large division from Spain. This did not amount to a true European army, as sometimes would be claimed later, but does demonstrate that certain aspects of Hitler's cause had a broader appeal.

German National Socialism could not participate in a genuine "European civil war" because, despite the salience of its anti-Communism, it was based on a biological racism and imperialism that lacked true universal appeal. Though its eastern war gained a number of allies, it could not engage in political proselytization on a completely international scale, because it did not believe in the validity or equality of international society, nor could it recruit defectors to the fullest extent, as for the most part Hitler refused to do in the Soviet Union, to the perdition of his cause. Late in the war, when Germany was clearly losing, Hitler tried half-heartedly and in a very contradictory manner to overcome such limitations, but it was too late. Conversely, Nazism was opposed by an extremely heterogeneous and internally contradictory alliance that ranged from Communists to ultra-reactionaries, united only by their anti-Nazism and the fact that they did share a general orientation toward social, moral, or religious interpretations of the world in contradistinction to biological racism.[7]

Stalin's war was quite different from that of Hitler. The "Stalin thesis" concerning Soviet policy toward a future conflict had been announced as early as 1925. When the "Second Imperialist War" (Sovietese for "Second World War") broke out, the Soviet Union's goal should be to stay out as long as possible, intervening at the last moment in order to determine the outcome and to take advantage of the resulting chaos and destruction to advance Communism. Nonetheless, the implacable hostility of Hitler had led Stalin to shift Soviet policy to "collective security" with the West in 1934–35, but this new policy failed to attract support, and in 1939 Stalin returned to the old policy in the Nazi-Soviet Pact, which required the official abandonment of Soviet antifascism.

The Western powers had resisted military alliance with Moscow as long as possible, at least in part because they had some perception of the Stalin doctrine and feared that any successful military action in which the Soviet Union was involved would lead to an advance of either Soviet imperialism or Communism

---

[6] R.-D. Müller, *An der Seite der Wehrmacht: Hitlers ausländische Hilfer beim "Kreuzzug gegen den Bolschewismus" 1941–1945* (Frankfurt, 2010).

[7] Cf. the formulation in D. Diner, *Cataclysms: A History of the Twentieth Century from Europe's Edge* (Madison, Wisc., 2008), 48–50.

or both. As it turned out, this perception was fundamentally accurate. Even the Czech prime minister, Eduard Benes, who was fundamentally pro-Soviet and believed some kind of social revolution in eastern Europe to be inevitable, hesitated in 1938 to insist on international military assistance, including that of the Soviet Union, for fear of starting a "second Spanish civil war," as he termed it, involving the specter of "sovietization" in Czechoslovakia or Poland.[8]

From 1934 on, Soviet policy emphasized the need for "new thinking" and tactical agility. The terms of the Nazi-Soviet Pact were nonetheless not foreseen, for, rather than guaranteeing Soviet neutrality, they established friendship and collaboration between Berlin and Moscow, not a full alliance but a very close understanding that permitted Stalin to undertake his own "parallel war" on the cheap.[9] Within less than twelve months, Soviet imperialism had swallowed up the Baltic states, eastern Poland, southeastern Finland, and northeastern Rumania – all at the cost of only three months of warfare with Finland. Thus the first major expansion of Communism came not at the end of the war, as planned, but at its beginning.

By the latter part of 1940, Stalin wanted even more, a complete division of all of eastern and far northern Europe, as well as control of the Turkish straits, a prelude to making the Soviet Union a Mediterranean and Middle Eastern power as well. At that point Hitler decided to delay no longer his assault on the Soviet Union.

The German invasion began the fourth phase of Soviet war planning, aimed simply at survival. During the second half of 1941, Stalin was apparently willing to make major territorial concessions (likening this to Lenin's deal with the Germans at Brest-Litovsk in 1918) in order to end the invasion and guarantee Soviet survival. Then, in the first part of 1942, he began to think for the first time that the Soviet Union could directly defeat Germany, and a year later, after Stalingrad, may have been willing to sign a separate peace only on the basis of the restoration of the borders of 1941, which Hitler would not agree to. Stalin was apparently willing to entertain some such possibility for two reasons: first, the Soviet Union had suffered gigantic losses yet continued to bear the main burden of the war against Germany; second, in part because of that, he suspected that the Western powers might yet sign a separate peace, and was not completely disabused of this notion until the summer of 1944 (exactly at the point when Franco, at the opposite end of Europe, also became convinced that Germany was on the road to total defeat).[10]

---

[8] M. Hauner, "Edvard Benes's Undoing of Munich: A Message to a Czechoslovak Politician in Prague," *Journal of Contemporary History*, 38:4 (October 2003), 563–77.

[9] The pact was officially justified by the Comintern in terms somewhat parallel to those of the Popular Front, as a tactical maneuver that would stimulate open warfare between the leading capitalist powers, thus within a few years providing much greater opportunity for revolution than ever before.

[10] V. Mastny, "Stalin and the Prospects of a Separate Peace in World War II," *American Historical Review*, 77 (1972), 1365–88; H. W. Koch, "The Spectre of a Separate Peace in the

The Comintern's policy for other Communist parties was not revolution but simply the antifascist "united front," dedicated to the military defeat of Germany. Thus, for different reasons, neither Hitler nor Stalin was interested in converting the conflict into a true *Weltanschauungskrieg*, an ideological and revolutionary European civil war. The only civil war sought by the Soviet Union was that waged by the antifascist Resistance. The principal exception lay in Yugoslavia, where conditions were unusually complex and chaotic, as Tito and his Communist Partisans partially disobeyed instructions and progressively converted their antifascist struggle into a revolutionary civil war. Later the Greek Communists began to do the same thing, but those among Italian Communists who sought to follow such a path were soon brought under control by their own leaders.

The fifth phase of Stalin's war strategy began to unfold late in 1943, with the prospect of a Soviet advance deep into east central Europe, achieving what Lenin had failed to do in 1920. This was even more ambitious than phase three, but rested on military conquest rather than revolutionary civil war (the "Stalin doctrine," so to speak), and that was the way the war ended, with vast amounts of territory occupied for the postwar satellite empire of "people's republics."

The war of the Allies was much more modest in its aims, though politically beset with contradictions. After the subjugation of Germany, the goal was restoration of the status quo, at least in Western Europe. Beyond that, the American government refused to subordinate military policy to political considerations, whatever different ideas Churchill might have had. Thus the status quo was restored only in Western Europe, opening the way for the golden age of Western European social democracy, but leaving a large part of the world open for the expansion of totalitarianism, an ironic outcome that partially reversed the announced American war aims, both in World War I and World War II.

PARALLEL WARS

The struggles of the great powers were accompanied by smaller "parallel wars," a term originally coined by Italian policy in 1939–40. By far the most important parallel war, however, was the Soviet advance in 1939–40, which Stalin hoped to extend much farther, still as a partner of Hitler.[11] Benito

East: Russo-German 'Peace Feelers', 1942–44," *Journal of Contemporary History*, 10 (1975), 531–49; K.-H. Minuth, "Sowjetisch-deutsche Friedenskontakte," *Geschichte in Wissenschaft und Unterricht*, 16 (1965), 38–45; I. Fleischauer, *Die Chance des Sonderfriedens: Deutsch-sowjetische Geheimgespräche, 1941–1945* (Berlin, 1986). See also the sources cited in G. L. Weinberg, *A World at Arms: A Global History of World War II* (Cambridge, UK, 1994), 1075–76.

[11] Recent research by Dzhakhangir Nadzhafov at the Moscow Institute of General History has turned up internal Soviet documentation, published in *Voprosy Istorii*, revealing that Stalin intended to annex parts of northwestern Iran and eastern Turkey, as well as the large Chinese district of Xinjiang (Inews.az/analytics/20090829104314684.html). (Thanks to Milan Hauner for these data.)

Mussolini, Hitler's only full ally, resented that very much, for he had begun Italian imperial expansion in Ethiopia in 1935, after consolidating control of Libya. His major goal was *"mare nostrum,"* meaning Italian domination of the Mediterranean, but this included the southern part of the Balkans. The idea was to carve out a separate Italian sphere in alliance with Hitler, something that the latter supported in principle, though the details each had in mind may have differed a good deal.

There were several "parallel wars" in eastern Europe. Having been invaded by Stalin in 1939, Finland fought its own "continuation war," as the Finns called it, against the Soviet Union in 1941, parallel to the German invasion but apart from it, to regain Finnish territory. Romania and later Hungary participated directly with Germany in the invasion of the Soviet Union, each hoping to score its own territorial gains. Marshal Antonescu, the Romanian dictator, wanted to regain Bessarabia and Bukovina, stolen by Stalin in 1940, and was awarded by Hitler the territory of "Transnistria," a slice of the southwestern Ukraine. Hungary sought to consolidate its expansion to the south, as awarded by Hitler in 1940, as well as possibly gaining some territory to the east.

Thus it is clear that General Franco's own concept, in Madrid, of a Spanish parallel war, of a military expansion into Africa on the coattails of Hitler, was in no way anomalous. A number of regimes were involved in equivalent enterprises, beginning with that of Stalin himself. Strangest of all was the policy of King Boris of Bulgaria, awarded by Hitler territory in Macedonia that Bulgaria had had to give up in 1919, at the price of absurdly declaring war on Britain and the United States – countries that Bulgaria could in no way combat – while remaining at peace with the Soviet Union.

NATIONAL LIBERATION WARS

In some Western countries that had been occupied by the Germans, the myth later developed that virtually the entire population had supported the Resistance, but this was not necessarily the case, particularly during the first years. The greater part of the population in most places did not participate, even indirectly. Collaboration in varying degrees was fairly common,[12] though in most cases collaboration was more passive than active. Attitudes and reactions also varied considerably according to the rhythm of the war. In France, for example, few people were engaged in the Resistance between 1940 and 1943, but when it became clear that Germany was losing and that the Allies might soon liberate France, the Resistance gained enormously in support.

To a greater or lesser degree, Resistance movements against foreign occupiers soon emerged almost everywhere, even during the Soviet occupation of Poland in 1939–41. By 1942 the Communists had become the most active

[12] See F. W. Seidler, *Die Kollaboration, 1939–1945* (Munich, 1995), and G. Eismann and S. Martens, eds., *Occupation et répression militaire allemandes: La politique de "maintien de l'ordre" en Europe occupée, 1939–1945* (Paris, 2007).

force of the Resistance in a number of countries and sometimes waged their own form of revolutionary class struggle under the banner of the Resistance, involving both a revolutionary civil war and a national liberation struggle. In most cases, however, they largely obeyed the Soviet injunction to participate in broad multiparty national fronts against the invaders, deferring any plans for a Communist takeover.

In Slovakia and Bulgaria, armed insurrections against the collaborationist policy and against the German forces broke out in the summer of 1944, with the goal of overturning the existing regimes and reversing their international alignment. Both of these risings were too weak to succeed, and both were suppressed, though the Bulgarian government did change its policy and seek too late to resume the role of neutral. Hungary sought independently to move in the same direction but was immediately occupied by German forces. In Rumania there was no revolt, but instead an internal coup d'etat to install a new government that reversed sides in the war, aligning Rumania with the Allies. During the last year of the conflict the Romanian army, which had fought for three years on the eastern front as an ally of Hitler, suffered more casualties fighting against the Germans than did the British army.

CIVIL WARS

Though World War II in Europe was not waged as a total revolutionary *Weltanschauungskrieg* by any of the aggressor states, all three of them represented ideological systems. Supporters and opponents of Fascism and Communism could be found in every country, and in some there was violent conflict between these factions, in addition to acts of resistance by patriots and nationalists of varying political hues. Civil war or internal violence during the war in Europe, as distinct from the violence of a foreign occupier, has normally been defined as a struggle between Fascists and anti-Fascists, sometimes conceived as a conflict between democracy and Fascism, or between Fascists and Communists or pro-Communists, or sometimes between left and right. These concepts, in turn, differ significantly from or even contradict each other. In Western Europe there was a genuine conflict between Fascists and democrats, but anti-Fascism embraced a broad spectrum. Extreme hostility between Communists and anti-Communists remained, but for most of the war was superseded by the formation of national fronts or united fronts against Germany.

Many political sectors changed positions, sometimes even twice, just as Stalin did, depending on the situation. At the beginning of 1939 Communists were ardent anti-Fascists, then became neutral or pro-Fascist for two years under the Nazi-Soviet Pact, after which they became ardent anti-Fascists once more. Many sectors of the right, if forced to choose, preferred Fascists to Communists, but there were many exceptions and variations. Many rightists, whether principled conservatives like Churchill or moderate authoritarians, remained anti-Fascists throughout. Others in France were simply forced into anti-Fascism by the war, after which they switched in mid-1940 to neutrality or a qualified pro-Fascism. The French army command became eager to end the war with Germany in June 1940 in part to avert the perceived danger of civil war, by analogy to events in 1871. In general, the radical right responded variously, depending on the wartime status of their countries. Their general tendency was pro-Fascism, but there were numerous exceptions. The moderate non-Communist left tended toward anti-Fascism, but again with some exceptions. Even democratic liberals could not be counted on to support anti-Fascism in every instance, though they were more reliable than most.

Collaborationist governments were formed in Slovakia, in half of France (the Vichy regime), in Croatia, in Serbia, in Greece, and later in Norway and in Hungary, and, by the autumn of 1943, they were joined by Mussolini's neo-Fascist Italian Social Republic in northern Italy. In addition, the independent governments of Hungary, Rumania, and Bulgaria became German allies. In all these countries it was theoretically possible to speak of potential civil war, and in each case, with the exceptions of Hungary, Norway, and Rumania, insurgencies developed at one time or another against the domestic government. The Resistance often operated on two fronts, against collaborationist compatriots, on the one hand, and against the invader on the other. The final phase of the war sometimes involved insurrections against a collaborationist regime or against the Germans, followed by a violent settling of accounts, sometimes featuring a mass slaughter of Fascists or of those deemed pro-Fascist or, at least, strongly anti-Communist. For these reasons, some commentators would later speak of aspects of domestic civil war in these encounters.

In 1941 the Comintern announced a policy of forming "united fronts," much broader and theoretically less radical than popular fronts, to struggle against Germany in each country. By 1942 the Communists had become the most active force of the Resistance in a number of them, including major Western countries such as France and Italy. Communists sometimes waged their own form of revolutionary class struggle under the banner of the Resistance, though in most cases they obeyed the Soviet injunction to participate in broad multiparty united or national fronts.

Full civil wars developed only in Yugoslavia and Greece. The independent variable there and elsewhere was the strength of Communism compared to that of rivals and opponents, though the final outcome would be determined by the international context. In extremely underdeveloped Albania, conversely, anti-Communists were not well enough organized to wage a serious civil war. The French and Italian Communist parties were stronger than those in any other part of Europe save the southern Balkans, but the other anti-Fascist forces were also much stronger, discouraging any prospect of revolutionary civil war, while their lands were occupied by the Americans and the British, not by the Red Army.

In France by 1944 there was violent conflict between the Gaullist Forces Françaises de l'Interieure and the Milices of the Vichy regime, as well as against the German occupation forces. This created what one historian has called "a climate of civil war,"[13] though not a genuine civil war, because the Free French government of De Gaulle was quickly installed as the legitimate government of France. Something similar might be found in other occupied western European countries.

The nearest thing to a genuine civil war in Western Europe was the conflict in northern Italy between 1943 and 1945 that pitted anti-Fascist Partisan forces, on the one hand, against German occupation troops and varied paramilitary and police forces of the reconstituted Fascist Social Republic, on the other. Some Italian historians simply refer to this as the "civil war," coming, in the Italian case, at the end of the dictatorship rather than, as in the Spanish case, at the beginning. It was a brutal three-way struggle in which an estimated 200,000 people died; the killings included the execution of hostages by the Fascists and Nazis and selective assassinations and other killings by the Partisans. This became a three-dimensional conflict: a war of national liberation against the Germans, a civil war of a multiparty front against Fascism, and also at times a revolutionary class struggle on the part of the Italian Communists, who comprised the largest single sector of the Partisans.[14] This kind of three-way conflict also took place in Yugoslavia and Greece, but there the dimension of revolutionary civil war came more directly to the fore, whereas in Italy it remained subordinate. In Italy the term "civil war" was used not infrequently after 1945, though it eventually was deemed politically incorrect, the reality of the situation becoming accepted by more historians beginning only in the 1990s.[15] After the fighting was finally concluded, however, the Italian Communist leadership restrained its revolutionaries and participated in a multiparty democratic coalition that founded a new republic, as in France.

The situation in Italy between 1943 and 1945 was the one that, in a very limited sense, most resembled the Spanish war. This was so not merely because Italy and Spain are the two large European countries that most resemble each other, but because there was a partial resemblance in the opposing forces. The differences, however, were even greater. In Italy, the civil war came at the end of the dictatorship, stemming from its disintegration, rather than constituting the origin of such a regime. The opposing political forces were, in the Italian case, more narrowly based on the Fascist side and much more broadly based on the side of the Resistance. Fascism sensu stricto was much stronger in Italy,

---

[13] O. Wieviorka, "Guerre civile à la française? Le cas des années sombres (1940–1945)," *Vingtième siècle*, 85 (2005), 10, quoted in E. Traverso, *A ferro e fuoco. La guerra civile europea 1914–1945* (Bologna, 2007), 232, fn 97. This theme is also treated in P. Burrin, *La France à l'heure allemande, 1940–1944* (Paris, 1995), 453.

[14] The most detailed source is E. Collotti et al., eds, *Dizionario della Resistenza* (Turin, 2006). One of the most notorious Communist attacks on a non-Communist Partisan unit is recounted in A. Lenoci, *Porzus: La Resistenza tradita* (Rome, 1998).

[15] The publication of Claudio Pavone's *Una guerra civile. Saggio storico sulla moralità nella Resistenza* (Turín, 1991) marked something of a turning point.

but few other than diehard Fascists supported the Social Republic, whereas Franco was supported by many non- and even anti-Fascists, all of them determined not to succumb at the hands of the revolutionaries. The Resistance in Italy was, conversely, much more broadly based than the Popular Front in Spain, for it included many more liberals, the equivalent of some of those slaughtered in the Spanish Republican zone, as well as the main new representatives of political Catholicism, most of whom would have been on the opposite side in Spain. The Resistance had no chance for victory so long as Germany occupied the country and could only assist the Allies, but without playing the major role. Much more in Italy than in Spain, the outcome was determined by foreign intervention; both the beginning and end there depended overwhelmingly on external factors, which could not be said for Spain.

Italian Communist leaders hoped to help lead a more moderate kind of regime that would eventually evolve into a people's republic, but the new system in Italy was much more broadly based and much more strongly oriented toward democracy than was the revolutionary Popular Front in Spain. The Italian Republic was a great deal more moderate, constructive, and obedient to law than the Second Republic in Spain, and soon moved to marginalize the Communists, even though the latter in some ways attempted to play a more conciliatory role in Italy than in Spain.

In Spain during World War II the national front sought by the Communists remained very weak, due to the strength of the Franco regime and the antipathy to Communism of most of the Spanish left, as a result of their experience in the civil war. The PCE finally launched an armed initiative from France in October 1944, a small trans-Pyrenean invasion that sought to reignite civil war. This was a complete failure, though irregular bands of varying political identities continued to operate with ever-decreasing effectiveness until 1952.[16]

The final phase of domestic conflict in Western Europe was the purge of collaborators and Fascists in 1945–46. Istvan Deak has calculated that this potentially affected about 2 to 3 percent of the population in the formerly occupied countries – some rather more, some rather less.[17] The most ferocious was the mass slaughter of the Fascist Ustashe and members of various other Croatian and Slovenian groups carried out by Yugoslav Communists in the northwestern zone of Yugoslavia, which initially liquidated at least 30,000 people, perhaps more, without the slightest judicial process, something more extensive, in both absolute and proportionate numbers, than Franco's post–Civil War executions in Spain. In recent years there has been much talk in Spain of disinterring "*fosas comunes*" (mass graves), but if a new one can be

---

[16] There is now a very extensive literature, most of it highly partisan, on what have come to be called the Spanish "Maquis," by uncertain analogy with France. One of the most recent, less romantic, and broadly synthetic treatments is J. Aróstegui, ed., *El último frente: la resistencia armada antifranquista en España, 1939–1952* (Madrid, 2008).

[17] The broadest single study is I. Deák, J. T. Gross, and T. Judt, eds., *The Politics of Retribution in Europe: World War and Its Aftermath* (Princeton, N.J., 2000).

found in Spain with the remains of twenty or thirty cadavers, it is a major event, whereas in Slovenia a single grave was unearthed in 2009 containing literally thousands of remains.[18]

In France the purge was more severe than in Italy, claiming more than 7,000 lives.[19] The exact figure in northern Italy is unknown, but has generally been estimated to total at least 3,000 summary executions, and perhaps many more than that, primarily by Communist groups.[20] In Norway, Denmark, and Holland, three stable and well-established democracies where the death penalty had been abolished in the nineteenth century, it was suddenly revived to apply to collaborators. In Belgium, some 400,000 cases were investigated, leading to 57,000 indictments and producing 2,940 death sentences, of which 242 were carried out.[21] In Czechoslovakia, which had also been a stable democracy, there were 700 legal executions, but many thousands of unarmed German civilians were slaughtered, beaten, or tortured by vengeful Czechs. Conversely, in Italy, the original homeland of Fascism, once the wave of killings by Partisans had passed, the Italian court system took a moderate approach. No more than 21,000 cases were investigated, of which no more than a third led to any kind of sentence, with only 91 death penalties carried out.[22]

After some years, the tendency was to move toward amnesty for the remaining collaborators. (The principal exception was Germany, which was slow to regain sovereignty, and then moved to a reverse rhythm.) Historically, amnesty has been a classic feature in the ultimate resolution of civil war and

[18] On the border region of Istria, see R. Pupo, *Il lungo esodo. Istria: le persecuzioni, le foibe, l'esilio* (Milan, 2006), and G. Baracetti, "*Foibe*: Nationalism, Revenge and Ideology in Venezia Giulia and Istria, 1943–5," *Journal of Contemporary History*, 44:4 (October 2009), 657–74.

[19] The first research was by Peter Novick, who calculated 7,306 killings in his *The Resistance versus Vichy* (London, 1968), which has generally been confirmed by the more detailed investigation synthesized by Marcel Baudot, "L'Épuration: Bilan chiffré," *Bulletin de l'Institut d'Histoire du Temps Présent*, 35 (1986), 37–53. Conversely, legal prosecution of collaborators was proportionately less extensive in France than in the smaller democracies to the north, which altogether indicted approximately 163,000 alleged collaborators. Of 7,037 judicial death sentences in France, 791 were carried out. There were 2,777 life sentences, 10,434 condemnations to forced labor, and 26,289 other prison sentences, as well as many other smaller penalties. P. Bourdrel, *L'Épuration sauvage* (Paris, 1988), 2 vols.

[20] Though some sources cite distinctly higher figures. See G. Oliva, *La resa dei conti* (Milan, 1999); G. Pisanò, *Il triangolo della morte: la politica della strage in Emilia durante e dopo la guerra civile* (Milan, 2003); and H. Woller, *I conti con il fascismo: l'epurazione in Italia, 1943–1948* (Bologna, 2004).

[21] M. Conway, "Justice in Postwar Belgium: Popular Passions and Political Realities," in Deák et al., eds, *The Politics of Retribution*, 133–56.

[22] L. Mercuri, *L'epurazione in Italia, 1943–1948* (Cuneo, 1988); R. P. Domenico, *Italian Fascists on Trial, 1943–1948* (Chapel Hill, N.C., 1991); R. Canosa, *Storia dell'epurazione in Italia. Le sanzioni contro il Fascismo, 1943–1948* (Milan, 1999). (Thanks to David Gress for some of these Italian references.) Perhaps the broadest inquiry of this sort will be found in the lengthy set of studies edited by S. U. Larsen, *Modern Europe after Fascism 1943–1980s* (Boulder, Colo., 1998), 2 vols.

major internal conflict, beginning with Athens at the close of the fifth century B.C. As Ernest Renan observed in the nineteenth century:

Forgetting, and even historical error, constitute an essential factor in building a nation, and for that reason progress in historical studies often represents a danger for nationality. Historical research, in fact, brings to light acts of violence that have accompanied the origins of all political formations, even those whose consequences have been beneficial.[23]

THE SOVIET UNION

The principal internal violence encouraged by the Germans in the vast territories that they conquered was to foment the murder of Jews by their fellow citizens in many parts of Eastern Europe, an activity in which sectors of the domestic population sometimes participated. The Soviet regime, by comparison, had been born in civil war, had actively promoted it in many countries for fifteen years, and consistently sought to exploit internal conflict between social and political groups. When it occupied eastern Poland between 1939 and 1941, the Soviet regime fomented interethnic violence and promoted large-scale ethnic cleansing to de-Polonize sizable districts. Paramilitary bands of Ukrainians and Belarussians were encouraged to murder and to dispossess sectors of the Polish population as part of the annexation of the entire territory to the Ukrainian and Belarussian SSRs. This constituted radicalization of the long-term Soviet policy to foment ethnic violence and civil war in Poland, carried out during the 1930s by small units of the NKVD that infiltrated eastern Poland. A low level of strife in that region had been a constant of the interwar years, and was then fanned to white heat by Soviet occupation policy.[24]

This continued to varying degrees and in various ways for much of the following decade. Under German occupation after 1941, Ukrainian nationalists carried out bloody pogroms against Poles,[25] as well as against Jews, acts that in a different manner were further encouraged by renewed Soviet occupation in 1944–46. Ultimately, at least two million surviving Poles were expelled.

Nonetheless, despite the progressive tightening of Soviet totalitarianism, minor irregular warfare and resistance against the dictatorship, particularly

[23] E. Renan, *Qu'est-ce qu'une nation?*, quoted in E. Traverso, *A ferro e fuoco: la guerra civile europea 1914–1945* (Bologna, 2007), 128. Traverso provides an excellent discussion of the problems of amnesty on pp. 125–29. See also the chapter "La 'guerra civile europea' e le sue conseguenze per l'idea di nazione e di Europa," in G. E. Rusconi, *Se cessiamo di esser una nazione* (Bologna, 1993), 101–23.

[24] See J. T. Gross, *Revolution from Abroad: Soviet Conquest of Poland's Western Ukraine and Western Belorussia* (Princeton, N.J., 1988).

[25] "It is estimated that between 1942 and 1944 100,000 Poles and 20,000 Ukrainians in the region were killed as a result of interethnic violence." J. Baberowski and A. Doering-Manteuffel, "The Quest for Order and the Pursuit of Terror," in M. Geyer and S. Fitzpatrick, eds., *Beyond Totalitarianism: Stalinism and Nazism Compared* (Cambridge, UK, 2009), 221.

ethnic resistance against Russian rule, had continued in the prewar Soviet Union for years. Historians generally conclude that this was finally fully suppressed in Soviet Central Asia by 1936. Such resistance was not purely spontaneous, since the intelligence services of Japan and the Soviet Union's western neighbors all sought to stimulate it.

The German invasion quickly revealed the disaffection of a significant part of the Soviet population, especially among the ethnic minorities. The massive capture of military prisoners by the Germans – more than 3.5 million in less than six months – was not due solely to the superior military prowess of the Germans. Though totalitarianism had eliminated all alternative political projects among the Soviet population, at first much of the Red Army was not highly motivated to fight for Stalin, and disaffection among some of the minorities was severe. They had been specially targeted for repression during the preceding decade,[26] and the anti-Soviet reaction among many Ukrainians, the Muslim peoples of the south,[27] and the recently conquered Baltic peoples was great. It would have been even greater had German policy made more of an effort to stimulate anti-Soviet nationalism, but Hitler's approach differed from that of Stalin in doing little to encourage internal revolt. It relied mainly on direct conquest and German race war until it was too late to change course effectively.

Even so, very large numbers of Soviet citizens served with the German forces as military auxiliaries, members of anti-Soviet partisan bands, volunteers in the Waffen SS, and finally even as Russian military units attached to the *Wehrmacht*.[28] Indeed, Jeffrey Burds, a specialist in this area, concludes that

In the second world war, nationalist armed collaboration was common in zones throughout the Soviet western and southern borderlands, eventually accounting for 2.5 million of 3 million armed collaborators with German occupying authorities in Europe. By 1945, one in eight German soldiers had been a Soviet citizen before the war.[29]

While this calculation may be somewhat exaggerated, there is no doubt that such mobilization could have been even greater had Hitler ever made it a priority. Though the bulk of Soviet citizens either remained loyal to or were

---

[26] Selected ethnic minorities suffered disproportionate rates of arrest, deportation, and execution during the 1930s: ibid., 223–24. See, more broadly, J. Baberowski and A. Doering Manteuffel, *Ordnung durch Terror: Gewaltexzesse und Vernichtung im nationalsozialis-tischen und stalinistischen Imperium* (Bonn, 2006). Timothy Snyder points out that during the first six years of the Third Reich (1933–39), the most severely repressed ethnic group in Europe were not Jews in Germany but Poles in the Soviet Union, of whom nearly 100,000 were executed during the Great Terror of 1937–38. *Bloodlands*, 89–109.

[27] P. von zur Mühlen, *Zwischen Hakenkreuz und Sowjetstern: Der Nationalismus der sowjetischen Orientvölker im Zweiten Weltkrieg* (Düsseldorf, 1971); J. Hoffmann, *Deutsche und Kalmyken, 1942–1945* (Freiburg, 1974).

[28] W. Strik-Strikfeldt, *Against Hitler and Stalin* (New York, 1971).

[29] J. Burds, "The Soviet War against 'Fifth Columnists': The Case of Chechnya, 1942–4," *Journal of Contemporary History*, 42:2 (2007), 267–314.

effectively controlled by the Stalinist regime, World War II in the Soviet Union had more the character of civil war than anywhere else in Europe, with the exceptions of Yugoslavia and Greece.[30]

Soviet policy responded with savage repression of its population and large-scale internal ethnic cleansing of more than three million of its unfortunate citizens,[31] hundreds of thousands of whom perished. At the end of the war, the Soviet government was a major participant in the greatest ethnic cleansing program in world history, involving the uprooting of nearly fifteen million Germans in eastern and east central Europe and the former eastern Germany. Of these, as many as two million may have died.[32]

Finally, low-intensity internal war continued for years in western portions of the Soviet Ukraine, as small Ukrainian, Lithuanian, Latvian, and Estonian guerrilla bands continued to resist for some time, though with ever-diminishing vigor. The Ukrainian nationalist resistance inflicted 35,000 fatalities on the Soviet military and police,[33] while several hundred thousand Ukrainians were killed in the repression. In Soviet-occupied Poland, a new Resistance began, which developed into a new insurgency against the Polish Communist army and police that lingered on for years, and in which perhaps 100,000 more died, though the main phase was over by the end of 1947.[34] Altogether, large numbers of people perished in these operations and in their ruthless suppression, by far the principal example of internal war in Europe after 1945, far surpassing, for example, the minor operations in Spain.

[30] For a broad if impressionistic treatment of Stalin's internal war during the era of World War II, see N. Tolstoy, *Stalin's Secret War* (New York, 1981).

[31] A brief summary may be found in N. Naimark, *Fires of Hatred: Ethnic Cleansing in Twentieth-Century Europe* (Cambridge, UK, 2001), 85–107.

[32] G. MacDonogh, *After the Reich: The Brutal History of the Allied Occupation* (New York, 2007).

[33] G. Roberts, *Stalin's Wars: From World War to Cold War, 1939–1953* (New Haven, Conn., 2008), 325.

[34] "These partisan efforts, coupled with violent labor and student protests, and along with the continued deportations to the Soviet gulags, became known as the Polish Civil War, and cost the lives of over 100,000 people." K. K. Koskodan, *No Greater Ally: The Untold Story of Poland's Forces in World War II* (Oxford, 2009), 249–50. This is treated briefly in A. J. Prazmowska, *Civil War in Poland, 1942–1948* (Houndsmill/New York, 2004), 143–90.

9

The Civil Wars in Yugoslavia and Greece

The two European countries that experienced full-scale civil war during or immediately after World War II were Yugoslavia and Greece. In both cases an analogy existed with the radicalization, breakdown, and civil strife that attended the end of World War I in eastern and central Europe, all of which merely reemphasizes the uniqueness of the Spanish case, in which civil war erupted in peacetime, initially without any direct exogenous influence or intervention.

The cases of Yugoslavia and Greece were contiguous geographically and chronologically, and both can be analyzed within the rubric of Communist/anti-Communist civil wars. Moreover, both were predominantly agrarian and underdeveloped countries, with a social basis in small family farms, but the parallels or similarities end there. All the other factors – politics, foreign policy, other aspects of social and economic structure, and the role of ethnicity – varied considerably. Because of these differences, the two cases must be discussed separately.

YUGOSLAVIA

Yugoslavia was one of several multinational European states created by the victors immediately after World War I and lasted seventy-two years, until its final dissolution in 1991.[1] With a population in 1940 approaching seventeen million, it was ethnically and geographically the most complicated country in the world, relative to its size. Originally named "Kingdom of the Serbs, Croats and Slovenes," it was in fact much more complex than that, with minorities of Albanians, Bosnian Muslims, Hungarians, Germans, Jews, and Macedonians (whose identity was contested among the Serbs, Bulgarians, and independent Macedonians).[2] No ethnicity constituted a majority, but

---

[1] A nominal state of Yugoslavia, consisting essentially of greater Serbia, continued to exist for some years after that. For a good survey, see J. R. Lampe, *Yugoslavia as History: Twice There Was a Country* (Cambridge, UK, 1996).

[2] See I. Banac, *The National Question in Yugoslavia: Origins, History, Politics* (Ithaca, N.Y., 1984).

the Serbs were the most numerous, amounting to more than 40 percent of the total population. The Serbian King Alexander became the constitutional monarch of Yugoslavia; the old Serb army constituted the basis of the new Yugoslav army; Serbian politicians largely dominated the new political system; and Serbian bureaucrats mostly staffed the administration. Interwar Yugoslavia was a Serb-dominated state that generated a good deal of dissidence, to which King Alexander replied by imposing a centralized royal dictatorship in January 1929. This lasted more than five years,[3] until the king was assassinated by terrorists of the Internal Macedonian Revolutionary Organization (IMRO) while on a visit to France in 1934. For the next five years, Yugoslavia was governed by a more moderate authoritarian system analogous to the contemporary Pilsudski regime in Poland. A new start was then attempted under the "Sporazum" (Agreement) of 1939, which arranged greater sharing of power among Serbs, Croats, and Slovenes, but considerable bitterness against Serbs persisted.

In 1941 Hitler was not initially interested in intervening militarily in either Yugoslavia or Greece, his main goal being a quiet Balkan rear guard while he proceeded with the invasion of Russia. In March 1941 he therefore coerced the Yugoslav government into signing the Tripartite Pact, a defensive alliance among Germany, Italy, Japan, and other countries, which in turn provoked a sudden coup by Serbian nationalist military commanders, who overthrew the ministry governing Yugoslavia. They charged it with not protecting Serbian interests and Yugoslav independence, though their new government assured Hitler that it would abide by the Tripartite Pact.[4]

By this time, Mussolini, Hitler's principal ally, had been bogged down for five months in a failed invasion of Greece (an operation that Hitler had never approved and that vexed him considerably). Both Greece and Yugoslavia, therefore, had become troublesome for German strategy, and Hitler made a quick decision to invade the two countries early in April 1941, rescuing Mussolini from his disastrous Greek adventure, occupying both Greece and Yugoslavia, and creating new puppet regimes that would guarantee a Balkan rear guard that was solidly pro-German.

The Yugoslav army collapsed so rapidly that the German invasion achieved complete success in a matter of days, the fastest of all of Hitler's *Blitzkrieg* operations. Yugoslavia was divided into a series of different zones and administrations, most of which were in turn divided between German and Italian areas of occupation. In Serbia proper, a puppet regime was installed under Gen. Milan Nedic, while Croatia was established as an independent state for the first time in modern history. The resulting entity, in fact a puppet or at best a satellite regime, was handed to the Croatian Fascist movement, the Ustashe

---

[3] See J. J. Sadkovich, "Il regime di Alessandro in Iugoslavia: 1929–1934. Un'interpretazione," *Storia Contemporanea*, 15:1 (February 1984), 5–37.

[4] Historians have never been able to explain fully the origins and motivation of the Belgrade coup, which remains a matter for debate. On its background, see J. B. Hoptner, *Yugoslavia in Crisis, 1934–1941* (New York, 1962).

(Insurgents), led by Ante Pavelic, and was known as the Independent State of Croatia, termed (from its acronym in Croatian) the NDH.[5]

Croatians harbored much resentment against the Serb domination of the previous two decades, but the enormous violence directed by the Ustasa regime against Serbs can hardly be explained by history alone. It stemmed from the violent and racist doctrines of the Ustashe, who considered the economically more advanced Croatians (Roman Catholic in religion, with a language, though much the same as Serbian, that employs the Latin alphabet), to be a completely superior and "Gothic" people, in contrast to the supposedly primitive, racially inferior, oriental, and Orthodox Serbs. A mixed Serb and Croat population existed in Bosnia-Herzegovina (most of which was awarded to the NDH), and even in parts of Croatia itself. The Ustashe unleashed an extraordinarily violent campaign of genocide against the Serbs, the only major campaign of genocide in Europe during the Second World War not directed against Jews or Poles. Many tens of thousands were slaughtered, often in the most grisly ways; large numbers were driven out and others forced into religious conversion, though in 1942 Pavelic also set up a separate Croatian Orthodox Church under his control. It will never be possible to tabulate exactly how many Serbs were slaughtered by the Ustashe, mainly during 1941–42. The statistic of 300,000 has often been used, though it is impossible to verify, and the number may have been smaller. There is no doubt, however, that it was one of the most extraordinary crimes of the greatest mass atrocity war in history.[6]

Altogether, there were four major Yugoslav political actors during the war – the Ustashe of the NDH, the Communist Partisan movement led by Josip Broz ("Tito"),[7] the Serbian Chetnik movement led by the Serbian army colonel Draza Mihailovic, and the Serbian puppet regime of Nedic, by far the least important. In the most confusing domestic scenario of all of World War II, the Ustashe at varying times fought against both the Partisans and the Chetniks, while massacring many civilians; the Chetniks at varying times fought against the Germans, Italians, puppet Serbs, Ustashe, and Partisans, while sometimes slaughtering non-Serb civilians in several regions; the followers of Nedic at

---

[5] On the Ustashe and the NDH, see S. P. Ramet, ed., "The Independent State of Croatia (NDH), 1941–45," a special issue of *Totalitarian Movements and Political Religions*, 7:4 (December 2006); J. J. Sadkovich, *Italian Support for Croatian Separatism, 1927–1937* (New York, 1987) and "Terrorism in Croatia, 1929–1934," *East European Quarterly*, 22:1 (March 1988), 55–79; L. Hory and M. Broszat, *Der kroatische Ustascha-Staat, 1941–1945* (Stuttgart, 1964); M. Ambri, *I falsi fascismi* (Rome, 1980), 129–97; and F. Tudman, "The Independent State of Croatia as an Instrument of the Occupation Powers in Yugoslavia, and the People's Liberation Movement in Croatia from 1941 to 1945," in *Les systèmes d'occupation en Yougoslavie, 1941–1945* (Belgrade, 1963), 135–262. For a brief summary, see my *A History of Fascism, 1914–1945* (Madison, Wisc., 1995), 404–11.

[6] E. Paris, *Genocide in Satellite Croatia, 1941–1945* (Chicago, 1960). The most nearly accurate macrostatistics on mass death in Yugoslavia during World War II will be found in B. Kocevic, *Zrtve drugog svetskog rata u Jugoslaviji* (London, 1985).

[7] P. Auty, *Tito: A Biography* (New York, 1970).

varying times fought against the Chetniks and the Partisans; and the Partisans at varying times fought against the Germans, Italians, Ustashe, Chetniks, and Nedic followers, while in 1941–42, and later in 1944–45, carrying out a kind of "Red Terror" against class enemies.

The only one of those forces to rise above extreme ethnocentrism was the Partisans, which was a major reason for their ultimate victory in 1944–45. The Yugoslav Communist Party (CPY) had been founded in 1919–20 and had achieved a certain appeal, not among urban "proletarians" (of whom there were few in Yugoslavia) but as a champion of poor peasants, particularly in Bosnia and Montenegro, thereby winning nearly 15 percent of the seats in the first Yugoslav elections of 1920. The early success of Yugoslav Communism, limited though it was, may be contrasted with the almost complete insignificance of Spanish Communism during the first fifteen years of the latter's existence.[8] Though the CPY was subjected to considerable repression and would not be able to build on its initial success for long, it remained practically the only political force in interwar Yugoslavia that sought to represent people from all regions and ethnicities, the only "all-Yugoslav" party.

The CPY, like nearly all Communist parties, had been thoroughly subjected to the control of the Comintern, and at the beginning of 1941 counted only about 12,000 members, though it had a potential following much greater than that. For two and a half months after the invasion, it was ordered to remain relatively quiescent, since Hitler and Stalin were still quasi-allies, but once Germany attacked the Soviet Union, Tito was instructed to devote maximal energy to developing an anti-German guerrilla force on the broadest basis, which quickly became known as the Partisans. In Yugoslavia, as in many other countries, the Communists showed their aptitude for military mobilization, with their centralism, strict discipline, firm leadership, and combination of pragmatism, ruthlessness, and extreme violence.

The ranks of the Partisans swelled with Serbian refugees from the Ustasha genocide, and their program of nominal autonomy and equal representation for all nationalities enabled them to attract followers from the other ethnicities as well. They quickly developed as the only all-Yugoslav resistance movement and hence also the only all-Yugoslav political movement, their status as a broad national liberation movement helping to disguise the almost complete control exerted by the CPY. Comintern leaders instructed all the Communist parties in occupied Europe to form broad multiparty (and, where appropriate, multinational) fronts that would concentrate on armed resistance and military support for the Soviet Union, with Communist political goals held in abeyance for the duration of the conflict. In Yugoslavia, however, the Partisans gained control of

[8] The only comparative study of the Spanish and Yugoslav revolutions will be found in P. B. Minehan, *Civil War and World War in Europe: Spain, Yugoslavia, and Greece, 1936–1949* (New York, 2006). See also I. Avakumovic, *History of the Communist Party of Yugoslavia* (Aberdeen, 1964), and A. Djilas, *The Contested Country: Yugoslav Unity and Communist Revolution, 1919–1953* (Cambridge, Mass., 1991).

small districts not held by other forces and during the first year of their struggle often imposed a kind of Red Terror against social and political opponents, though to some extent this proved counterproductive. Much more appealing was their emphasis on a broad all-Yugoslav national front; this attracted many, and remained the political platform of the Partisans well into 1944.

Tito waged a revolutionary war in the sense that he was building a broad new popular movement that could ultimately lead to a Yugoslav Communist regime, but he was also fighting a liberation war that devoted considerable effort to irregular combat against the German and Italian occupiers. He was not deterred by the harsh German reprisal policy, which announced that it would execute 100 civilians for every German soldier killed, but adopted a Leninist position of "the worse, the better" in the accurate calculation that extreme German repression would alienate Yugoslav civilians and convulse society, providing grist for the Partisan mill and increasing the potential for ultimate revolution. By contrast, the Serbian Chetniks of Mihailovic sought to preserve the old order, conserving their strength in order to reimpose it when the general war ended.[9] Thus more and more they avoided attacks on German forces that would bring brutal reprisals against Serbian civilians, while devoting themselves increasingly to struggle against ethnic enemies, with attacks at various times on Albanians, Bosnian Muslims, the Ustashe, and the Partisans. By 1942 there coexisted with the national liberation struggle against Germany and Italy a confusing triangular civil war among Serbs (mainly Chetniks), the Croatian Ustashe, and the multinational Partisan movement. Whereas initially Mihailovic had been recognized as internal leader of the anti-Axis struggle by the Yugoslav government in exile, and hence had received most of the arms and other support provided by Great Britain, by the beginning of 1943 British support had shifted decisively to the Partisans, who were judged by far the most effective anti-Axis force, and for the remainder of the war they would be the chief beneficiaries of British assistance, enabling them to become stronger than ever.[10]

Yugoslavia was the only area, aside from the occupied portions of the Soviet Union, in which the resistance created a serious military problem for the Germans, requiring the commitment of many troops to repress the Partisans and Chetniks, primarily the former. Three different offensives were launched against the Partisans between the latter part of 1941 and the first half of 1942. Though fighting was sometimes severe and losses heavy, the Partisans continued to gain recruits and by the end of 1942 may have had nearly 100,000 men

[9] L. Karchmar, *Draza Mihailovic and the Rise of the Chetnik Movement, 1941–1942* (New York, 1987), 2 vols.; and J. Tomasevich, *War and Revolution in Yugoslavia, 1941–1945: The Chetniks* (Stanford, Calif., 1975).

[10] F. W. D. Deakin, *The Embattled Mountain* (London, 1971); W. Roberts, *Tito, Mihailovic and the Allies, 1941–1945* (New Brunswick, N.J., 1973). For a pro-Chetnik critique, see M. Lees, *The British Role in Tito's Grab for Power, 1943–1944* (San Diego, Calif., 1990), and D. Martin, *The Web of Disinformation: Churchill's Yugoslav Blunder* (San Diego, Calif., 1990). The most recent account is S. K. Pavlowitch, *Hitler's New Disorder: The Second World War in Yugoslavia* (New York, 2008).

under arms, a small portion of them organized as a regular army. In Bosnia in November 1942, Tito convened the first assembly of his Anti-Fascist Council for the National Liberation of Yugoslavia (AVNOJ – pronounced "avnoy"), his political umbrella organization that managed partially to disguise its domination by the CPY. The German command feared an imminent Allied invasion of Yugoslavia and, with fourteen German divisions stationed in the country, launched two more offensives in the southern part of the country to destroy the Partisans. Despite heavy losses, the main group managed to slip away again. With the collapse of Fascist Italy in the summer of 1943, the Partisans captured many Italian weapons and were even joined by several thousand former Italian troops. By the latter part of 1943 they were stronger than ever, and able to withstand continued, but diminishing, German pressure during the first half of 1944. Over half of Tito's troops were Serbs, but there were also many Croatians, as well as Slovenes and Bosnian Muslims. The German invasion had completely destroyed most of the old political forces, and in this vacuum the egalitarian and multinational Partisans enjoyed greater popularity than most of the ethnic-based groups, most of which were also violent and authoritarian.

Though Tito had originally been appointed by the Comintern, the strength of his movement assured him broad autonomy. Stalin still preferred the political cover of a non-Communist regime, as he had in Spain, and wished to avoid political conflict with other Yugoslav forces, partly in order to concentrate on the military effort and partly to avoid friction with Britain. Military supplies from the latter increased in the first half of 1944, and by September the British had convinced the Yugoslav king in exile to recognize Tito as leader of all the resistance forces. That notwithstanding, when Tito made a secret trip to Moscow the same month he bluntly told Stalin that the king would not be allowed to return and that at war's end he would install a Soviet-style regime. The Red Army broke into Yugoslavia the following month, enabling Tito to enter Belgrade, but the Yugoslav leader maintained full control of his forces, and, with the Soviet military concentrated against German resistance in Hungary, his country never fell under Soviet control. The Partisan army completed occupation of all Yugoslavia by May 1945, carrying out a mass slaughter of the final captured Croatian and Slovene soldiers. During the establishment in 1945–46 of a new regime modeled on the Soviet Union, there were approximately 100,000 violent deaths, most of them executions, but some the result of military actions to eliminate the last members of the opposition.[11]

---

[11] This is the reasoned conclusion of J. R. Lampe in *Yugoslavia as History*, 223–24. Croatian sources refer to approximately 50,000 prisoners slaughtered in northwestern Yugoslavia alone during May–June 1945, though Lampe considers that something of an exaggeration. Precise research on this kind of topic is extremely difficult. See S. Guldescu and J. Prcela, eds., *Operation Slaughterhouse: Eyewitness Accounts of Postwar Massacres in Yugoslavia* (Philadelphia, 1970). The Croatian version is presented in "La Tragedia de Bleiburg," a special number of *Studia Croatica* (Buenos Aires, 1963).

The history and achievements of the Yugoslav Partisans during the Second World War were unique, for they constituted the principal case during this period of European history in which a partly guerrilla movement fought a series of major engagements with the occupier and not merely survived, but went on to gain complete military and political control of the country. The only equivalent occurred in the small, backward neighboring state of Albania. The Partisan achievement was possible only because the German invasion completely destroyed the old structure of things, while all the competing forces were violent and repressive groups based on a single ethnicity. Even so, the Yugoslav Partisans revealed extraordinary toughness, capacity for organization, high morale, flexibility, and combat potential. Their achievements were thus comparatively unique, even if made possible in part by the fact that by 1943 the British had become willing to subordinate everything else to the military struggle, strongly supporting the Partisans even though that meant running the risk of a Communist and totalitarian postwar Yugoslavia. In 1945 a Soviet-style regime was established and, though it began to grow more moderate in the 1950s, continued to govern Yugoslavia until the country finally broke apart in 1991. There then ensued four more years of civil war, accompanied by genocide and ethnic cleansing, during which the idea of Yugoslavia disappeared altogether.

In the Spanish war, the British government had practiced nonintervention, calculating that even if this meant victory by Franco, such an outcome was not incompatible with British interests, even though just barely so. In Yugoslavia, the opposite occurred; Britain ended by intervening to some extent on behalf of the Communists, emphasizing military issues above all else, hoping that this would not lead to a Communist regime but also calculating that even the risk of a postwar Communist Yugoslavia might somehow be compatible with British interests. Indeed, after Tito and Stalin became bitter foes in 1948, this would turn out to be the case. Following numerous complications, then, the opposing British policies in the Spanish and Yugoslav civil wars led indirectly to outcomes that eventually became acceptable to British foreign policy, but for some years this was not at all clear in either case.

GREECE

Civil war in Greece was similarly a consequence of a convulsion wrought by exogenous forces, not an endogenous self-immolation, as in Spain. Modern independent Greece dates from the 1820s, and for a century the country lived under the typical constitutional monarchy of that era, with universal male suffrage introduced in 1864, much earlier than in most countries. The political party system was also typical, with two clientelistic parties, one liberal and one conservative, that mobilized peasant votes and shared power. All of this was rather similar to the Spain of the Restoration, though a major difference was that the Greek Orthodox Church never became the ground of basic political cleavage, as was often the case with religion in Roman Catholic countries. Socially and economically, this very small country (scarcely half the size of today's Greece) was a land of smallholding farmers, which resulted in a conservative and mesocratic, if impoverished, society. The most sophisticated sector was a small mercantile elite engaged in international commerce, which developed a merchant marine disproportionate to the size of the country.

The greatest single issue in the late nineteenth and early twentieth centuries was irredentism, since more than half the Greek-speaking population still lived under Ottoman rule outside independent Greece. The more ardent nationalists espoused the "*Megali* Idea," the goal of a greater Greece that would extend into the Balkans, regain Constantinople, and cover the entire Aegean and the western part of Anatolia as well. All this was simply the Greek version of similar ambitions in Serbia, Bulgaria, and Rumania, since in every case independence had been won by the Balkan countries on limited terms, and each aspired to more territory and the incorporation of coethnics (or those deemed to be so). When the Greek army tried to act on behalf of this ambition in 1897, it met disaster at the hands of the Turks, though the great powers freed Crete from Ottoman rule. The role of nationalism and the question of "Greater Greece" during this period meant that Greek national politics and aspirations were much more similar to those of Portugal than to those of Spain.

A turning point came in 1909, when a successful military revolt, the first since 1843, introduced a more liberal and even more nationalist orientation. Eleutherios Venizelos created a new Liberal Party and reformed the constitution, dominating much of Greek affairs for the next two decades. This set the stage for the first great division in public life, the *ethnikos dichasmos* (national schism) between conservative monarchists and more radical liberals oriented toward republicanism. For twenty years, from 1916 to 1936, Greece had the most convulsive political history of any country in Europe. One king was deposed in 1917, then soon restored, only to be replaced by a republic a few years later, after which the crown prince eventually was called back to assume the throne once more in 1935.[12] The armed forces became highly politicized, but Greek leaders managed to move through these kaleidoscopic changes without civil war, while continuing to preserve a parliamentary system of sorts. Universal male suffrage prevailed, and party competition became fully institutionalized. The system thus worked after a fashion, not unlike parliamentary government in Spain and Portugal, if even more chaotically.[13]

---

[12] To be more precise, King Constantine, deposed by the pro-Entente Liberals in 1917 in order to bring Greece into World War I, was succeeded by his son Alexander, who suddenly died of an infected monkey bite in 1920. Constantine then returned to the throne but, after the military disaster in Anatolia in 1922, was forced to step down and later was officially deposed after a referendum in 1924. His elder surviving son returned as George II in 1935.

[13] The best treatment of Greek politics during this era is G. Mavrogordatos, *Stillborn Republic: Social Coalitions and Party Strategies in Greece, 1922–1936* (Berkeley, Calif., 1983). Comparative analyses of the southern European polities may be found in G. Arrighi, ed., *Semiperipheral Development: The Politics of Southern Europe in the Twentieth Century* (Beverly Hills, Calif., 1985), and N. P. Mouzelis, *Politics in the Semi-Periphery: Early Parliamentarism and Late Industrialization in the Balkans and Latin America* (New York, 1986).

The great achievement of the nationalists was nearly to double the size of the country through the annexations achieved in the Balkan wars of 1912–13. Greece was then forced into the world war on the side of the Entente in 1917, and afterward, amid the chaos attending the break-up of the Ottoman empire, was encouraged to invade Anatolia in 1921–22, which resulted in a major disaster and helped to provoke the temporary transition to a republic. An exchange of population took place that moved 400,000 Muslims to Turkey but added 1,300,000 refugees to a Greece of fewer than six million people.

After one temporary six-month military dictatorship in 1926, the parliamentary system finally came to an end ten years later when a more permanent dictatorship was imposed under the former army general and right-wing party leader Ioannis Metaxas, who ruled until his death at the beginning of 1941. As dictator, Metaxas was more than Primo de Rivera and less than Franco. He aspired to a permanent authoritarian and corporative system and, if not very popular, ruled with an iron hand, though with only limited violence.[14]

During this period Greek society began to change significantly, for its average industrial growth rate of 5.7 percent annually during the 1930s was the highest in the world – a little-known fact. Urbanization and social differentiation increased, with the expansion of labor unions and a Communist Party (the KKE) that had 15,000 members in 1936 – a rather large membership relative to the size of the country. The fact that the KKE had come to hold the balance of power between the republicans and the monarchist populists was a major argument used to justify the dictatorship.

As mentioned earlier, Mussolini's disastrous attack on Greece in 1940, effectively repelled by Metaxas, created a situation in which Hitler rather reluctantly invaded Greece in the spring of 1941 in order to save his ally. A puppet administration was installed in Athens, and the country was divided into German, Italian, and Bulgarian zones of occupation. The British navy blockaded all German territory, a disaster for Greece, which imported much of its food from abroad. Suffering was even worse than in Spain, for absolute famine set in during the winter of 1941–42, with as many as 300–400,000 people dying – nearly 5 percent of the population. After that, British policy relented and allowed food supplies to reach Greece.

Axis occupation resulted in great suffering, economic destruction, and loss of life, but at first did not subject the population to such extreme brutality as in Poland or occupied Soviet territory.[15] It also eliminated the old political leaders and parties, so that the lead in organizing resistance activity

---

[14] J. V. Kofas, *Authoritarianism in Greece: The Metaxas Regime* (Boulder, Colo., 1983).

[15] H. Fleisher, *Im Kreuzschatten der Mächte: Griechenland 1941–1944* (Frankfurt, 1986); J. Hondros, *Occupation and Resistance: The Greek Agony, 1941–1944* (New York, 1983); M. Mazower, *Inside Hitler's Greece: The Experience of Occupation, 1941–1944* (New Haven, Conn., 1994); A. Mouchtouris, *La culture populaire en Gréce pendant les années 1940–1945* (Paris, 1989).

was taken by the KKE, though more moderate groups later developed their own resistance organizations. Like all Communist parties, the KKE received instructions from Moscow to form a broad multiparty front and not to aim initially for establishment of a Communist regime. However, political polarization in Greece had grown because of the dictatorship of 1936–41, and, for the time being, the old parties had been eliminated. The KKE organized a multiparty National Liberation Front (EAM), which also included a number of very small and unrepresentative leftist groups, but not the center-left republicans, and created a National People's Liberation Army (ELAS). EAM was much narrower than the Spanish Popular Front, and, unlike the latter, was controlled by the Communists.

The first phase of civil war suddenly erupted in the autumn of 1943, when ELAS began to attack the smaller non-Communist resistance groups.[16] Since a minority of Greeks collaborated with the puppet government in Athens, KKE leaders alleged that ELAS attacked only collaborationists and merely sought to unify the resistance, but this is doubtful. In a number of countries during World War II, the Communists attacked political rivals on the grounds of collaborationism, a convenient excuse with which to eliminate competition. Moreover, the KKE leaders' denial of political ambition was scarcely convincing, particularly since the Communists had initiated a Red Terror against civilian opponents in some of the areas they controlled. In one region in southern Greece, the victims almost equaled in number the civilians killed by the Germans.[17] Assaults on non-Communist groups in Greece paralleled similar attacks by the Communists in Yugoslavia and Albania. By 1943, "collaborationism" had

[16] There is a sizable literature on the Greek civil war. C. M. Woodhouse, *The Struggle for Greece, 1941–1949* (London, 1976), remains perhaps the best account. Among the better works are Woodhouse, *Apple of Discord* (London, 1948); D. G. Kousoulas, *Revolution and Defeat: The Story of the Greek Communist Party* (London, 1965): J. Iatrides, *Revolt in Athens: The Greek Communist "Second Round," 1944–1945* (Hanover, N.H., 1972); Iatrides, ed., *Greece in the 1940s: A Nation in Crisis* (Hanover, N.H., 1981); Iatrides, *Greece at the Crossroads: The Civil War and Its Legacy* (University Park, Pa., 1995); L. Baerentzen et al., eds., *Studies in the History of the Greek Civil War* (Copenhagen, 1987); D. H. Close, ed., *The Greek Civil War, 1943–1950: Studies of Polarization* (London, 1993) and *The Origins of the Greek Civil War* (New York, 1995); and J. S. Koliopoulos, *Plundered Loyalties: Axis Occupation and Civil Strife in Greek West Macedonia, 1941–1949* (London, 1999). A clear summary may be found in J. S. Koliopoulos and T. M. Veremis, *Greece, the Modern Sequel: From 1831 to the Present* (New York, 2002), 68–98, and there is a comparative treatment in Minehan, *Civil War and World War in Europe*.

[17] See the detailed study of the Argolid district in the Peloponnesus in S. N. Kalyvas, *The Logic of Violence in Civil War* (Cambridge, UK, 2006), 248–329, as well as his chapter, "Red Terror: Leftist Violence during the Occupation," in M. Mazower, ed., *After the War Was Over: Reconstructing the Family, Nation, and State in Greece, 1943–1960* (Princeton, N.J., 2000), 142–83. By the latter part of 1943, EAM had, in good Communist fashion, created its own Cheka, the squads of OPLA (standing for "Organization for the Protection of the People's Struggle"), which began the execution of civilians described as "reactionaries." This came as an enormous shock to villagers, unused to any such arbitrary violence since the time of the Ottomans. Attacks by the security battalions of the collaborationist government in Athens, as well as by German troops, produced an escalation of violence in 1944.

become a convenient excuse with which to crush political opposition. ELAS succeeded in destroying much of the non-Communist resistance, clear proof that fighting the Germans was not necessarily its main priority. The KKE enjoyed major advantages. There had never been a single strong Socialist party in Greece, as distinct from petty rival groups, allowing the KKE to dominate the worker left, and in 1944 it possessed the only national political organization in Greece. Its message of patriotic resistance was also attractive to many, bringing numerous volunteers to ELAS.

Anticipating the country's liberation, the Greek government-in-exile had moved to Cairo, and there the KKE instigated a mutiny among Greek army and navy units in an effort to gain the dominant voice in the regular armed forces. This failed, and in May 1944 its leaders agreed to join a multiparty "National Government," just as the Italian Communists entered Italy's Badoglio government that same year.

Meanwhile, with the German occupiers on the verge of retreat, the KKE consolidated its position in many small towns and in much of the countryside, eliminating opposition. Wartime convulsions had enabled a marginal political grouping to become a major force, the only well-organized one on the Greek mainland. To increase its military strength, ELAS conscripted peasants and made an opportunistic deal in the north with Slavic Macedonians, many of whom had collaborated militarily with the occupiers, bringing about 15,000 Macedonians into its ranks.

There the KKE was playing a dangerous game. In Yugoslavia, Tito had been winning over Macedonians, who had often tended to collaborate with Bulgaria and the Axis in order to break away from Greece, with his promise of an autonomous republic of Macedonia inside a federal Yugoslavia. The KKE saw Macedonians as useful military recruits and as providing a broader connection to Communist forces in Yugoslavia, but Macedonian ambitions undermined Greek sovereignty over their territory. ELAS argued that it had "disarmed" and won over those deceived by the Germans and believed that it held the upper hand, but a thousand of the new recruits took advantage of the German retreat to leave Greece with them. All this only underscored the cynicism with which EAM/ELAS suppressed genuine resistance groups as "collaborators."

In October the government-in-exile returned to Athens to administer the country, but it controlled little more than the capital, since EAM occupied possibly as much as 70 percent of the countryside. King George II was strongly backed by the British, but he was not very popular in Greek society because he had supported the prewar Metaxas dictatorship, a situation rather similar to that of Alfonso XIII in Spain in 1930. EAM spoke of freedom and democracy for Greece, and benefited from the aura of being the major resistance force, but its leaders were uncertain how to convert their military strength into political legitimacy. The royal government taking power in Athens was a national unity government that included KKE ministers, but it was dominated by the older political forces, which proposed to build a regular national army, undercutting ELAS. When police fired on EAM demonstrators in Athens in

December 1944, the KKE was tempted to use the superior numbers of ELAS to seize power directly, launching an insurrection to gain control of Athens and the entire country, though the decision seems to have been impromptu and the action not well organized. This has usually been termed the Greek Communist "second round," the nominal first round having been the offensive against non-Communist resistance forces in the autumn of 1943. John Koliopoulos and Thanos Veremis argue, however, that it was merely the climax of a fairly continuous offensive against non-Communist forces begun nearly fifteen months earlier, and this interpretation seems plausible. The KKE was pursuing the same course as Communists in neighboring Bulgaria, Albania, and Yugoslavia, all of whom were in the process of taking over their countries by violent and highly authoritarian means.

ELAS was by some distance the strongest military force in the country; the reason for its failure lay not in domestic conditions or the resistance of the small and weak non-Communist Greek army, but in international power relations, about which the KKE leaders were uninformed. They knew nothing of the recent agreement between Stalin and Churchill that had consigned Greece to the British sphere of influence, and were proceeding on their own, encouraged not by Stalin but by neighboring Communist leaders. What thwarted the attempted takeover was not Greek resistance, which could not match ELAS, but the swift reaction of Churchill, who in 1944 was determined to achieve in Greece what he had not been able to achieve in Russia twenty-five years earlier. He quickly moved in veteran British combat units from Italy, which subdued ELAS forces within the greater Athens area in a week or so.[18] The British intervention came as a shock to KKE leaders, who had consigned only part of their strength to the capital because they were concerned to conquer other districts at the same time. ELAS was effective in irregular warfare; some of its best units were led by cashiered republican army officers who had been expelled from the Greek army at the time of the monarchist restoration in 1935, in somewhat the same way that thousands of former tsarist officers commanded Red Army units in Russia.[19] ELAS, however, had never dared fight *Wehrmacht* forces in direct confrontation, and could not stand up to British regulars. Conversely, ELAS excelled at repression of civilians, murdering at least 2,000 in the Athens area, sometimes after gruesome torture, and seizing thousands of hostages. Peace was restored by the Varkiza agreement of February 1945, whereby EAM accepted an amnesty for "political crimes," agreed to disband ELAS, hand over its arms, and participate in peaceful political competition.

---

[18] See G. M. Alexander, *The Prelude to the Truman Doctrine: British Policy in Greece, 1944–1947* (Oxford, 1982), and, for the subsequent phase, H. Richter, *British Intervention in Greece: From Varkiza to Civil War, February 1945 to August 1946* (London, 1985). More broadly, see S. Xydis, *Greece and the Great Powers, 1944–1947: Prelude to the Truman Doctrine* (Thessaloniki, 1963).

[19] Though in fact even more ex-republican officers had served in the security battalions of the collaborationist government, according to Prof. Stathis Kalyvas.

There followed a confused interim during 1945–46, which may be compared to that between November 1934 and February 1936 in Spain. Just as
the leftist parties in Spain never renounced the October insurrection, so the
remnants of ELAS hid many of their arms, and 5,000 members were soon
undergoing further military training in Tito's Yugoslavia. Moreover, small
rogue elements of ELAS continued to operate as guerrilla fighters in several
rural districts.

During 1945 the Greek government, like that of Spain a decade earlier,
prosecuted revolutionaries accused of atrocities, while also indicting other
Greeks who had been most conspicuous in collaborating with the Axis occupation. This conformed to the somewhat ambiguous terms of the peace agreement, which specified that "from this amnesty shall be excluded common-law
crimes against life and property which were not absolutely necessary to the
achievement of the political crime concerned."[20] In addition, however, elements of the new National Guard and right-wing volunteers hunted down
a number of Communists, or Communist sympathizers, and killed them.
Repression therefore existed in three different dimensions: judicial prosecution by the court system, violent actions by former ELAS bands, and reprisals
by elements of the right. At no time did political violence come to an end, in
a situation much more extreme and confused than that of Spain in 1935, and
one that the newly restored institutions of the Greek government were too
weak to control.[21]

Historians have not succeeded in fully and convincingly defining the strategy of the KKE leaders at this point. On the one hand, the latter maintained
hidden arms caches and trained future insurrectionists in Yugoslavia, but,
on the other, they claimed to pursue a normal and peaceful political life and
probably lacked the power to control certain small rogue ELAS groups in
the countryside that had never disarmed. The activities of the latter served as
justification for the government to arrest more and more leftists, and the KKE
finally announced that it would therefore boycott the first regular postwar
elections, scheduled for 31 March 1946. By that point the sadistic crimes committed in the second round had considerably reduced popular sympathy for
the Communists.

In the meantime, the situation was further complicated by the initiatives
of Slavic Macedonian nationalists in northeastern Greece. Some of them had
formed armed bands that had collaborated with the occupiers, only to pass
later into ELAS. Tito had established a Macedonian Republic as part of the
federated republics of Communist Yugoslavia, modeled on the multinational
Soviet Union. Leaders of the Macedonian Republic, in turn, claimed that
their borders should expand southward to include southern "Aegean" (that

[20] J. O. Iatrides, *Revolt in Athens: The Greek Communist "Second Round," 1944–1945*
    (Princeton, N.J., 1972), 320–21.
[21] Despite its title, A. Gerolymatos, *Red Acropolis, Black Terror: The Greek Civil War and the
    Origins of Soviet-American Rivalry, 1943–1949* (New York, 2004), is more illuminating
    about these domestic events than about international affairs.

is, Greek) Macedonia. During 1945 about a thousand irregulars crossed into Greece to harass Greek authorities, and the resulting repression by the Athens government in Greek Macedonia led to increasing sympathy for the nationalists among the inhabitants of that region, though that in turn shifted the loyalties of many of the Greek refugees from Anatolia who had previously supported the left.

The official position of the KKE espoused equal rights for all ethnic groups. It had compromised with Macedonian nationalists in 1944 and then had broken with them, but their support was important, and the KKE continued to back Macedonian autonomy.[22] During the course of 1946 Tito ordered the nationalists active in Greece to subordinate themselves to the KKE. By the summer of 1946 larger numbers of Macedonian and Greek Communists had crossed the frontier and, later organized as the "Democratic Army of Greece" (DAG), began to carry out armed operations to occupy Greek Macedonia and also as much as possible of northern Greece. The DAG set up regular local governments and conscripted more and more peasants, presenting its offensive as the patriotic continuation of the war against Axis occupation and its collaborators. Economic conditions remained poor, and there was much suffering in the countryside. The KKE had always enjoyed disproportionate support among former refugees and their descendants in the northeast, though that support had begun to shift. The DAG stressed its Communist identity more than had EAM and gained a certain following among poor peasants, enabling it to create a relatively cohesive if primarily conscripted military force, though one that increasingly emphasized coercion and the seizing of hostages.

This marked the beginning of the main phase of the civil war (the third round), though at first the KKE claimed that it was not involved, but that popular "armed bands" were springing up in the countryside. (This may be compared to the relationship between the Popular Front and the disorder in Spain during the spring of 1936, which was obviously more chaotic and less organized than Communist violence in Greece.) During the first months the DAG seemed to possess more combat vigor than the government forces, more and more members of which deserted. The DAG promoted a program not very different from that of the Spanish Popular Front in January 1936: a democratic republic, for the most part based on private property. Theoretically, at least, its program was not as revolutionary as that of Tito's AVNOJ in Yugoslavia in 1943–44.

International conditions once more played a major role. In February 1947 the British government, which had been supporting the Greek army, informed Washington that it could no longer bear the burden. The response was the Truman Doctrine, announced by the American government a month later, which pledged military and other assistance to governments such as those of Greece and Turkey, and possibly others, that were threatened with subversion

[22] E. Kofos, *Nationalism and Communism in Macedonia* (Thessaloniki, 1964); E. Barker, *Macedonia: Its Place in Balkan Power Politics* (London, 1950).

from abroad. This is taken by some historians to mark the formal beginning of the Cold War, as major American assistance strengthened the government forces more and more.[23]

By February 1947 the KKE leadership had decided to commit itself to armed struggle and civil war, having received guarantees of major military supplies from Yugoslavia and a degree, at least, of encouragement from Moscow. Though significant numbers of weapons were supplied by the former, Stalin remained cautious,[24] and the new American commitment would prove decisive, also beginning to alleviate the widespread economic distress that had benefited the DAG.

The year 1947 was a time of fluctuation, the first full year of civil war that led finally in December to the formation of a Provisional Democratic Government controlled by the KKE, though nominally resting on the DAG. At that time it controlled a significant part of the countryside, primarily in the north, but no major city. Time was not on its side, however, as the Americans built up the forces of the Athens government, and in March 1948 the formal split between Moscow and Belgrade was announced, rendering external assistance to the DAG more problematic.

Perhaps because of these factors, Nikos Zahariadis, the DAG leader, in May 1948 ordered his forces, numbering perhaps 30,000 troops, to seize the initiative in regular warfare against the government army in order to force a more rapid decision. The DAG was considerably outnumbered and not prepared for such operations, suffering heavy casualties that eventually resulted in a retreat to the far north, by which time at least half the DAG forces were made up of Slavic Macedonians, whose devotion to any genuine Greek cause was doubtful. During the final phase Communist discipline became ever more draconian, leading to further atrocities, a feature of the war on both sides.

By the beginning of 1949, the situation grew more desperate by the month, and the KKE announced a more radical stance, for the first time coming out in favor of an immediate socialist workers revolution and also endorsing the right to nationalist secession and independence. This did little good, for most of the DAG's support was not based on Communism or any kind of revolutionary socialism, and association with Macedonian separatism could only make it more unpopular with the Greek majority.

The KKE and its affiliates were never anything other than a minority force, though highly disturbed conditions and the Communists' proficiency at organization and militarization had given them disproportionate influence. In the summer of 1949 government pressure became overwhelming, and the remaining Communist forces slipped across into Yugoslavia. They committed what many considered the last great atrocity of the war – the deportation

---

[23] J. Jeffery, *Ambiguous Commitments and Uncertain Policies: The Truman Doctrine in Greece, 1947–1952* (Lanham, Md., 2000).

[24] P. Stavrakis, *Moscow and Greek Communism 1944–1949* (London, 1989).

of 25,000 children, both Greek and Macedonian, whom the Communists claimed would be mistreated in "monarcho-fascist" Greece. A certain portion of the Slavic Macedonian population then emigrated to Yugoslav Macedonia. During the course of the war, the DAG committed many atrocities,[25] and in 1947–48 the government authorities also executed hundreds of prisoners, especially Macedonians, accused of the most violent crimes. A major effort was made to suppress the KKE altogether.

Casualty statistics are as hard to arrive at as in the other cases. One calculation is that the Axis occupiers killed 40,000 civilians during 1941–44 and the resistance (mainly EAM) another 15,000, while 5,000 or more Greeks died in military action. The fighting in Athens in 1944 took several thousand lives, including nearly 2,000 executed by the Communists. The resulting "White Terror" may have killed 3,000 leftists in 1945–46. The main round of civil war resulted in about 20,000 deaths for the DAG and 15,000 for the government forces, while the former executed 4,000 civilians and the latter carried out 5,000 executions by court-martial of military captives when the latter were accused of violent crimes.[26] This total of 120,000 or more is much smaller than the number who died in the famine of 1941–42, but occurred in a small population of little more than seven million. The number of strictly military deaths was limited; between Axis occupiers and the Greek forces, the greater number of fatalities occurred among civilians.

The revolution and civil war in Greece was the last example in a long series of cases in Europe from 1905 to 1949. It partially overlapped chronologically with and also paralleled one of the leading cases in Asia, that of the revolution and civil war in Indochina. In both Greece and Indochina, the Communists first gained strength as a resistance movement during World War II, moving on to a full revolution that combined both revolution and nationalism and came to play a significant role during the Cold War.

Greece constituted one of the cases, along with Finland, Latvia, Estonia, and to a degree the Weimar Republic, in which the civil war was won by a parliamentary regime. At no time had anything approaching a majority of the Greek population supported the Communists, and by 1948 most sectors had rallied to the government, fearful not merely of domestic Communism but also of Soviet imperialism – despite the absence of Soviet intervention – and resentful of Macedonian separatism. Nearly twenty years later, Greece again fell under a temporary military dictatorship, which governed from 1967 to 1974, the only such interlude in the history of any NATO country save Turkey

---

[25] Some of them most graphically presented in *Eleni* (1983), the memoir by Nicholas Gage about his mother, one of the numerous victims.

[26] Most of these statistics are taken from Kalyvas, *The Logic of Violence*, 249. The final round of executions by the government forces on the basis of courts-martial was similar to that conducted by the Franco regime in 1939–41, though proportionately less extensive. The repression by both sides in Greece, though severe, was proportionately less intense than that by both sides in Spain. The history of political prisoners is treated in P. Voglis, *Becoming a Subject: Political Prisoners during the Greek Civil War, 1945–1950* (New York, 2002).

and Portugal. Parliamentary rule was restored in 1974, after which the KKE was again legalized, but most of its clientele was won over by the new Greek Socialist party, PASOK, which governed from 1981 to 1989.

Political commentary and historical writing was dominated by the right down to the end of the dictatorship in 1974, stressing the danger of Communism and defining the civil war as a struggle of the "national-minded" versus "traitors" motivated by foreign powers. The restoration of democracy, followed later by the victory of PASOK, resulted in a new hegemony of the left in the media and the universities, which produced a revisionist historiography that redefined the civil war as a continuation of the resistance against the Germans, a struggle between "patriots" and "collaborationists/reactionaries," which the latter won. Between 1945 and 1974, "almost two out of three books published was anti-left," whereas between 1974 and 2004, "four out of five books were left-wing."[27] Needless to say, in the latter discourse not merely was the identity of the Communists disguised, but their political violence against civilians was largely ignored.[28] By 1989–90 a political reconciliation had been achieved under the new government alliance of the conservatives and the post-Communist "Coalition," which passed legislation to designate the conflict simply as the "civil war" and to provide equal pension benefits to participants on both sides.[29] Only in recent years, however, has greater professionalism and objectivity been achieved in Greek historiography, with serious attention given to the role of political violence.[30]

[27] N. Marantzidis and G. Antoniou, "The Axis Occupation and Civil War: Changing Trends in Greek Historiography, 1941–2002," *Journal of Peace Research*, 41:2 (2004), 223–31.
[28] This historiography was initially developed abroad, where the most widely read work was D. Eudes, *The Kapetanios: Partisans and Civil War in Greece, 1943–1949* (New York, 1972).
[29] D. Close, "The Road to Reconciliation?," in P. Carabott and T. D. Sfikas, eds., *The Greek Civil War: Essays on a Conflict of Exceptionalism and Silences* (London, 2004), 257–78.
[30] Thanks above all to the efforts of Stathis Kalyvas. In addition to the works previously cited, see Kalyvas, "Cómo me convertí en revisionista (sin saber lo que esto significaba): Usos y abusos de un concepto en el debate sobre la Guerra Civil griega," *Alcores*, 4 (2007), 125–42.

Conclusion

The first half of the twentieth century was the time not only of the most extensive international violence in European history but also of the greatest internal conflict. When that period ended, the era of classical modernity would soon begin to come to a close, and the factors that stimulated the world wars – outlined at the beginning of this book – had also for the most part begun to pass from the European scene. Intense nationalism, the rivalry of multiple empires and would-be empires, the ideologies based on vitalism and conflict, and autarchist economic competition had all either disappeared or were in serious decline. The transformation of the media and information technology helped to bring to an end the classic age of political propaganda, while the quantum leap in weapons technology discouraged direct war between the powers. Thus stage three of the twentieth-century world revolutionary process did not bring World War III but the much different Cold War – long, expensive, and destructive, but not another military holocaust.

Revolutionary civil war in Europe was stimulated by some of the same factors, but also by different ones. As suggested earlier, the stage had been set by the emergence of classical modernity, roughly between 1890 and 1930. Features that encouraged the sharpening of internal conflict included: 1) the increasingly rapid pace of change and modernization, unprecedented in its rhythms, which pressed issues of democratization, participation, and egalitarianism, accompanied by the decline of classic liberalism; 2) the interaction of the major modern revolutionary ideologies, most of which in one way or another espoused extreme measures, violence, and authoritarian solutions; 3) the acceleration of economic development and of social transformation, with the expansion of education and literacy, stimulating new ambitions, resentments, and conflicts and encouraging the psychological revolution of rising expectations, with the influence of these factors sometimes magnified by the effects of economic crisis; 4) increasingly frequent regime changes, as well as mounting demands for further regime change; 5) the growth of nationalism and the incipient dissolution of empires, accompanied by intense demands for national liberation in some countries; and 6) the traumatic consequences of foreign war. Civil wars and grave internal conflict were features of the twenty-year crisis from 1917 to 1939, which set off the most complex set of political and social radicalisms in mutual conflict ever seen in European history, climaxed by two final civil wars that began during World War II. The interplay of these factors may be contrasted with their sharp decline after about 1947.

Totalitarianism created a state monopoly on internal violence in the eastern half of Europe, while in the west, with the exception of the Iberian peninsula, social democracy stabilized and matured, accompanied by the drastic decline of revolutionary ideologies. Beginning in the late 1940s, rapid economic growth continued for a quarter-century and, when it finally faltered, avoided major depression, completing a social transformation without precedent. All this obviated further demands for violent change. Throughout Western Europe, the response to the trauma of World War II was much more positive and constructive than had been the response to World War I, the strong leadership of the United States helping a great deal. This made it possible to transcend the era of internal conflict.

Civil war, or the major threat thereof, appeared in three kinds of situations: in struggles for political and social modernization in the largely undeveloped peripheral countries of the south and east between 1905 and 1936; in completely new polities, from Finland to the First Republic in Portugal and the Second Republic in Spain; and in lands traumatized by foreign conquest or military defeat. The only fully developed country examined in this study – Germany – was impacted by the third situation and also had to develop a new political regime, but managed to avoid full civil war. Two generations earlier, France had experienced all three situations, producing a short, bloody civil war directed against the dominant forces in the nation's capital. Some combination of these three situations affected every country that suffered full-scale civil war, while the lands of northwestern Europe, which enjoyed more advanced economies and already possessed stable and representative institutions, were never destabilized, though they underwent moments of volatility.

An additional factor was sometimes political contagion. Finland, though politically precocious and in some ways remarkably advanced, suffered contagion from the Russian revolution, the consequences of imperial military defeat (though it resulted in national liberation), and all the problems associated with establishing independence and building a new political system. Spanish politics under the Second Republic also suffered contagion from radical and violent policies that were being pursued elsewhere.

The cases of Finland and Latvia were the only ones in this group in which civil war attended the founding of national independence. Such a circumstance is not unusual, however, for severe internal strife has often attended national liberation wars and/or the gaining of political independence. The degree of civil war involved in the American Revolutionary War has often been downplayed by standard historiography, and intense internal strife – sometimes amounting to full-scale civil war – has accompanied or followed the struggle for independence in many new countries in the second half of the twentieth century. The case of Latvia, however, is hard to deal with because of limited sources, inability to read the language, and the complex involvement with Soviet and German intervention.

Most commonly, civil wars and intense internal strife were triggered by the consequences of foreign war, however much they also reflected other tensions. This was especially the case in countries that already suffered from severe domestic conflict, as in Russia, Latvia, Yugoslavia, and Greece (and even, to some degree, Finland). In this regard, the uniqueness of the Spanish war always stands out, as does the fact that, more than any other, it became a war of religion. In general, the civil wars were not significant as military contests, either because of limited mobilization or duration, or because of insignificant weaponry and technology, though here again to some extent the Spanish war was exceptional on both counts.

The role of Communism was fundamental. All these conflicts were Communist/anti-Communist civil wars, with the exception of the post–World War I crisis in Italy and the partial exceptions of Spain and Germany.[1] Even in the latter cases, Communism became semihegemonic in the revolutionary Spanish Republic and eventually dominated leftist revolutionary activity in Germany. In only two countries did the Communists win, but this does not negate the fact that they developed a totalitarian model uniquely well designed for war, even if it was frequently unable to overcome all the obstacles that it faced. The Bolshevik model featured total dictatorship and something approaching total mobilization, though this also required the great demographic and economic resources of the Russian heartland in order to triumph. Tito's Partisans faced more severe odds, and their achievement was the greater, using the same model, combined with the development of a multinational front of considerable popular appeal. The challenge in Spain was especially complex in political terms, and there the Communists attempted a mixed policy, more distant from the classic Bolshevik model, which achieved some success but could never be fully implemented.

Normally there was considerable incentive for one or more foreign powers to intervene, since the radical nature of the conflicts had international ramifications, even if the goal of the intervening power at first might simply be to advance the process of subversion, as in the case of Germany in Russia in 1917–18. The character and importance of such intervention varied, being particularly important in the cases of Russia, Latvia, Hungary, Spain, and Greece, and less so in the others. Foreign intervention more commonly favored counterrevolution, but, in the two cases where the revolutionaries won, the most crucial intervention favored them, pointing up its importance. In both

---

[1] One might also add the case of Finland, but, though the revolutionary Finnish Social Democrats were not Bolsheviks, they were closely allied with and played the same role as the Bolsheviks.

Russia and Yugoslavia the Communists at times enjoyed significant backing from non-Communist powers, a paradox made possible only by the exigencies of world war. This is not to deny that in both these cases the Communists developed considerable strength on their own. Only in Germany was a long intermittent insurgency contained without significant foreign assistance, though in this case the insurgency never reached the level of full-scale civil war. In Finland, the fact that the Bolsheviks were simply in no position to intervene significantly left the counterrevolutionaries in a position to consummate their victory largely, though not entirely, on their own.

Successful counterrevolution normally resulted in parliamentary democracy, but not always. The victory of the reaction in Hungary restored the old nineteenth-century regime with only minor reforms, producing a system considerably less than democratic, while the Franco regime began its very long history as a semi-fascist system. Once again the Spanish case stands out, though, in this regard, its very timing – in the late 1930s – was a crucial factor.

The international significance of the civil wars also varied. Generally, the conflicts in the larger countries had the greatest influence abroad. The Greek civil war was more important than the other cases involving small countries, because of its relationship to the great powers and the beginning of the Cold War. The Spanish struggle was perceived by many to have enormous international significance, but it has been argued in this book that such significance was secondary and indirect.

The historical importance of most of these conflicts was considerable. The outcome of the Russian war would help to determine much of the course of the twentieth century; the war in Spain decided the future of that country for four decades; and the Greek civil war played a role in crystallizing the Cold War. These three were the ones with the greatest historical influence, though the outcome of the Finnish war helped to consolidate Finland's modern parliamentary system, which has governed the country ever since, and helped to produce one of the most productive, progressive, and prosperous small societies of the twentieth century. The outcome of the war in Latvia guaranteed the beginning of national independence, while the defeat of the revolutionaries in Germany consolidated liberal democracy for a decade, though no longer. Conversely, it might be argued that a victory in Germany for the pre-Communist revolutionaries in the winter and spring of 1919 was the only case in which revolutionary victory might have had a positive, rather than negative, effect on world history.

After the end of the era of world wars, the Cold War took the place of World War III and has sometimes been described as an "international civil war." Such a dimension at times existed, but armed conflict did not take place in Europe, and the concept is somewhat exaggerated. More specifically, as far as the two great adversaries were concerned, it became a world war by proxy, which sometimes produced civil war in other parts of the world. Armed conflict during this long era of more than forty years took place almost exclusively in what came to be known as the "Third World," mainly the Afro-Asian world, avoiding direct confrontation between the superpowers. The two major wars of the second half of the century, in Korea and in Indochina, both involved broad dimensions of civil war. The only lengthy war of the late twentieth century that was strictly international was the Iran-Iraq conflict.

For Europe, the massive changes that occurred after World War II – mostly productive changes in the western half of the continent – together with the terms of the Cold War introduced a long period of both internal and external stability. Revolution had come to Eastern Europe, but not by insurrection and civil war, as posited by Marxism-Leninism. It came on the bayonets of the Red Army (the Stalinist doctrine), with the exceptions of Yugoslavia and Albania. Complete Soviet domination meant that there was only limited disorder, but much oppression. Communist parties also temporarily played major roles in France and Italy, but were unable to destabilize those societies. The principal new outbursts of political revolution in Europe would come from the opposite direction, in the form of rebellions against Communism in East Germany (1953), Hungary (1956), Czechoslovakia (1968), and Poland (1980). The only international military actions in Europe during the Cold War were the Soviet invasions of Hungary and Czechoslovakia. The Cold War had set a boundary to Communist expansion in Europe, so that revolutionary civil wars moved to other continents, first reaching a climax in China between 1945 and 1949.

The only leftist revolution to occur in Western Europe during the later twentieth century was the Portuguese revolution of 1974, which overthrew the long-standing Portuguese dictatorship, replacing it with a mixed regime led by victorious military factions, which declared that they were leading Portugal to "socialism." For more than a year, the country was increasingly divided between a conservative, Catholic north and a radical, secularized south, a potential setting for civil war. The military government, however, also pledged support for democracy and held general elections within a year. The balloting of 1975 was won by anti-Communist moderates, so that a formal commitment to free elections, combined with internal division inside the military and the influence of Western European democracy, undercut the revolutionary thrust and permitted the conservative instincts of much of Portuguese society to find expression. A controlled insurgency against Portuguese Communism occurred in the conservative north during the summer of 1975, producing much destruction of local party headquarters but extremely little violence against persons. The guarantee of free elections and civil rights thus resulted within a year and a half in the triumph of democracy, though all influences of left-wing military pretorianism were not eliminated until 1982.

Beyond that, a metapolitical perspective would be provided by cultural philosophers who suggest that classic modernity pretended to objectivity and produced revolutionary explosions, sometimes leading to civil war. The subjectivity of the postmodern era, on the other hand, tends toward subjec-tvity and implosion, not explosion.

If the era of civil war in Europe had ended, the new era of civil war in the world at large was just beginning. By the 1960s, the focus of violent revolution seemed to have passed from Europe to Latin America, sparked by the triumph of Fidel Castro in Cuba. Ideologically based insurgencies and terrorist movements appeared in several Central American countries and also to varying degrees within various parts of South America. These conflicts sometimes polarized the society and threatened political stability, but the consequence was usually military regimes and more authoritarian government. These insurgencies never produced a full state of civil war, save for a time in Guatemala and El Salvador, though the "Shining Path" insurgency continued for years in Peru.

During the second half of the twentieth century, civil war, not international war, became the predominant form of violent conflict in the greater part of the world. There were several reasons for this. One was that, as mentioned, the Cold War itself sometimes encouraged civil war in what was called the Third World. Since the atomic stalemate left the superpowers disinclined to fight each other directly, they supported opposing participants in various kinds of internal conflict abroad. Soviet leaders found that the easiest way to oppose Western interests was often to promote "national liberation move-ments" (a policy instituted initially by Lenin in 1918), irrespective of whether they were Communist in identity. A second influence was decolonization and the emergence of many new states in Africa and Asia, whose territory, lead-ership, political systems, and ethnic hegemony were in varying ways often violently contested internally. Governments in newly established states often faced internal rebellion, which only encouraged them to become clients of a superpower. Thus many of the factors that had encouraged internal war in European countries before 1945 – radical ideologies, social conflict, foreign manipulation, ethnic secession – were much more common in other parts of the world after that time. The focus of nationalism shifted to Asia and Africa, provoking efforts at secession or direct interethnic civil war, occasionally end-ing in genocide. During the Cold War, some of the most intense conflicts had to do with communist/anticommunist civil wars, but, especially in the later twentieth century, other rivalries came to the fore.

The end of the Cold War in no way lessened the frequency of civil war or major internal conflict, particularly in Africa and the greater Middle East. Ideological divisions of the Cold War were immediately replaced by a new emphasis on ethnicity and/or religion. Civil war returned to Europe for a few years with the break-up of Yugoslavia, and threatened to break out in some of the post-Soviet states, though it assumed significant form only as ethnic revolt in Chechnya and in the Caucasus. Ideological civil war persisted in a number of African states,[2] mixed with ethnic conflict, but in general the new fault lines

---

[2] And at one point in the Middle East, South Yemen even featured an intra-Communist civil war.

lay along ethnic and religious divisions. Added to this is the problem of the "failed state" in Africa, South Asia, and even possibly Latin America, which exposes further internal conflict. The European civil wars associated with classic struggles of modernization, radical ideologies, and the consequences of disastrous international conflict came to an end in 1949, but in the world as a whole internal war has replaced international war as the predominant form of strife in the twenty-first century.[3]

---

[3] For a discussion of some of the recent literature on contemporary civil wars, see S. Tarrow, "Inside Insurgencies: Politics and Violence in an Age of Civil War," *Perspectives on Politics*, 5:3 (September 2007), 587–600.

Index

29, 41–43, 62, 78–80, 104–7, 110–12, 184, 196–97, 200; Germany's invasion of, 199; Greece and, 222; imperial designs of, 61–62; internal violence in, during World War II, 205, 226; international revolutionary strategy of, 24, 33, 47–49, 54–58, 62, 70, 96, 106, 230; invasion of Poland and, 54–58, 65, 77, 197; invasion of Yugoslavia and, 213; liberation wars against, 199–200; pogroms in, 59, 205; repression in, 9–10, 58–61, 66–68, 207, 229; Spanish civil war and, 129–30, 141n8, 159–63, 170–72, 174, 178, 181–83, 188–89; World War II strategy of, 196–99, 205–8. *See also* Comintern; Lenin; Stalin

Spain: collectivization in, 145–48, 150, 172; Communist Party of, 169–70, 173, 179; economic conditions of, 168; fascism in, 108, 150; interwar turmoil of, 89–91; maps of, *139, 142, 177–78*; pre-revolutionary violence in, 123–26, 130–32; repression in, 125, 148–53; revolution in, 117–36; succession conflicts in, 1–2; terrorism in, 10, 19, 148–53. *See also specific politicians and parties*

Spanish civil war: academic studies of, 173n69; air forces in, *139*, 159, 175–76, 183; arming of trade unions and leftists, 137–38, 142–45; atrocities in, 148–53, 203–4; civil conflicts within, 1, 169–73, 179–80; Finland civil war as analogous to, 27, 30–32; foreign intervention in, 9, 90, 128, *139*, 141, 157–65, 168–72, 174–75, 178, 181–83, 185–89, 203; German civil strife's analogies to, 118, 125–28, 134; inevitability of, 128–29; International Brigades and, 44, 141, 189; Nationalist strategies in, 138–39; propaganda in, 5, 125, 141, 148, 173, 175–76, 176n74, 182–83; religious dimension of, 11–12, 153–57, 165, 167, 174; Republican strategic failures in, 137–38, 140–41, 145–48, 150, 152–53, 176–78; revolutionary beginnings of, 117–36; Russian civil war's analogies

to, 37, 45, 59–60, 63–65, 118–19, 136, 140, 142–43, 146–48, 150, 153–55, 165, 168, 170, 173–75, 180; sea war and, 178–79; significance of, 181–89, 197; terrorism in, 10, 19, 148–53; uniqueness of, 2, 227–28

Spanish Socialist Party (PSOE), 89
Spartacists (in Germany), 72–74, 124
SPD (German Social Democrats), 70–71, 73, 76–77, 98–99, 101
SS (secret police), 9, 196, 206
Stahlhelm (PCL), 99
Stalin, Iosef: economic thinking of, 35, 66–67, 87, 146; international revolutions and, 81; military strategies of, 56–57, 184–86, 196; "Socialism in One Country" and, 96–97; Spanish civil war strategy of, 159, 162–63, 182; Tito and, 213–14; totalitarianism of, 66, 110; underestimation of Hitler and, 101, 105; on World War I, 47. *See also* Comintern; Soviet Union
Stamboliski, Alexander, 93–94, 118
Sternhall, Zeev, 18n7
Stone, Norman, 35
Strelkii (regiments), 40, 86
Stresemann, Gustav, 81
Sturm-Abteilung (SA), 99, 101n14
succession wars, 1
Svinhufvud, P. E., 26
Sweden, 133n21
Switzerland, 109

Tamames, Ramón, 146n17
Tanner, Vaino, 31
Technische Nothilfe (TN), 82
terror and terrorism: Finnish revolutionary war and, 27–28; French Revolution and, 12, 17; in Latin America, 230; as revolutionary tactic, 10, 17, 19, 94; in Spain, 89
Teshkilat (secret police), 9
Thirty Years War, 8, 34, 95
Thucydides, 4, 11
Tito (Josip Broz), 153, 198, 210–14, 218, 220–21, 227
Tocqueville, Alexis de, 4, 6
Togliatti, Palmiro, 162